Simon Morley is the author of *Writing on the Wall: Word and Image in Modern Art*; *Seven Keys to Modern Art*; *The Simple Truth: The Monochrome in Modern Art*; and *By Any Other Name: A Cultural History of the Rose*; and the editor of *The Sublime: Documents in Contemporary Art*. He has contributed to numerous publications including *Third Text, World Art, Art Monthly* and the *Independent on Sunday*, and has taught at Sotheby's Institute, Winchester School of Art and Dankook University, Republic of Korea, where he was Assistant Professor of Fine Art. He is also an artist.

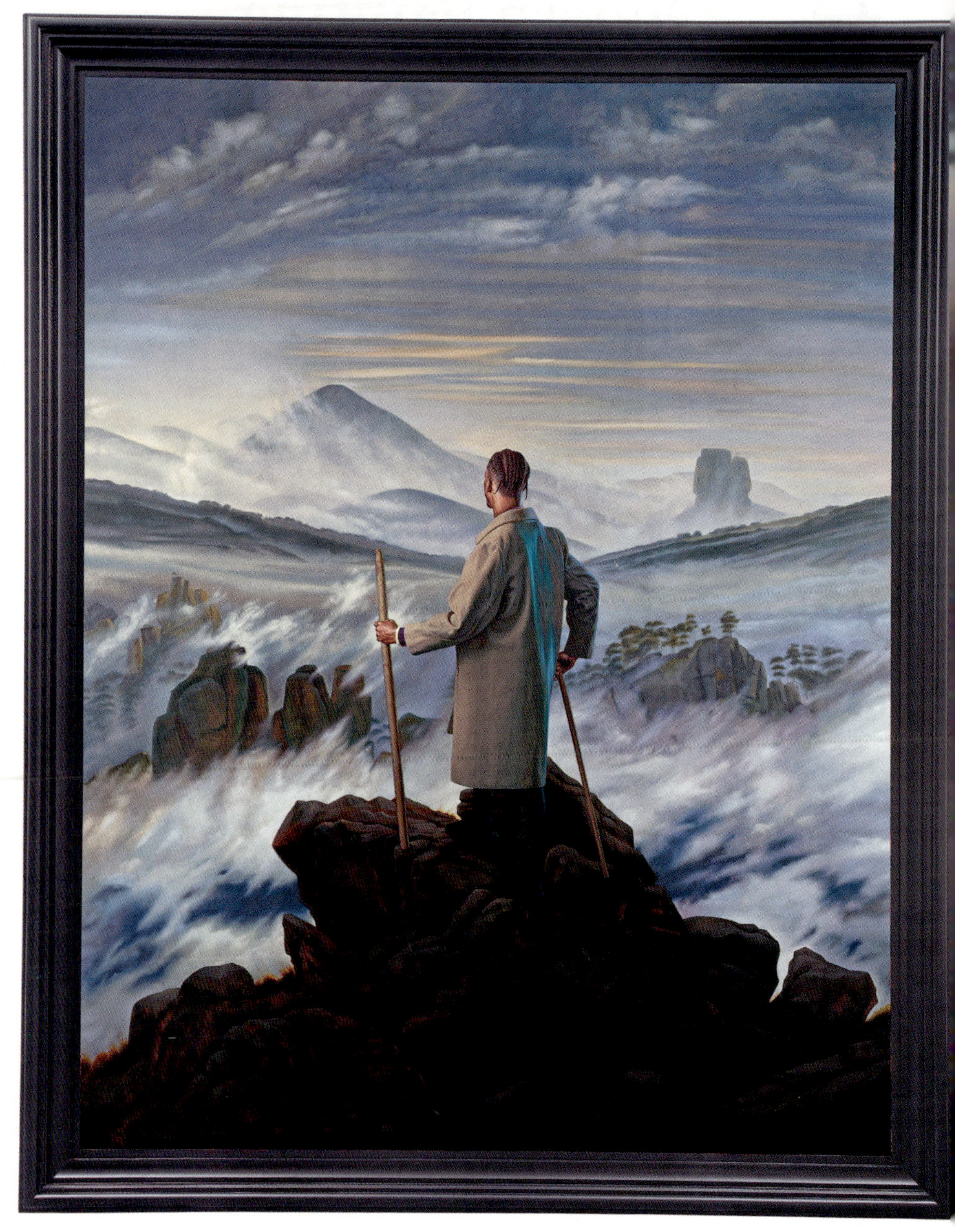

1 Kehinde Wiley, *The Prelude (Babacar Mané)*, 2021

Modern Painting
A Concise History
Simon Morley

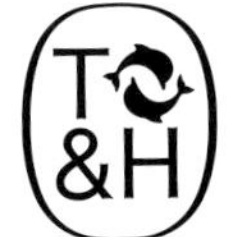

First published in 2023 in the United Kingdom
by Thames & Hudson Ltd, 181A High Holborn,
London WC1V 7QX

www.thamesandhudson.com

First published in 2023 in the United States
of America by Thames & Hudson Inc.,
500 Fifth Avenue, New York, New York 10110

www.thamesandhudsonusa.com

Art direction and series design by Kummer & Herrman
Layout by Adam Hay Studio

British Library Cataloguing-in-Publication Data
A catalogue record for this book is available from
the British Library

Library of Congress Control Number 2023935851

ISBN 978-0-500-20489-4

Printed and bound in Malaysia through Asia Pacific
Offset Ltd

Contents

Acknowledgments

This concise history of painting has been gestating for quite some time. An especially important influence has been the experience of living since 2010 in the Republic of Korea, and of teaching studio classes in painting at a university within a department that is still called 'Western Painting' – as opposed to the other one called 'Oriental Painting'. This context has certainly helped put things in a more multicultural perspective.

Thanks to James Elkins, probably the best art historian writing on painting, for some useful comments on a draft of this book, and thanks to others too numerous to name here for conversations and exhibitions over the years. Big thanks to the team at Thames & Hudson: Roger Thorp for commissioning me to write this book, Mohara Gill for helpful early editorial feedback, Ilona de Nemethy Sanigar for managing the editorial process, pre-press controller Mark Bracey, production controller Julie Bosser, Michela Parkin for incisive final edits and Nikos Kotsopoulos, the resourceful picture editor.

Preface

It may come as a surprise that the predecessor to the present book in the renowned World of Art series is Sir Herbert Read's *A Concise History of Modern Painting*, first published in 1959, revised by Read in 1968, and finally reprinted with an additional concluding chapter by Caroline Tisdall and William Feaver in 1974. Read's history assumes without question the importance of painting, or at least some forms of painting, as a vitally 'modern' art medium. One of the reasons for the delay in the appearance of a new survey in the World of Art series is that around the time Read published his book, and certainly when it was revised, painting's status fell into question. The experimental impetus driving art forward, the desire to innovate, seemed to have ended up producing blank canvases, or near enough. At the same time, painting as a medium was condemned by the artistic avant-garde as outdated and too much of a commercial product. Instead, various conceptual practices that were anything *but* paintings took centre stage. But times have changed. Within contemporary art, paintings in many, many styles have secured valued places alongside a host of other practices that embrace radically expanded ideas about art.

Read began his history with the French artist Paul Cézanne – that is, in the late nineteenth century. This new volume starts about one hundred years earlier, with the emergence of Romanticism in European art. Read's choice was primarily motivated by the fact that for him the honour of being called a *modern* painter was only to be awarded to those who made certain kinds of paintings. He argued that it was not enough for an artist to 'belong to the history of art in our time' in order to be described as 'modern' in the specific way he defined it. His narrative drew a line between late nineteenth-century Post-Impressionism and what came before, as well as a line around types of painting associated with less innovative styles that

did not reject the conventions of optical realism forged in the
Renaissance. Read saw 'modern' art as being geared towards
challenging these conventions and dedicated to perpetual
innovation – with one style trumping and making redundant
what came before as art moved inexorably towards what Read
described as the goal of 'making visible' rather than 'reflecting'
the visible (which is what he assumed realistic painters did). In
stylistic terms this boiled down to either abstract art and the
repudiation of any obvious reference to the visible world, or the
dreamlike imagery associated with Surrealism.

This new concise history tells a more inclusive story than
Read's, one that places painting in a broader stylistic, historical,
geographical, and gender and ethnic frame. It is structured as
a loose timeline. Where it seemed interesting to do so, I have
quoted the words of the artists themselves, but I have avoided
quoting from critics, theorists and art historians. At the end
of the book there is an Appendix in the form of a series of
questions that the reader might like to ask of the artists and the
ideas discussed, but also of the text itself. This is followed by a
Further Reading section for those that want to dig deeper.

I hope this new history allows the artists and paintings
it discusses to be appreciated within a diverse and inclusive
intellectual, historical and social framework. I am certain that,
especially from the perspective of the new plural centres of the
globalized contemporary artworld, the story told in these pages
will still look overtly centred on Europe and North America.
But the concept of 'modern art' was born in western Europe,
and it is inextricably bound up with the forces of westernizing
modernity. Furthermore, there is no escaping the fact that
'art history' as a genre is in itself a fundamentally western
discipline invented for organizing cultural artefacts and their
relationships within specific categories across time and space.

Finally, I want to stress that there is no substitute for
knowledge by acquaintance. Only by seeing *real* paintings in
museums and galleries will we be able to develop valuable
relationships with them. This truth is especially important to
recognize nowadays, since we are becoming more and more
dependent on experiencing the world via digital media. While
the Internet allows easy and free access to an unprecedented
number of images of paintings, compensating generously
for the inevitable difficulties involved in seeing real ones, we
should always remember that a photograph of a painting is
just that, a small-scale, flat, synthetically coloured, digitally
generated reproduction. But, more concerningly, a photograph
of a painting on a screen or in a book displaces it into a context
in which we experience it sitting down within the kinds of

spaces that encourage the more cerebral or intellectual modes of thinking associated with word-based knowledge. Real paintings, by contrast, are meant to be experienced in three-dimensional environments within which we physically move around, and where we are open to more embodied, sensual forms of experience and knowledge.

Chapter 1
The Roots of Modern Painting *c.* 1789–*c.* 1848

Modernity and the Artist

If humanity's past 300,000 years of existing on earth were visualized as a twenty-four-hour day, the period covered by this book would be the last minute. But in terms of social and cultural change it was within these sixty seconds that almost everything happened. For the modern period has been one of momentously rapid transformations and upheavals globally, caused by the convergence of complex social and economic forces and new ways of understanding human nature primarily emanating from the west.

In the first few seconds of the last minute of human history – the end of the eighteenth century and early part of the nineteenth century – European artists began responding to the material and intellectual changes going on around them by forging radically new styles and proposing new ideas about the meaning and value of art. The English artist and writer William Blake (1757–1827) reacted with special originality, seeing the dawning of an age that was shining with exciting new freedoms. In making *The Dance of Albion*, also known as *Glad Day* (c. 1793), Blake was inspired by the recent American and French Revolutions to express his faith in the birth of a liberated 'modern' humanity capable of freely embarking on the task of self-discovery and creation. But there were also artists who reacted to the darker implications of these momentous changes. The Spaniard Francisco Goya's (1746–1828) horrific painting *Saturn Devouring His Son* (c. 1820–23), which was made towards the end of his life directly on a wall of his house and was never intended for public exhibition, is haunted by a very different vision of the new world coming into existence. A popular saying of the period was that, like Saturn,

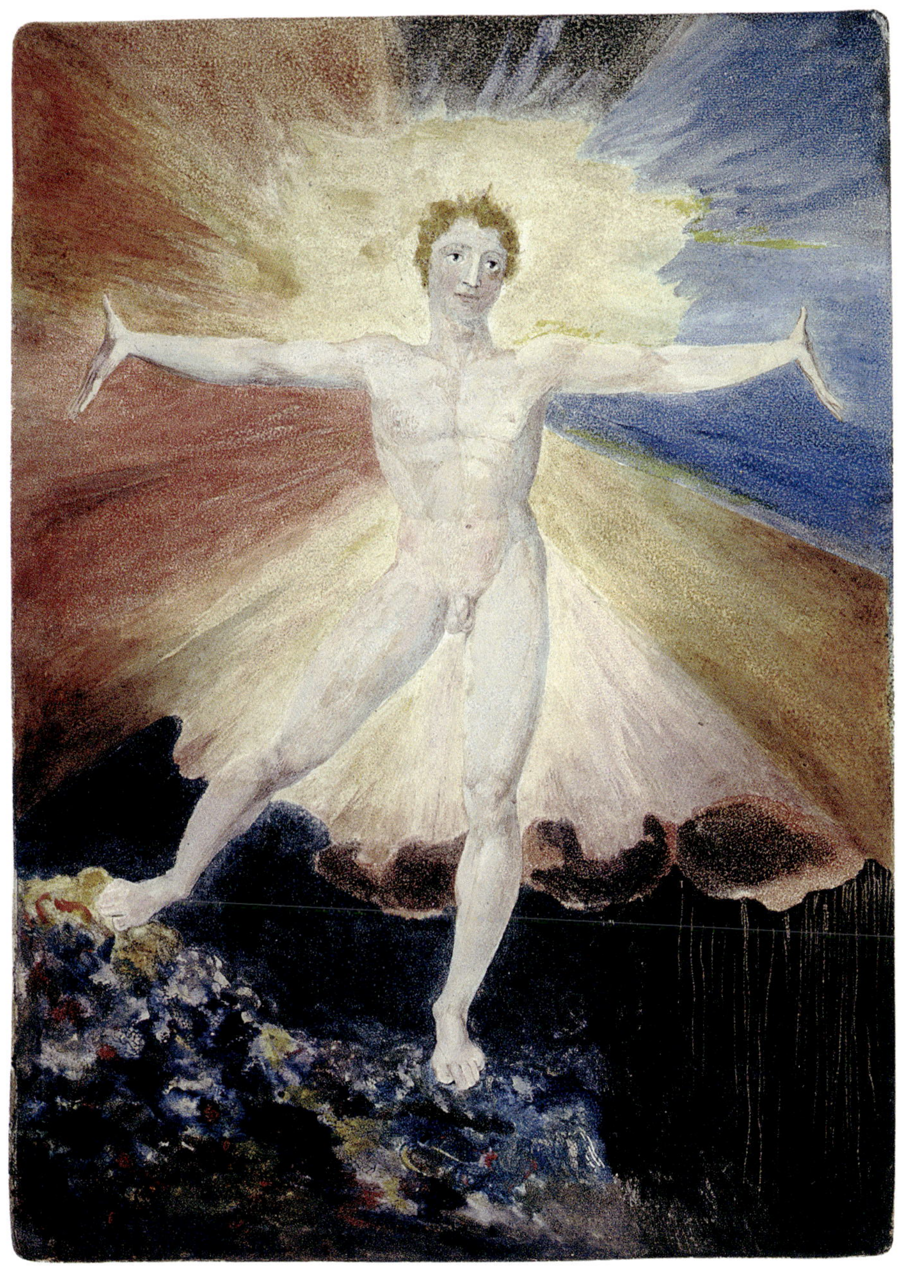

2 William Blake, *The Dance of Albion* (also known as *Glad Day*), c. 1793

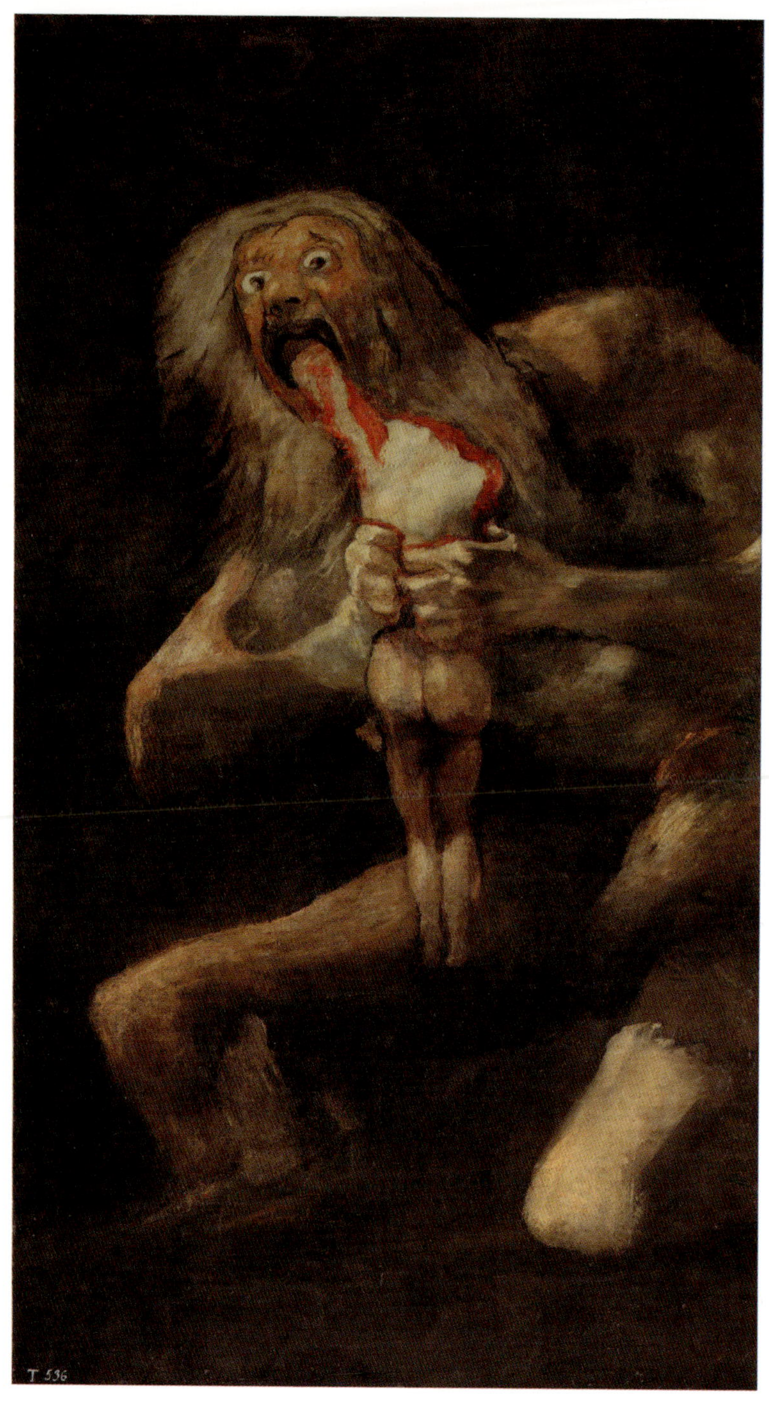

3 Francisco Goya, *Saturn Devouring His Son*, c. 1820–23

the Classical god of Time, the French Revolution had devoured its own children, that the great hopes it initially inspired had been dashed. Goya's painting was a consequence of his first-hand witnessing of the violence and turmoil unleashed by the twenty years of European war that followed the Revolution and especially devastated his native Spain.

The social and political upheavals of the American and French Revolutions were in part a consequence of what is called the Enlightenment, a multifaceted intellectual, political and social movement that radically changed the way westerners understood their place in the world, imbuing them with newfound confidence and faith in progress. The Enlightenment thinkers argued that if traditional beliefs and practices were not tested and revised, each new generation was condemned to inherit the superstitions and prejudices of its predecessors. They exposed the irrationality, violence and injustice spread by the religious clerical orders that dominated European society and over the centuries had sanctioned bloody Crusades, witch-hunts, book-burnings, the suppression of scientific enquiry and innovation in all areas of society. They advocated a secular and humanistic society based on faith in progress in which the only reliable source of knowledge was reason, which, so they declared, was universal and independent of tradition.

At the same time as humanity's relationship to the world was being transformed by the thinkers of the Enlightenment, deep changes in the structure of the western economy were also occurring, specifically the emergence of the economic infrastructure that came to characterize the modern developed world: industrialization. This transformation began in England, because of the convergence there of new ideas about trade and economic markets that combined with ample fossil fuel resources in the form of coal, newly invented and vastly more efficient machinery for harnessing and converting energy, and a relatively open and tolerant government. Industrialization eventually led to a fundamental restructuring of the whole of western European – and then North American – society away from agriculture and around technology, factory labour and urbanization, and caused a massive increase in western economic power through dominance of world trade and military conquest.

Together, these developments give birth in Europe to what we now call 'modernity': a dynamic form of society that required continuous material growth, technologically driven acceleration and cultural innovation – a society full of aspiration and promise that was moving forwards towards a better future. But it was also a society that, as Goya's painting suggests, was deeply troubled. Science was proving hugely successful at analysing the laws of the world and separating facts from values and emotions, but as a result, personal, spiritual and imaginative responses to the world were increasingly equated with the 'childish', the immature and the 'merely' subjective. In the new industrial and capitalist society, economic efficiency was becoming the sole end of life, the principal indicator of personal and collective progress. In fact, the new rational worldview seemed to understand the world only to better control and manipulate it. Nature was seen as a neutral resource, the 'outside' of human society, open to profitable and limitless exploitation.

The Impact of Modernity on European Painting

Social, economic and political forces were pushing artists into unfamiliar roles or towards the social margins. As society became increasingly secular, the Roman Catholic Church, a traditional source of patronage in much of Europe, lost its dominance and no longer supported the arts. The nobility, another traditional client, was also ceding its position to the new commercial middle class who drove forward the Industrial Revolution. In place of the old patrons, the newly established nation-states took on leading patronage roles, seeking to direct culture towards the celebration of the values they claimed to represent. As a result, new subjects and styles were demanded. But it was by no means clear what these innovations should be.

In the period before the French Revolution, the most important European institution where the art of painting was taught was the Académie Royale de Peinture et de Sculpture in Paris, founded in 1648 and admired and imitated throughout Europe. The Académie and the state-organized exhibitions showing the works of its alumni, known as the Salon, set the standard by which most artists throughout western Europe pursued their goals and careers. For the Académie, the absolute measure by which art was judged was the achievements of Classical Greece and Rome, as well as those of Renaissance artists such as Raphael and Titian and the seventeenth-century French artist Nicolas Poussin, who was especially admired for his devotion to the idealizing and ennobling principles associated with the Classical tradition. This was founded on *mimesis* or optical realism; a painting was meant to produce a convincing illusion of three-dimensional space on a two-dimensional surface by using two basic principles: perspective and modelling of forms in light and shade.

These methods had been partly developed in Classical Greek and Roman art, then lost during the Middle Ages;

but in the early fifteenth century in Italy a major innovation occurred – the invention of a much more optically convincing illusion called linear perspective – which provided the means by which to imitate three-dimensional space as it would be seen by a stationary person standing in front of a scene (and, technically speaking, looking with one eye closed). This illusion was produced by organizing a painting's composition using orthogonal lines converging at a single 'vanishing-point', as if in the far distance. This geometric structuring device was then supplemented by the rendering of forms within the illusionistic space as if a source of light – most probably daylight – was striking them from a particular direction at a particular moment in time. The 'illuminated' side of a form was painted lighter and the 'shadowed' side darker, and the effect of a shadow cast by the form on the surrounding area was also simulated.

The materials artists used to produce this optical realism were also born in the Renaissance: oil paint applied with paintbrushes, usually to canvas. Most of the paintings discussed in this book, especially before the 1960s, were made using these media. Oil paint is a mixture of coloured pigments which, until European chemists started synthesizing new colours in the late eighteenth century, were all derived from natural sources such as mineral salts, earth and even living organisms. Some pigments were very expensive, such as ultramarine blue, derived from the semi-precious stone lapis lazuli, which could only be sourced from what is now Afghanistan. These pigments were suspended in oil, usually linseed, and the result was a viscous paint medium that dried slowly and could be either thinned down to create semi-transparent glazes or built up into cumulative layers of thick paint, called 'impasto'. The canvas support, which was woven in linen or cotton, was stretched taut over a wooden frame and 'sized' or sealed with a liquid to make it non-absorbent. As a result, a painting could be of various proportions, and easy to transport because it could be removed from the support and rolled up. The stretched canvas was usually propped vertically on an easel and painted on by the artist (and their assistants) from a standing or seated position parallel to the surface.

By the seventeenth century these technical devices and procedures were being skilfully marshalled to represent broadly three kinds of optically real pictorial world: portrayals of Christian stories intended to function as part of the Catholic rite; 'History Paintings', or grand narratives embodying the noble, idealizing values associated with the Classical world, as well as portraits of the wealthy who commissioned paintings

to memorialize and ennoble them; and depictions with a more
'naturalistic' look, such as still-lifes, landscapes, portraits
and 'genre' scenes (everyday life subjects), in which a painting
seemed to directly describe the visual world as it appeared to
the eye without evident attempts at conveying the experience
of religious transcendence or an idealized world. The first two
uses of the picturing system dominated southern Europe and
Roman Catholic countries, while the third was common in
the Protestant north, where the religion proscribed the use of
imagery in relation to the divine and there was thus a shift to
forms of painting based on more secular themes.

But in 1793 the Académie was closed by the new
Revolutionary government because it was judged to be a
symbol of the oppressive old order. However, in the event, the
Revolutionaries continued the pre-Revolutionary convention of
looking to Classical Greece and Rome and the Renaissance for
role models, which they now saw as embodying the admirable
values of reason and republicanism. Artists were called upon
to 'Classicize' recent historical events. But the unprecedented
speed, novelty and violence of the transformations taking place
challenged them not only also to strive to equal and surpass
the achievements of the past, but also to search for new ways of
representing the world they experienced. In *The Death of Marat*
(1793), Jacques-Louis David (1748–1825) – an ardent supporter of
the Revolution and a direct participant in events – aimed to
produce a eulogy to a recently murdered politician, and to this
end he employed the techniques he learned and successfully
practised in pre-Revolutionary France. But the stark realism
with which he ended up portraying Marat slumped dead in
his bath, and the void-like emptiness of the space above his
inert body, jar with the goal of achieving the mood of noble
poise and masterly detachment that is central to Classicism,
suggesting a far less confident and assured vision of reality.

The allegiance of artists to the fundamental principle upon
which David's painting – indeed, all western art since the
Renaissance – was founded began to be questioned. Artists
no longer felt obliged to show obedience to the tenets they
had learned, and were freed from believing that the ideals
and methods bequeathed by the past unquestionably offered
credible guidance in how to represent the experience of
the modern world. This crisis deepened as artists acquired
greater knowledge of art history, which revealed alternative
picturing conventions within Europe's past. But the sense of
the superiority of western art was to be even more profoundly
challenged by increasing contact with non-western cultures
brought about by world trade and colonial conquest. As we

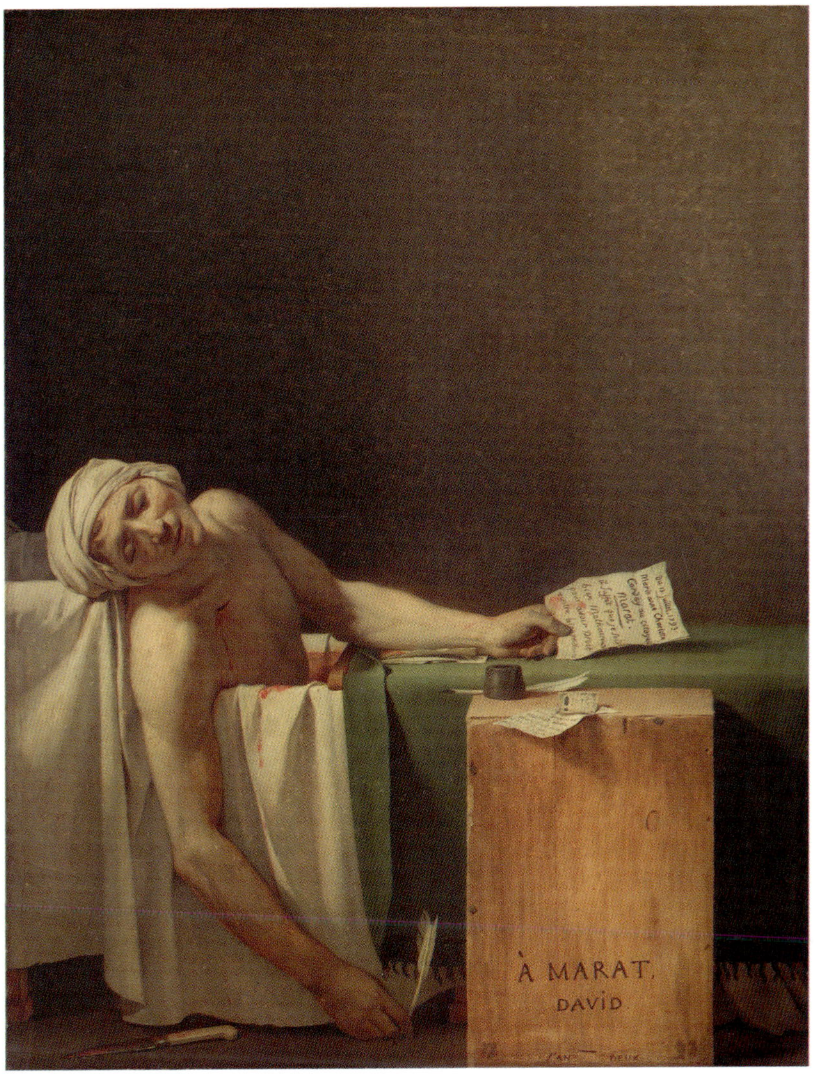

4 Jacques-Louis David, *The Death of Marat*, 1793

will see, these encounters would lead some artists to invert the
hierarchy of values and to declare that non-western cultures
and the art they produced were aesthetically, spiritually and
morally superior to the west's.

Across the English Channel, the works of J. M. W. Turner
(1775–1851) were especially pervaded by an acute awareness that
the conventional language of painting based on the careful
organization of a composition using linear perspective, no

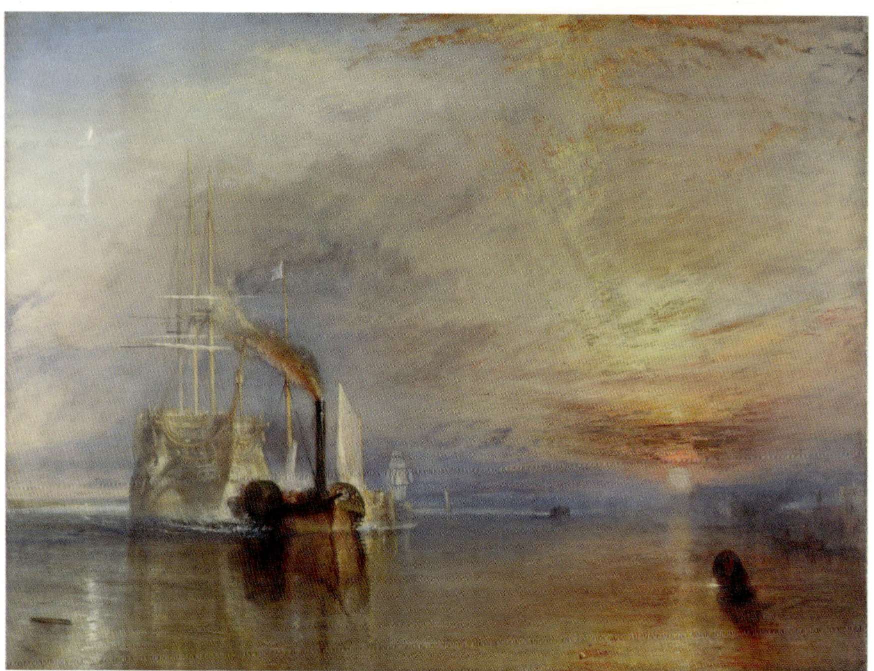

5 J.M.W. Turner, *The Fighting Temeraire tugged to her last berth to be broken up, 1838*, 1839

longer sufficed to evoke the vertiginous realities of modern life. In appearance, Turner's painting is clearly very different from David's. In abandoning the bounding and controlling line central to linear perspective, and composing his picture out of vague zones of colour, Turner conveys the sensation that the image on his canvas is transient and extends beyond its four edges rather than being contained within it. To some extent, Turner was developing stylistic traits explored by Leonardo da Vinci in the Renaissance and by artists during the Baroque period of the seventeenth century, where the conventions of geometric, rigid linear perspective and clear modelling in light and dark were countered by a more ambiguous and mercurial construction of space and light. But Turner pushed these tendencies much further. One contemporary described his paintings as 'too much abstractions of aerial perspective.... All is without forms and void. Some one said of his landscapes that they were pictures of nothing, and very like.'

The vessel named in the title of Turner's painting *The Fighting Temeraire tugged to her last berth to be broken up, 1838* (1839) is a wooden battleship that participated in the Battle of Trafalgar in 1805, when the British defeated a Franco-

Spanish fleet. At that time, Europe's state-of-the art sailing ships were already the most advanced in the world, but when Turner made his painting, they were becoming obsolete due to a newer invention: the steam-powered ship. But soon, paddle boats like the one shown in Turner's painting, would themselves be replaced by the faster and more efficient technology of the screw propeller-driven ship. Turner has produced a vivid visual correspondence between the fire and smoke streaming from the funnel of the squat and ugly paddle steamboat and the rays of the setting sun, suggesting perhaps that the new technology was in the process of making humanity a rival to nature itself. The venerable 'ship of the line', as it was termed (and a useful pun, in that the vessel is composed of actual lines, unlike the rest of Turner's painting), looks like an ethereal ghost, a magical but useless revenant from the past. The future would lie with the internal combustion engine and carbon-based fuel, like coal, of which, by geological chance, England proved to have an easily extracted abundance. This in its turn gave Britain the chance to lead the way in forging a society based on a carbon-economy and driven by high levels of consumption.

Romanticism

Turner's paintings, like Blake's and Goya's later works, are representative of a new cultural tendency that embraced all the arts and became known as Romanticism. The Romantics emphasized the novelty of the present and the constraining and deadening influence of the past. In accordance with the Enlightenment's vision, they were committed to the dignity of the individual and highlighted the paramount importance of the freedom of the inner life. But while they celebrated the desire to throw off the stranglehold of the past, they also recognized that the newly emerging society nurtured novel kinds of domination, appropriation and exploitation. They welcomed the openness encouraged by the spirit of the Enlightenment, but were acutely aware of the dangers of an excessive commitment to the narrow rationalistic vision of reality, and of the elevation of science to the status of a new religion. They therefore opposed what they saw as the reign of the mechanical, of *quantity* rather than *quality*, within the new scientific and technological culture, challenging the claim that science was the only authoritative source of human knowledge, and that all other potential sources – religious, pre-modern, indigenous non-western, imaginative – were irrelevant or to be sequestered away at the harmless margins of culture. As a result, the Romantics often sought to turn art

into a cultural space within which to explore more personally
meaningful relationships to the world, and to use the arts
to address the kinds of existential and spiritual concerns
that formerly were expressed within the Christian religion.
Frequently, Romantic works are also pervaded by nostalgia and
suffused by a craving for closer union with 'nature', for a lost
time when humanity supposedly lived in harmony, untainted
by the tragedy of history.

This new conception of art highlighted the centrality of
the individual's imagination. Feeling was the supreme source
of authority, and art was re-cast as a private realm in which
to represent the world as 'seen through a temperament', as
the nineteenth-century French novelist Emile Zola put it. Art
was understood to be inspiration, and even to involve forces
beyond the artist's own desires and aspirations, intentions
and understanding. The idea was established that art deals
with an obscure authority that speaks *through* the artist but is
not the artist. Its sources are fundamentally inaccessible, and
unreachable with mere training, skill and practised technique.
Before this period a European painting was usually likened to
a window or a mirror, implying that it was a painted copy of an
existing three-dimensional reality out there 'behind' it in the
world of people, objects and events. But now, increasingly, a
more apt metaphor would be that of a lamp providing access to
something shrouded in the darkness, in the soul of the artist.
The object of reference was still 'behind' the painting, and it
was still represented using linear perspective and modelling,
but now this reality was to be seized through the expressive
intentions of an artist standing heroically apart from a society
characterized as dull, ossified and conformist.

In opposition to this alienating social environment the
Romantics presented works that expressed their hope for
reconciliation with the world. Art was a haven from which to
resist the forces of oppression and to criticize the status quo
and its legacy of terror, exploitation, deviancy and apathy, a
sanctuary from which they could also explore self-realization
and transformation, openness, freedom, pleasure and joy. They
saw art as dealing with the realm of values (what 'ought to be')
rather than of facts (what 'is'). Sometimes, the Romantics made
art into a substitute for religion and claimed to see the future,
taking over the prophetic roles traditionally played by religious
clerics. Above all, the Romantics encouraged the idea that
people should not be content with things as they are. In these
ways, they turned art into the restless conscience of modernity.
And as a result of this new multifaceted vision, the audience
for Romantic art would be obliged to take on a new and

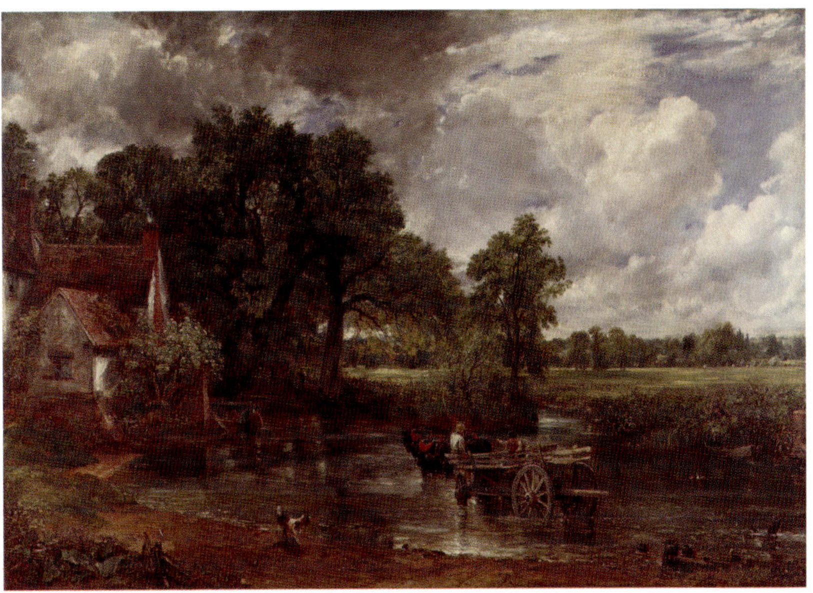

6 John Constable, *The Hay Wain*, 1821

more active role as it sought to engage with works of art, and to enter into open-ended dialogues in search of some kind of personal transformation.

The Romantics dedicated themselves in particular to exploring personal and emotional relationships to nature. For example, unlike artists schooled in the Classical tradition, who sought to paint an idealized reality, the English artist John Constable (1776–1837) focused almost entirely on depicting ordinary places in the region of south-eastern England he knew well from childhood, like the river and mill in his most famous painting, *The Hay Wain* (1821). 'My limited and abstracted art is to be found under every hedge, and in every lane,' Constable declared, 'and therefore nobody thinks it worth picking up.' In writing this, he was indicating that for him painting was intrinsically involved in what was at hand but neglected and overlooked. For Constable, conscious awareness of the art of the past was not the basis for making exemplary art in the present but rather an impediment to the free expression of one's own true feelings, which arose from direct experience of the world. He observed: 'When I sit down to make a sketch from nature, the first thing I try to do is, *to forget that I have ever seen a picture.*' Constable thereby gave expression to a characteristically modern idea: painting must be original.

The Beautiful and the Sublime

For the Romantics, a landscape could have two general aspects:
the 'beautiful' and the 'sublime'. As an aesthetic quality, the
'beautiful' evokes emotions of oneness and love that are positive
and pleasurable. A 'beautiful' landscape is harmonious, well-
formed, self-contained, clear and bright – like Constable's *The
Hay Wain*. The 'sublime' in nature, by contrast, expresses the
physically powerful, awe-inspiring and terrifying – the infinite
magnitude of nature manifest in the ocean, volcanos, mountains,
fog and mist. An interest in the sublime inclined artists to
seek out the extraordinary and melodramatic. Technically, it
led to the loosening of the firm grid of linear perspective so
that compositions seem to be more ambiguous, dynamic and
unstable. Turner's paintings are 'sublime' in this sense, as are
works by the French artist Jean-Louis-André-Théodore Géricault
(1791–1824), such as *The Raft of the Medusa* (1818–19), which depicts
an episode drawn from the account of a recent shipwreck, when
– after thirteen days adrift – the survivors, who had been driven
to resort to cannibalism, see a ship in the distance. Géricault's
melodramatic staging of the tragedy, which accentuates the
suffering of the human body under extreme conditions, directly
challenged artistic conventions that celebrated the value of
detachment and order.

7 Jean-Louis-André-Théodore Géricault, *The Raft of the Medusa*, 1818–19

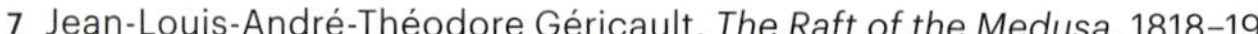

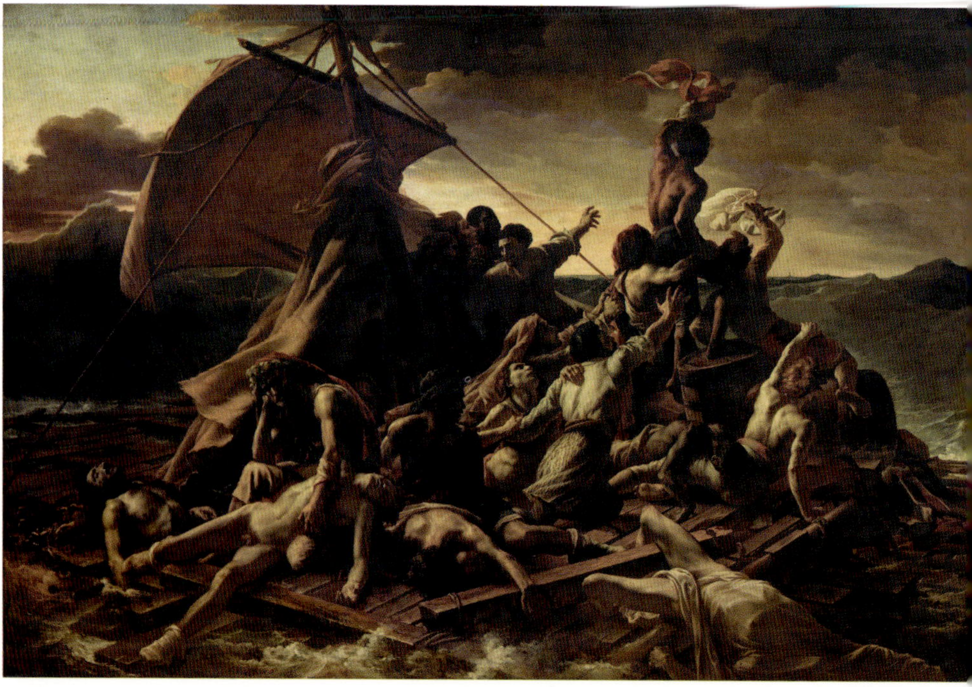

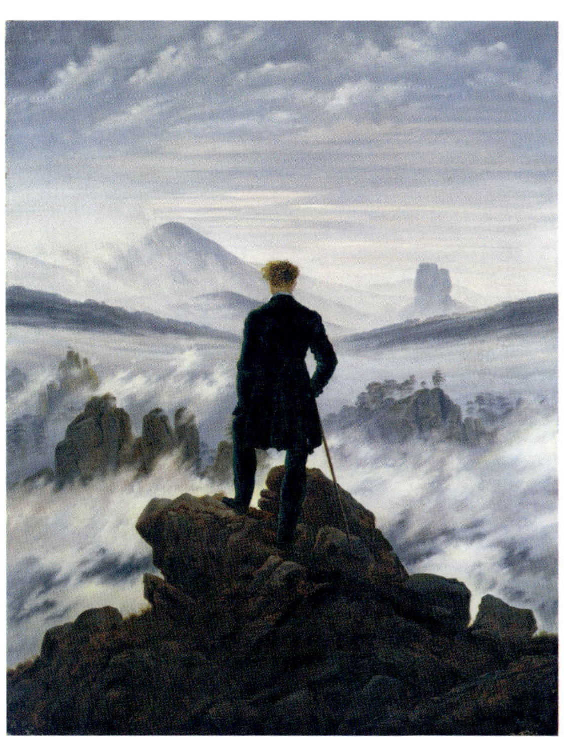

8 Caspar David Friedrich, *Wanderer above the Sea of Fog*, c. 1817

But the sublime is also the transcendent, the wondrous and inspiring in nature. The English word comes from the Latin *trans-*, meaning 'beyond', and *scandare*, 'to climb', an indication that the concept was intended to restore an elevated dimension to experience in a period when the traditional Christian distinction between the lower 'profane' world and the higher 'sacred' world was being eroded. In *Wanderer Above the Sea of Fog* (*c.* 1817), the Dresden-based artist Caspar David Friedrich (1774–1840) suggests that the sublime is about reaching the limits of experience or transcending ordinary existence. Friedrich used the pre-existing tools of pictorial illusionism, but repurposed them to produce a dramatic sense of a threshold. From the high vantage point that has brought the 'wanderer' – the artist himself – closer to the realm of the Gods, humankind seems endowed with god-like powers. The concept of the sublime pushed painting into the realm of the invisible, the paradoxical and the mysterious, and encouraged the exploration of enigmatic, evocative and changeable states of mind and mood to replace the desire to communicate a clear message.

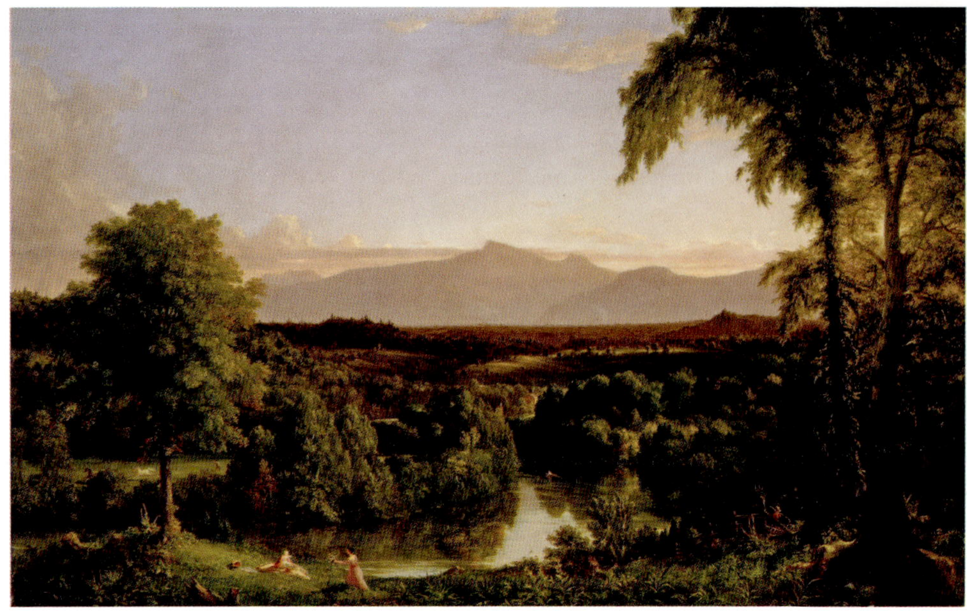

9 Thomas Cole, *View on the Catskill – Early Autumn*, 1836–37

Across the Atlantic, in the 'New World' of North America,
the sublime proved an especially attractive idea to artists,
such as those associated with the Hudson River School,
including Albert Bierstadt (1830–1902), Frederic Edwin Church
(1826–1900) and Thomas Cole (1801–1848). The concept of the
sublime became a means through which to understand the
awe-inspiring experience of the vast unknown wildernesses that
were being encountered by European settlers. In *View on the
Catskill – Early Autumn* (1836–37), for example, the British-born
Cole, the leading member of the School, employed the language
of the Romantic sublime to evoke the dramatic, awe-inspiring
mountains and valleys around the Hudson River in upstate
New York.

But Romantic landscape paintings, both 'sublime' and
'beautiful', are far from spontaneous recordings of real-life
views. In retrospect, one can see that they were a consequence
of the increasing separation of humanity from nature as
western society became urbanized and industrial. They are
symptoms of a specifically modern relationship to nature that
treats it as a resource to be exploited – in this artistic context,
by turning nature into an object for aesthetic enjoyment or
source of the awe-inspiring. Often, Romantic landscapes
ignore or actively conceal the signs of human transformation,

unrest and exploitation in their quest to create a consoling
vision. Cole's many paintings of the Hudson River valley are
far from accurate representations of what was a genuinely
unspoiled wilderness. During the 1830s, swathes of the virgin
forests of the region were felled to make way for a railroad,
and the Indigenous Americans who had lived in the region for
centuries had already been chased from their hunting grounds
by settlers. When they do appear in Cole's work, they function
as exotic novelties. The relationships with nature that Romantic
artists so convincingly depict are actually inspiring acts of
the imagination.

Romanticism versus Neo-Classicism

The Romantics pitted themselves against slavish allegiance
to the principles of art inherited from the Renaissance. Under
the influence of these traditional principles, students were
taught that making a painting was divided into two broad and
strictly demarcated stages: the sketching stage, which was
generative and explorative and intended to be private, and the
finished and public stage, the exhibited painting itself – what
in France was called *la grande machine* ('the great machine').
This final stage, which embodied in definitive form the artist's
conception first mapped out in the sketches, was expected to
be clearly composed using linear perspective, outlines in-filled
with colour, and clear modelling of forms in light and dark.
Sketches, often done in pencil on paper, were usually made
quickly, as they were regarded as merely visual aids in the
development of the final painting. But sketches in oils were also
required, and these were generally comprised of what is called
in French *taches* – quickly applied strokes of paint that remain
on the surface as dabs, blots or patches. These *taches* are the
traces left behind by the movements made by the artist holding
(usually) a paintbrush, and are evidence of the decisions and
bodily actions that went into the making of a picture.

But increasingly, it seemed to artists attracted to
Romanticism that the explorative, expressive, relatively
unconstrained dimension of what they did should be given
more centrality, and even be what their audience saw. As a
result, more free and 'unfinished' effects, like those explored
by Turner and Constable, began to take precedence over the
executive and controlling techniques necessary for making
a conventionally completed work. There were historical
precedents for such 'painterly' painting in the work of artists
from the Venetian Renaissance of the sixteenth century and
Baroque artists of the seventeenth century such as Rembrandt
van Rijn and Peter-Paul Rubens. But now, colour in the form of

fluid or lumpy oil paint began spreading across and enveloping compositions, and increasingly gained dominance over the tidy bounding and controlling line.

Inspired by these painters, and especially by the contemporaneous example of John Constable, the French artist Eugène Delacroix (1798–1863) started drawing more attention to the status of his paintings as flat surfaces covered in coloured brushmarks by building his works out of a sequence of rapid, skilled gestures made with a paintbrush. The subjects Delacroix depicted became vaguer and more elusive, and his painting's presence – the physical fact of its existence in a specific place, rather than what it represented – was increasingly dominant. Even in his more clearly composed works, such as *Liberty Leading the People* (1830), Delacroix radically disrupted the ordered spaces that linear perspective and modelling were intended to create, producing instead a far more confusing, immersive and ambiguous pictorial space. The French poet and critic Charles Baudelaire described Delacroix as 'the most suggestive of all painters' – he made more room for the viewer's own speculations concerning intention and meaning. In this work, Delacroix celebrated not the Revolution of 1789 but the smaller and, in the event, rather muted July Revolution of 1830 that led to the deposing of Charles X and the establishment of a constitutional monarchy under Louis-Philippe. He employed dynamic and expressive brushstrokes to bring vividness and poetry to a contemporary event. Although the painting obeys some of the conventions of Classicism – the female figure symbolizing Liberty was inspired by the Classical Greek sculpture the 'Winged Victory of Samothrace' (*c.* 190 BCE) which Delacroix could see in the Louvre Museum – the artist deliberately depicted the central subject as a woman of modern Paris, and placed her at the head of and atop a seething mass of human bodies.

It was against the still powerful forces of cultural reaction – which, it should be emphasized, included the most materially successful and publicly celebrated artists of the age – that the Romantics like Delacroix positioned themselves as a progressive alternative. In France, the most important rival artistic movement comprised members of the French Académie, which had been reinstated on the restoration of the monarchy in France in 1816, and whose members continued to adhere to what was known as Neo-Classicism. In the period after 1815 and the defeat of Napoleon and the restoration of the monarchy in France, the leading exponent and arch-opponent of Delacroix was Jean-Auguste-Dominique Ingres (1780–1867). His *Odalisque with Slave* (1842) reflects the growing European fascination for non-western culture – in particular in this period, Muslim North

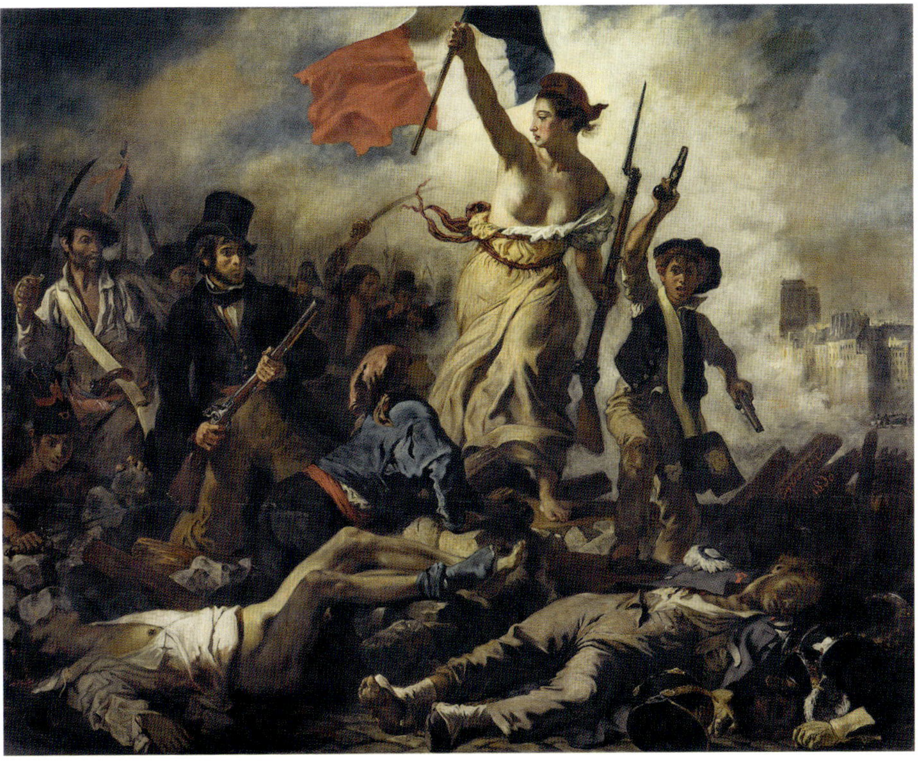

10 Eugène Delacroix, *Liberty Leading the People*, 1830

Africa and the Middle East. An 'odalisque' was a concubine in a harem. Here, in a tacit celebration of racial superiority, her luminous whiteness is contrasted with the darker skins of the Abyssinian musician slave and the African slave eunuch. Ingres painted this work and others depicting harems at a time when changing attitudes within Europe towards the inhuman practice of slavery in general, and most especially the trade in Africans, led to the abolition of the slave trade (first in Britain in 1807) and then of slavery itself (also first in Britain, in 1833). In France, slavery was abolished in 1848, six years after this painting was made. But for Ingres, the Near Eastern region dominated by the Ottoman Empire provided for his European male audience the setting for a fantasy of sexual availability and domination.

Artists allied to the Neo-Classical tendency celebrated very different values to those of the Romantics, values they shared with the elite audience for their works – the Court, the aristocracy, state officials and the *haute bourgeoisie* (the new monied class who had benefited most from capitalist industrialization) who chose to emulate the nobility and shared an idealized vision of the world they inhabited and of themselves. This was a social alliance that required a very specific style and circumscribed collection of subjects that were intended to clearly mark out the space of painting as distinct from and superior to that of everyday life, and that was dedicated to the celebration of the values and privileges of their social class and resisted any change that might threaten them. The Academicians were committed to painting as the visual embodiment of the values of order and a firm connection to the idealized past. Linear perspective, and the bounding line clearly dividing the picture into recognizable and evenly illuminated forms and spaces, were deemed sacrosanct. According to the conventions of the Académie, the traces of paint and bold colours admired by the Romantics were signs of poor workmanship and bad taste, and should be absent from a finished painting, which was to possess what has been described as a 'licked-on surface'.

Historically, the skills displayed by an artist in constructing space using linear perspective and the line to define forms signalled the paramount cultural values of control and measured thought. Colour was denigrated as overly 'feminine', emotional and too ambiguous when compared to the 'masculine', rational, ordering principles imposed by the line. But it was precisely the unstable and emotional possibilities of colour and fluid, dynamic brushstrokes that now appealed. In favouring the coloured and dynamic *tache*, the Romantics were therefore doing more than simply making an innovation in style. The Romantics were rebelling against the dominance of the values of clarity, order and reason not just within painting but within society as a whole. They were embracing feeling, the spontaneous and the liberating power of the imagination. They bequeathed to the art of the entire modern period its most striking characteristic: that true art must be a continual search for the new, for more than existing art can offer. They forged the idea that modern art must be the dramatization of society's rupture with the past and its perpetual development. They also gave birth to the quintessentially modern idea that art was valuable in itself – and not because of any cause it served, be it religious, political or a ruling elite. In fact, art's very lack of social purpose made it seem the highest form of meaning and hope. As something beautiful and thought-provoking, a source of solace and comfort, art was *intrinsically* meaningful and life-affirming, an aesthetic response to an all too often alienating and silent world. It was the play of the possible in a world dominated by the dull routines of the probable.

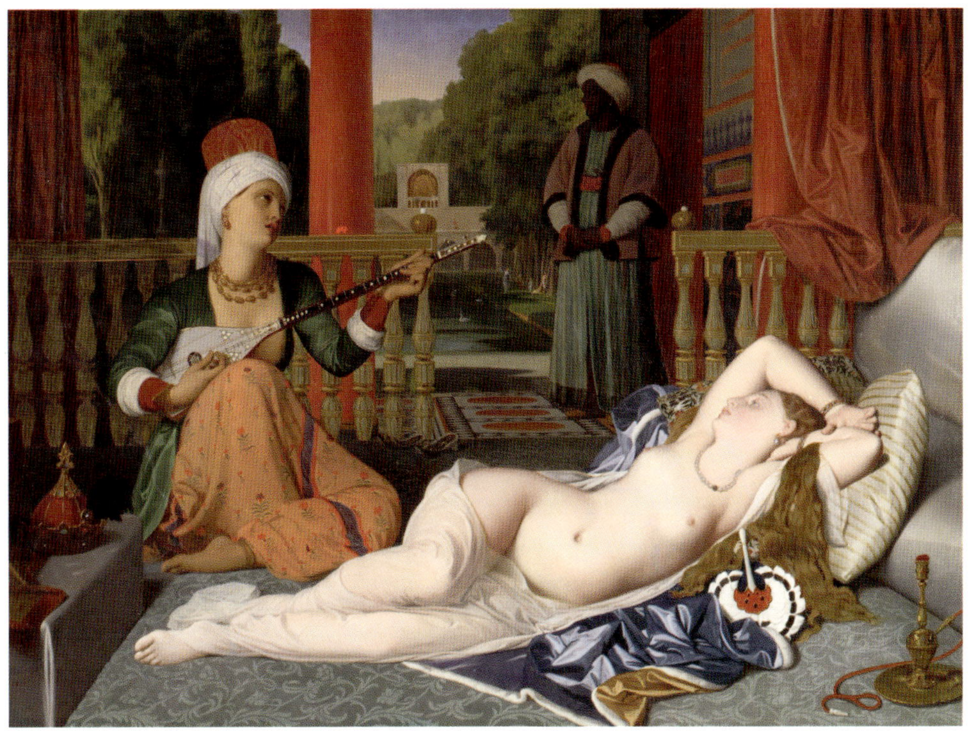

11 Jean-Auguste-Dominique Ingres, *Odalisque with Slave*, 1842

Love and Fear of the New

In retrospect, the confrontation between Romanticism and Neo-Classicism in painting reflects in microcosm the emergence of two radically different but interdependent ways of responding to the unprecedented conditions of modernity which involve beliefs and actions that still very much concern the people of today. On the one hand are the neophiles – the lovers of the new. They embrace the values of innovation and individualism, and are almost always politically progressive or radical. They recognize that while the once familiar borders and boundaries that circumscribed existence no longer constrain the present, causing new levels of uncertainty, this also means they have the freedom to openly enjoy unprecedented potential and reshape their lives from the ground up. They are open to encounters with other cultures, finding them enriching, and they feel comfortable in a multicultural society. Artists of this kind will therefore welcome the emancipation of the present from the past, and will see their task as engaging in dynamic and progressive struggle.

As they understand that how and what one sees is dependent on context, that it is never only a question of perceiving 'reality' but of *interpreting* it, they will explore new ways of representing the world. They are curious and ready to learn from other cultures, and accept and even welcome the discovery that their own culture does not have a unique claim to truth and is not inherently superior.

But there are also the neophobes – the fearers of the new. They experience the complexity, contingency, fragmentation and uncertainty of modernity as a threat. The loss of historical continuity is seen as detrimental for society, and they emphasize the importance of maintaining traditions and recovering lost power. They value the ideal of the homogeneous community more than the freedom of the individual, and seek control through the simplification of values. The dominant impulse is therefore to resist change and demand the re-establishment of the old boundaries, the beliefs and patterns of life within which to live securely and fruitfully. The neophobe prefers to live in a monoculture that is secure in its sense of cultural superiority, its unique relationship to truth. As a result, the neophobe is usually politically conservative or reactionary. For those wary of innovation, and anxious about the uncertainties that inevitably come with freedom, the act of seeing will always tend to be associated with the need to establish limits. So, for the neophobic artist, innovation and novelty are dangerous because they threaten familiar values and ways of life. They consider the art of other cultures as inherently defective, inferior to their own and of little value other than as exotica. Their art will be characterized by narrowness of vision, by dogmatism, rigidity, inflexibility and the desire to exclude.

These opposing worldviews are, of course, not wholly distinct, not least because people are far from consistent or rational in their beliefs and actions. Often the young are neophiles, while the old are neophobes, which means that at some stage in any individual's life, their experiences can force upon them a change of values. Modern art includes both neophilic and neophobic tendencies. Like anybody, an artist might display traits from both attitudes simultaneously or change camps as they mature. The Romantic's nostalgic evocations of a prelapsarian past, for example, and the perception of modern society as a corruption of human virtue, fed hostility to progress. While Constable's art can be described as neophilic on the level of technical innovation and the commitment to the truths of subjective experience, politically speaking he became increasingly conservative.

To the educated audience of his time, the intimate visions of the tranquil English countryside would have been understood as corresponding to the call for greater social order and harmony grounded in traditional values of the Christian religion and resistance to the forces agitating for greater political freedom. And, as we will see, throughout the modern period, radical artists' hostility to the 'bourgeois' status quo could make them seek out the simplicity of grand ideas and schemes that promised to impose order on change – such as when they embraced communism or fascism – so as to make the future fall into line with their own beliefs.

Chapter 2
The Birth of the Avant-Garde *c.* 1848–*c.* 1880

The Birth of the Avant-Garde

By the 1840s, the largely optimistic and progressive spirit
that had inspired the Romantics' belief in an open future in
which life would inevitably become more free, equal and just
was being severely challenged by the tenacity of the old order.
For those committed to radical change, the failures of the
popular uprising of 1830 in France, celebrated in Delacroix's
painting of *Liberty Leading the People*, and of the much more
serious unrest throughout western Europe in 1848, showed
that despite a growing desire for change the old elites were
holding doggedly onto power. Karl Marx's theory of society as
class conflict seemed an increasingly accurate diagnosis of a
European society founded on the oppression of the majority
by a small and ruthless minority. This was a society that was
dangerously out of balance, and that encouraged the relentless
monetarization of life. Marx argued that the abject bondage
of the poor to the soil was being replaced by a far worse one:
servitude in the factory and submission to the efficacy of the
timetable and rational uniformity. Industrial labourers were
nothing more than 'wage slaves' of the capitalist owners of the
'means of production'. Marx described capitalist society as a
world in which *everyone* – including the capitalist owners – was
alienated from themselves, their fellow human beings and the
world. But, he declared that the 'proletariat' would soon rise
up, violently shake off its chains, and then become the new
collective masters of a far more benign 'classless' society.

This vision of revolution leading to sudden change for
the better was very appealing to radical artists, who saw
themselves as pitted against the indifference and reactionary
interests of the ruling class who controlled and exploited the

masses and only seemed interested in purchasing technically
proficient but superficial art. Feeling increasingly marginalized
and estranged from the dominant values and routines of
modern life, some artists began styling themselves as an
avant-garde. This term derives from military strategy, where
it refers to troops sent out ahead of the main army, and an
artistic avant-garde was meant to imply a cultural force set
apart from and in opposition to mainstream society, one that
is heroically ahead of its times and politically allied with the
forces of democractization and, increasingly, revolution. For the
avant-garde felt deceived and betrayed by the moderate liberal
forces within society that advocated gradual reform, and they
saw hypocrisy and self-interest everywhere. As a result, they
embraced the ideals of resistance and antagonism towards
'bourgeois' art and society and advocated the perpetual 'shock
of the new'. Indeed, authentic proof of vanguardist credentials
lay in producing artworks that were deliberately offensive to
the old elite and to the new capitalist bourgeoisie who were
increasingly gaining power and status.

Salon Painting versus Realism

Especially in France, a belligerent but inherently co-dependent
relationship developed between two rival artistic factions:
the Neo-Classical Academic 'Salon' painters and the avant-
garde Realists (the term 'Salon' referred to the annual
official exhibitions in which works were presented to the elite
audience). The Realists derisively dubbed the former *Pompiers*
('firemen') because Salon painters often painted Classical
scenes with warriors sporting helmets that looked like those
worn by the French firemen of the period. The goal of the Salon
painters was to create their *grande machines* – the large-scale
paintings destined for a public building or museum, displaying
a high level of technical skill and containing instantly readable
images that were both visually clear and symbolically familiar
and reassuring. Deference to the values of tradition was
simultaneously an attempt to block the dangerous incursions
of 'vulgar' modernity. Thomas Couture's (1815–1879) enormous
painting *The Romans of the Decadence* (1847), for example, was
destined to be installed in one of the French state's public
buildings. But it is also an instance of a 'Salon' painting
that has absorbed some useful lessons from Romanticism,
especially Delacroix's more dynamic organization of figures.
Like the Realists, Couture was Republican and anticlerical,
and this work was made a year before the 1848 revolution that
toppled the July Monarchy, and was perceived at the time as a
'realist allegory' of contemporary French decadence. But the

12

underlying intention was to still produce a work that allowed the elite audience to simultaneously enjoy a sexually provocative subject and savour their rights and privileges. Despite its critical dimensions, they would have been reassured that there was a secure bridge back from the present to the Classical past.

In his 'Manifesto for Realism' (1855) Gustave Courbet (1819–1877), the most important artist of the European avant-garde at mid-century, decried what he considered the mortifying vacuity of Salon paintings and declared he wanted 'to create living art'. In practice, this goal meant Courbet produced paintings that were antithetical in both style and content to those of the *pompier* enemy. But Courbet's self-proclaimed brand of Realism was also intended to challenge the Romantics, whose cult of feeling and imagination he saw as leading away from the complexities and injustices of social reality. Courbet wanted to make painting more natural, more 'real', a copy of aspects of life that the Salon painters found unworthy of their attention. His goal was to destroy the hold of the ideal *and* the imagination over painting. To this end, Courbet confronted his audiences with the raw and tragic facts of life in the impoverished region of eastern France where he was born. Such subject matter was for him the sole basis for authentic art.

The Stonebreakers (1849), shown at the Paris Salon of 1850 – where to Courbet's satisfaction it caused a scandal – exemplified the new Realist values. The subject of humble labourers was meant to bring the 'vulgar' countryside to the city, and

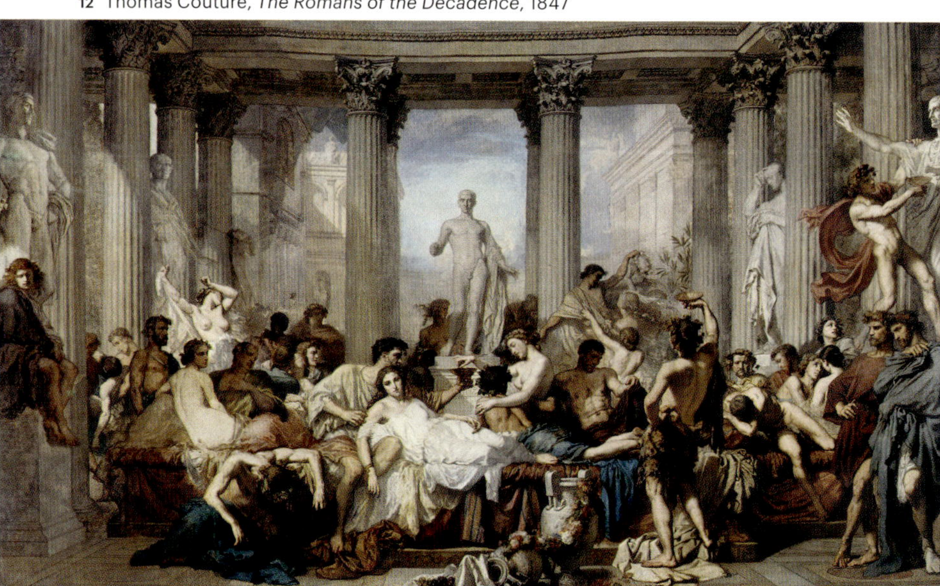

12 Thomas Couture, *The Romans of the Decadence*, 1847

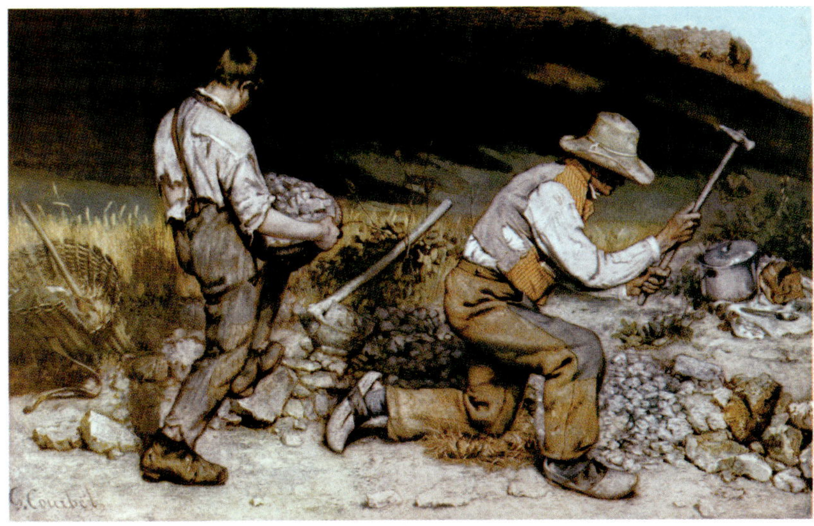

13 Gustave Courbet, *The Stonebreakers*, 1849 (destroyed during the Second World War)

Courbet was judged by his critics to be deliberately aiming at 'ugliness-for-ugliness's-sake'. This was also manifest in the execution of the work. Courbet produced a roughly textured surface, applying paint not just with paintbrushes but also the palette knife, rags, sponges and his fingers. As a result, he drew attention to the status of painting as a raw physical fact, a presence on the wall, as much as a representation of something out in the world. When looking at such a painting, the contemporary audience was necessarily prised away from their habits of viewing, forced by its novelty and intensity to focus on an unfamiliar range of potential meanings and goals.

Naturalism and the Pre-Raphaelites

Less obviously abrasive alternative forms of the painting of everyday life also emerged during this period, styles pandering to a growing public interested in art that was a more direct reflection of the world they could see around them, but at the same time, not too controversial or unsettling. These were modern styles that avoided the extremes of Classicizing idealism or Romantic 'art-for-art's sake', but also Realist ugliness. In France, *juste milieu* ('middle way' or 'happy medium') painting developed, which, as the term suggests, aimed at a balance between the Classicizing and the anti-Classicizing impulses. Schools of landscape painting developed that drew on the more naturalistic aspects of Romanticism and on Realism. In France, the Barbizon School, which included the artists

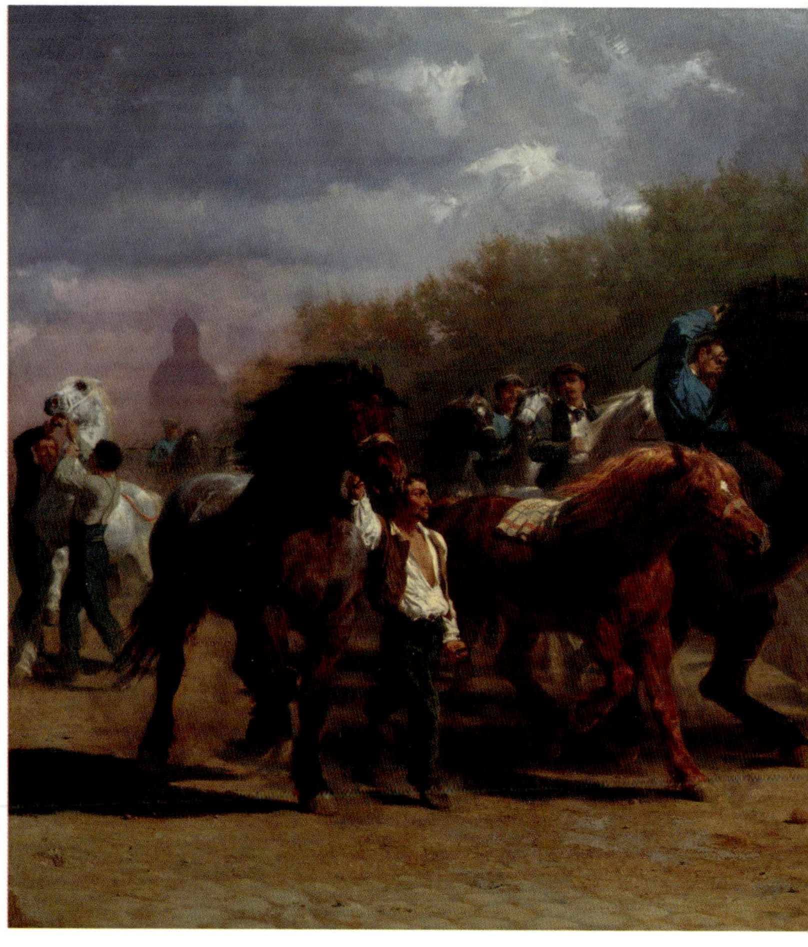

Jean-Baptiste-Camille Corot, Charles-François Daubigny and its
most prominent figure, Théodore Rousseau, especially revered
John Constable, who was admired for his dynamic, heavily
layered dashes of different colour and use of white highlights,
techniques that resulted in the animation of the whole surface
of Barbizon School paintings. Genre or narrative painting
also developed, merging Romanticism and Realism in the
concept of 'naturalism' – depictions of subjects without obvious
idealization or Romantic emotionalism, but also without the
overt 'ugliness' of Courbet's vision. For example, Rosa Bonheur
(1822–1899), the most successful and celebrated woman artist
of her time, in *The Horse Fair* (1852–55) painted an everyday
scene in Paris. To achieve such an accurate depiction, she made

14

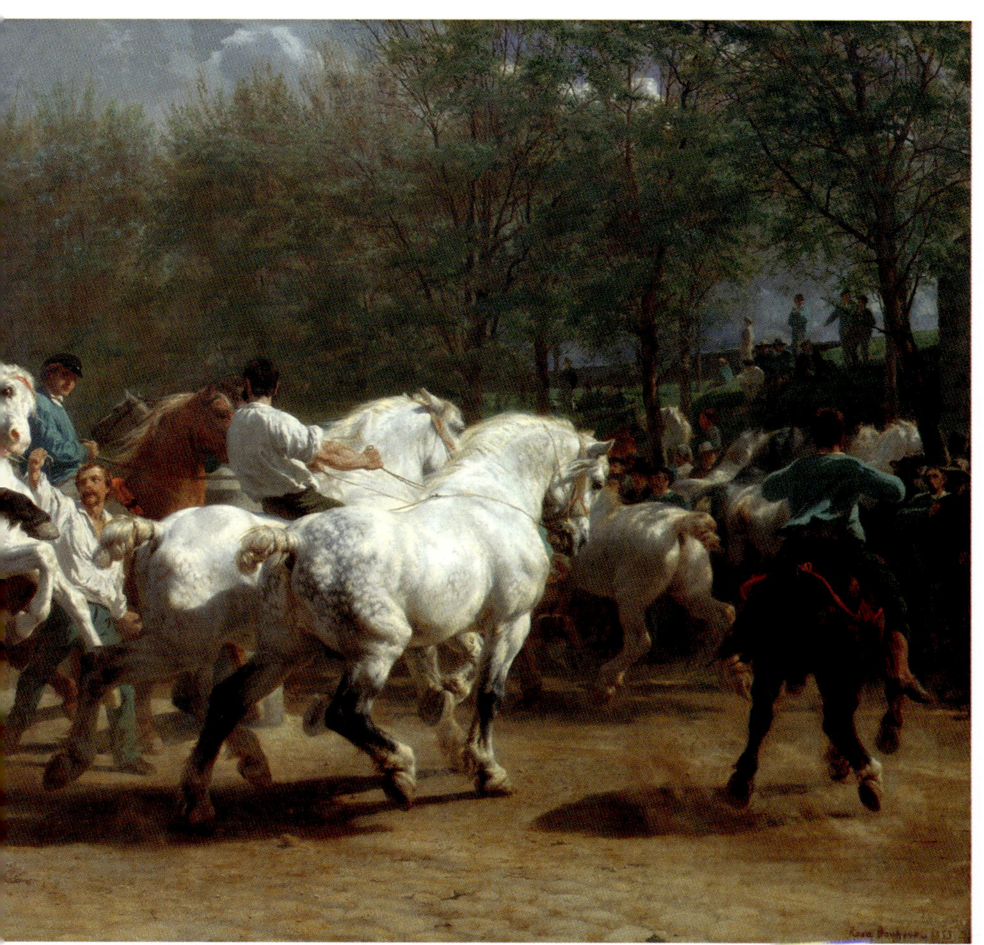

numerous sketches on the spot, which obliged her to dress as
a man to avoid attracting attention, unconventional behaviour
for which she had to get official permission.

In Britain, where Romanticism was especially important
and was opposed by the entrenched values of the Royal
Academicians, Britain's equivalent to the Salon painters, the
Pre-Raphaelite Brotherhood rebelled by embracing the new
sobriety of naturalistic painting. Founded in 1848 by, amongst
others, the painters William Holman Hunt, John Everett
Millais and Dante Gabriel Rossetti, by calling themselves
'Pre-Raphaelite' they announced an alignment with the art
of the late medieval and early Renaissance periods – with
artists then known as the 'Primitives'. This allegiance was

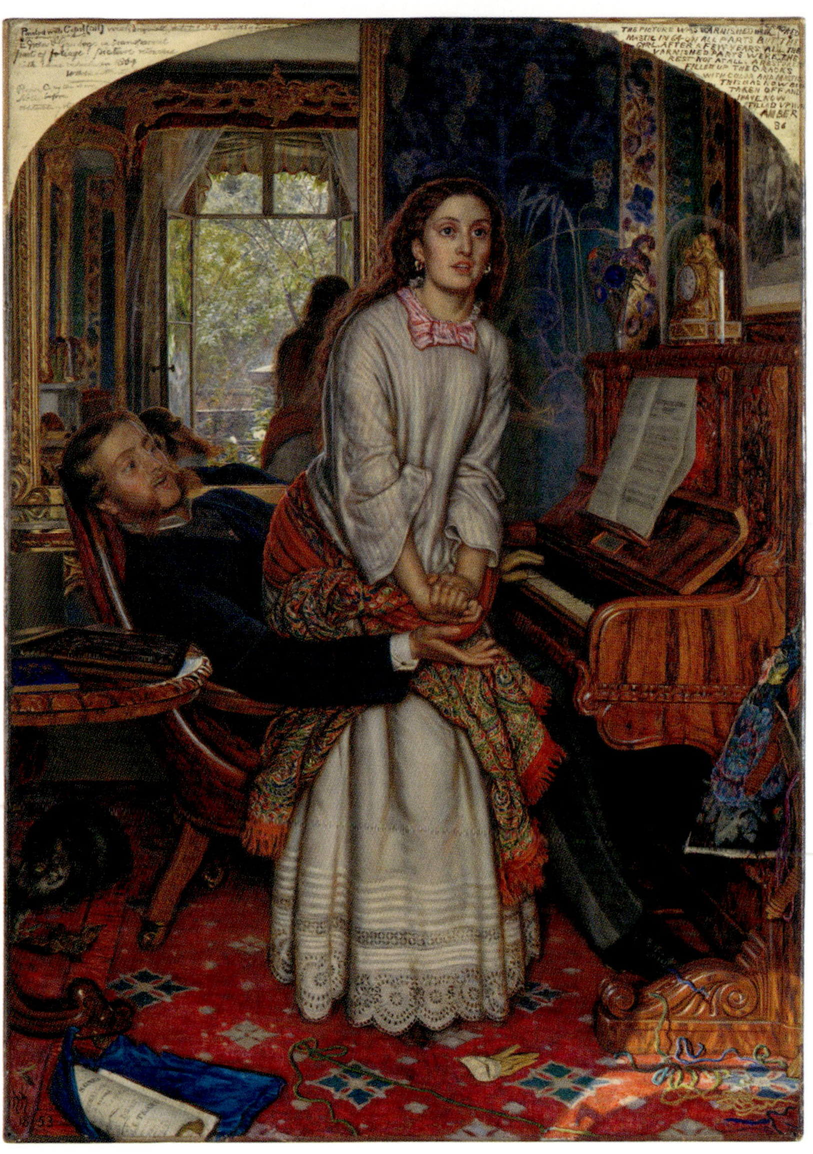

15 William Holman Hunt, *The Awakening Conscience*, 1854

therefore to the art of a largely denigrated historical period in Europe, but one the Pre-Raphaelites saw as offering a subversive alternative to the dominant art tendencies. The result, in practice, were works in a laboriously detailed linear style in-filled with strong colour. The preference was for genre or narrative scenes based on modern life. William Holman Hunt's (1827–1910) *The Awakening Conscience* (1854), for example, is a jewel-like composition sparkling with details. But its mood is deliberately deceptively cheerful, and an analysis of the carefully placed clues within the painting allows one to identify a far from edifying narrative. The young woman – the whiskered gentleman's mistress – has suddenly realized that his honeyed words are empty and that she is nothing more than a pretty thing to be played with then discarded, just like the bird on the rug menaced by a cat, at bottom left.

Across the Atlantic in the United States, Winslow Homer and Thomas Eakins developed forms of realism that sought to capture the unique characteristics of the emerging culture of the United States, forging an idea of art freed from the idealism that still plagued European art. As Eakins declared: 'It is well to go abroad and see the works of the old masters, but Americans....must strike out for themselves, and only by doing this will we create a great and distinctly American art.'

The novelty of social change made it difficult for artists to know just what to pay attention to out there in the world, what aspects of the new reality were worthy of attention and how best to depict them. The Americans committed to realism even more strongly than the Europeans in the belief that to be a 'modern' artist meant to rely on the self for inspiration and values, rather than refer to models handed down from the past. Modern experience, the reality of life in the industrial metropolis, could no longer be so securely attached to traditional pre-given roles and conventions, and demanded new forms of art rooted in the ambivalence and uncertainties of personal experience and vision.

Beyond Realism and Naturalism

'The artist today does not say, "Come and see faultless works," but rather "Come and see sincere work",' declared the French artist Edouard Manet (1832–1883), a former student of Thomas Couture and friend and admirer of Courbet. Manet's emphasis on sincerity and authenticity, and on the ambiguity and openness of the possible meanings of the work of art – rather than the masterful display of technical skill and the communication of clear and reassuringly morally ennobling values – reflected the impact of both Romanticism and Realism. Manet recognized that painting based excessively on the desire for integration with the past, that spoke of connectedness and secure attachment to the authority of tradition, inevitably lacked the authentic individuality that made a work of art a true expression of modern life. Manet believed that artists should be involved in re-imagining what painting can be based on novel ideas and visual sources coming from personal experience, awareness of social change, and in response to new developments within the realm of ideas. Like Courbet, he was suspicious of the free flights of the imagination central to Romanticism and wanted to root painting in the tangibility of the here-and-now. But he also saw that Courbet and his followers were still adhering to rules of pictorial space founded on optical realism, as if this convention provided a true, objective picture of the world. He increasingly felt that as part-and-parcel of the quest for authenticity these rules themselves needed to be rigorously interrogated.

Manet was also aware that while styles of art that emphasized uniqueness and overt differences from the past possessed individual novelty and accomplishment, as a result, they risked becoming mired in superficiality and egotism. Therefore, so Manet argued, only when a painting was somehow the result of two basically incompatible impulses – the desire to emulate authoritative past greatness *and* the drive for innovation in response to the present – could art avoid the dual vices of conformity and self-centredness. He believed that, henceforth, the intelligent painter should be involved primarily with the almost impossible task of finding a balance between conflicting forces and obligations. They should strive to imitate the best in already existing paintings, not only because some achievements of the past remained worthy of emulation and continued to speak to the present of human experience, but also because, as a specific material medium, painting is essentially self-organizing – that is, it is able to produce, maintain and evolve itself by continuously creating from its own constituent parts, independently from any sources external to itself. But, at the same time as focusing on painting's autonomy, Manet argued that artists should be striving to depict the characteristic features and events of the modern world around them.

In 1863 the poet and critic Charles Baudelaire echoed Manet's thinking when he too considered the challenges posed to the artist by the new society that was coming into existence around him in Paris. He wrote: 'Modernity is the transient, the fleeting, the contingent.' But he immediately added that there was also another equally significant 'half of art' – what he described as 'the eternal and the immutable'. Baudelaire's paradoxical

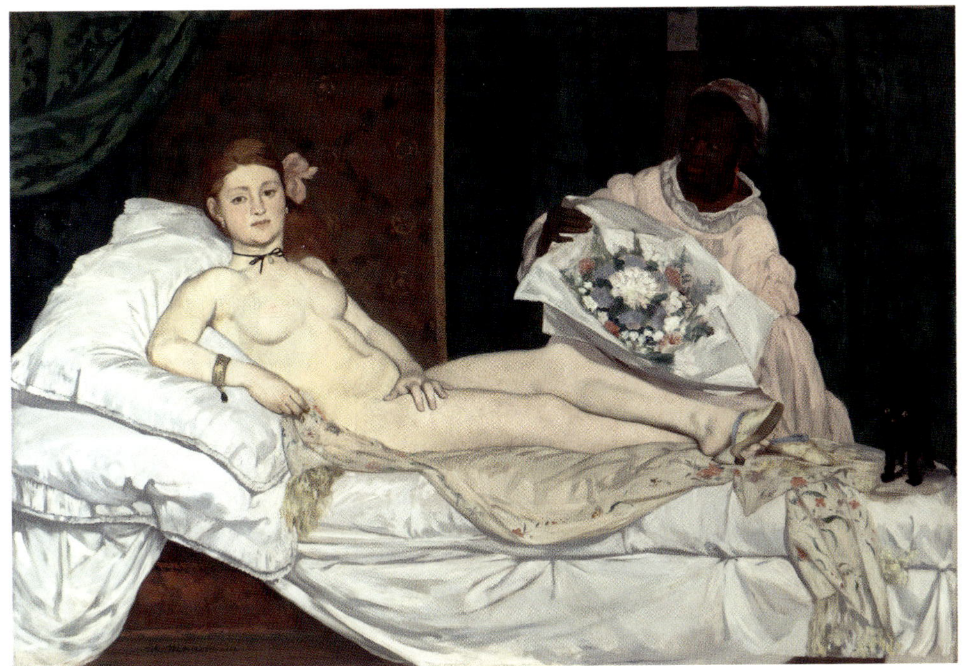

16 Edouard Manet, *Olympia*, 1863

blending of apparent opposites also reflects the recognition
that modern artists were being led away from the past and
towards freedom and innovation in the present moment, but
that they were also inevitably linked to the authority of the past.
Like Manet, Baudelaire saw that the novel conditions of modern
life posed a seemingly impossible challenge for the artist,
who must somehow bring together conflicting realities that
pit the experience of unstable, contingent, instantaneous and
subjective perceptions in the present against the continuities
and stability provided by a bond with eternal truths.

16 Manet's painting *Olympia* (1863) exemplifies this productive
tension between innovation and tradition. It is a portrait of a
well-known courtesan of the kind the gentlemen who would
have viewed the painting patronized (at mid-century there were
approximately 10,000 such high-end prostitutes in Paris, known
colloquially as *grandes horizontales*). This one is attended by
her Black maid, who presents a bouquet of flowers that has
been sent by a client. The appearance of a person of colour
in a nineteenth-century European work of art is unusual,
and a reminder that France was a colonial power. Within
the conventions of the period – even the progressive ones

of Manet and his circle – the Black woman would have been interpreted as symbolizing 'dark' and dangerous sexuality, the transgressive culture of the *demimonde*, and she was therefore intentionally included to enhance the scandalously contemporary nature of the painting.

But it was not just the modern and scandalous subject – the brazenly confrontational gaze of the courtesan and the inclusion of a Black maid – that shocked the audience of 1863. Manet conjoined his scene from decadent modern Paris with an overt reference to a Classical goddess and a famous Renaissance painting: *Venus of Urbino* (*c.* 1534) by the sixteenth-century Venetian artist Titian, making a barely subliminal connection between an aggressively modern subject, and the mores it reflected, and the noble themes and masterpieces of the Renaissance – the very themes that were so dear to Academic Salon artists. But that was not all. The way Manet painted his subject was also deemed a deliberate affront to public decency. To many of his contemporaries, Manet's manner of painting seemed inherently faulty. He was said to have an insufficient mastery of linear perspective and modelling, and to deliberately flaunt weak drawing skills, making his work excessively flat and two-dimensional and much too highly contrasted in colour.

The influence of Manet on the future of painting would prove to be profound. He helped foreground the untapped potential of working more consciously in the gap between painting as a two-dimensional surface and painting as a 'window' onto a world – between the 'reality' of painting as an image and the reality of 'painting' as an object. To understand this twofoldedness more clearly it is useful to make an analogy with the familiar experience of looking through a car windscreen. Normally, one focuses one's attention on what lies beyond the glass surface. In fact, looking at the glass while driving is very likely to lead to an accident. Similarly, the conventions of painting in Europe had come to place the lion's share of importance on what is seen beyond the screen – beyond the flat surface upon which paint is applied in an illusionary three-dimensional space. While it is impossible for an artist to wholly ignore their working surface, to a far greater extent than in other cultures, such as the Chinese, for example, European art was dedicated to producing a convincing imitation of a reality seen beyond the 'screen' and therefore to minimizing the viewer's awareness of that 'screen'. But what artists were now beginning to consider more assiduously was the surface of the painting itself as inherently aesthetically interesting, and a carrier of valuable information.

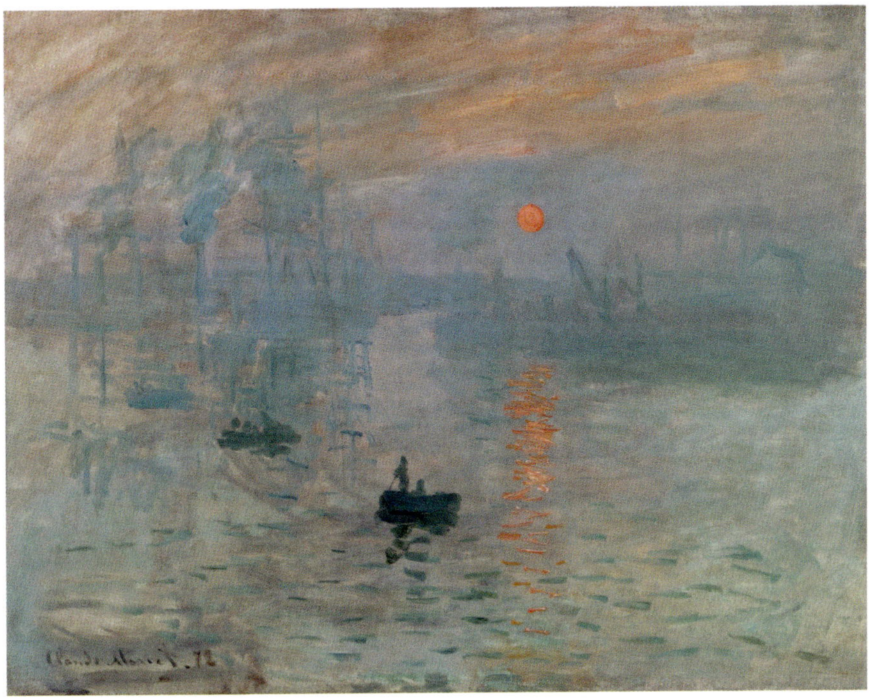

17 Claude Monet, *Impression – Sunrise*, 1872

Impressionism

The challenges to the role of painting as a medium of representational imitation intensified when artists discovered they had a powerful new rival: a technological invention utilizing a glass lens and a chemical process to reproduce an image that was apparently a seamless copy of its referent. Compared to photography, painting's traditional function as a hand-made copy of the visible world seemed comparatively awkward and arbitrary, even redundant. Some artists saw photography as a rival, a threat or even a death sentence, but others recognized that it opened up whole new possibilities and were challenged to determine what was still unique to the medium of painting – what it could do that this new machine could not – and what role it might still play in society alongside photography. For example, some artists understood that the instantaneousness of photography could be a powerful new model of how to convey a heightened sense of lively presence, of the authentic reality of the moment. Rather implausibly, perhaps, these artists thought to use the labour-intensive medium of painting in oils with a brush to mimic the visual immediacy delivered by photography.

17 *Impression – Sunrise* (1872) by Claude Monet (1840–1926)
epitomizes this interest in creating a convincing image of a
specific moment in time, an interest that brought to painting
a new kind of illusion: instantaneity. The work's title proved
to be the inspiration for the new movement's name, and it was
exhibited in the First Impressionist Exhibition, which took place
in a private gallery in Paris in 1874. The exhibition was a financial
failure, but it brought the innovative new style to the attention
of the – suitably outraged – public for the first time. Other
artists associated with Impressionism include the French artists
Gustave Caillebotte, Edgar Degas, Eva Gonzalès, Berthe Morisot,
Camille Pissarro, Pierre-Auguste Renoir and Alfred Sisley; the
Americans Mary Cassatt and James Abbott McNeill Whistler and,
subsequently, a younger generation including Childe Hassam;
and the British artists Philip Wilson Steer and Walter Sickert.

Impressionist paintings appear to be, and often really
were, made very quickly and outdoors. Two further new
technologies became available in this period that assisted in
this activity, and also helped push painting towards a new
materiality and immediacy: synthetically produced oil colour
and ready-mixed paint packed into metal tubes. From the
beginning of the nineteenth century, the coloured pigments
that artists needed were increasingly not derived from natural,
sometimes expensive, sources, nor were they artisanally made.
Instead, colours were derived from the chemical industry and
mass-produced. For example, the colour mentioned in Chapter
One known as ultramarine blue, which was made from a rare
semi-precious stone, was synthesized in the 1830s and became
available as a much cheaper pigment. From the 1840s, oil paint
was being manufactured to fit in ready-made metal tubes,
making available a commercial product that was standardized
according to industrial norms. These tubes were cheap and
easy to transport, making painting out-of-doors more feasible,
and this new technology became indispensable to artists like
the Impressionists who often wanted to paint *en plein air* –
in the open air.

In effect, these artists were arresting the production of a
painting at the preliminary 'sketch' stage and presenting it
as the finished work, making it appear to be capturing an
instant in time – like a photograph. They abandoned the soupy
brown grounds that had served Constable, Delacroix, the
Realists and the Barbizon School artists, and which to modern
eyes (and largely thanks to Impressionism and the paintings
made afterward) seem to neutralize and dull colour. A typical
Impressionist painting, by comparison, looks chromatically
far brighter and more vivid.

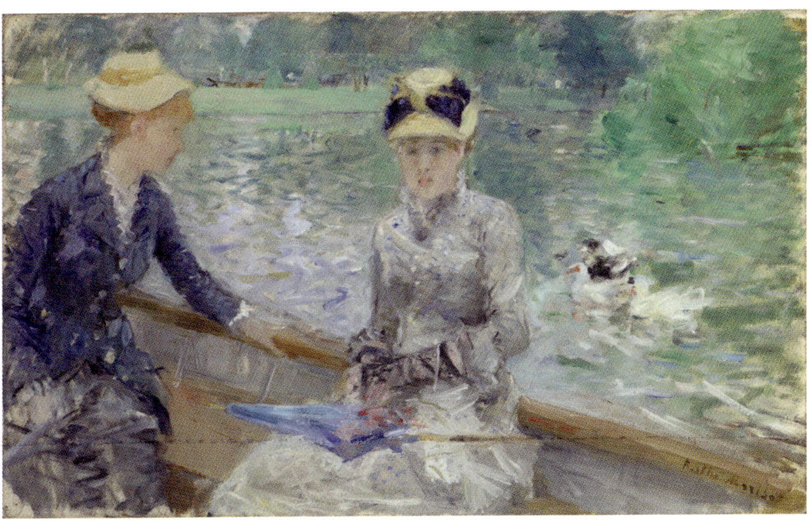

18 Berthe Morisot, *Summer's Day*, c. 1879

18

In *Summer's Day* (c. 1879), Berthe Morisot (1841–1895) exploited
the convenience of portable paint in tubes to convey a powerful
sense of the here-and-now, giving the viewer the sensation that
they too are seated in the boat with the two women enjoying
themselves at the Bois de Boulogne, near Paris. But the flurry
of zig-zag brushstrokes also makes us aware that this is a
hand-made image, and by leaving areas of the canvas bare (for
example, at bottom right) Morisot suggests the work has not so
much been tidily finished as casually arrested at a particular
moment in time.

Another importance source for the unorthodox compositions
of Impressionist paintings was the influence of Japanese prints.
Like neighbouring China and Korea, Japan had maintained a
closed-door policy and rebuffed encroachments by westerners,
but in 1854 it was forcibly opened to trade with the world by the
United States, whereupon its leaders perceptively recognized
the superiority of western technology, trading policies
and military might, and very quickly set about a scheme
of successful westernization. This also involved the active
promotion of its own heritage and, at the Paris International
Exhibition of 1855 and again at the 1867 World's Fair, Japan
held large-scale exhibitions to showcase its rapidly vanishing
traditional culture. These events helped launch a vogue for
what became known as *Japonisme*. Particularly important
for the Impressionists was the genre of coloured woodblock
prints called *Ukiyo-e* – 'pictures of the floating world'– such as

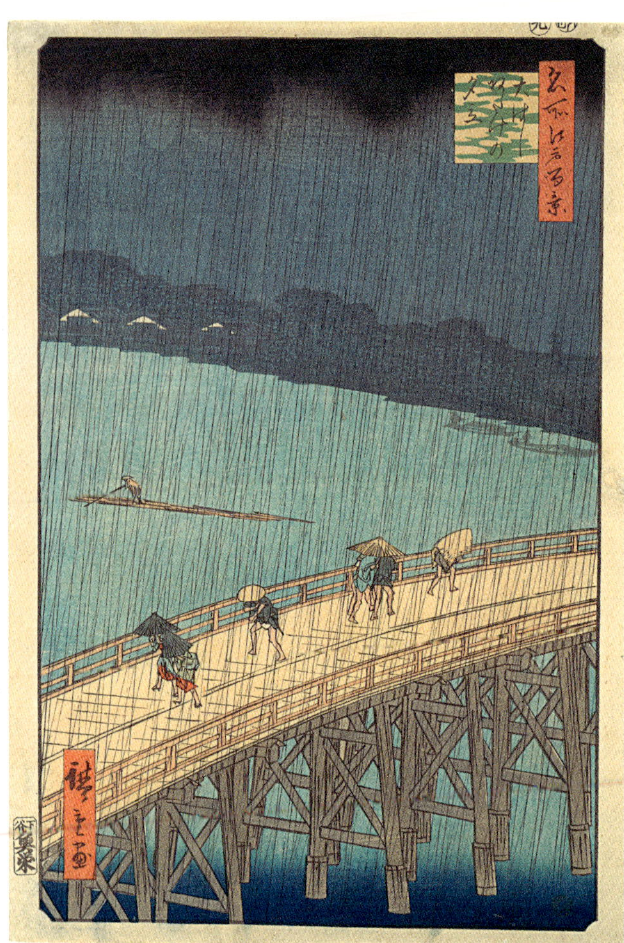

19 LEFT Utagawa Hiroshige, *Sudden Shower over Shin Ohashi Bridge and Atake*, 1857, from *One Hundred Famous Views of Edo*
20 OPPOSITE James Abbott McNeill Whistler, *Nocturne: Blue and Gold – Old Battersea Bridge*, c. 1872–75

19 Utagawa Hiroshige's (1797–1858) *Sudden Shower over Shin Ohashi Bridge and Atake* from an album of prints entitled *One Hundred*
20 *Famous Views of Edo* (1857). *Nocturne: Blue and Gold – Old Battersea Bridge* (*c.* 1872–75) by the American artist James Abbott McNeill Whistler (1834–1903), who lived in London and Paris, in its radical simplification of form and unorthodox composition is indebted to the example of such prints, and may even be directly inspired by one.

For westerners, the exotic and unfamiliar subjects of Japanese prints were an invitation to imagine the world differently, to step outside the relentless onward rush of European modernity. Until this period, Europeans had believed that the technical apparatus based on optical realism they had for picturing the

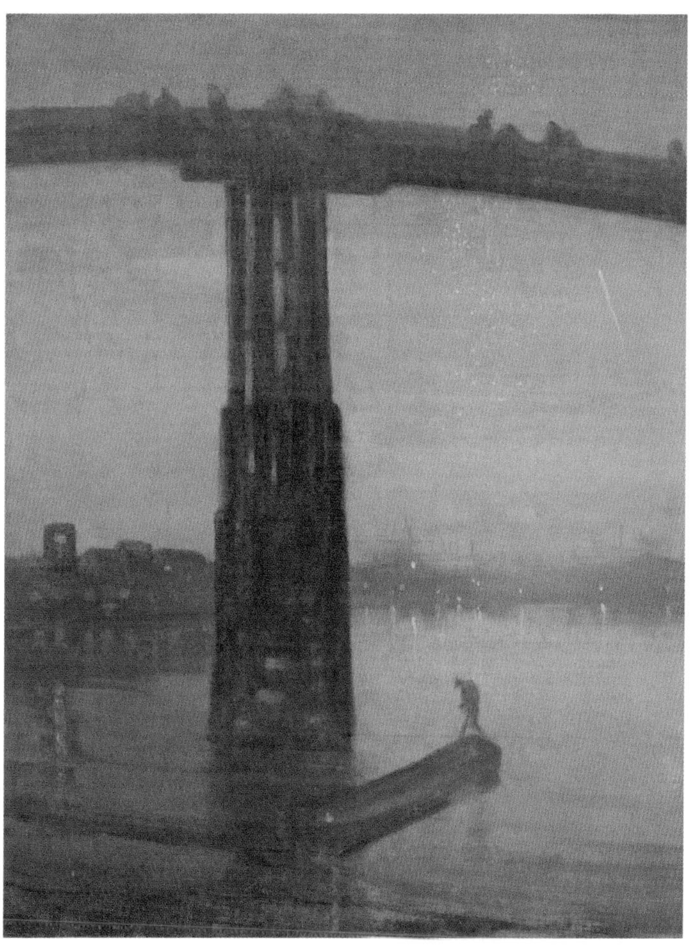

world was the most accurate way of imitating reality and was superior to all other forms of painting. But in an isolated world with little or no contact with other cultures – in a monoculture – there is no way of distinguishing between 'reality' and the conventions and rules of one's own society. Now, however, the opening up of Europe to the wider world through trade and conquest was making it increasingly obvious that culture was not a reflection of a 'reality' but of a specific perspective, thereby opening the way towards multiculturalism – the incorporation of distinct and multiple cultural and ethnic groups within the same society. Yet these encounters with the non-western did not immediately shatter the self-confident sense of cultural – and indeed racial – superiority held by the vast majority of

westerners. For them, their way of doing things remained the
only way. But for some, by contrast, the increased knowledge
of the wider world made it obvious that the western attitude
was in need of radical reassessment. For artists, this meant
the recognition that the principles upon which their art was
based were culturally contingent, that elsewhere very different
styles and ideas about art existed. The western ideal had been
conceived in Classical Greece and Rome, and became dominant
in western Europe alone after the Renaissance. In short, linear
perspective and shading using the medium of oil on canvas
mirrored how Europeans saw their place in the world, not how
the world actually is.

European artists were discovering that painting could have
very different goals and appearances, that the kinds of subject
matter considered suitable varied enormously – for example,
that depictions of the female nude were unknown in Islamic
countries and East Asian art, but far more erotically charged
ones than those made in the west were common in Hindu
India. Westerners discovered that they were unique in using
oil-based paint, were even unusual in choosing to paint on a
vertically oriented surface and in assuming that a painting
was something to hang vertically on a wall to be looked at
from directly in front. In Japan, as in the rest of East Asia, for
example, artists used ink and water-diluted colours, and when
they made their works they positioned the unstretched piece
of paper or silk on which they worked horizontally. A finished
painting was not then stretched on a wooden support or framed
but rather mounted as a scroll to be rolled and unrolled, or on a
multiple panelled folding screen. Sometimes, East Asian artists
used an alternative perspectival model called 'axonometry',
which simulated three-dimensional objects and space without
being based on optics. As a result, the perceptual distortions
experienced in optical realism were not included. Artists also
routinely incorporated calligraphic writing in their works, as
can be seen in Hiroshige's *Sudden Shower* print.

But, in fact, a Japanese print like Hiroshige's is a pictorial
hybrid. It is a fusion of Japanese *and* western conventions, in
that it exploited the linear perspective that Japanese artists
learned from seeing examples of western art but fused it with
indigenous conventions, ideas and goals. In Hiroshige's work,
for example, linear perspective is used for the top of the bridge,
but axonometric perspective, where lines remain parallel
rather than converge, for the bridge's wooden supports. So,
while on a technical level Japanese prints suggested to western
artists new asymmetric and dynamic ways of composing a
picture, of combining pictorial flatness with a sense of depth,

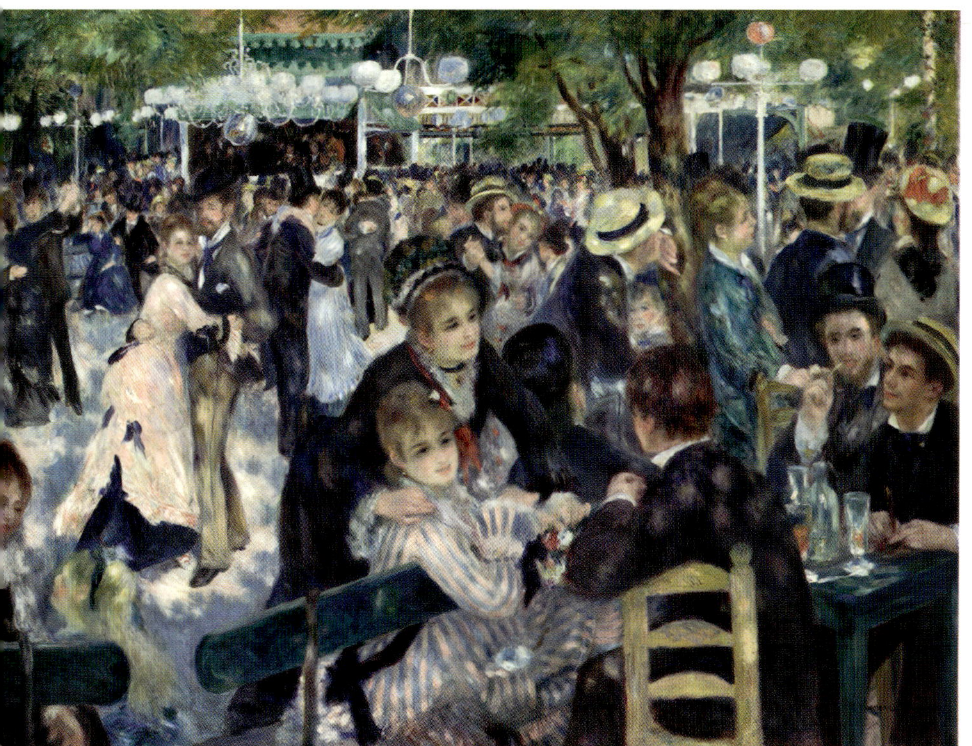

21 Pierre-Auguste Renoir, *Dance at le Moulin de la Galette*, 1876

as well as the potential of areas of bold flat colour, they were still recognizably linked to the goals central to the western tradition, and therefore easier to assimilate.

The Impressionists found the example of Japanese prints and the new technical innovation of photography indispensable in their quest to capture the novel experience of modern life in Paris, the city in which many of them lived. In *Dance at le Moulin de la Galette* (1876) Pierre-Auguste Renoir (1841–1919) simulated photography's appearance of spontaneity and, using small, rapidly applied *taches* or dabs of paint, skilfully imitated the fugitive nature of dappled sunlight, setting areas of light and dark in contrast to one another to add vibrancy to the scene. The work's informality greatly enhances the painting's capacity to evoke a confident vision of city life as leisure, pleasure and privilege: modern living as an eternal weekend. The people depicted in the painting, many of whom were Renoir's friends, are enjoying an afternoon at a popular Parisian open-air dancehall near Renoir's studio in

Montmartre. But the impromptu aura, and the way the painting appears to capture a single moment in time, are actually consequences of Renoir's meticulous planning and the intensive labour that went into realizing such a large canvas in his studio.

Mary Cassatt (1844–1926), another American living in Paris, drew on the example of Japanese prints and photography to make it appear that the viewers of her painting *In the Loge* (1878) are eavesdropping on a momentary event, witnessing a fashionable young lady attending a play at the Comédie Française. The composition is a bold juxtaposition of light and dark, and organized so that a viewer's eyes are drawn to those of the woman, who is looking across the theatre at unseen members of the audience through a pair of opera glasses. In the background, upper left, a gentleman directs his gaze towards her. The viewer completes the triangle, making Cassatt's painting an interesting study of the devices invented to record or enhance the visual gaze, and the different values and meanings of that gaze within the spaces of modern society.

As a woman painting another woman, Cassatt's understanding of the power and significance of this gaze must have been substantially different from that of the male artists of the period. The fact that there were several female Impressionists – among them Berthe Morisot and Eva Gonzalès as well as Mary Cassatt – is also a sign that western society was radically changing, becoming more open in ways that challenged traditional hierarchies. In later chapters of this book we will encounter the paintings of many women artists, but for most of the earlier period the systemic inequalities of western society made it exceedingly difficult for women to study art, let alone pursue a career and succeed. Within a culture that made a fundamental distinction between the male public realm of history, politics and important events, and the private and domestic world of the female, in which the family was the basic social unit, ambitious painting was inherently gendered 'male', that is, assumed to be an activity that required specifically 'masculine' skills and experience, and a profession suited only to men.

The conventional role of a woman within the artworld was as muse and/or spouse, and, sometimes, supportive patroness. There were many basic institutional impediments in the way of women competing professionally with men in the field of art. For example, the art academies and schools, such as the most prestigious of all – the Ecole des Beaux-Arts in Paris – were almost exclusively only open to men. But even when women were admitted to art academies, they were placed at an inherent

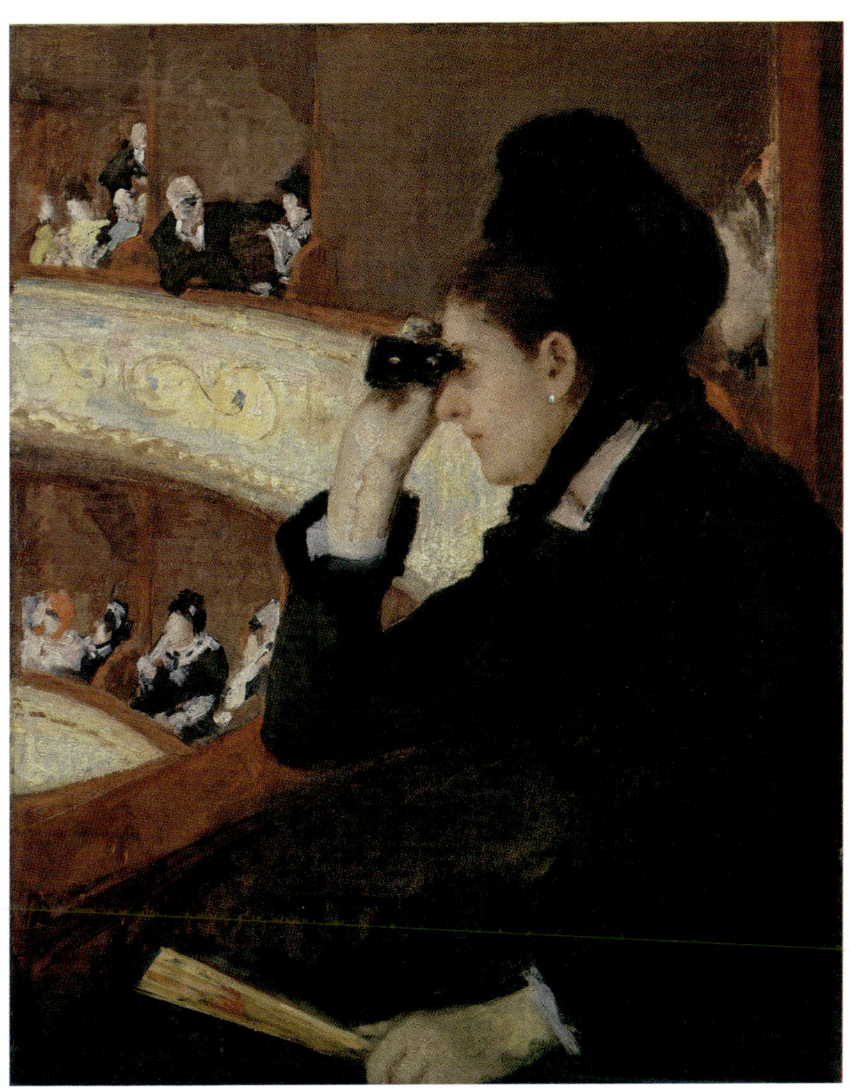
22 Mary Cassatt, *In the Loge*, 1878

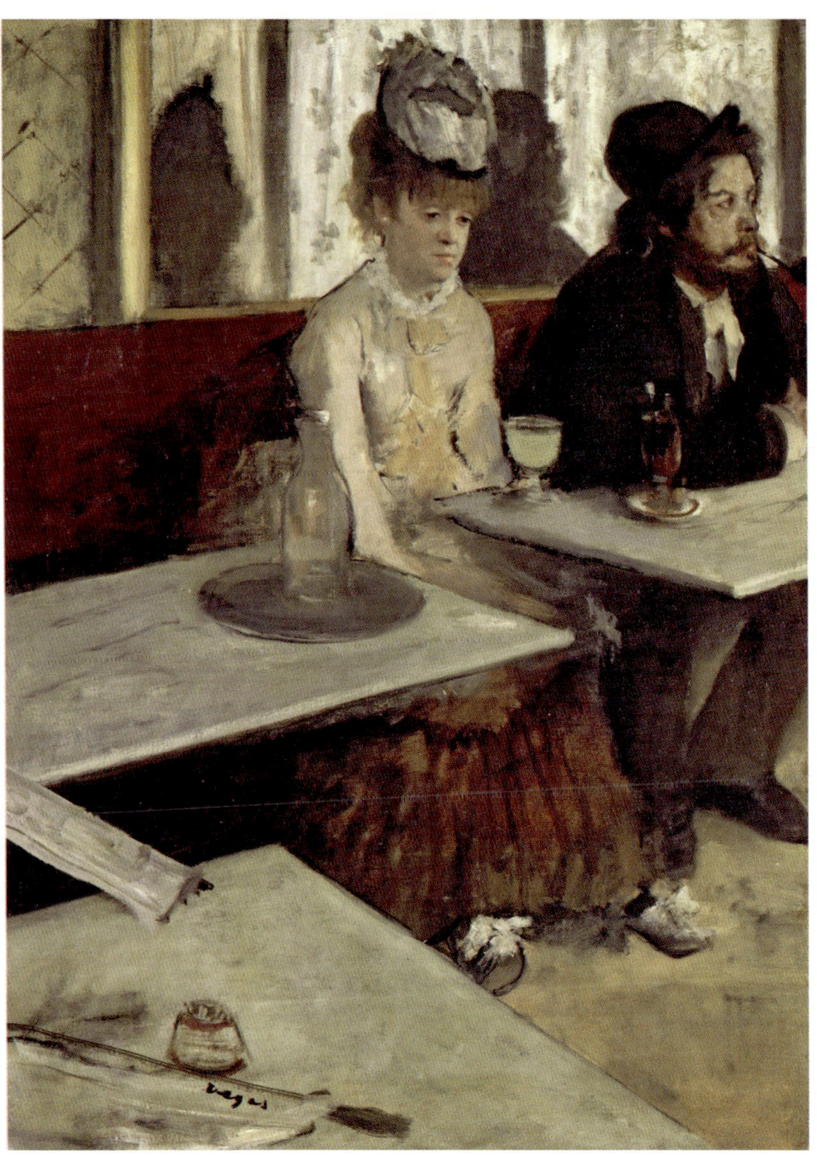

23 Edgar Degas, *In a Café* [*Absinthe*], 1875–76

disadvantage. Cassatt attended the Pennsylvania Academy
of Fine Arts in Philadelphia, where 20% of students were
female. But they could not take life-drawing classes, in which
students studied from the nude model, and were therefore
inhibited in acquiring some of the most basic skills necessary
for a mainstream artistic career. However, in Cassatt's case,
a wealthy and relatively enlightened family (they eventually
became major collectors of Impressionist art) sanctioned her
studies in Paris in the private studios of, amongst others, the
Academician Thomas Couture. But Cassatt soon abandoned
this more traditional mentorship for that of radicals like
Edouard Manet and Edgar Degas.

The Impressionists did not only respond to the glamour,
excitement and leisure activities of modern city life. On
occasion, they also revealed its darker side. In the painting
by Edgar Degas (1834–1917) *In a Café [Absinthe]* (1875–76) the
forlorn couple seem tragically estranged from each other and
their surroundings. The woman in particular looks morosely
marooned in her own dejected mental universe. One reason
for her stupor is the drink on the table, referenced in the
alternative title: absinthe. This herbal and floral alcoholic
beverage would eventually be banned in France and other
countries because it was reputed to cause hallucinations, and
its very high alcohol content when coupled in some brands
with an enticingly cheap price made it a serious health hazard.
Notice how the marble-topped tables in the painting seem to
be floating without supporting legs. Degas's picture reflects his
awareness that Paris was far from a place of new pleasures and
diversions for the majority of its impoverished inhabitants.

Impressionism and its Audience

In 1863 Napoleon III, the Emperor of France, granted the
Académie des Beaux-Arts independence from the government,
changing its name to the Ecole des Beaux-Arts. This led to
greater independence from state control, and it was there
that several of the Impressionists studied. The monopoly of
the official Salon exhibition was also being challenged by
'unofficial' events, such as the Salon des Refusés, inaugurated
in 1863 as a venue for the entries 'refused' by the official Salon.
It was there that the Impressionists showed their work. From
1884, the Salon des Indépendents became another key Parisian
art event, one where many of the avant-garde artists who are
featured in the next chapter of this book exhibited.

At the same time, art was becoming more fully integrated
into the burgeoning capitalist market economy. Increasingly,
progressive art like Impressionism could be seen in group and

solo exhibitions in the newly established private galleries, like that of Paul Durand-Ruel, for example, who represented artists in return for a percentage of sales or placed them on retainers, thereby controlling the viewing and marketing of their work. The private gallery system, involving dealers or brokers, became increasingly central to the artworld and, within this market, American collectors such as Alfred C. Barnes, who were the benefactors of a dynamic, prosperous and more forward-looking society, proved especially important. Durand-Ruel, for one, saw the potential of the transatlantic market and in 1887 opened his first gallery in New York.

But Impressionism made painting increasingly challenging to appreciate and demanded new skills from its audience. A more indeterminate relationship between the viewer and the picture was being created that required the willingness on the former's part to collaborate in the creation of the latter's meaning. A painting was more and more like a work-in-progress, an open-ended record of a performance without clear symbolism or narrative content, and something that seemed to have a tentative relationship to anything beyond itself. As the solid architecture provided by the bounding line and modelling in light and dark were abandoned – along with the familiar subjects of art – and artists came to rely on meshes of rapidly applied, dynamic skeins, smudges and dabs of paint, it seemed they were deliberately courting obscurity and the possibility that what they did had no meaning beyond itself. 'When you go out to paint, try to forget what objects you have before you, a tree, a house, a field, or whatever,' Claude Monet advised, taking Constable's wish to forget about other paintings one step further. 'Merely think here is a little square of blue, here an oblong of pink, here a streak of yellow, and paint it just as it looks to you, the exact colour and shape, until it gives your own naïve impression of the scene before you.'

Emphasis was shifting to the value of the insularity of a painting, its self-sufficiency as an aesthetic visual experience. The idea was taking hold that a painting was no longer primarily related to the creation of an illusion – to the interpretation of some optically perceived subject matter or the presentation of symbols within a simulated three-dimensional space. Rather, painting was increasingly conceived as about the activity of perception itself, about seeing marks and colours on a canvas surface arranged in a certain order, and then making sense of and enjoying the effect. This transformation would have immense repercussions for the future of painting. 'It was the catalogue that told me that that was a haystack. I numbly felt that the object was missing in this picture,' wrote the pioneer of abstract art, the Russian Wassily Kandinsky in 1895 on seeing a late work by Monet. 'Painting received a fabulous power and magnificence. Unconsciously the object was also discredited as the inevitable element of the picture.' But, as a result, the connection between the events and experiences of modern life and painting began to become more tenuous, as it grew increasingly to be painting (a noun, the work) about painting (a verb, the action). And so, rather than the self-conscious avant-garde, ironically it was to be the works of the Academic artists, the defenders of tradition, that established themselves as the models for a truly popular 'modern' art – the kind to be found on chocolate boxes, magazine covers and posters. In fact, the avant-garde was casting itself as the defender of a rarefied form of 'high art' characterized by a rapid proliferation of ever more extreme and, for the general public, controversial and alienating styles.

Chapter 3
Post-Impressionism to Expressionism
c. 1880–*c.* 1900

Neo-Impressionism and Post-Impressionism

In the 1880s a reaction against Impressionism set in amongst the new generation of progressive artists. The Frenchman Georges Seurat (1859–1891) aimed to reintroduce elements that he recognized were absent from Impressionist art by applying a much more rigorously rational and empirical working method. In the huge *A Sunday on La Grande Jatte – 1884* (1884–86), for example, Seurat boldly announced his commitment to the painting of everyday life by choosing a popular location next to the Seine, but also overtly distanced himself from Realist and Impressionist styles through the construction of a large-sized work of the scale usually associated with 'Salon' painting which was characterized by a formal simplicity that bestowed on the banal everyday a sense of 'Classical' and timeless monumentality. Seurat also took the interest in colour shown by the Impressionists in a more overtly scientific direction by researching optical and colour theory to discover the underlying rules informing the subjective and embodied nature of the visual impression. In this 'Divisionism' or 'Pointillism', as he called it, points of primary (red, blue, yellow) and secondary (violet, orange, green) colour were painted adjacent to each other and organized into a rational system. Rather than the artist mixing the colours on the palette, the viewer's eye mixes them while perceiving the work.

The French artist Paul Cézanne (1839–1906) was from the same generation as the Impressionists, and worked for a time in that style, but he eventually chose a quite different path. Cézanne also came to believe that Impressionism's pursuit of an instant in time had led to an unstructured and excessively 'passive' form of painting, in the sense that Impressionism was

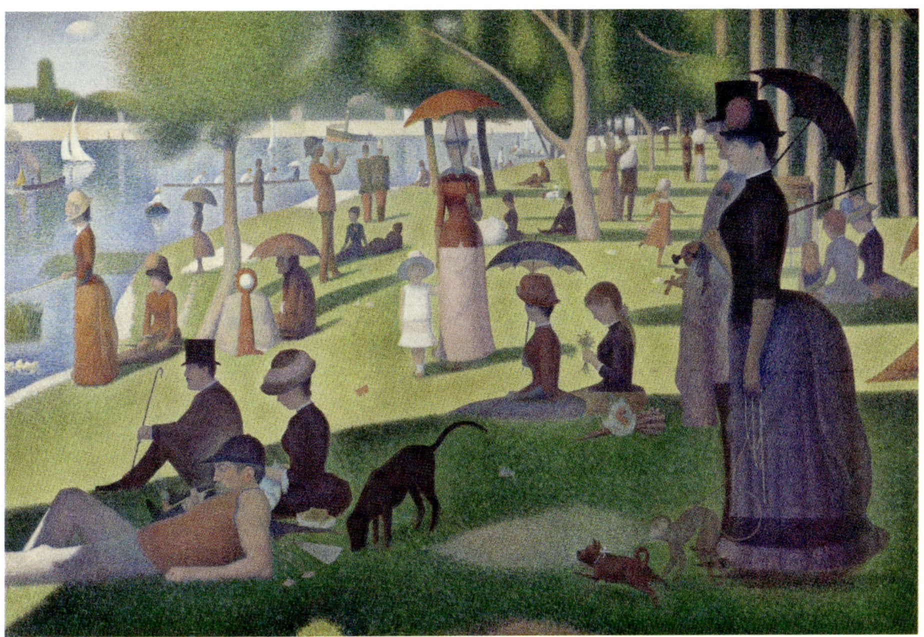

24 Georges Seurat, *A Sunday on La Grande Jatte – 1884*, 1884–86

conceived as the attempt to simply record with paint and brush
on canvas sensations generated by a visual phenomenon. Instead
of this goal, Cézanne sought to re-establish an objective and
more permanent dimension to painting by creating a decidedly
unorthodox connection with the Classical tradition. He declared
his goal was the 'making of Impressionism something solid and
lasting like the art of the museums', but, Cézanne said, he would
do it 'after nature'. As a result, his painting *Mont Sainte-Victoire
with Large Pine* (*c.* 1887) differs from a typical Impressionist
painting by being more solidly structured compositionally. This
effect was created through a process of geometric simplification
and the organization of muted colour-tones applied in
regular dashes of paint. In other words, Cézanne consciously
reorganized what he observed to bring out the underlying formal
relationships within the composition of his painting, adjusting
the branches of the pine tree in the foreground, for example,
so they rhythmically echo the profile of the distant mountain,
thereby creating a kind of theatrical proscenium arch.

Cézanne's special importance for his contemporaries
and for later artists lay in this willingness to break with
the conventions of illusionistic painting based on linear
perspective and modelling while nevertheless remaining

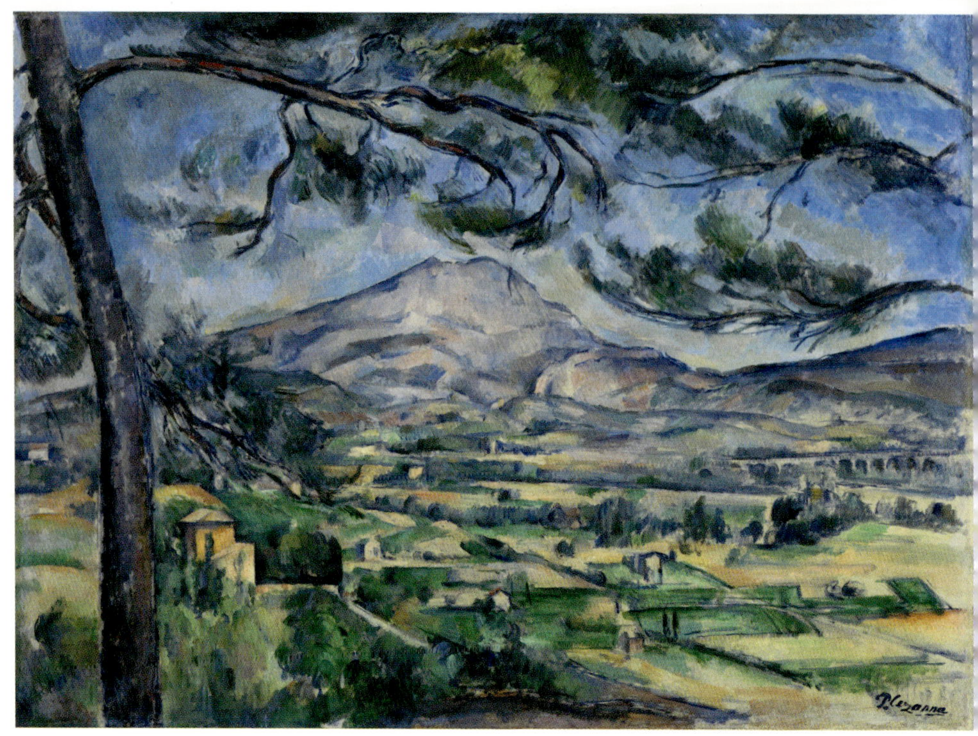

25 Paul Cézanne, *Mont Sainte-Victoire with Large Pine*, c. 1887

loyal to the idealizing and ordering principles of the Classical tradition. He said he aimed to paint like Nicolas Poussin, the paragon of the Academicians who was admired for his rigorously structured and harmonious compositions, but without recourse to the subjects or techniques associated with this tradition. Instead, Cézanne said he relied only on his own sensations, on his capacity to order what he perceived into an aesthetically pleasing whole.

By contrast, the Dutchman Vincent van Gogh (1853–1890) was less interested in constructing a vision of timeless order than in expressing his restless experience. To this end, the liberation from linear perspective and modelling, and a willingness to embrace gesture and colour, took painting in a very different direction. Shapes and colours were not only determined by what Van Gogh observed, but also imposed so as to better communicate powerful emotional states. Of his intentions in general, Van Gogh noted: 'I retain from nature a certain sequence and a certain correctness of placement of the tones, I study nature so as not to do anything silly, to remain reasonable – but – I don't

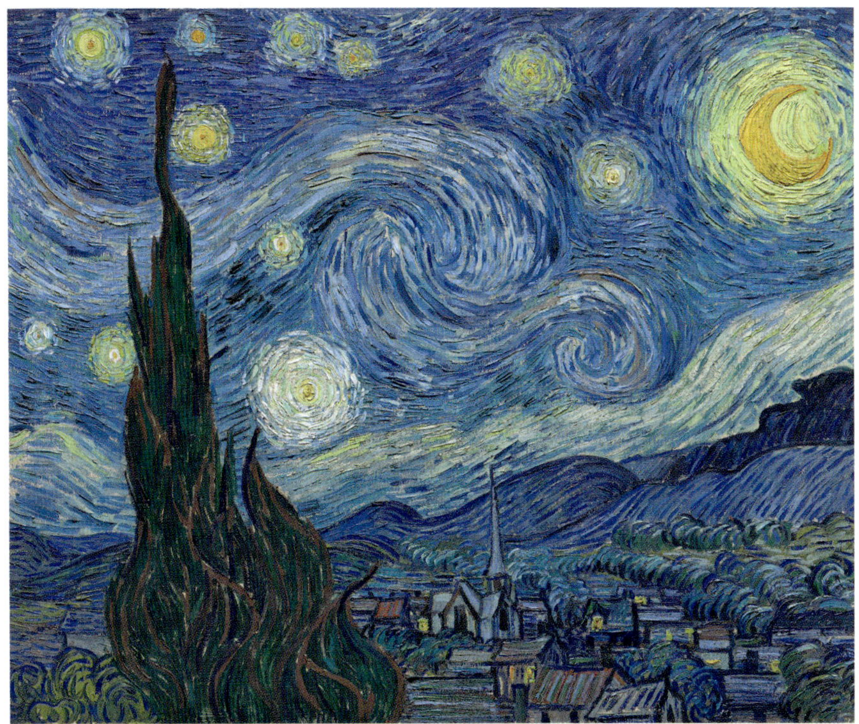

26 Vincent van Gogh, *The Starry Night*, 1889

really care whether my colours are precisely the same, so long
as they look good on my canvas, just as they look good in life.'

Van Gogh moved to the south of France because he wanted
to escape what he saw as the shallow, soul-destroying life
in Paris. But he seems to have been hoping a geographical
relocation would allow him to quit more than just city life –
he was looking to escape the torment of modern existence
in general. By the end of 1888, however, he had had a nervous
breakdown. He suffered from what today would be called a
comorbid illness or bipolar mood and personality disorder,
experiencing acute anxiety which was exacerbated by excessive
alcohol intake. A few months after his breakdown, he
voluntarily admitted himself to a mental asylum near Arles,
which is where he painted *The Starry Night* (1889). The swirling
serpentine brushmarks and deep blue colouration powerfully
evoke feelings of awe that are mixed with restlessness and
heightened emotions.

Van Gogh's example as an artist – of what the purpose of
making art should be in the modern world – proved especially

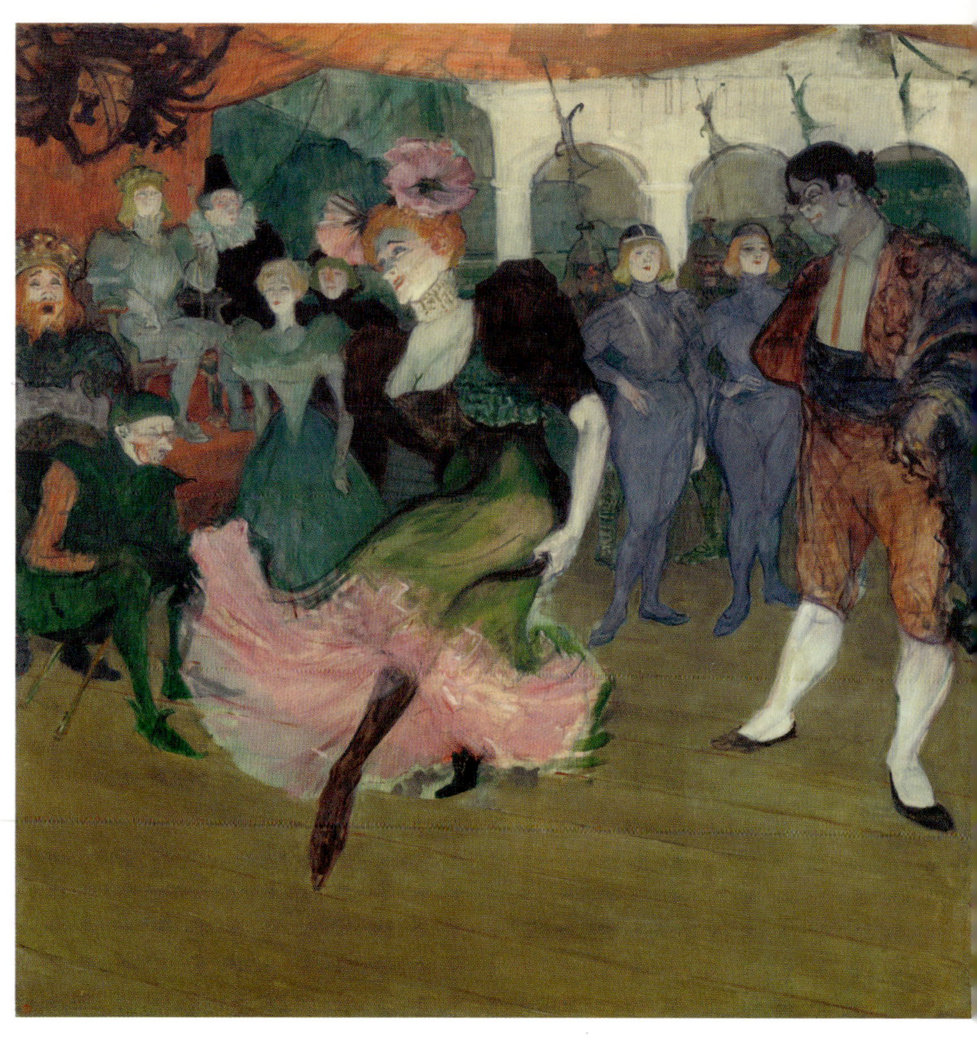

27 Henri de Toulouse-Lautrec, *Marcelle Lender Dancing the Bolero in 'Chilpéric'*, 1895–96

important for the next generation, demonstrating that painting could be used to extend one's personal anxiety and suffering into a general critique of contemporary existence. His life story has also helped propagate one of the most popular clichés concerning the modern artist: that their 'strange' distorted works are a direct consequence of mental anguish. Research has shown that there is indeed often a close correlation between styles of modern art and the symptomology of the psychopathologies suffered by artists. But Van Gogh, and other artists who had mental illnesses, created their works despite their afflictions as much as because of them. In fact, his enormous output over a period of only five short years speaks as much of extraordinary conscientiousness as it does of psychotic obsession.

While Van Gogh said he hated Paris and sought to distance himself from its toxic influence, there were other artists who, in ways pioneered by the Impressionists, made art that revelled in the experience of the city. However, they sought to convey their enchantment more vividly than the Impressionists through selective exaggeration and distortions that drew attention to their own psychological states. Henri de Toulouse-Lautrec (1864–1901), for example, made the alluring decadence of the French capital the central theme of his paintings and posters. In *Marcelle Lender Dancing the Bolero in 'Chilpéric'* (1895–96) he catches the magnetic eroticism of one of his favourite subjects, the red-headed actress Marcelle Lender, as she dances in a theatrical performance in an establishment in the bohemian Montmartre, a district known for its dance halls, cabarets and brothels. The style of the work owes something to Edgar Degas, but unlike the Impressionist, Lautrec distorted and exaggerated forms and colours to convey a more expressive relationship to his chosen subject.

With the work of Seurat, Cézanne, Van Gogh and Toulouse-Lautrec, decisive steps were being taken away from the convention that still dominated western painting: illusionistic imitation. What we begin to sense within their works is the potential of painting when it is redirected towards, on the one hand, the power of the expressive image and, on the other, being envisaged as an intrinsically valued aesthetic experience independent of any representational content.

Orientalism and 'Primitivism'

Van Gogh's desire to escape the horrors and tedium of urban 'bourgeois' life, but equally the celebration of the bohemian *demimonde* loved by Lautrec, was also fired by fascination with the exotic 'otherness' of cultures beyond the west. As has been touched upon already, the depiction of non-western cultures, for example, and the influence of Japanese prints was a staple

27

of art in the nineteenth century, both Academic and avant-garde. In the previous chapter we encountered Ingres's painting *Odalisque with Slave* of 1842, for example. The broader context for such interest was the fact that, fired by the prospect of vast new markets and resources, but also by what the British called 'the white man's burden' and the French *la mission civilisatrice* – 'the civilizing mission' – the western powers had set about aggressively and successfully colonizing the world.

This Age of Imperialism, as it became known, created new forms of economic and social bondage, and the vogue for the global exotic in the arts was in this sense bankrolled by colonial conquest. But while for the Academic artist choosing an 'Orientalist' theme afforded the opportunity to indulge in romantic dreaming, salacious voyeurism and feelings of cultural superiority, for the avant-garde, encounters with non-western cultures became a way of extending their assault on 'bourgeois' values by embracing what they termed the 'primitive' as a dangerous but reformative force. Non-western cultures, of which artists actually had very little direct knowledge, were imagined to embody deep sources of wisdom that Christianity had forgotten and to which a society based on science and materialism was oblivious. This cult of 'primitivism' opposed the cold, convention-ridden world of urban society to the lively expressiveness of peoples who, so it was believed, were still immersed harmoniously in nature. For, in contrast to modern westerners who lived in alienating cities controlled and regulated through bureaucratic structures governed by reason and dominated by economic priorities that reduced them to anonymous cogs in a machine, the 'noble savage' was said to enjoy unrestrained sensual fulfilment. In this sense, the idea of the 'primitive' expressed the growing belief amongst westerners that modernity was not about progress – the liberation of humanity – and instead was characterized by oppression and cultural decline. People in the modern west were losing the possibility of meaningful existence through being compelled to excessively focus on an idea of 'development' based on purely scientific and economic goals. The result was a loss of community, new forms of enslavement and the destruction of nature.

A powerful desire to move beyond the shadow of tragic western history was growing amongst artists. We have seen that for the Impressionists' generation Japan had proven a major source of inspiration. Van Gogh collected as many as six hundred Japanese woodblock prints and painted his own variations on some of them in oils, including a version of Hiroshige's *Sudden Shower over Shin Ohashi Bridge and Atake*. But Van Gogh also believed these prints had ethical significance, that they were the creations of purer minds and a better civilization. If he had lived longer and been less antisocial and mentally unstable, it is possible Van Gogh would have followed the example of his friend and more confident rival, the Frenchman Paul Gauguin (1848–1903) – who had joined him in Provence in the south of France for a few months – in leaving Europe altogether, travelling to Tahiti in 1891 and later to the Marquesas Islands in the South Pacific in search of what he called the 'savage'.

Gauguin had already tried Brittany in north-west France, which, like Provence, was then a remote and backward region. There, in a fishing village he established what became known as the Pont-Aven School, a group of artists that included fellow Frenchmen Emile Bernard and Paul Sérusier. Gauguin advocated what he called 'Synthetism', proposing that a painting should blend the direct perception of nature with a generous portion of imagination, abstracting form and colour to create a subtle mood or deep symbolic meaning. 'Don't copy nature too closely,' he advised. 'Art is an abstraction; as you dream amid nature, extrapolate art from it.'

Gauguin consciously made a link between childhood innocence and non-western peoples, who, so he assumed, still possessed 'child-like' qualities: 'No more Pegasus, no more Parthenon horses!' he declared. 'One has to go back, far back.... as far back as the dada of my childhood, the good old wooden horse.' His sense of frustration with western society demanded a more drastic kind of renunciation and relocation than Van Gogh's, although like the Dutchman he was fired by the conviction that beyond Europe – beyond the prison of history, the mortifying touch of industry, technology, trade and the bourgeois values he himself had once upheld (Gauguin left behind a wife and family in Paris, where he had worked in a bank) – life was much, much happier. 'Barbarism', he declared, meant 'rejuvenation'. As already noted, encounters with 'barbarism' also meant evidence of ideas about art that were very different from those that dominated Europe. Indeed, for Gauguin as for other advocates of 'primitivism', it seemed that far from being evidence of western culture's superiority – superiority manifested in its painting's ability to 'master' reality – the conventions of western art were actually proof of cultural sickness, of the failure to fully embrace and celebrate real human capacities.

Convinced he was doing more than just dreaming of utopia, of a paradise on earth, Gauguin booked a ticket to Tahiti, an island which had been a French protectorate since 1842 and was annexed as a colony in 1880. By the time he arrived in 1891, Tahiti was already much affected by western presence (and infected

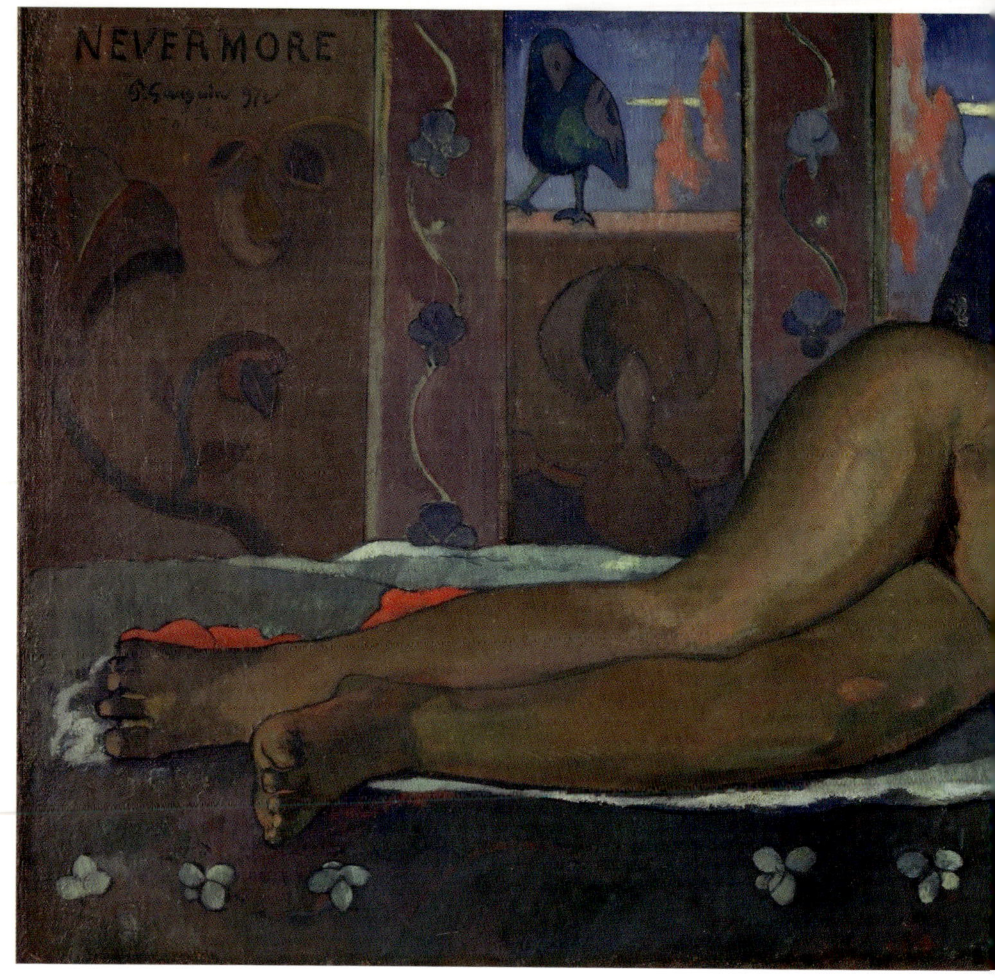

by westerners' diseases to which the local population had no immunity). Nevertheless, for his artistic purposes, Gauguin opted to mostly ignore the complex reality before his eyes and stuck instead to the simplicity of his dream, and art's role in propagating it. Technically, Gauguin rejected linear perspective and modelling in favour of a more flat, frieze-like space in which only some forms are modelled in light and dark while others remain more two-dimensionally rendered. In *Nevermore* (1897), for example, Gauguin's flaunting of western norms regarding the depiction of a female nude are far more radical than those in Manet's painting illustrated in the previous chapter. Regarding

28

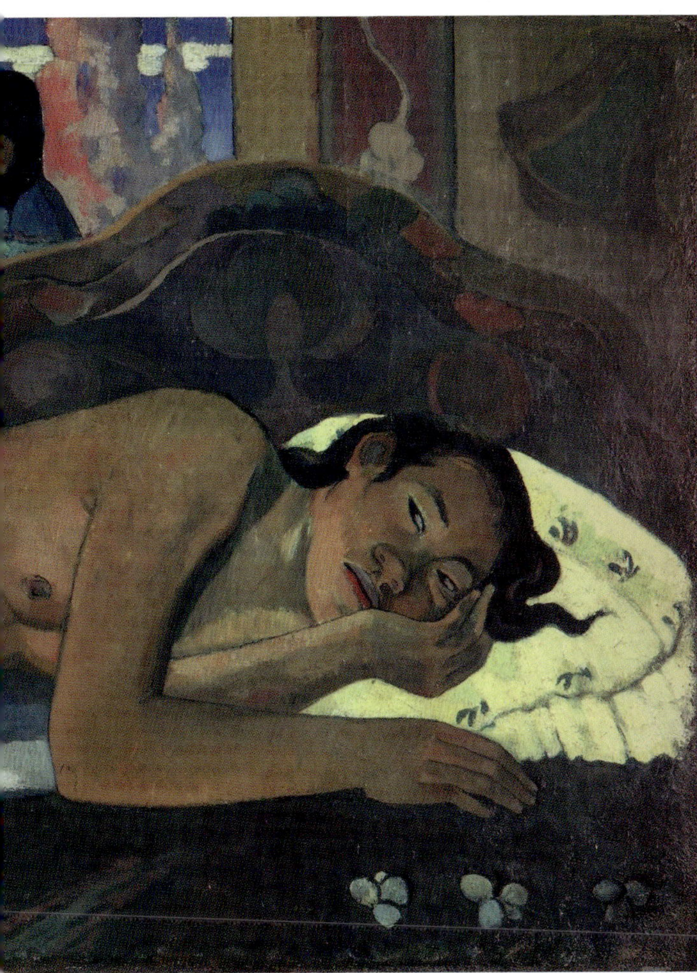

his picture, Gauguin explained: 'I wanted to make a simple
nude suggest a certain barbaric splendour of times gone by.'
The girl on the bed was actually one of Gauguin's teenage
Tahitian 'wives', who had just lost their first child. This may
explain the ominous-looking bird, and the title – borrowed from
a poem by Edgar Allan Poe. Gauguin entered into several sexual
relations with young girls in Tahiti, 'marrying' two of them and
subsequently fathering children. In this sense, he exploited his
position as a westerner to make the most of the sexual freedoms
available to him. It is also worth noting that Gauguin had
recently learned that back in Paris his favourite daughter by

his legal wife had just died, aged twenty, from pneumonia caught on her way home from a ball.

'Primtivism' was part of a more general tendency in the culture of the end of the century to escape inwards, to retreat from contamination by the past and the present, from a plethora of unstable and uncomfortable realities, into the relative insularity of the imagination and art. 'Primitivism' thereby extended the essentially Romantic belief in the self as the sole arbiter of truth by incorporating the artefacts of non-western cultures into a counter-cultural movement based on the idea that beyond the local and historical differences lay a timeless, essential, integral and cohesive humanity. In this sense, 'primitivism' meant the aestheticization of the world, or the reduction of global artefacts to a single formal standard amenable to western taste, understanding and goals. This effectively uncoupled non-western art and artefacts from their connection with local historical, religious, symbolic, political and utilitarian contexts, making them available for exploitation in the services of westerner's frustrations, desires and dreams.

The fascination for 'elsewhere' could take strange pictorial forms. Unlike Van Gogh and Gauguin, Henri Rousseau (1844–1910) never left his native Paris, although this proved no obstacle to his vivid imaginings of exotic faraway places. A mood of self-conscious escapism and innocence pervades *Tiger in a Tropical Storm* (*Surprised!*) (1891), which drew inspiration in part from Rousseau's visits to the hothouse in the botanical gardens and the Natural History Museum in Paris. Rousseau made his living as a customs officer in Paris – hence his nickname 'Le Douanier'. The unusual style reflects the fact that he had no schooling as an artist – in other words, he had not learned the skills necessary for structuring pictorial space using linear perspective and modelling in light and dark. But the important point is that for Rousseau this deficit was no obstacle. Like Van Gogh and Gauguin, who also received no formal art-school training, a lack of conventional technical skills was no deterrent, because mastery of these skills was now no longer what made an artist an artist. Indeed, they were more likely than not to be an impediment to freedom of imagination and expression.

In retrospect, 'primitivism' within the arts can be seen as a reflection of the contradictions and ambivalence experience by Europeans in this period towards a wider world with which it was increasingly coming into violent contact. The modern world was being shaped through conquest and genocide, through destabilizing encounters whose consequences still reverberate today. In one sense 'primitivism' therefore mirrors the 'might is right' values that underpinned imperialism. But it also reflects

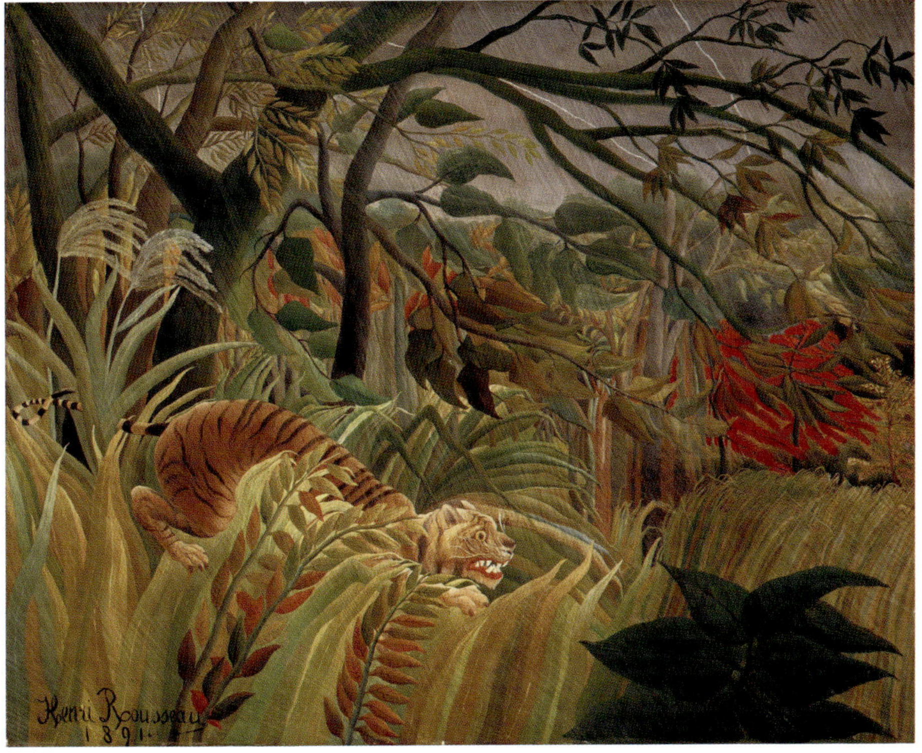

29 Henri Rousseau, *Tiger in a Tropical Storm* (*Surprised!*), 1891

the growing awareness amongst Europeans that contact with other cultures is intrinsically valuable, and that as they learned from these cultures they also learned about their own.

Symbolism

The imaginative retreat from the values of 'bourgeois' modernity with which 'primitivism' was involved was also evident in the emergence of the pan-European movement called Symbolism. To an even greater extent than the Romantics, the Symbolists celebrated the mysterious, the unrepresentable, the impossible. The act of painting was understood to involve a wilful avoidance of clear or familiar meanings and the cultivation of realms of the potential. The goal was to ensure the optimum conditions for free imaginative exploration. Within Symbolism, a painting was transformed into a space for refined and intangible moods, equivocal chimeras and mysteries, and expressions of the 'spiritual', all of which were marshalled in opposition to the vulgar materialism of everyday life.

Some Symbolists adopted the visual language of optical realism and repurposed it to convincingly visualize an inner psychological world, a timeless, silent, meditative atmosphere redolent with restless desires, melancholy and foreboding. The Swiss artist Arnold Böcklin (1827–1901) imbued his realistic scenes with a powerful inner mood, and in works such as *Island of the Dead* (1880) created a melodramatic and morbid meditation on death. The reality is more psychological than empirical. The French Symbolist Odilon Redon (1840–1916), by contrast, engaged in much greater stylistic innovation, flattening pictorial space and creating decorative patterned surfaces. Redon described works like *The Cyclops* (c. 1914) as 'dreaming accompanied also by thought', in which 'the logic of the visible' was put 'in the service of the invisible'. He also announced the birth of what he termed a new 'suggestive art', which 'cannot furnish anything without having its sole recourse to the mysterious play of shadows and the rhythm of mentally conceived lines'.

The French Symbolist group named the Nabis (Prophets), which included the artists Paul Bonnard, Maurice Denis, Paul Sérusier and Edouard Vuillard, took it as a fundamental principle that there were communicable correspondences between the forms painted by an artist and specific emotions, an equivalence between the outer visual world and the inner invisible world of thought and feeling, that functioned irrespective of any depicted or narrative content. The basic materials and principles of art – line, colour, shape, balance, rhythm, pattern – were said to be sufficient ingredients for

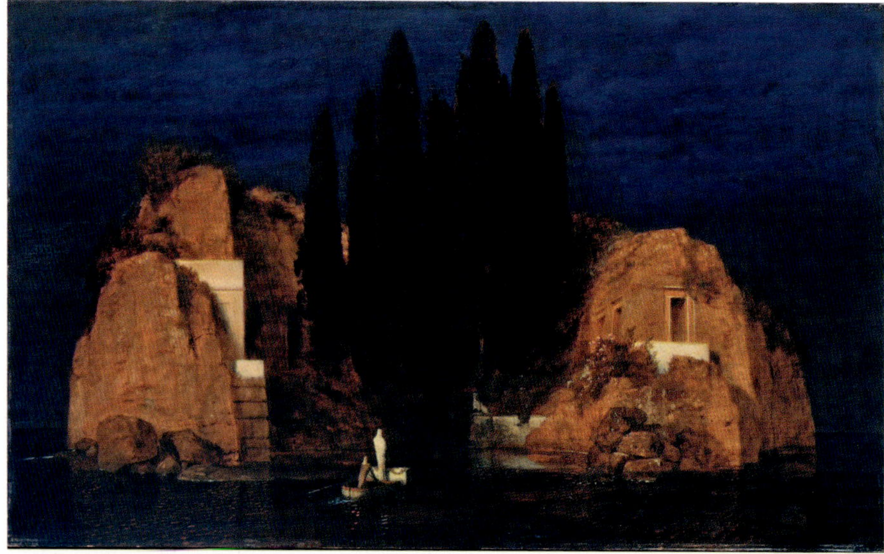

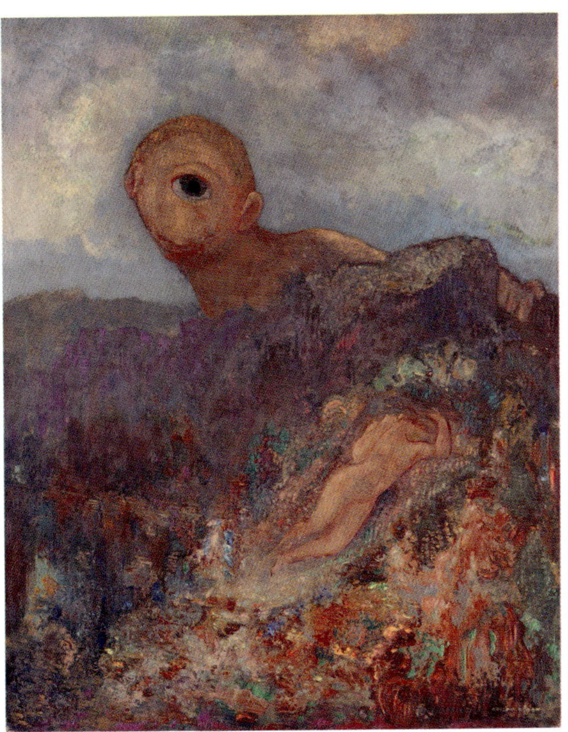

30 OPPOSITE Arnold
Böcklin, *Island of the
Dead*, 1880
31 RIGHT Odilon Redon,
The Cyclops, c. 1914

making direct visual equivalents for primary emotions or states
of mind, and it was argued that in the quest to secure this
visual correspondence between the outer and inner, the world
of things – and their presence in art – was actually an obstacle.
As Maurice Denis announced in clear and unequivocal terms:
'A painting before being a warhorse, a naked woman, or some
anecdote or other, is essentially a flat surface covered with
colours in a particular arrangement.' Denis used the preposition
'before', which implies his awareness that a painting is both an
image *and* an object. But these two interrelated dimensions –
the 'fictive' and the 'factual', or the 'illusionary' and the 'real' –
would be increasingly prized apart.

An important consequence of these varied developments was
that colour was increasingly understood to be independent from
the visible world and absolute, losing its descriptive function
and becoming instead a decorative or expressive force in its own
right. As we saw in Chapter Two, the growing fascination with
the possibilities of painting as a medium of pure colour was
facilitated on a practical level by a revolution in the manufacture
of synthetic colour pigments. Along with this development

there also came theoretical and scientific interest in the optics of colour. In addition, thanks to new technologies, the appearance of the industrialized environment of the city was literally becoming more colourful and, from the late nineteenth century, walls, screens, paper surfaces, casings, aluminium and steel structures, glass, electric lighting, advertisements and textiles began to shed their dull surfaces and embrace polychromy. In this sense, the new colour-centred painting was not only about attending to the intrinsic properties of the medium or inspired by examples of non-western art like Japanese prints, but also mirrored developments within the infrastructure of western society that was undergoing radical transformations.

Art Open to the Talents

As also noted in the previous chapter, there were almost unsurmountable obstacles in the way of women seeking to pursue careers as artists, but increasingly, thanks to the growing openness of western society, women began to find it possible to forge careers alongside and in competition with men. The German artist Paula Modersohn-Becker (1876–1907), for example, embraced 'primitivism' and focused on the female nude, challenging convention and transforming the meaning of the female image in art. The case of the French artist Suzanne Valadon (1865–1938) is especially indicative of how the rigid conventions of society had begun to weaken and open up new possibilities not just for women but for the lower classes. Valadon began life in the artworld as a model for such artists as Renoir and Degas. Unlike Berthe Morisot, Mary Cassatt and Modersohn-Becker, who were born into privileged bourgeois families, Valadon's mother was unmarried, and she grew up poor in Paris. For Valadon, therefore, the struggle to become an artist was even more socially challenging; but she was also less constrained by her upbringing and, as a result, forged a career as an artist of considerable originality. *Adam and Eve* (1909), for instance, shows the influence of Gauguin, but the mood could not be more different. It is also the first painting by a female artist of a nude man and woman together to be publicly exhibited and, while the title indicates that this is ostensibly a work with a religious theme, the woman is clearly Valadon herself and the man is her young lover of the time.

Fauvism

In 1905 the French artists André Derain and Henri Matisse spent the summer painting in and around the fishing village of Collioure in south-west France, and in the autumn they

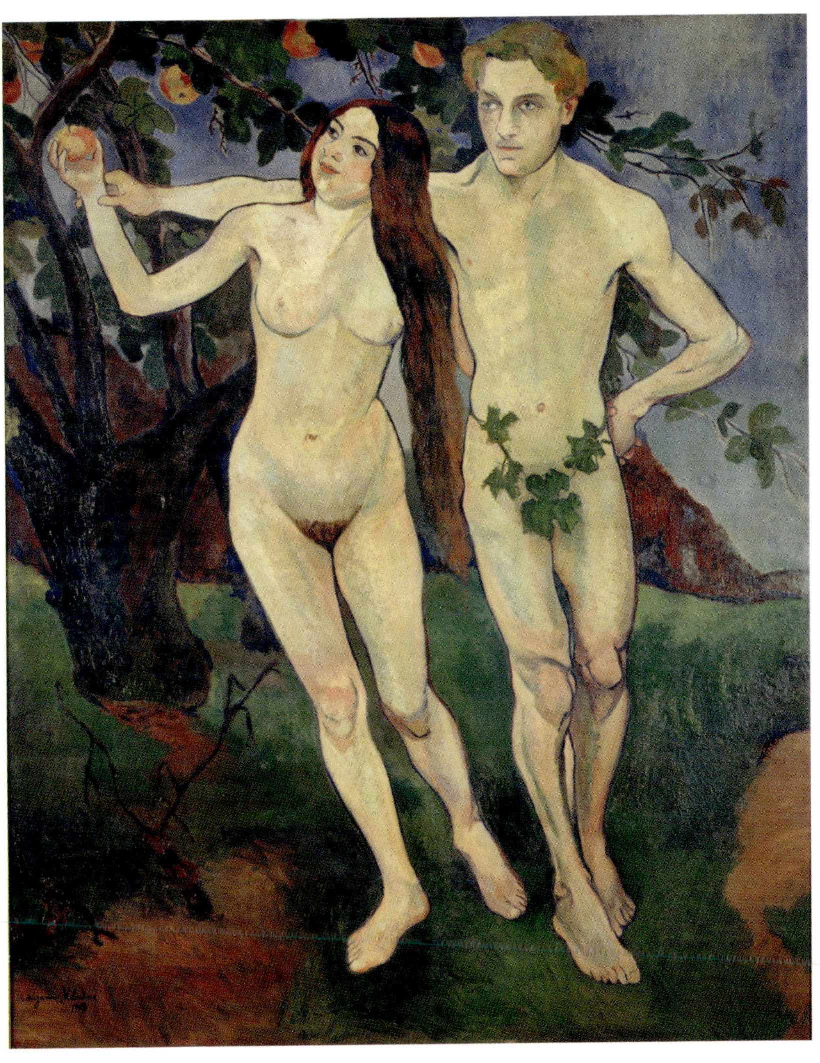

32 Suzanne Valadon, *Adam and Eve*, 1909

exhibited the results in Paris along with some of their friends, including fellow Frenchmen Maurice Vlaminck and Raoul Dufy, and a hostile critic likened their works to those made by *'fauves'* (wild beasts), because they seemed to take the 'primitivizing' impulse to a dangerously uncivilized extreme. But the artists themselves happily adopted the slur and so became known as the Fauvists. In contrast to the term 'impression', the Fauvist preference was for 'expression'. The distinction was intended to indicate that, rather than transcribing the visual sensation of phenomena, Fauvism was above all concerned with using painting to record an artist's spontaneous feelings as triggered by some phenomena – especially a landscape – through dynamic brushwork and non-naturalistic colour. Fauvism therefore involved an active pushing out of feelings from within the artist rather than a passive taking in of sensations from without, like Impressionism. In practice, this meant that in works such as *Mountains at Collioure* (1905) André Derain (1880–1954) dispensed with the naturalistic coloration of Impressionist painting and marshalled highly coloured brushstrokes to create a lively decorative surface. Compared to an Impressionist painting, Derain's is far more radical in its abandonment of perspective, modelling and naturalistic hues. Instead, the viewer is confronted by a vividly coloured surface comprised of a mesh of painted marks.

Henri Matisse (1869–1954), who quickly became the most prominent spokesman for the new expressionistic tendency and would go on to be one of the most admired and influential artists of the first half of the twentieth century, declared in 1908: 'I put down my colours without preconceived plan….To paint an autumn landscape I will not try to remember what colours suit this season, I will be inspired only by the sensation that the season gives me.' Matisse's preoccupation with sensation led him to deliberately confuse and dissolve the clear distinctions that usually structure pictorial space, but unlike in Impressionism and Post-Impressionism, which had reduced the canvas into an all-over field of small coloured patches, Matisse organized his work's surface using flat areas of colour and simple structuring lines, producing a clearly constructed and tangible surface pattern. In *The Dessert: Harmony in Red* (1908) a field of cadmium red – a pigment recently invented by chemists – spreads out across almost the entire canvas, confusing the perspectival structure that organizes the composition. What are solid objects and what is empty space, what is near or far? Japanese prints were an important influence on Matisse, as were also encounters with Persian art at the Paris World's Fair in 1900, exhibitions of Islamic art and – a few years after he

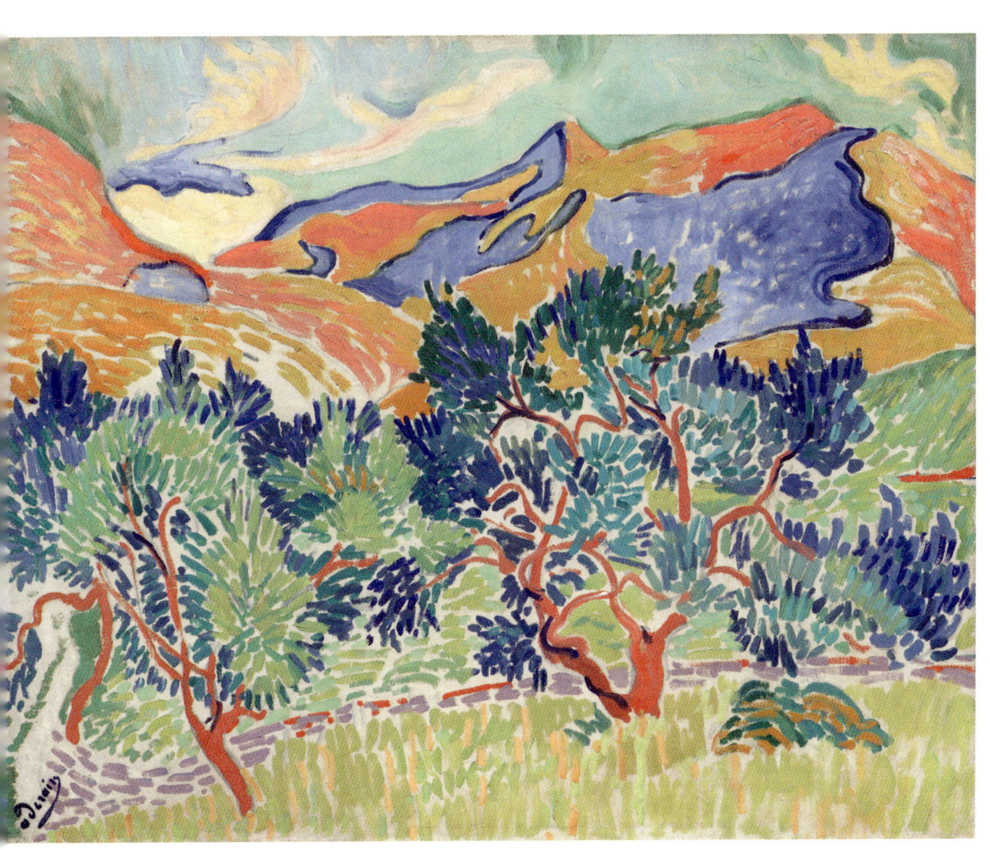

33 André Derain, *Mountains at Collioure*, 1905

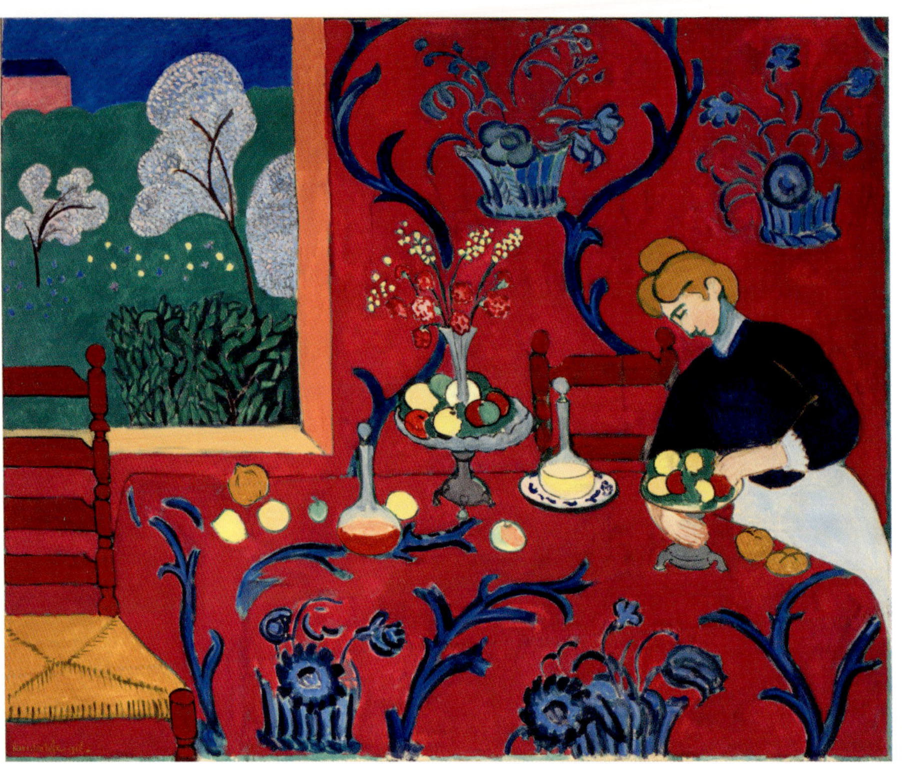

34 Henri Matisse, *The Dessert: Harmony in Red*, 1908

made this work – visits to the Alhambra and other Moorish
sites in southern Spain and Morocco. From such sources,
Matisse reconceived western painting as bright unified fields
of colour and linear arabesques – like a carpet. The central
goal of western painting since the Renaissance was decisively
abandoned in favour of a decorative and expressive surface.
Matisse also saw this new kind of painting as having a specific
role to play within modern society, observing: 'What I dream of
is an art of balance, of purity and serenity, devoid of troubling
or depressing subject matter, an art which could be for every
mental worker, for the businessman as well as the man of
letters, for example, a soothing, calming influence on the mind,
something like a good armchair which provides relaxation from
physical fatigue.'

From Symbolism to German Expressionism
The world revealed through the release of colour from
the straitjacket of realism – and the free rein given to the

unfettered imagination – would not always be a serene one of 'balance, of purity and serenity'. A sense of alienation, fear and anxiety could be graphically expressed, emotions that reflected a deepening social crisis. For over a thousand years before the forces of modernity shattered the confident conviction, Europe was dominated by an overarching belief in God as the ultimate source of meaning, and Christ as the world's Saviour. But as science supplanted the old mythical and religious explanations of the meaning of existence, replacing them with a more 'objective' and 'true' explanation, the values that once brought certainty and meaning began to fracture catastrophically. For example, Charles Darwin's theory of evolution, which was put forward in a book published in 1859, was a triumph of scientific enquiry but it dramatically undermined the theological edifice upon which human life had been securely built. The nineteenth-century German philosopher Friedrich Nietzsche argued that the inevitable consequence of the whole 'project' of the Enlightenment, discussed in Chapter One, was not a more free and egalitarian society but rather nihilism – literally, 'nothing-ism' – or the belief that life is inherently meaningless, that all choices are equally empty. Nihilism, Nietzsche argued, resulted from the removal of God from the world. But while secular society now lacked something vital, daily life carried on as if nothing important had changed. Nietzsche observed that while everything could now be explained without God, people unconsciously continued to live as if traditional meanings forged centuries before around God's image still gave their lives meaning. Though ordinary people could live with their salutary illusions, the seeker after truth must be exemplary in staring heroically into the abyss, where they would see the dreadful truth: 'God is dead, and we killed him', as Nietzsche famously announced.

When assessed in this context, the role of an artist was understood as leading in two directions: they could set themselves the task of relentlessly exposing the illusions and alienation inherent in modern existence, or seek strategies to counter present-day nihilism through their art, working to restore a sense of inner connectedness and resonance with the world. The Norwegian artist Edvard Munch (1863–1944) chose the former path. Like Van Gogh, he suffered from acute mental illness; as a young man he experienced great personal tragedy and later in life had several nervous breakdowns. Munch wrote: 'sickness, madness, and death were the black angels that guarded my crib.' As a result, his work dwelt obsessively on loss, sickness, death, melancholy, resentment, jealously, anxiety, fear, unfulfillable dreams, but also stoic defiance in a pitiless universe. In his now iconic work *The Scream* (1893), for example, Munch used line, colour, rapidly applied brushstrokes and distorted forms to powerfully communicate the feeling of humanity engulfed or crushed by a terrifyingly alien reality.

The Belgium artist James Ensor (1860–1949) also set out to represent the ominous and grotesque side of life, turning away from the visible world in favour of an inner world of unsettling fantasy. But unlike the work of Munch, Ensor's is pervaded

by a spirit of macabre humour. For *Death and the Masks* (1897) he used the masks sold for carnival processions in the family's curiosity shop below his studio in Ostend to create a tragicomic meditation on death. In terms that seem to place the sources of art wholly beyond reality and to locate it deep in the unconscious, Ensor declared: 'Reason and nature are the enemy of the artist.'

In Germany, artists such as Alexej von Jawlensky, Wassily Kandinsky, Ernst Kirchner, August Macke, Franz Marc, Gabrielle Münter and Emil Nolde, and in Austria Oskar Kokoschka and Egon Schiele, can be seen to have vacillated between the two paths laid out by Nietzsche's prognosis. They explored the hypocrisies of the status quo but also the new freedoms offered by modern life through dramatic and provocative subject matter, using vigorous and speedy brushwork, anti-naturalistic colours, extreme deformation, asymmetrical compositions and a flattened picture space.

The artists of Die Brücke (The Bridge), several of whom did not formally study painting, were firmly committed to the belief that youth carried the future in its hands, and that this must be expressed in their paintings. 'With faith in progress and a new generation of creators and spectators we call together all youth,' declared their manifesto of 1906. 'As youth we carry the future in us and want to create for ourselves freedom of life and of movement against the long-established older forces. We claim as our own everyone who reproduces that which drives him to creation with directness and authenticity.' Central to their credo were the 'primitivist' ideals of the instinctual and of maximum spontaneity. They had absolute confidence that their feelings possessed natural purity and value, and that their paintings were the direct embodiment of their inner life. Emil Nolde (1867–1956), for example, who was associated with Die Brücke but preferred the isolation of the countryside to the urban life adopted by the others, collected masks from different world cultures, and in

works such as *Masks Still Life III* (1911) painted them in thick, quickly applied paint and vivid, jarring colours. But, like other western artists, Nolde was less interested in understanding

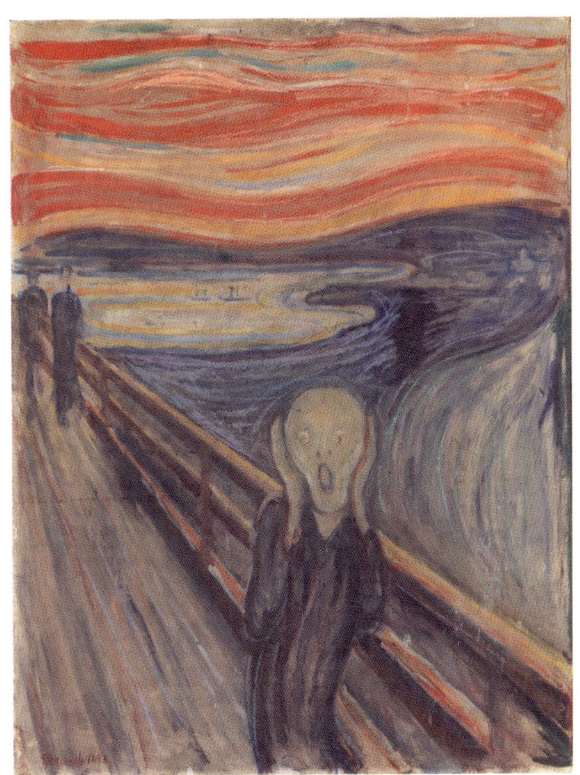

35 RIGHT Edvard Munch,
The Scream, 1893
36 BELOW James Ensor,
Death and the Masks, 1897

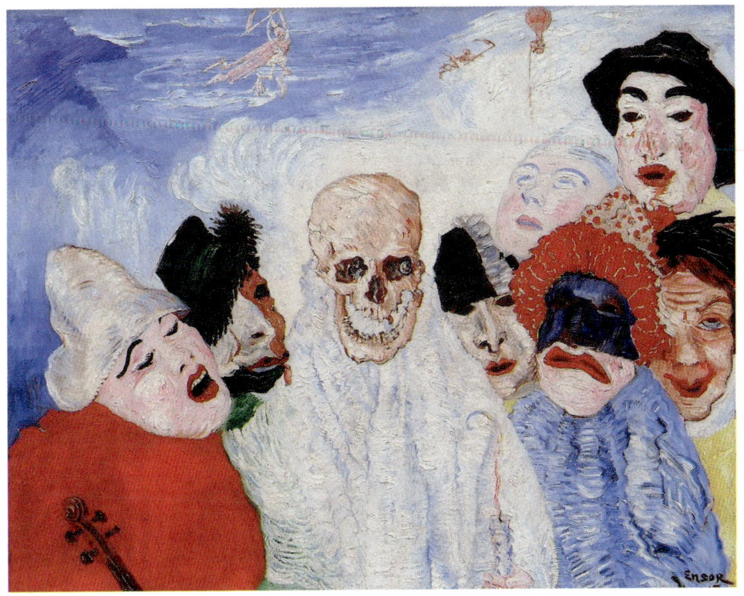

non-western cultures than in idealizing them as the antithesis of the decadent culture of the west, observing: 'Primitive peoples....create their works with the material itself in the artist's hand, held in his fingers. They aspire to express delight in form and the love of creating it. Absolute originality, the intense and often grotesque expression of power and life in very simple forms – that may be why we like these works of native art.'

The courting of the 'primitive' and the yearning for spiritual renewal were especially central to the other important German Expressionist group, which was based in southern Germany: Die Blaue Reiter (The Blue Rider), named after an almanac compiling images and texts published in 1912. The leading figure was the expatriate Russian Wassily Kandinsky (1866–1944), whose work evolved from paintings reminiscent of Russian folk and religious art, via Impressionist-style landscapes to, by 1910, landscapes greatly influenced by Fauvism. But, as we will see in the next chapter, this would prove only the prelude to a far more radical innovation.

Other Blue Rider artists included von Jawlensky, Macke, Marc and Münter. As Franz Marc (1880–1916) declared in terms that spoke for his entire generation of the avant-garde: 'the wasteland of the nineteenth century was our nursery.' In the

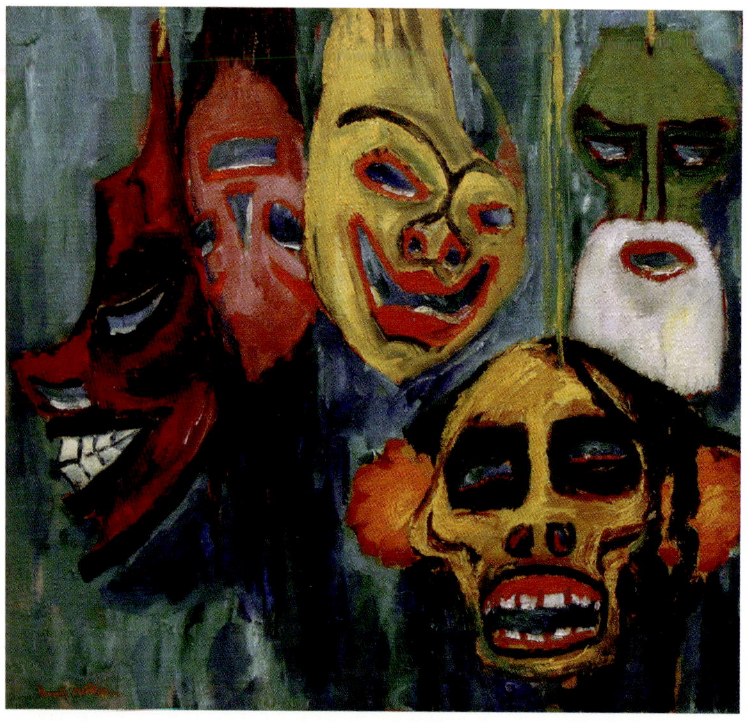

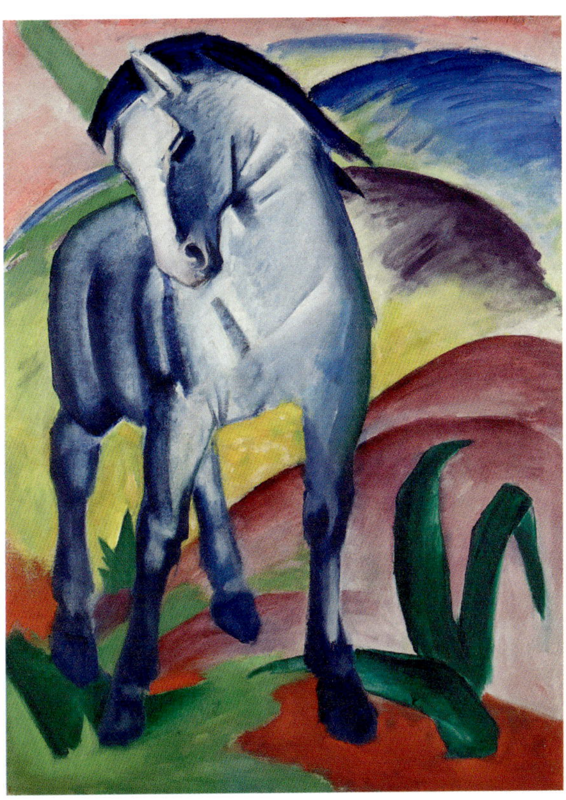

37 OPPOSITE Emil Nolde, *Masks Still Life III*, 1911
38 RIGHT Franz Marc, *Blue Horse I*, 1911

quest for spiritual regeneration, they waged war in the name of innovation, because, as Marc put it, 'New ideas kill better than steel and destroy what was thought to be indestructible.'
38 In *Blue Horse I* (1911) Marc celebrated the strength and beauty of the horse. He wrote: 'I seek pantheist empathy with the vibration and flow of the blood of nature – in the trees, in the animals, in the air....I see no happier medium for the "Animalization" of art, as I would like to call it, than the animal picture.' But Marc also transposed the animal into the world of the human imagination by painting his horse blue, the symbolic colour of the spiritual, the impossible, the ineffable.

In Austria, the Vienna Secession movement, formed in 1897, was allied with Symbolism and led by Gustav Klimt (1862–1918).
39 In *The Kiss* (1907–8), Klimt created a vision of a sensual and pleasurable world through a decorative style that emphasized richness of surface detail and texture. But amongst younger Austrians this vision soon ceded to Expressionism-inspired works that reflect a far darker and more troubled relationship

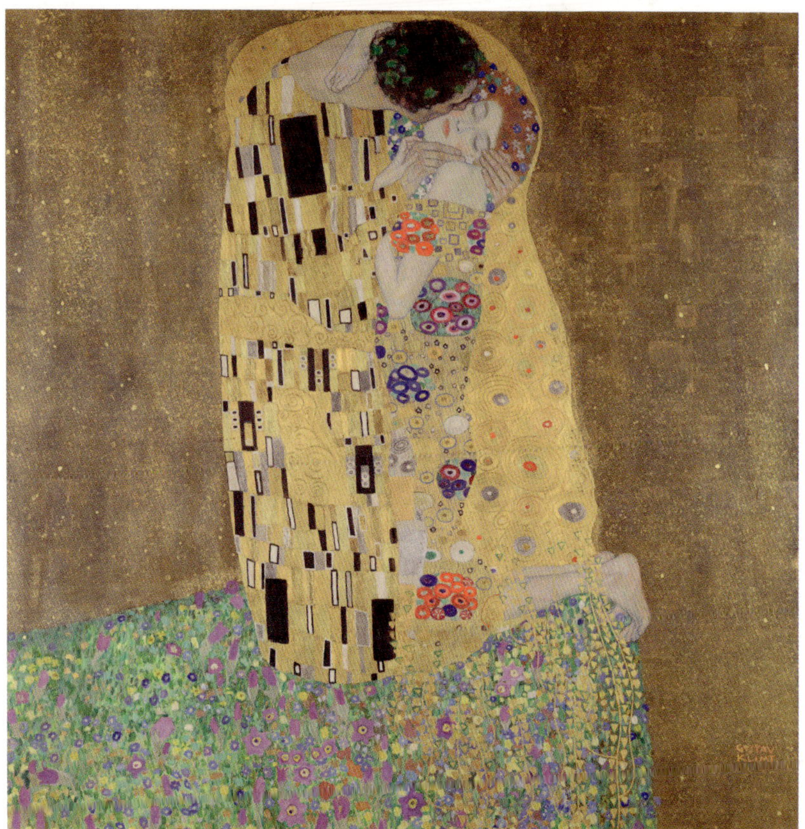

39 Gustav Klimt, *The Kiss*, 1907–8

to reality, one in which artists were willing to address the taboos and destructive dimensions of human existence.

One of Klimt's former students, Egon Schiele (1890–1918) depicted provocative and erotically posed male and female models isolated within empty spaces. In *The Self-Seers II (Death and Man)* (1911) Schiele meditates morbidly but seemingly prophetically on the closeness of death to life, as he died tragically young in 1918 in the Spanish Influenza epidemic. The pandemic also took the lives of his pregnant wife and Gustav Klimt.

The transition from Klimt's decorous and sensual idiom to the far more unsettling and unsettled works of Schiele reflects the fact that a rift was growing within western culture, one that divided the experience of the world along the lines suggested by Nietzsche in *Birth of Tragedy* (1872), in which he interpreted

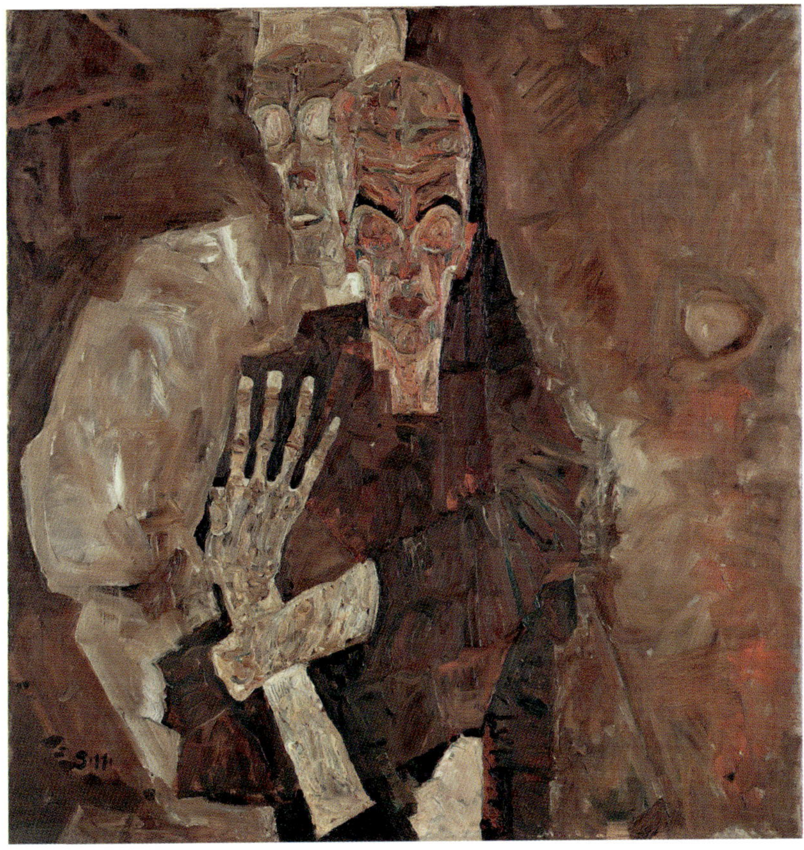

40 Egon Schiele, *The Self-Seers II (Death and Man)*, 1911

the symbolic meaning of the Greek gods Apollo and Dionysus. The 'Apollonian' artist aimed at what Matisse called 'an art of balance, purity and serenity', while the 'Dionysian' embraced disruption, chaos and negation, or all that lies beyond reason – beyond thought itself. The Apollonians sought to reinforce the boundaries that produce a sense of individual and social equilibrium, and aimed to communicate positive values and emotions, shielding themselves from the horrors of existence. The Dionysians, by contrast, heroically threw themselves into a formless and turbulent reality, and worked to erase boundaries and dismantle the self. They willingly encouraged inner unrest to liberate the dynamic energies that lie suppressed within normal, commonplace life.

Chapter 4
Cubism to Dada
c. 1900–*c*. 1920

Abstract Art and the Spiritual

The word 'abstract' has already been encountered on several
occasions in these pages. The artists or critics who used the
term were referring to the fact that a painting is inevitably a
process of 'abstraction' because it extracts from or simplifies
a complex visual referent so as to translate it on a flat surface
into a coherent and personal pictorial statement. 'Abstraction'
in this broad sense means the process by which exclusion is
prioritized over inclusion, and all paintings are thus inevitably
'abstract'. But while the roots of the 'abstract art' of the
twentieth century lie in this general meaning, the implication
of the act of exclusion was transformed to mean broadly three
things: the emptying of painting of its accumulated historical
clutter so it becomes pure and more essential, and therefore
ostensibly more 'modern'; the transfer of attention away from
painting as an activity concerned primarily with narrative, with
telling stories in pictures, towards painting as a self-sufficient
entity; and, thirdly, the total rejection of not only the traditional
task of optical realism, but of all pictorial languages aimed
at representing the visible world. Painting was thus re-cast
as a medium for the expression of invisible thoughts, ideas,
moods, feelings and spiritual realities. Often, the impulse
towards abstraction within a specific artist's work will mix all
these different intentions. For, to achieve the last two forms of
abstraction, it is necessary to engage in the iconoclastic activity
of the first.

This period saw the first attempts to unite what westerners
knew of traditional non-western religion and philosophy with
the latest breakthroughs in philosophy and science. Westerners
became aware that the word 'enlightenment' could have two

distinct cultural meanings. On the one hand, as we have seen,
it can refer to a style of thought that values conclusions based
on evidence and reasoning, promotes a science-based worldview
and encourages the humanist pursuit of social and individual
wellbeing and justice. But from a global perspective, a very
different meaning of 'enlightenment' is significant, one which is
seemingly at odds with the western version. This relates to belief
in the human capacity to gain an accurate and deep intuitive
understanding of the totality of reality, and which values
mystical experience and the possibility of 'awakening'.

The second, non-western, idea of 'enlightenment' served as
the foundations for the impulse towards abstraction aimed at
visualizing an invisible 'spiritual' dimension. It was particularly
appealing to westerners because, as part of the systematic
'disenchantment' and rationalization of society, modern
scientific-technological culture seemed to be increasingly
limiting 'reality' to the visible – what the organs of perception
allow one to respond to – thereby omitting everything invisible
and beyond the reach of the senses. But this notion of the
'visible' as containing far more than conventional painting
allowed was also being reinforced by the discoveries of science
itself – by what the microscope revealed of the very small, and
the telescope of the very large. For some, the limited world
made visible by science also seemed to suggest that painting
should address everything science could not embrace: the
wholly transcendent realms of the spirit – the ineffable and
numinous world of religious experience, altered states of
consciousness, the paranormal and the supernatural.

Hilma af Klint (1862–1942) was a Swedish artist, mystic
and occult medium who used image-making as a way of
communicating her visions. *The Ten Largest, No. 2, Childhood*
(1907) is one of a series that Af Klint called 'The Paintings
for the Temple', which eventually amounted to 193 works, all
made between 1906 and 1915. In relation to these works, she
explained that they 'were painted directly through me without
any preliminary drawings and with great force' by channelling
a spirit from beyond the grave. The fact that Af Klint was a
woman – most spirit mediums were women – is indicative
of the fact that the quest for trans-rational and 'spiritual'
alternatives to the materialism that dominated western society
in this period was often pioneered by social groups deprived of
access to the dominant sources of power and authority. In the
art circles of the period, and right up to the 1980s, Af Klint
was a very marginal, even cranky figure, and mostly unknown.
Today, however, she is considered one of the great pioneers
of abstraction.

41

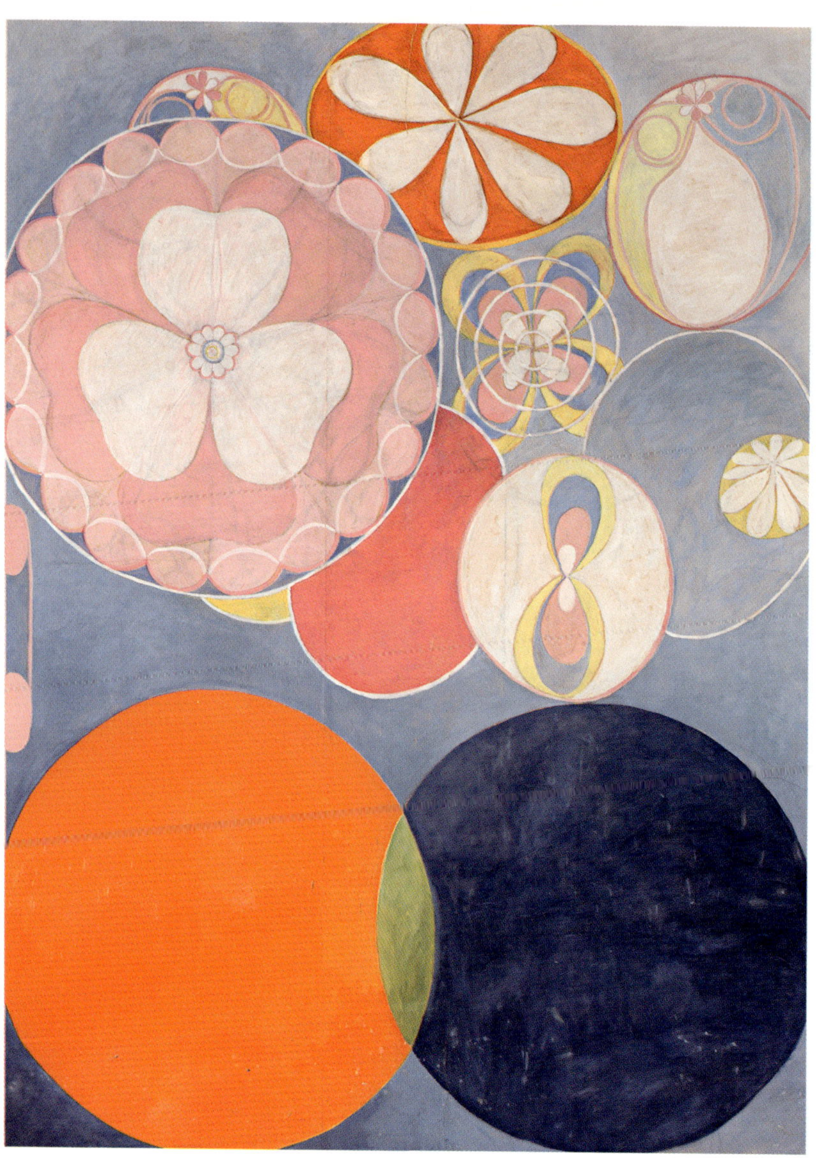

41 ABOVE Hilma af Klint, *The Ten Largest, No. 2, Childhood*, 1907
42 OPPOSITE Wassily Kandinsky, *Composition VI*, 1913

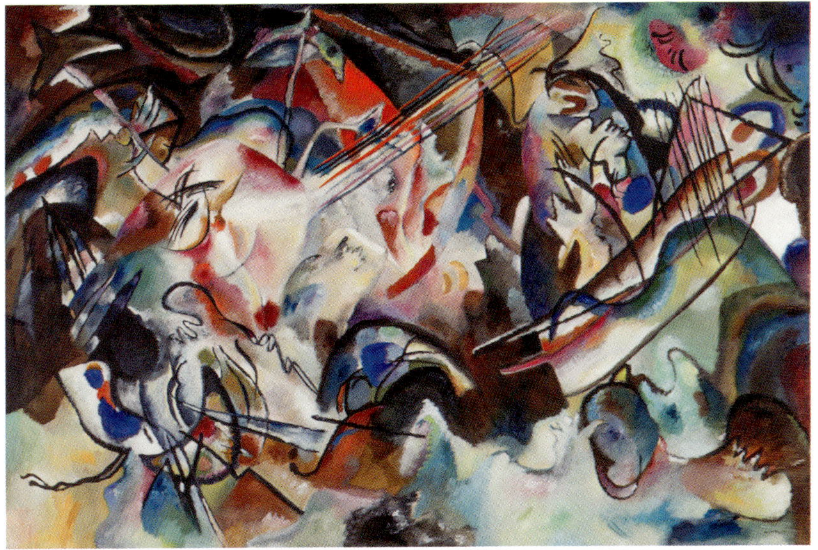

The first male artist to self-consciously evolve a form of 'abstract' painting that was overtly 'spiritual' was Wassily Kandinsky. In his influential book *Concerning the Spiritual in Art* (1910), Kandinsky drew on the teachings of Theosophy – which attempted to blend eastern and western knowledge with the goal of offering an alternative to what it saw as an increasingly 'soulless' modern world – and argued that there were three categories of painting: the 'impression', 'the improvisation' and the 'composition'. While an 'impression' draws on exterior reality, the 'improvisation' and 'composition' arise from the artist's mind. As the title suggests, *Composition VI* (1913) reflects Kandinsky's attempt at the third kind of painting. There are no recognizable objects, no clear sense of illusionistic space – of what is up and down, near and far. Kandinsky obliges the viewer to concentrate attention on the physical presence of the painting. But this was not simply in order to enhance appreciation of its decorative aesthetic and sensory qualities. Rather, Kandinsky believed he was transforming painting into a more expressive and profound medium in relation to the transcendent and immaterial dimensions of existence.

With the emergence of such 'non-objective', non-figurative or 'abstract' art, painting's reference point is no longer located 'behind' the painting, out there in the world, but 'within', inside the arena of painting itself conceived as a visualization of the mind of the artist. Like Af Klint, Kandinsky also avidly read and debated the writings of mystical and spiritual sages hoping to remedy what he perceived as the deadening materialism of western culture. As we saw in Chapter Three, Kandinsky was a founding member of the expressionistically inclined Blaue Reiter group in Germany, and it was from within this context that he evolved towards abstraction, severing the link with an external referent and focusing instead on the capacity of shapes and colours to convey deep and meaningful thoughts and feelings. But it should be noted that when Kandinsky used the German word *geistige* or 'spiritual', he did not mean it in the same sense as Af Klint, who was referring to an existence beyond the grave. Rather Kandinsky's goal was a refined, internal level of consciousness connected to an essential 'reality' lying beyond mere appearances and 'impressions'.

Cubism

Around the same time that Kandinsky was tentatively pushing towards the 'spiritual', 'abstraction' was being pursued in Paris with very different goals in mind. The style that became known as Cubism began to emerge as a recognizable tendency in 1907 and initially entailed 'abstracting' in the older sense of the term – extracting, removing or simplifying selected elements from an external referent. Cubist works made by such artists as Georges Braque, Albert Gleizes, Juan Gris, Fernand Léger and, most famously, Pablo Picasso signalled a shift in painting towards balancing the inner world of the imagination and thought and the outer world of observation and experience.

In their quest for an art that was geared less overtly towards self-expression and more to the measured analysis of the visible, in the period 1910 to 1912 the works of the two pioneers of Cubism, Braque (1882–1963) and Picasso (1881–1973), became almost indistinguishable, and were characterized by the selection of an unprepossessing subject – for example, a nude figure or still-life – which was then painted as if observed from multiple viewpoints and reconstructed using faceted or linear 'cube-like' or gridded forms. The works were also primarily painted in an almost monochromatic palette of black, grey and muted ochres, so an all-over, homogenous surface was produced. Often, Cubist artworks substituted an abstract sign for an image based on pictorial resemblance. Rather than using perspective and modelling or simulating an 'impression' of a visual stimulus, thereby producing a representation of a static theme as seen from a particular point of view, a Cubist painting introduced the movements involved in scanning the visual field that are part of normal vision. It also relied far more than was usually the case in painting based on observation on the memory of what things

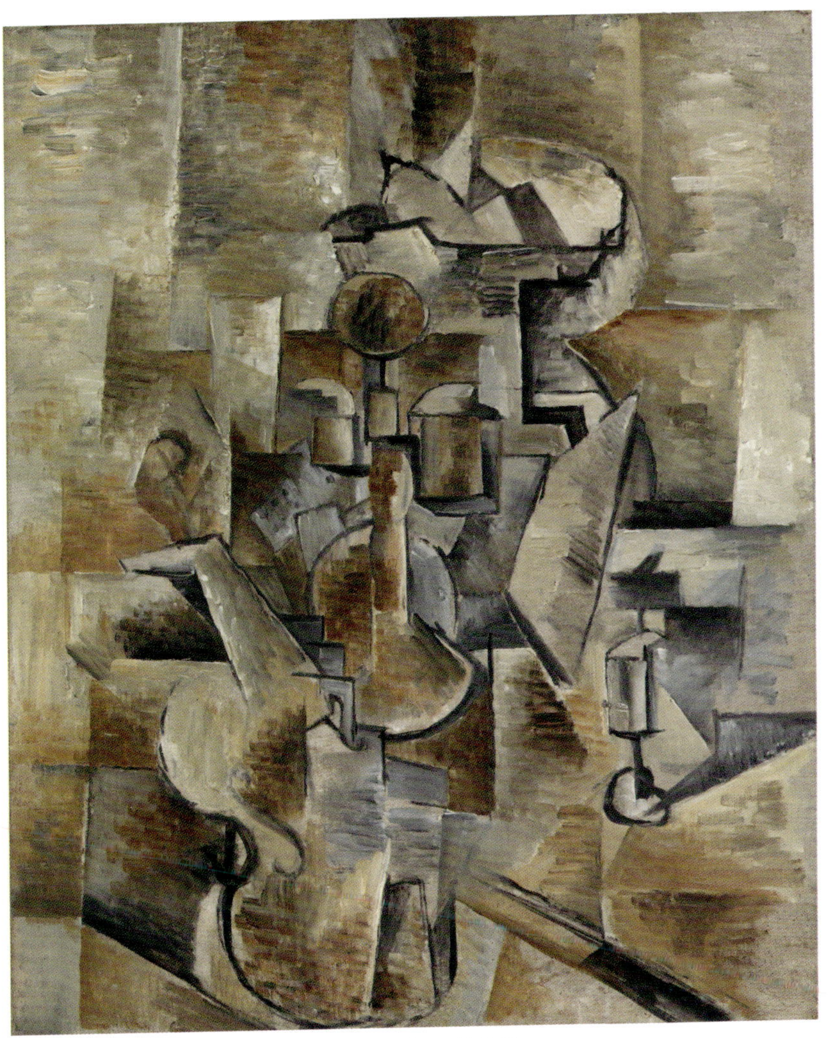

43 Georges Braque, *Still Life (Violin and Candlestick)*, 1910

look like, on a repertoire of repeated visual units designating
familiar objects. This was a new kind of pictorial script or
visual code that had to be learned, like writing. But it was also
a reminder that all paintings – however seemingly 'natural' or
'realistic' – rely on a code that must be learned.

In practice, the deconstruction and reconstruction process
became so complex that in some cases, such as Braque's *Still Life
(Violin and Candlestick)* (1910), it is difficult to discern at first the
objects described in the work's title. But on closer inspection,

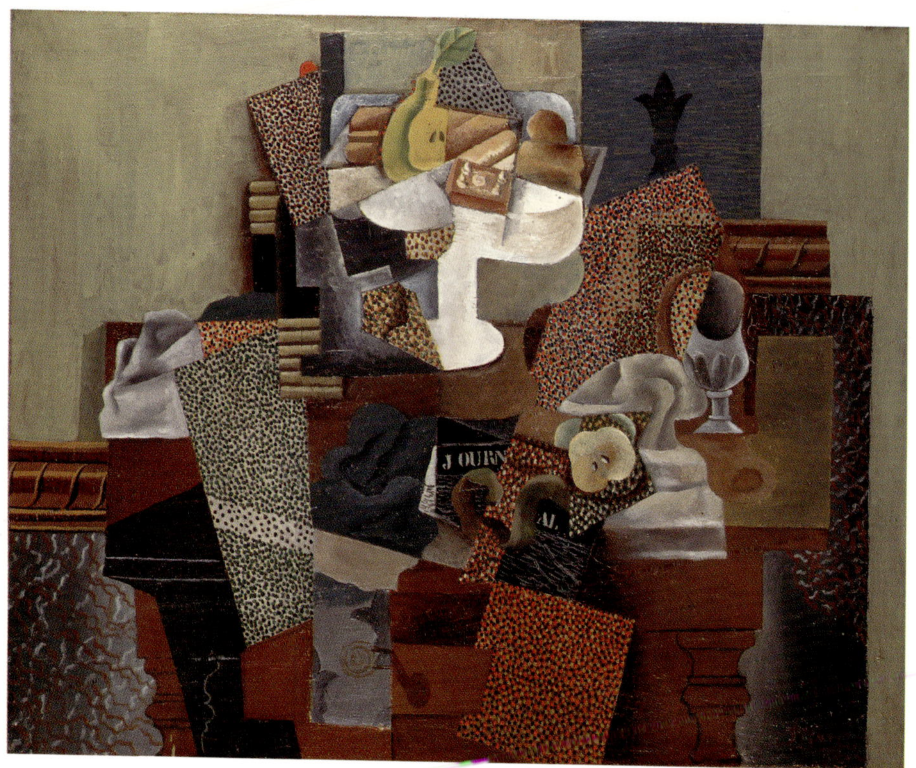

44 Pablo Picasso, *Still Life with Compote and Glass*, 1914–15

the characteristic shape of a violin's neck, peg box, centre bout, F-holes and tailpiece can be made out bottom left, and above in the centre there are the round base and vertical shaft of a candlestick holding a candle. One can also make out a wine glass in profile to the right and, at the top middle, a *compotier* holding fruit.

Paintings of the early period of Cubism are often termed 'analytic' or 'gridded' because they are based on the observation of a specific subject perceived by the artist which is reduced to a geometric superstructure. But they also still included aspects of the old illusionistic system of painting, such as employing light and dark contrasts to create internal spaces, as seen here in Braque's picture, where the violin casts a shadow. But the whole language of painting has been deliberately rendered ambiguous. Braque has included multiple points of view and fragments of different kinds of visual code. He noted: 'What greatly attracted me – and it was the main line of advance of Cubism – was how to give material expression to this new space of which I had an inkling. So I began to paint chiefly still lifes, because in nature there is a tactile, I would almost say a manual space...that was the earliest Cubist painting – the quest for space.' Crucially, this new kind of space was subjective; it was dependent on the individual's selection and organization of what was observed into a compositional unit. As an early supporter of Cubism, the poet Guillaume Apollinaire, wrote in 1913: 'Authentic Cubism.... would be the art of depicting new wholes with formal elements borrowed not from the reality of vision, but from that of conception.' In other words, Cubism pushed to an extreme the distinction between seeing (the physical act of visual perception) and knowing (reflecting on this act).

But in the next phase of Cubism, termed 'synthetic', which began in 1912, Cubist works shifted decisively towards the latter. For now, they were based not on direct observation of something in front of the artist but rather on the imaginative rearrangement of a repertoire of visual signs developed in the earlier stage, which is further deconstructed and reconstructed on the surface of a work. This transformation was largely the result of the introduction of a wholly new dimension to painting, which is the second important innovation of the period: collage. The term collage derives from the French word for glue – *colle* – and indicates that elements within a composition have been pasted onto a (usually) paper surface rather than painted. Collage opened up several new pathways, while also undermining some of painting's most sacrosanct and seemingly inviolable – even to the avant-garde – conditions. A typical Cubist collage is made up of fragments of planar, two-dimensional artefacts culled from the outside world – such as newspaper, posters, wallpapers, tickets and so on – which have been directly imported into the work rather than imitated in paint.

44 In *Still Life with Compote and Glass* (1914–15) Picasso took the collage-effect he and Braque had pioneered through cut-out papers glued down on small-sized paper surfaces, and mimicked it in a work on canvas done entirely in oil paint. Small oases remain of a more familiar pictorial language – in the wine glass, middle right, for example, and the fruit in the *compotier* – but most of the work has been composed of flat interlocking planes of different colour, or parodies of 'Divisionist'-like *taches* of paint. Some of these 'collage' shapes plausibly define elements within the representation, but others seem to fly free of any such descriptive function and are purely juxtapositions of flat angular forms. One practical consequence of this is that the work is no longer quite the puzzle Braque's painting poses, as it is easier to 'read' the various elements as standing in for things

in the world – a newspaper, a wine glass, crumpled cloths, a table stood against a wall – as well as the *compotier* full of fruit.

In a far more explicit way than in any of the works discussed in the previous chapters, collage drew attention to the status of painting as something visually *present* – a flat surface upon which shapes and colours have been arranged, not an illusion of a three-dimensional space. Furthermore, collage offered a way beyond the expressionistic – and now increasingly commonplace amongst the avant-garde – painterly *tache*, replacing it with flat coloured surfaces. As a result, the collage technique radically simplified the composition, giving it a more pronounced sense of tangible structure (defined by the cut edges of the collaged elements) and consequently of perceived order. By using hard-edged and material properties, collage also drew painting closer to the characteristic forms of technology and the urban environment, which are typically geometric and flatly coloured, thereby moving painting away from its dependence on the organic forms of the natural world. Collage also suggested that a modern painting need not depend on conventional materials or practices, nor on the traditional skills associated with using them. It foregrounded the improvisational and unplanned properties of a painting by emphasizing its status as a surface upon which elements are arranged and rearranged before coalescing into a final composition. Lastly, by employing 'low', ready-made media, and by directly incorporating elements from the modern everyday world, collage showed that painting could be 'modern' through its status as an amalgam or hybrid of explicitly different and borrowed stylistic and semantic categories.

While Picasso would go on to explore other ways of painting, even returning in the 1920s to the more conventional space of linear perspective and modelling, Cubism would prove decisive in that it liberated him from the constraints of any particular style, and made central the importance of the subjective and improvisatory, as well as of the role played by the viewer in giving meaning to what they see. As Picasso said in 1935: 'A picture is not thought out and settled beforehand. While it is being done it changes as one's thoughts change. And when it is finished, it still goes on changing, according to the state of mind of whoever is looking at it. A picture lives a life like a living creature, undergoing changes imposed on us by our life from day to day.'

These developments within art were also a direct result of major changes in society and advances in technology and science that were leading to new ways of thinking about and experiencing time and space – ways that, today, people in the developed world take for granted. The period between 1880 and 1910 saw the invention of new machines that greatly increased the speed and scope of communication, transportation and entertainment: the telephone, the airplane and the defining technical invention of the modern age – the automobile – as well as the defining entertainment medium, the cinema. Enhanced manufacturing efficiency was being ensured by the development of such equipment as the electric sewing-machine and the introduction of scientific management techniques in the workplace, improving economic efficiency by replacing traditional practices with empirically tested methods. In medicine, the X-ray machine and medical breakthroughs like vaccines led to mortality rates dropping significantly, especially amongst infants. In scientific research, the electron and radioactivity were discovered, and Quantum and Relativity theories presented. Sigmund Freud published *The Interpretation of Dreams* in 1900, heralding the birth of a new and ostensibly scientific theory of the mind. Increasing numbers of people, male and female, had access to education, and so levels of literacy increased, and with them the breadth and depth of knowledge and capacity to think independently. The professions were being systematically transformed into meritocracies, thereby facilitating greater social mobility. Mass media emerged to service the newly literate and leisured populace, leading to the dissemination of information faster and more widely than ever before, and giving birth to new forms of popular culture. Free and independent thought and expression were increasingly taken for granted and protected by law. Several western governments moved towards greater democracy by enfranchising their citizens, and women began to agitate publicly for equal rights with men, including the right to vote.

On a global level, the western capitalist nation-states now hugely outperformed other countries in terms of trade, industrial development and military might. They also sought direct political authority over large portions of the world, hoping to exploit natural resources and populations, while also bringing some of the benefits of modernization with them – for example, in relation to medicine and education. By 1914, the west controlled one quarter of the land surface of the planet and, as the American historian Henry Adams declared in 1900, it seemed that the era of the 'Virgin' – of the reign of superstition, religion, inertia and fatalism – had given way to the triumphant era of the 'Dynamo', of reason, science and progress.

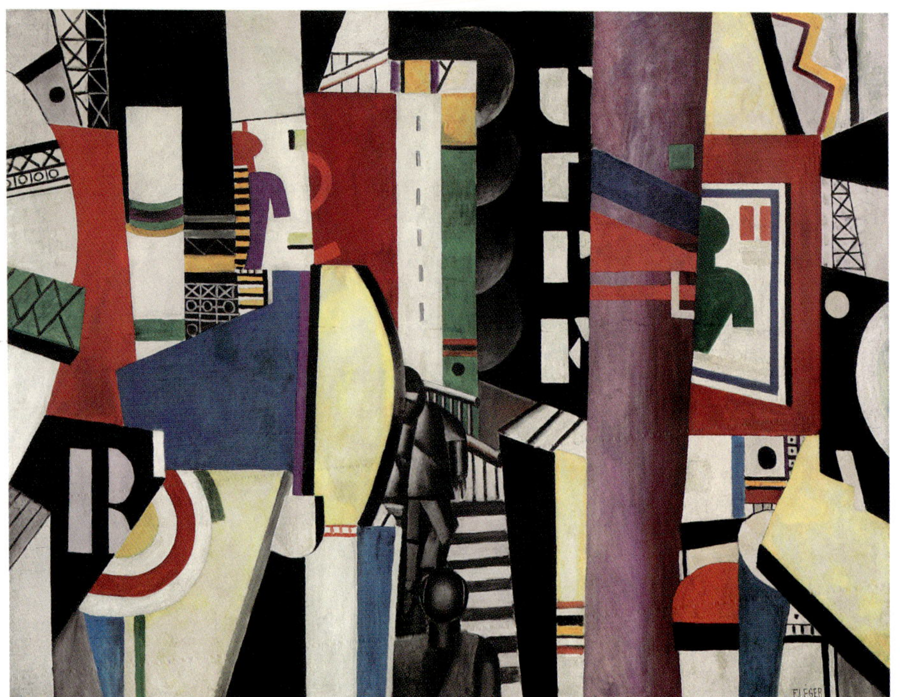

45 ABOVE Fernand Léger, *The City*, 1919
46 OPPOSITE Marc Chagall, *I and the Village*, 1911

Beyond Cubism

Cubism proved an extraordinarily fertile breeding ground for artists and led to a plethora of new developments. One possibility was to deploy the formal geometric structures of Cubism while continuing within a style still founded on the principles of depicting a subject from a single point of view. The Paris-based Italian artist Amedeo Modigliani (1884–1920) and French artist Marie Laurencin (1883–1956), for example, rooted their work in the sober palette of Cézanne and the simplification and 'primitivism' adopted by Picasso and Braque in their initial move towards Cubism; but Modigliani, in his portraits of friends and lovers, and Laurencin in her portraits (especially of women) and bucolic fantasies, maintained a more homogenous perspectival space, and ensured that a clear linear outline around forms made their subjects easily recognizable.

The Symbolist aesthetic was also revived through an injection of Cubist-inspired formal innovation. In the work of the Jewish-Russian artist Marc Chagall (1887–1985), who also lived in Paris, Cubism was drawn upon not only in relation to

the flattening of colours into distinct, hard-edge fields that
organize the composition, but also to create a dreamlike vision.
In *I and the Village* (1911), a memory of his hometown of Vitebsk
in Russia, Chagall used Cubist deformation to confuse space
and scale, and to defy the laws of gravity (note the upside-down
female figure at the top).

By contrast, Fernand Léger's (1881–1955) encounter with
Cubism led to the creation of paintings that celebrated the
urban environment and the lives of the working people who
lived within it. Léger took the 'cubes' and flat planes of Cubist
collage to signal an affinity between painting and machinery,
factories and modern design, but also the rational, scientific
spirit of the modern age. This in turn is evidence that dominant
material aspects of the environment work unconsciously
to mould preferences for specific shapes and colours. To
construct the solid architectural space of *The City* (1919) Léger
used predominantly vertical and horizontal lines, and clearly
delineated zones of flat colour. The result is a monumental
effect that forges out of Cubist collage a new kind of modern
Classicism. Indeed, the metropolis evoked by Léger over one
hundred years ago looks surprisingly undated and could still
be a credible image of a city of the present day.

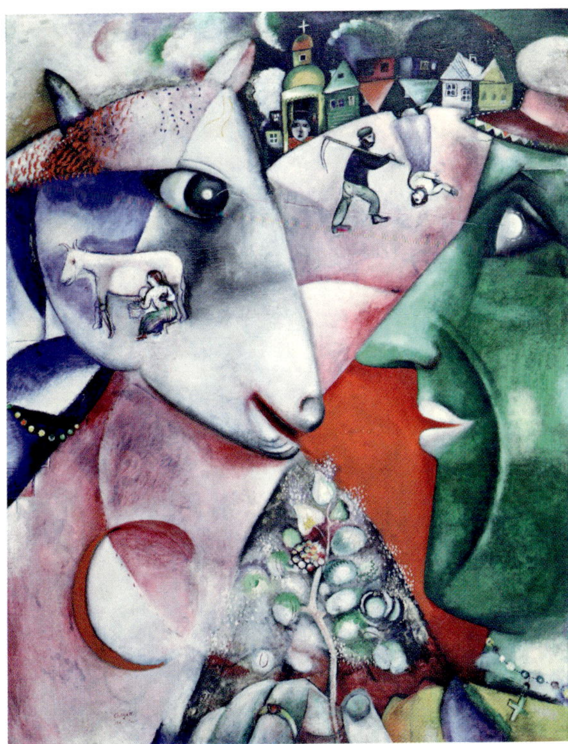

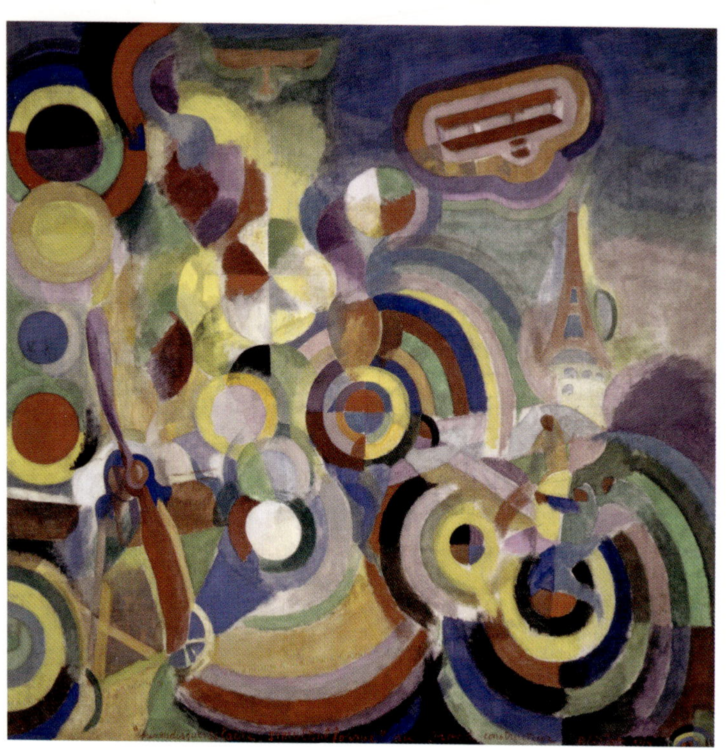

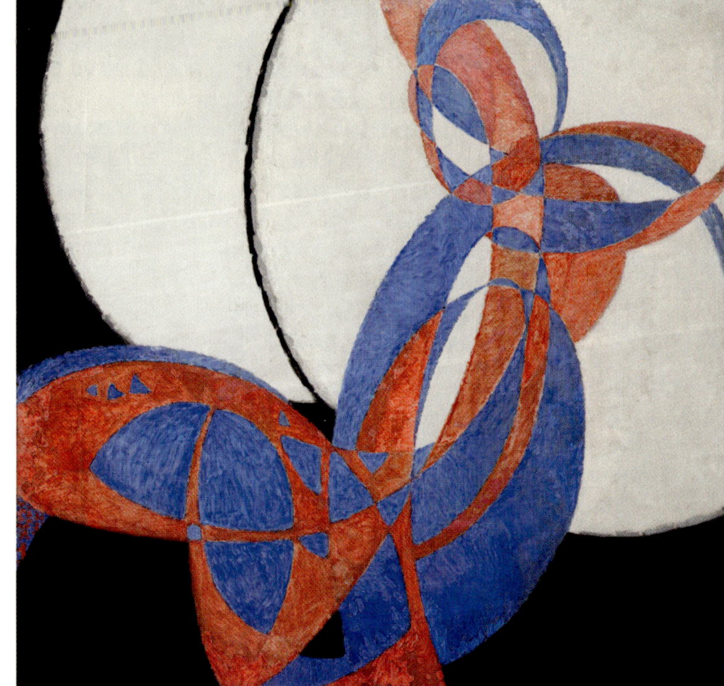

47 ABOVE Robert
Delaunay, *Homage
to Blériot*, 1914
48 RIGHT František
Kupka, *Amorpha, Fugue
in Two Colours*, 1912

For the French couple Robert (1885–1941) and Sonia Delaunay (1885–1979), Cubism was an invitation to develop a genre of painting based on pure colour relations in simple and repetitive shapes, which they argued also reflected the inherent multi-sensory dynamism of the city. They termed their style Orphism, and drew from Cubism an optimistic spirit inspired by the technological wonders of the period. Orphist works explored the borderline between recognizable imagery and what at first seem to be purely abstract shapes. Robert Delaunay's *Homage to Blériot* (1914), for example, blends abstract forms of vibrantly coloured 'solar' discs with the characteristic shape of the Eiffel Tower alongside representations of the aeroplane used by the famous French aviator Louis Blériot to cross the English Channel in 1909 (top middle) and its propeller (bottom right), as well as a more contemporaneous biplane (top right).

Delaunay's work pushes towards full-blown abstraction of the sort being explored at this time by Kandinsky in Germany, but another Orphist, the Czech artist František Kupka (1871–1957) more resolutely severed his 'non-objective' works from reference to the visible world, producing geometrically shaped, two-dimensional forms that were self-sufficient and without representational function but, so Kupka believed, capable of communicating a non-material, spiritual dimension to existence that brought it close to music. He declared: 'I can find something between sight and hearing and I can produce a fugue in colours as Bach has done in music.'

Futurism and Vorticism

A group of Italian artists calling themselves the Futurists were especially inspired by how Cubism heralded a new urban art that celebrated the wonders of modernity. Multiple viewpoints, and the embrace of the everyday world, became for the Futurists an invitation to explore what they saw as the radically new experience of time and space produced by machines like the automobile and the aeroplane, and the frenetic pace of urban life. They were also interested in a recent invention – cinema – for here too was evidence of a radically modern way of organizing time and space. But what made the modern world different, and superior, to the past was *speed*. As the leader of the group, the poet Filippo Marinetti declared: 'We affirm the world's magnificence has been enriched by a new beauty: the beauty of speed. A racing car hood is adorned with great pipes, like serpents of explosive breath – a roaring car that seems to ride on grapeshot is more beautiful than the Victory of Samothrace.'

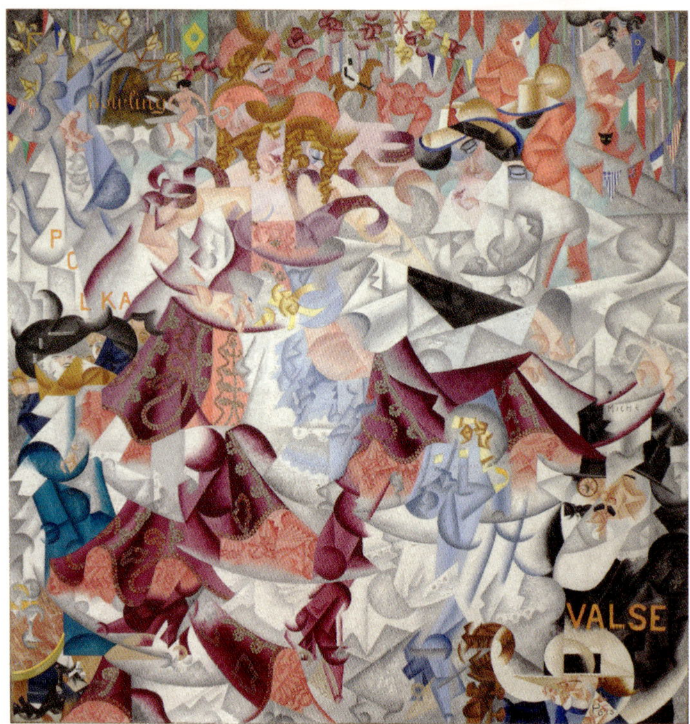

49 LEFT Gino Severini, *Dynamic Hieroglyphic of the Bal Tabarin*, 1912
50 OPPOSITE David Bomberg, *Ju-Jitsu*, c. 1913

Giacomo Balla (1871–1951) attempted to simulate in paint the effect of an automobile speeding by on a road, breaking up the lines into vectors of energy transecting the canvas, while Carlo Carrà (1881–1966) transformed a demonstration in a city street into a spiralling cacophony of collaged and painted texts evoking the frenetic and noisy experience of urban life.

In *Dynamic Hieroglyphic of the Bal Tabarin* (1912) Gino Severini (1883–1966) conveys the animated ambience of a Parisian nightclub by employing the Cubist device of collapsing space into a complex merger of foreground, middle-ground and background, and by breaking up forms into interrelated lines of force and shard-like facets. At the centre, one can make out two dancing women, one with sequins attached to her purple dress, and, sitting bottom right, a man with a monocle. Also note the tiny naked woman astride a pair of scissors top left. The term 'hieroglyphic' indicates that Severini conceived of his work as a stylized – abstracted – fusion of image and word, creating a new kind of visual language.

In Britain, a group of artists calling themselves the Vorticists, masterminded by the artist and writer Percy

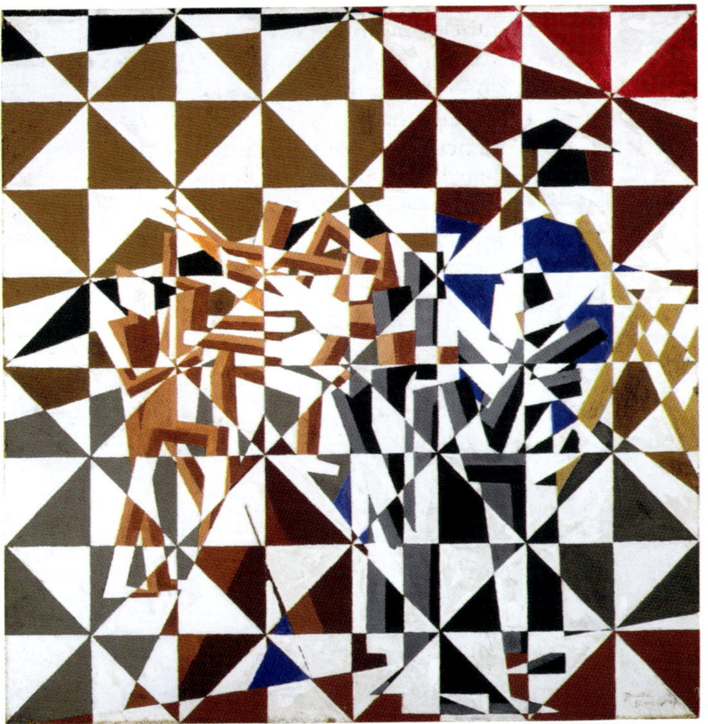

Wyndham Lewis and including the artists Jessica Dismorr,
Christopher R. W. Nevinson, Helen Saunders and Edward
Wadsworth, also embraced the ideal of a modern art modelled
on the new material forms and the spirit of industry and
the city. They set themselves up in rivalry to the influential
Bloomsbury Group – which included writers such as Virginia
Woolf, her sister the artist Vanessa Bell, the painter Duncan
Grant, the critic Clive Bell and the critic and curator Roger Fry –
who were the principal conduit of the art and ideas surrounding
Post-Impressionism coming from France discussed in the
previous chapter, but who proved reluctant to embrace the
newer, more brash and urban trends. In their magazine,
entitled provocatively *Blast* (1914), the Vorticists declared: 'We
are primitive mercenaries in the Modern World.' Associated
with Vorticism, though not technically a member of the group,
David Bomberg (1890–1957) aimed, in paintings such as *Ju-Jitsu*
(*c.* 1913), to capture the new experiences of the bustling port of
London near where he grew up, declaring: 'I want to translate
the life of a great city, its motion, its machinery, into an art that
shall not be photographic, but expressive.'

50

Cubo-Futurism and Suprematism in Russia

In Russia, artists including Alexandra Ekster, Natalia Goncharova,
Mikhail Larionov, Kazimir Malevich and Liubov Popova dubbed
themselves Cubo-Futurists to indicate their dual allegiance to the
latest developments. Once again, the emphasis was primarily on the
celebration of modern life, especially the dynamism of urban living.
In *Painterly Architectonic (Still Life: Instruments)* (1915) by Liubov
Popova (1889–1924) the connection to an external reality becomes
much more attenuated and can probably only be recognized
through consulting the work's title, although it is possible to infer
the presence of a guitar from the characteristic pink shape on the
right. The title is in fact double, and the former aspect indicates
Popova's primary interest in the juxtaposition of interlocking shapes
that seem to float or rest one on top of another and produce a
unified structure reminiscent of architectural design.

Like several artists during this period, the Ukraine-born
Kazimir Malevich (1879–1935) worked in various styles –
Impressionist, Post-Impressionist, Symbolist and Cubo-Futurist –
on the way to naming his very own: 'Suprematism'. Here, pictorial
'architectonics' become dominant. In a typical Suprematist
painting, clusters of flatly coloured geometric shapes angled on
the diagonal stand out or float on a flat, usually white, ground.
'Only when the habit of one's consciousness to see in paintings
bits of nature, Madonnas and shameless nudes has disappeared,
shall we see a pure-painting composition,' Malevich announced

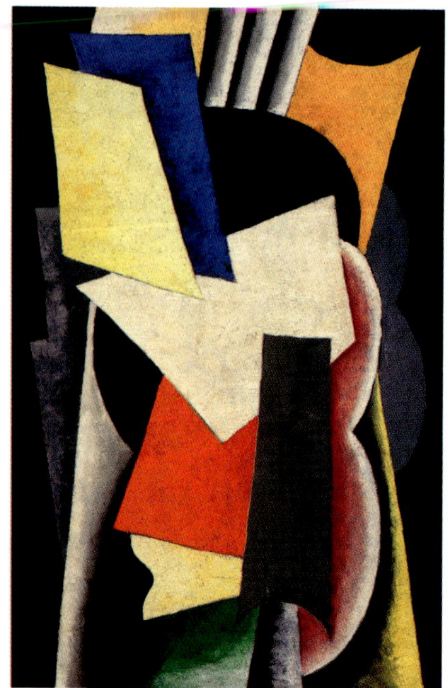

51 LEFT Liubov Popova,
*Painterly Architectonic
(Still Life: Instruments)*, 1915
52 OPPOSITE Kazimir Malevich,
Black Square, 1915

in 1915. But his goal was far more radical than simply the
formal abstraction of an object. For, as he put it, he sought
to fill painting with 'the spirit of non-objective feeling, which
penetrates everything'.

52   Malevich's *Black Square* of 1915 was at that date the emptiest
western painting ever made. It is a starkly minimal diagram of a
non-visual but nevertheless real world that, so Malevich insisted,
is inaccessible to rational analysis and can only be grasped
through intuition, a higher state of consciousness characterized
by 'pure feeling'. Malevich cast his paintings as serving a similar
role to the icons of Russian Orthodox Christianity, and thereby
sought to distinguish the Russian avant-garde from its western
European counterparts. Like an icon, a Suprematist work
was a visual form that made the ineffable tangibly present. As
Malevich noted: 'My acquaintance with icon painting convinced
me that the point is not the study of anatomy or perspective, nor
in depicting the truth of nature, but in sensing art and artistic
reality through the emotions.'

The international rivalries that had led to the violent carving up of the world into imperial spheres of influence and colonial rule contributed to a dangerous arms race in the first decade of the twentieth century that would eventually lead to the first global war. The essentially optimistic and utopian mood of the avant-garde, its faith in the possibility of transforming society, was to be sorely tested when in August 1914 the tensions between the European nations finally led to the 'Great War' (1914–18), as it was known. In fact, the conflict was at first welcomed enthusiastically by many progressive artists and intellectuals on both sides, because they saw it as a way to reinvigorate their dull, bourgeois, commercial society. In Italy, for example, the Futurists were aggressively nationalistic and welcomed Italy's belated entry on the side of France, Britain and Russia in 1915. Their leader, Filippo Marinetti, described the heroic nature and cleansing potential of conflict, calling war 'the world's only hygiene'. Ironically, Cubism was to have an unexpectedly direct real-world impact and contribute to the war effort when artists helped in the development of camouflage – deforming colouration on ships and military hardware in order to disguise and conceal it from the enemy.

But the horrific experience of mechanized warfare quickly obliterated romantic idealization. The British artist Paul Nash (1889–1946) was conscripted as a second lieutenant in the Hampshire Regiment and his painting *We Are Making a New World* (1918) shows a devastated environment, the tragic antithesis to John Constable's Romantic landscape idylls of almost one hundred years before. Compared to the radical experiments evident in the paintings reviewed so far in this chapter, Nash's work also relies more on the convention of optical realism to communicate his direct experience of standing before such a landscape. Nash must have spoken for many soldiers when, in a letter in the autumn of 1917, he wrote: 'I am no longer an artist interested and curious. I am a messenger who will bring back word from men fighting to those who want the war to last forever. Feeble, inarticulate will be my message, but it will have a bitter truth and may it burn their lousy souls.'

George Grosz (1893–1959) volunteered for the German army in 1914, was discharged on health grounds in 1916 and then drafted again in 1917, whereupon he had a nervous breakdown and was committed to an asylum. As a result, his paintings are suffused by an aura of violence and a deep sense of disgust with the society that encouraged, glorified and sustained war. The influence of Cubism is evident in

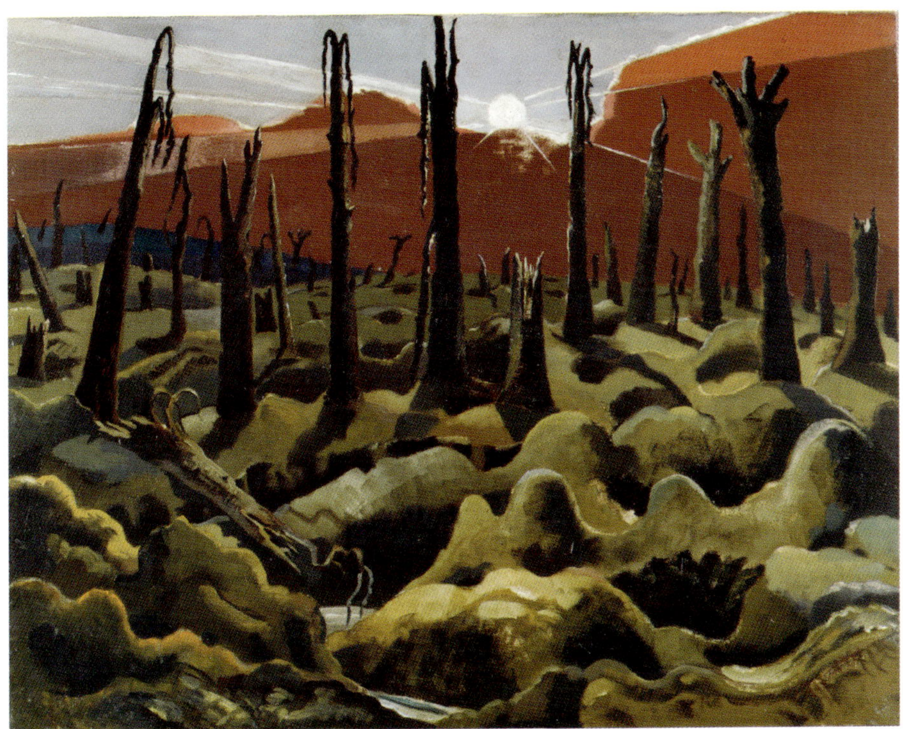

53 Paul Nash, *We Are Making a New World*, 1918

his angular disruptions of space, but now fragmentation is used to enhance an expressionistic mood of violence and ugliness, and a powerful sense of unease, social dislocation and moral collapse. A similar use of Cubist fragmentation pervades the work of another German, Max Beckmann (1884–1950), who volunteered as a medical orderly in the army. His harrowing experiences at the Front also sharpened the edge of his tragic vision of humanity. In *The Night* (1918–19) a man and woman are being tortured in a claustrophobic room while a child looks on demurely. The presence in the bottom foreground of a gramophone player's trumpet adds an element of sinister modern banality to the horrific scene. But while stylistically, the solid yet fractured compositional architecture of Beckmann's painting is heavily indebted to Cubism and Expressionism, it also looks back to medieval German sculpture and, in this sense, such paintings were intended to signal continuing faith in the capacity of art to transfigure pain and affirm cultural continuity – Beckmann's belief that, despite everything, art can triumph over the horrors it depicts.

54

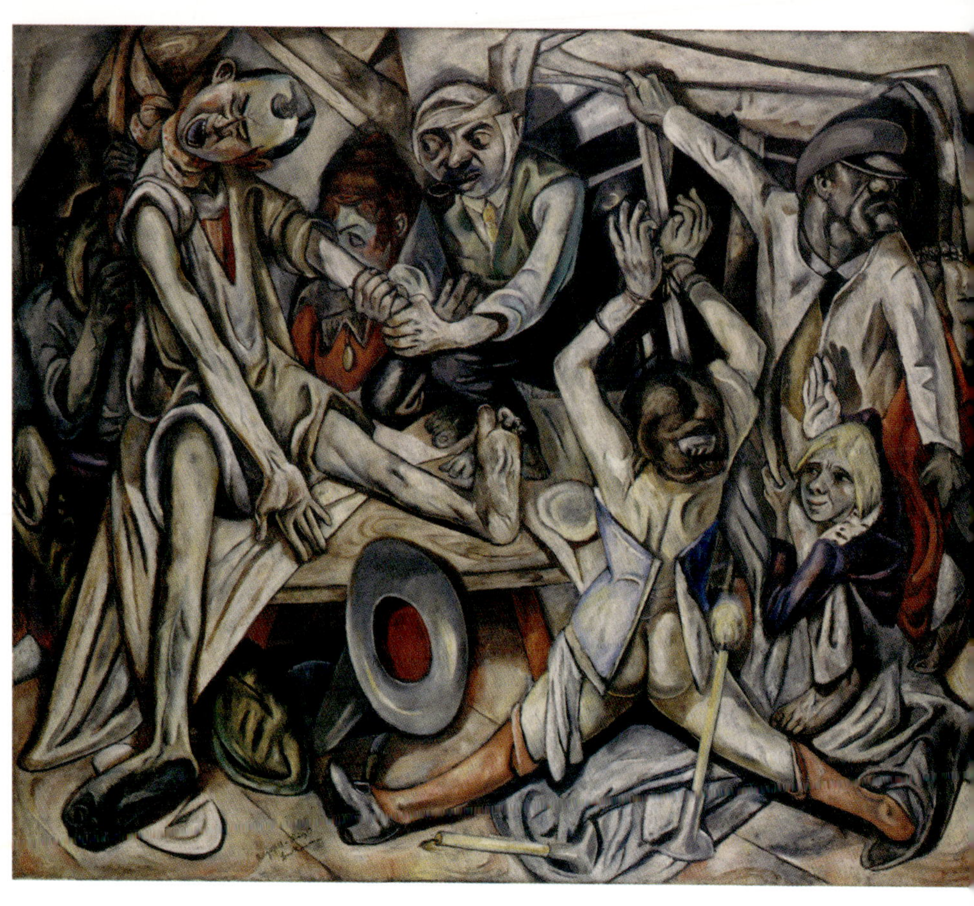

54 Max Beckmann, *The Night*, 1918–19

Dada

As the war raged, and then in the immediate aftermath of
the carnage, many artists inevitably asked themselves how such
brutality could occur amongst the apparently most civilized
nations on earth. For some, like Grosz and Beckmann, the
war revealed the deep eternal truth about humanity's barbaric
nature. For others, the violent abuse of power was a direct
consequence of a modernity that had spawned a dehumanized
culture excessively wedded to rationalism, science and
technology. It was also argued that perhaps *art* itself was not
so much a potential antidote to the cultural sickness that
led to war and all the other signs of human depravity, but
actually part of the sickness itself. If this was true, and art
was inextricably associated with a murderous society, then it
seemed obvious that it had somehow to be wrested free of the
malign association.

Traumatized by the realities of mechanized warfare, artists
felt compelled to push even further away from convention
by embracing absurdity, randomness, chance, spontaneous
expression – the antitheses of all that society valued. For
some, this meant abandoning painting altogether as
hopelessly aestheticizing and tied to the traditional values
of society. The most dedicated exponents of such iconoclastic
rage and strategic disruptions were the Dadaists, a term
chosen because of its explicit childish meaninglessness.
During the war, the Dadaists, such as Jean (Hans) Arp
and Sophie Taeuber-Arp, and the poets Tristan Tzara and
Hugo Ball congregated in neutral Switzerland. At the height
of the Battle of the Somme in 1916, Hugo Ball declared:
'What we call Dada is a harlequinade made of nothingness in
which all higher questions are involved, a gladiator's gesture,
a play with shabby debris, an execution of postured morality
and plenitude.'

After the end of the war in defeated and chaotic Germany,
Dada was especially influential, and several artists explored
the possibilities of photocollage. Kurt Schwitters (1887–1948)
fused an interest in the iconoclasm of Dada with continuing
allegiance to the ideals of Expressionism, leading to works that
he believed expressed a uniquely modern kind of spirituality
that transcended the baseness of the material world while at
the same time being firmly rooted in the here-and-now. To this
end, Schwitters rummaged through his pockets and the trash
and produced what he called 'Merz' collages, a nonsense title
apparently derived from abbreviating the name of a bank: the
'Commerz- und Privatbank'. In the process, Schwitters pushed
collage towards a densely allusive abstraction built out of

found elements from everyday life. In *Merz Picture 25A: The Star Picture* (1920) Schwitters included scraps of newspaper, stamps, a metal lid, string, fragments of cardboard, a wooden slat with a name plate on it, and a piece of metal mesh, all overlaid with murky oil paint.

56

In works such as *Machine Turn Quickly* (1916/18) the French artist Francis Picabia (1879–1953) engineered awkward and ridiculous unions between the realm of the mechanical and the amatory, culling imagery from technical manuals to create fantastic, sexualized hybrid machinery. Picabia aimed to expose the absurd disjunction between a modern world increasingly dominated by the scientific and technological and basic human desires and values. 'Farce, farce, farce, farce, farce, my dear friends,' declared the artist.

Another Frenchman, Marcel Duchamp (1887–1968), took the subversive ideal behind Dada perhaps the farthest. In New York, where Duchamp moved to escape the war, he became involved in organizing Dada-inspired activities and, as a ruse, purchased a man's urinal at a showroom, tilted it sideways, signed it 'R. Mutt 1917', called it *Fountain* and entered it anonymously in an exhibition of which he was an organizer. The exhibition was non-juried, that is, all entered works were meant to be accepted, but the organizing committee – despite all being dedicated advocates of the progressive in art, like Duchamp – baulked at the mass-produced and vulgar ceramic object and rejected it. This, however, was Duchamp's intention. A few years earlier, with his *Bicycle Wheel* of 1913, he had invented the 'readymade' – a pre-existing artefact that an artist elects to elevate to the status of 'work of art'. Duchamp thereby exposed the inherent contradiction within the avant-garde gambit, which rather than truly being open to the 'new', also had its own parameters and rules that must be obeyed. But beyond that, Duchamp suggested that the true purpose of the avant-garde was to challenge the very meaning of 'art' by asserting that anything can be art, and anyone an artist. His action was therefore part of the wider assault on art itself launched by Dada.

In 1915 Duchamp had begun a work enigmatically entitled

57

The Bride Stripped Bare by her Bachelors, Even, also known as *The Large Glass*, which would take him until 1923 to complete. The piece is comprised of two vertical free-stranding glass panels attached to a wooden base. The effect is to detach it from the wall, drawing the surrounding space into the work, and thereby shifting the experience of painting towards one that is more usually associated with sculpture. At some point during construction the glass cracked, however, and the work was set aside and left to gather dust, which Duchamp

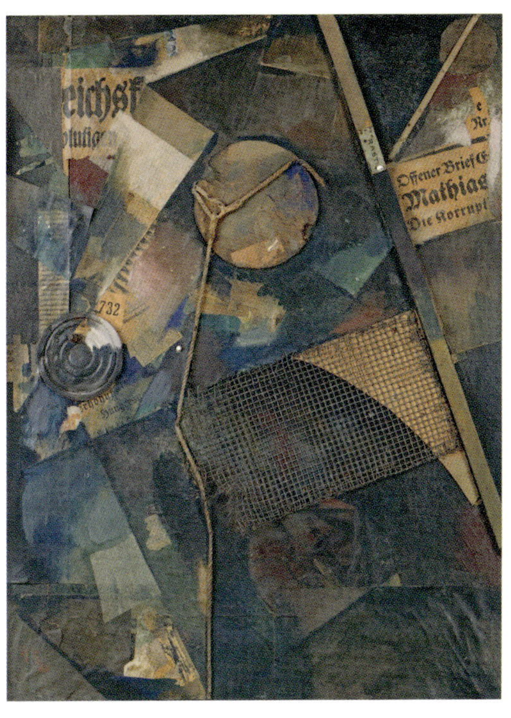

55 RIGHT Kurt Schwitters, *Merz Picture 25A: The Star Picture*, 1920

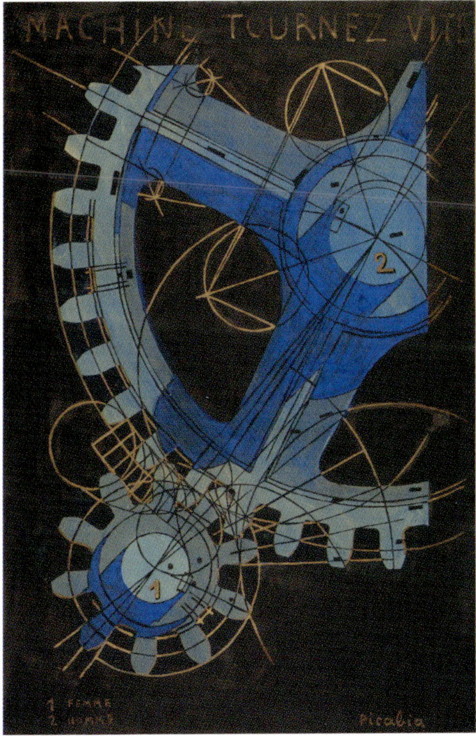

56 LEFT Francis Picabia, *Machine Turn Quickly*, 1916/18

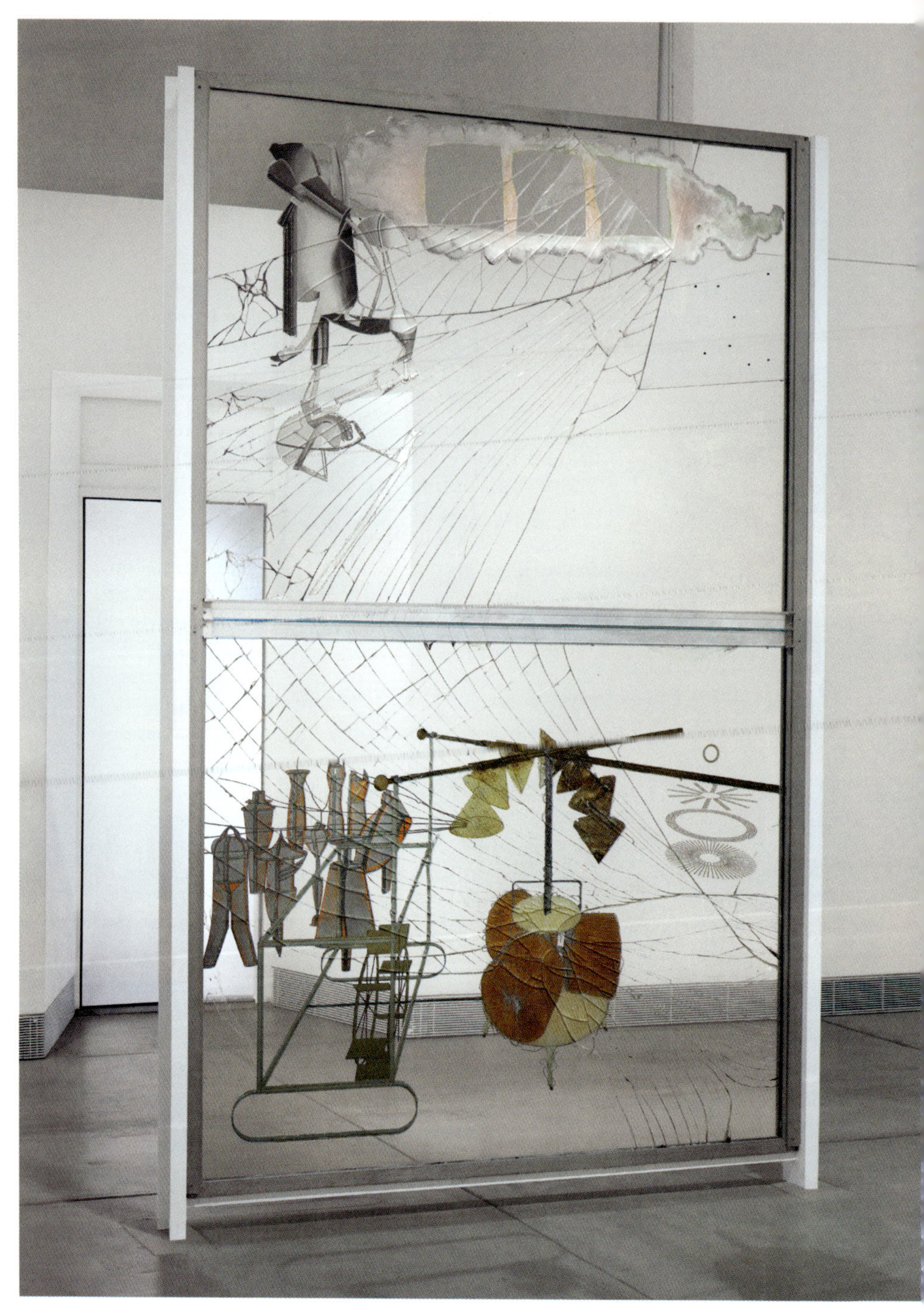

57 Marcel Duchamp, *The Bride Stripped Bare by her Bachelors, Even (The Large Glass)*, 1915–23

subsequently decided to incorporate into the piece when he recommenced work on it. Sandwiched between the panels are painted and collaged designs reminiscent of Picabia's amatory machines. The upper section represents the 'bride', the lower 'the bachelors', and consummation is suspended perpetually. Duchamp was also fascinated by the absurdities generated by the incompatibilities of machinery and human desire within modern society.

In an interview in 1946 Duchamp tried to explain his motivation: 'I wanted to get away from the physical aspect of painting. I was much more interested in recreating ideas in painting....I wanted to put painting once again at the service of the mind.' But by this time, Duchamp had abandoned painting altogether. As he explained in the same interview, one reason for inventing the 'readymade' and reorienting his practice towards ideas had been that he was tired of hearing the expression 'stupid as a painter', by which he meant he felt the art of painting was too limited to what he termed 'retinal art' – making a copy of what the eye could see – and, in general, aesthetics and self-expression. In Duchamp's opinion, modern art should strive to become a realm of speculative and philosophical ideas realized in novel forms. The artist was to be remodelled as a subversive thinker in and through the visual.

Chapter 5
Painting Between the Wars *c.* 1920–*c.* 1945

Surrealism

Is it an elephant, a machine or a giant pot we see ominously looming at the centre of *Celebes* (1921) by the Dada-inspired German artist Max Ernst (1891–1976)? He had served as an artillery engineer during the recent war, and later expressed the traumatic experience as follows: 'On the first of August 1914 M. E. died. He was resurrected on the eleventh of November 1918 [the day the war ended] as a young man who aspired to find the myths of his time.' Bearing this in mind may lead one to conclude that perhaps the grey-green object has military connotations. Maybe it's a tank. But Ernst himself explained that he had in mind a children's rhyme about an elephant from Celebes – though clearly this isn't the kind of animal one will find in a zoo or roaming the African savannah. It is also known from Ernst's remarks that the cylindrical form was based on a photograph of a Sudanese corn-bin. The more we look, learn and reflect, the more confusing the painting becomes.

A decade previously, in northern Italy, the Italian artist Giorgio de Chirico (1888–1978) had begun exploring a similar psychological *terra incognita*. In fact, it was Ernst's encounter with pictures of de Chirico's work in an art journal in 1919 that proved the catalyst for his own enigmatic art. What Ernst found so exciting was how de Chirico employed the familiar language of perspective and modelling in light and dark to depict a decidedly unfamiliar, invisible, mental world that seemed to resonate at a deep, pre-rational level that was uncanny and mysteriously poetic. De Chirico drew on Symbolism, especially the painting of Arnold Böcklin, perceiving in the nineteenth-century Swiss artist's work a new model of figurative painting that preserved the familiar forms of the visible

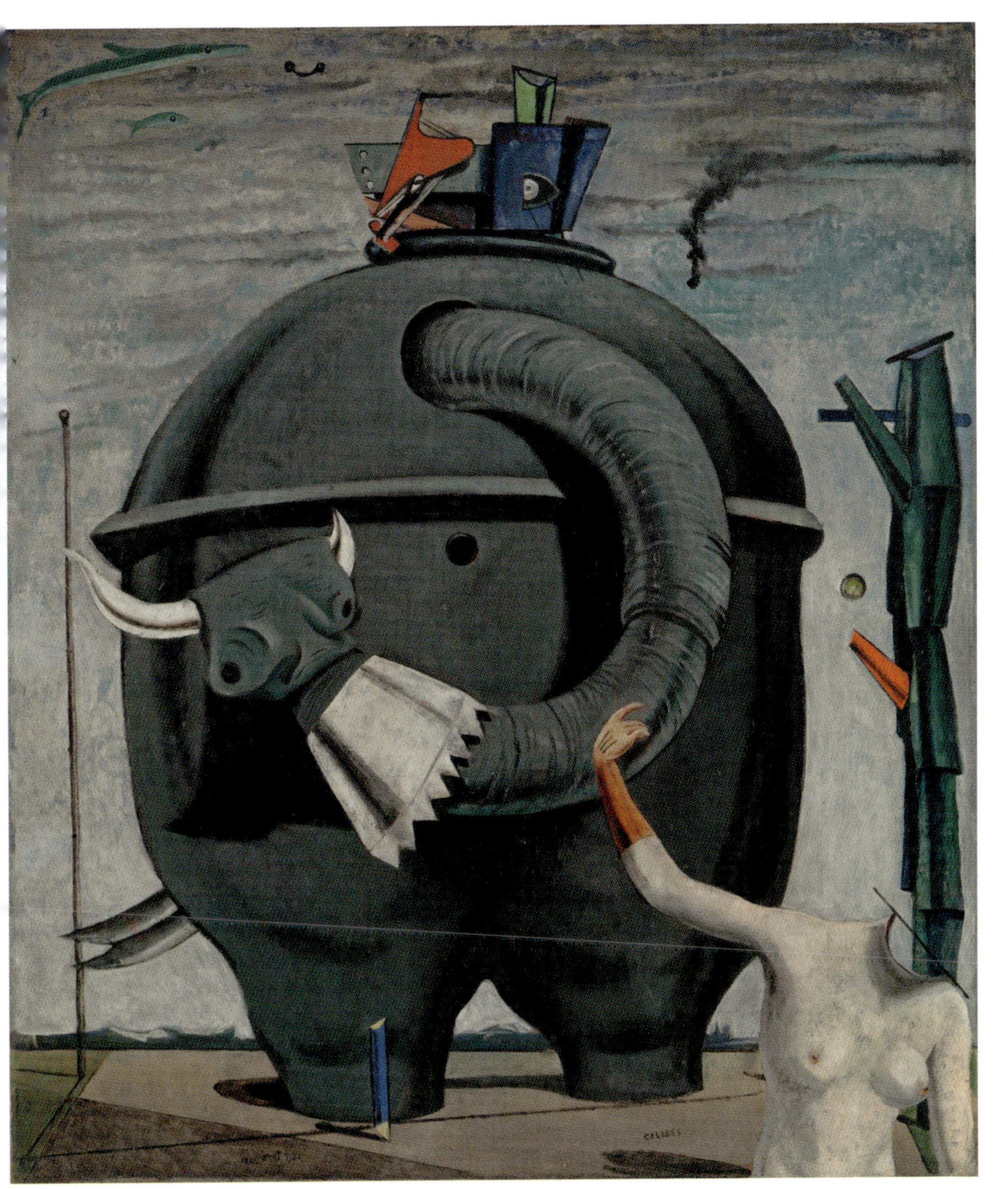

58 Max Ernst, *Celebes*, 1921

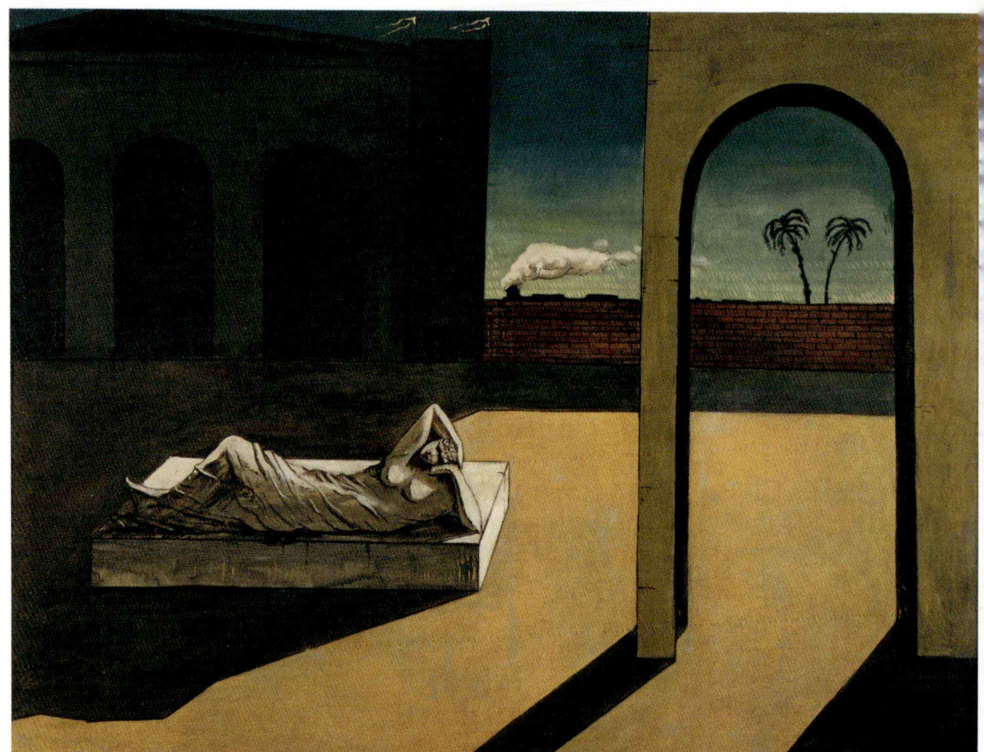

59 Giorgio de Chirico, *The Soothsayer's Recompense*, 1913

world of appearances but imbued them with a powerfully mysterious mood. In works like *The Soothsayer's Recompense* (1913), which de Chirico termed his *Pittura Metaphysica* (Metaphysical Painting), he presented a form of painting that evoked an invisible mental reality while employing familiar stylistic means for depicting aspects of the visible world. As he explained: 'Every object has two appearances: one, the current one, which we nearly always see and that is seen by people in general; the other a spectral or metaphysical appearance beheld only by some rare individuals in moments of clairvoyance and metaphysical abstraction, as in the case of certain bodies concealed by substances impenetrable by sunlight yet discernible, for instance, by X-ray or other powerful artificial means.' In the other 'spectral' world represented in *The Soothsayer's Recompense*, the old pictorial conventions for depicting space exist, but that space is now interior and does not fully conform to the laws of physics nor linear perspective. And the sense of time seems fluid and subjective.

In 1917, the French poet André Breton (1896–1966), who was
working at the time as a medical orderly treating shell-shocked
soldiers, saw de Chirico's paintings in the shop window of
a picture dealer in Paris and was also deeply impressed.
Later Breton declared: 'it is to Giorgio de Chirico that credit
must go for preserving for eternity the memory of the true
modern mythology which is in formation.' Breton argued that
contemporary artists were faced with a basic dilemma: 'The
old model, taken from the external world, was no longer viable.
That which was to succeed, taken from the interior world,
had not yet been discovered.' According to Breton, abstract
art and Cubism had failed, marking the end of a concept of
art in which the representation of the external world was still
the paramount goal. But, like Ernst, Breton recognized in de
Chirico's paintings the birth of a new model, one that meant
the imagery in art was 'taken from the interior world'.

Four years later, Breton saw for the first time some of Ernst's
work – paper collages (in which illustrations from books
were pasted together to create bizarre hybrid realities), which
had been sent to Paris for an exhibition, and immediately
recognized that Ernst was also creating a modern painting
based on the illusionism of the inner life. This was no longer
visual realism but intellectual or *conceptual* realism. By 1924,
the new art of the 'interior world' had a name – Surrealism –
and its many international followers included poets, such as
Breton himself, novelists, philosophers, photographers and
film-makers, and many painters: Balthus, Tarsila do Amaral,
Paul Delvaux, Leonora Carrington, Salvador Dalí, Leonor Fini,
Frida Kahlo, Paul Klee, René Magritte, André Masson, Roberto
Matta, Joan Miró, Kay Sage, Yves Tanguy, Dorothea Tanning
and Remedios Varo.

It seemed to the surrealists that there was evidence of a
deepening social and cultural crisis in the west everywhere
they looked. Traditional religious belief was waning, but
nothing substantial was taking its place, no belief-system
capable of bringing deep meaning to existence. Sociologists
described modern westerners as suffering from *anomie* (a term
coined by Emile Durkheim for the breakdown of social values
and sense of connection), or as living in an 'iron cage' (Max
Weber). Sigmund Freud characterized his patients' various
psychopathologies as nothing more or less than the price that
must be paid for being 'civilized', which required the repression
of the natural animal instincts within humanity. But the 'Great
War' had revealed how shallow were the roots of so-called
civilization, and how readily modern technological societies
could engage in and justify inhuman actions. As the iniquitous

influence of capitalism at home and oppressive imperial domination abroad became more and more obvious, the call for revolutionary change was increasingly heard.

In response to these unsettling realities, the Surrealists gave supreme importance to the irrational, but not, like Dada, as a purely cleansing and purging infusion of deliberate nonsense and meaninglessness. Rather, they saw the irrational as the deepest truth, and so Surrealism turned Dadaist iconoclasm into a constructive movement aimed at the liberation of the mind. As we have seen, an interest in the irrational was already central to Romanticism and was also an important dimension of the ideals associated with the term 'primitivism'. Breton declared: 'Surrealism is based on a belief in the superior reality of certain forms of previously neglected associations, in the omnipotence of the dream, in the disinterested play of thought.' In place of western society's cult of reason and objectivity – the mathematical reign of quantitative data – Surrealism elevated the organic, imagination, intuition and feeling, all within the reign of quality. Within the safety of the arena provided by art, the ecstasy and horror of the repressed instinctual life could be endlessly explored, a symptom of freedom from the mundane realities of the despised 'bourgeoisie'.

In Belgium, René Magritte (1898–1967) had also come to believe that artist's role was to represent a hidden 'superior reality', and he spoke for Surrealism in general when he declared: 'The mysterious is not just one of the possibilities of the real. The mysterious is what is absolutely necessary for the real to exist.' Magritte also stated: 'The real value of art is a function of its power of liberating revelation.' In stylistic terms, Magritte painted more solidly illusionistic dream-realities than either de Chirico or Ernst by reverting to a more homogenous pictorial space and adopting a simplistic figurative manner common in the advertisements and illustrations of the period. But what he populated it with was far from familiar – at least from waking life. What is *represented* in *The Central Story* (1928) is transparently clear, but the *meaning* of this strange gathering of objects certainly is not.

The Spaniard Salvador Dalí (1904–1989) also adapted a familiar painting style to explore even more fantastical reaches of the proposition that the role of painting was to depict a 'superior reality'. He mixed extreme distortions of form and space with a conventional representational style that deliberately harked back to the 'licked on' smoothness of nineteenth-century Academic art. Once again, stylistically, the origins of the strange world into which Dalí draws us are to be found in the work of de Chirico and Ernst, but he added a new characteristic – the 'melting' or

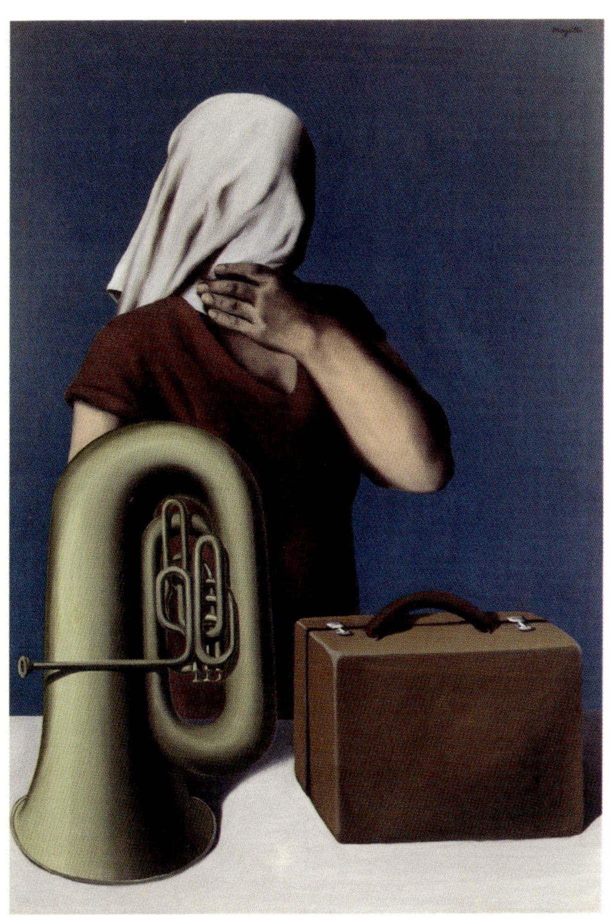

60 René Magritte,
The Central Story,
1928

'softening' of forms so that they reject their real-world material properties and appear to blend into each other. *The Great Masturbator* (1928) is one of Dalí's most provocative works, and the title leaves us in no doubt as to the sexual implications. Dalí described his method as 'paranoia-criticism', by which he meant, as he stated, 'a process of a paranoiac and active character, it is possible (simultaneously with automatism and other passive states) to systematize confusion and thus help to discredit completely the world of reality'. The term 'paranoia' in medical parlance refers to a delusional psychosis, but for Dalí, as for the Surrealists in general, it was precisely this mental disruption, which was an implicit affront to dull 'bourgeois' consciousness, that gave birth to original works that expressed a deeper 'reality'.

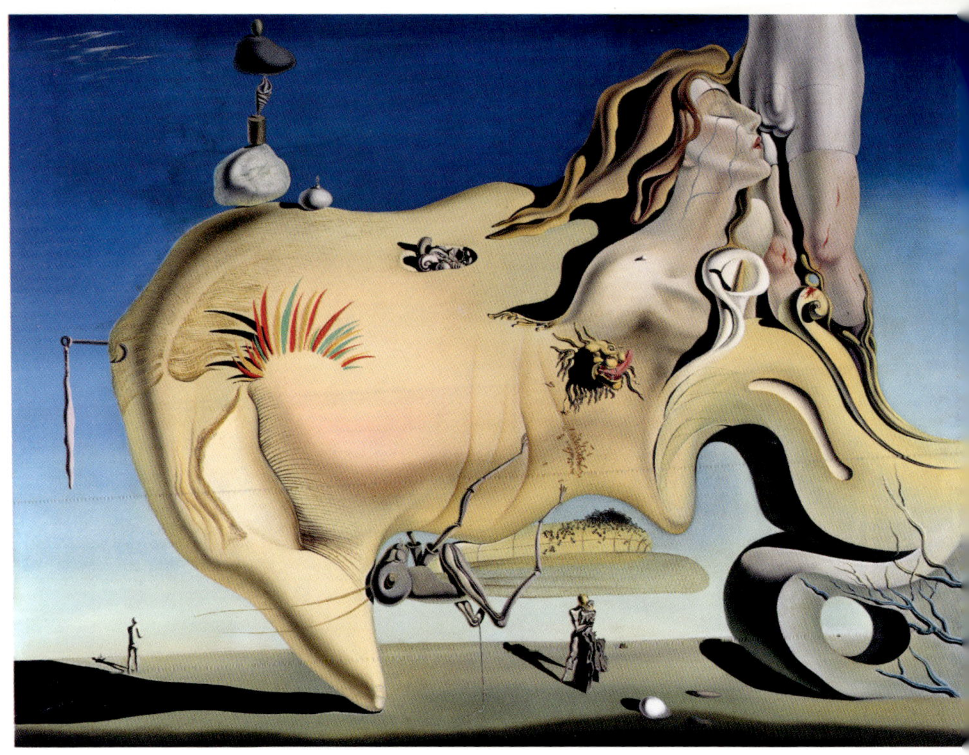

61 Salvador Dalí, *The Great Masturbator*, 1928

For Magritte and Dalí, as for the Surrealists in general, a significant new catalyst was Freud's psychoanalytic theory, which provided a seemingly scientific validation for ideas that had until them seemed wholly opposed to the modern scientific spirit. Freud likened the human mind to an iceberg, with the conscious part just the small portion above water, which is dominated by the Ego. This is the person we think we are. But Freud argued that the Ego is in perpetual struggle with two psychic forces: the Libido, coming from our instinctual life characterized by basic appetites that dominate the iceberg below water level, and the 'Super-ego'. This is the moral sense derived from the disciplining influence of parents and social institutions, such as school and religion, that consider the instincts as demeaning animalistic dimensions and, as such, a threat to social order. Freud believed that dreams are one way in which the unconscious conflict between the instinctual forces, which involve predominantly sexual and violent desires on the one side and the idealizing demands of the Super-ego on the other, are enacted at levels inaccessible to the conscious mind. Psychoanalysis offered 'scientific' credentials for the unfettered exploration of everything that affronted the conscious and rational mind and the conventional values of 'bourgeois' society.

In his statement above, Dalí mentioned two key Surrealist tenets – 'automatism' and 'passive states' – as primary means of achieving his goal. In relation to these key principles, in the 'Surrealist Manifesto' of 1924, Breton had defined the movement as follows: 'SURREALISM, n. Psychic automatism in its pure state, by which one proposes to express – verbally, by means of the written word, or in any other manner – the actual functioning of thought. Dictated by thought, in the absence of any control exercised by reason, exempt from any aesthetic or moral concern.'

In their quest for imaginative works that exemplified these uncommon and provocative qualities, the Surrealists celebrated the conventionally unskilful, nonsensical and obsessive art of the mentally ill and other socially marginal people. Here, they argued, was art in touch with life. *Japan = Thurn* (1920) is not a work by someone who considered himself a professional artist. It is a painting by a Swiss man who suffered from severe

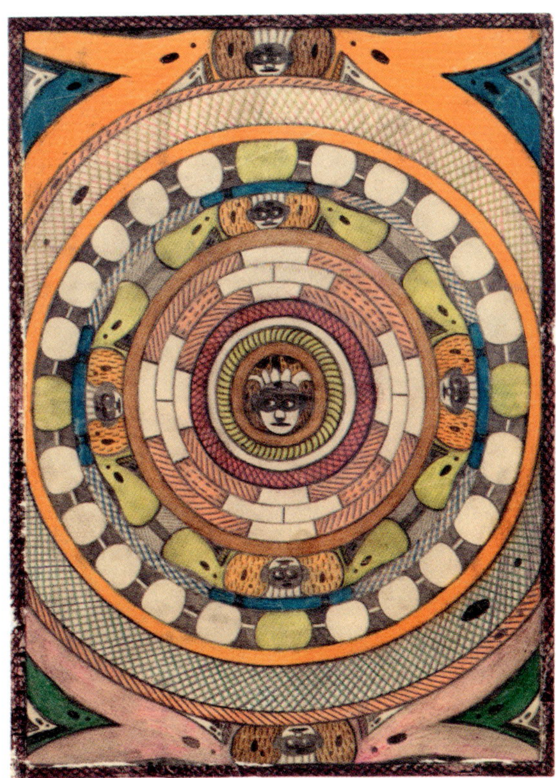

62 Adolf Wölfli,
*Japan Tower
(Japan=Thurm),*
1920

psychosis and frequent hallucinations and lived most of his
adult life in a psychiatric hospital: Adolf Wölfli (1864–1930).
In 1908 Wölfli began a semi-autobiographical series of works
mixing words and images, which eventually contained over
25,000 pages and 1,600 illustrations. His work was brought to
the Surrealists' attention though a publication by a psychiatric
doctor that set out to study the art of the mentally ill. The
Swiss artist Paul Klee's (1879–1940) *Bird Garden* (1924) reflects
this interest in the works of 'outsider' artists like Wölfli, and
was the result of a spontaneous image-generating process
which he believed approximated to the liberated image-making
practices of such people. Klee often worked on a small scale
and in mixed media to enhance the intimacy of his work. He
described drawing as 'taking a line for a walk', indicating the
extent to which art was an extension of natural capacities, and
he stressed the central importance of maintaining a close bond
with nature.

Joan Miró's (1893–1983) *Composition (Painting)* (1933) has
much in common with doodling, that is, the making of marks
and images without conscious attention or intention. Strange
shapes float over a hazy ground, and some take on zoomorphic
(animal-like) form. This is a more overt kind of 'automatic'
painting that does not so much mimic the visual appearance
of dreams, like Magritte or Dalí did, but rather simulates the
actual *processes* involved in the act of dreaming, in the sense
that such works were made as 'automatically' or spontaneously

63 BELOW Paul Klee, *Bird Garden*, 1924
64 OPPOSITE Joan Miró, *Composition (Painting)*, 1933

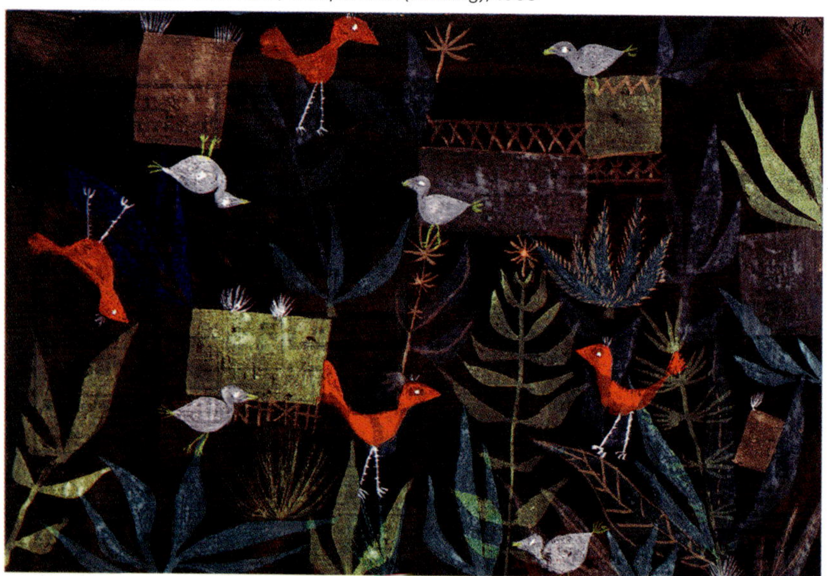

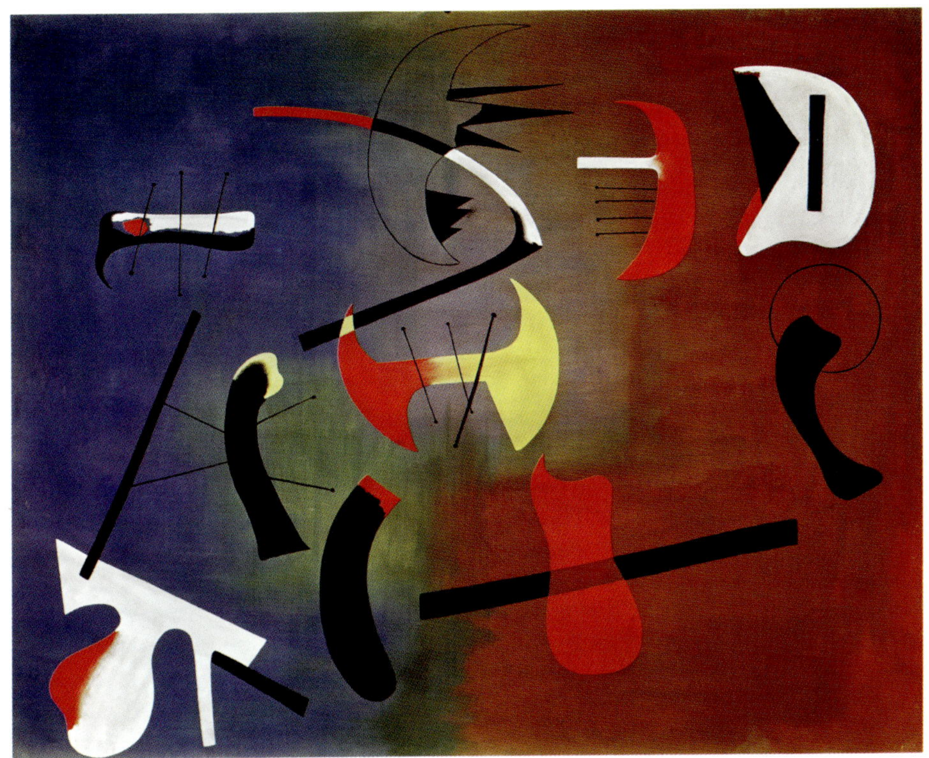

as possible, without conscious control. That Miró and Klee's
works seem deliberately 'child-like' is an indication that
children were also a primary inspiration for the Surrealists.
As with pictures by the mentally ill, children's pictures are not
motivated by the attempt to record what is seen but rather by
what is *known* by the child. In other words, children's art is a
variety of image-making based on Breton's 'internal reality'.
As Breton wrote: 'the mind that plunges into surrealism relives
with burning excitement the best part of childhood. Childhood
comes closest to one's real life – childhood where everything
conspires to bring about the effective, risk-free possession
of oneself.'

Constructivism and Soviet Russia

Because of the Bolshevik Revolution of 1917, art in Russia
evolved in very different directions to western Europe and
America. Many of the Russian avant-garde encountered in the
previous chapter welcomed the Revolution, which ended the
moribund and reactionary Czarist regime, and they quickly

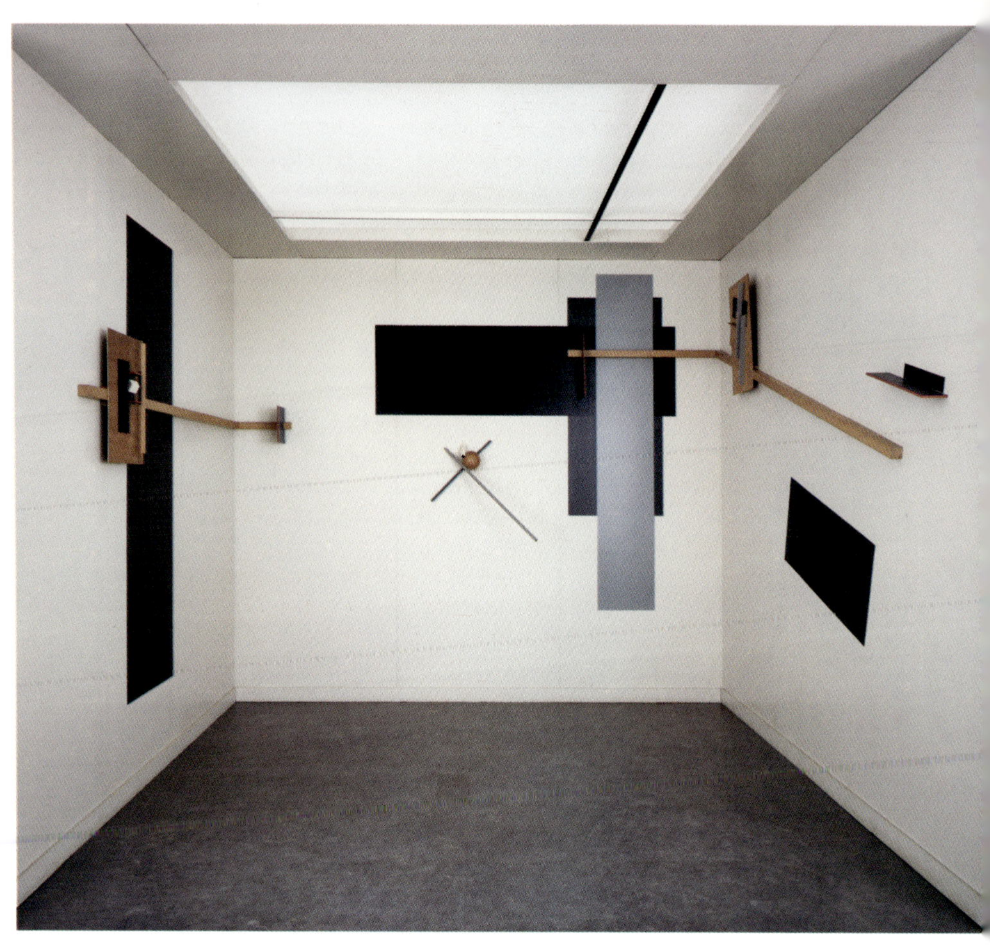

65 El Lissitzky, *Proun Room*, 1923, reconstructed 1971

set to work furnishing the Bolsheviks with a new culture.
Wassily Kandinsky, pioneer of abstraction, returned to his
homeland in 1918, excited by events, and helped organize the
Institute of Artistic Culture in Moscow, believing that under
the new political leadership his vision of an 'objectless' art
would be well-received. While in the Soviet Union, his style
evolved, becoming more hard-edged and geometric under the
influence of both Cubism and the most avid advocates of the
union between art, modernity and politics – the Constructivists
– who took a very different view of the role of art to that upheld
by the Dadaists and Surrealists.

The Russian Constructivists argued that to think of art in
terms of the exploration of spiritual values, the imagination,
self-expression or an 'interior world' continued to betray an
artist's bourgeois roots and was wholly inappropriate in the
new 'classless society'. Drawing on Marxist analysis of the
dependent relationship between the superstructure (culture) and
the base (economics), they argued that in the new Communist
society art must prove its value through direct social utility,
connecting the artist to the forces of production. In the words
of one advocate of Constructivism, the theorist Aleksei Gan,
artists must become 'constructors in the general work of arming
and moving the many-millioned human masses'. In a gesture
that was meant to signal the end of 'bourgeois' painting, in
1921 Alexander Rodchenko (1891–1956) presented a triptych of
three all-over coloured canvases: *Pure Red Colour, Pure Yellow
Colour, Pure Blue Colour.* This was painting reduced to its
constituent elements and thereby rendered purely material...
and superfluous. Henceforth, Rodchenko announced, he would
dedicate himself to more practical work designing posters and
using the contemporary medium of photography. But if painting
was to continue to have any relevance within the new society, it
had to move into the more functional context of architecture and
design. El Lissitzky (1890–1941), for example, invented his own
sub-category of Constructivism called 'Proun', which he defined
as 'the station where one changes from painting to architecture'.
Like the Constructivists in general, El Lissitzky emphasized
the need to eschew traditional materials as well as traditional
subjects and forms, and instead to use modern industrial
materials like glass, plastic and steel. The goal was to transform
art into a practical tool in the service of Communist society. In
1923 he installed a group of works in a room that consciously
set out to blur the boundaries between painting, sculpture
and architecture. The original installation is only known from
photographs, so the image reproduced here is a reconstruction.

Geometric Abstraction

While Constructivism in the Soviet Union reflected the
impact of specific cultural forces, it was also linked to a broader
tendency throughout Europe in the post-war period that led
artists away from the imaginative world of the Surrealists
towards what became known as the 'machine aesthetic'. It
was argued that Cubism had shown that a truly contemporary
painting must be based on a universal language of geometry,
reason and utility – the cornerstones of the scientific worldview
– and the primary shapes of the new urban environments
within which more and more people lived and worked. The
visual embodiment of progress was mechanization, and the
new and exciting technologies supported by mathematical
principles that were materially manifest everywhere in the
industrialized modern world. It seemed self-evident to some
artists that to be truly modern, art must therefore strive to
emulate these new forms – the ways of thinking they embodied,
and that reflected the radical transformations in the experience
of time and space.

The Dutch group, De Stijl (The Style), which included
the artists Theo van Doesburg, Georges Vantongerloo, Piet
Mondrian and the architect Gerrit Rietveld, played an especially
influential role in the European avant-garde from its formation
in 1917 until 1931. De Stijl shared in the Constructivists' desire
to break down the boundaries that kept the various plastic
arts apart, so they could function not as adjuncts to daily life
but as an intrinsic part of it. The goal of the new 'constructive'
or 'concrete' art was to use the intrinsic resources and rules
of painting, without borrowing from external phenomena or
transforming them, like Cubism did. De Stijl advocated the
reduction of the various arts to what was perceived as their pure
essence.

Piet Mondrian (1872–1944) used the term 'Neoplasticism'
to describe his own rigorously plotted painting system, and
in works such as *Painting 1* (1921) the western tradition of
linear perspective and modelling is decisively repudiated. But
Mondrian believed he was creating much more than simply a
purified aesthetics of geometric shapes and colours. His study
of Cubism, wedded to an interest in esoteric philosophy but
also recent scientific research, had led him to the conclusion
that the most important goal for the artist should be the
directing of art along trans-rational grounds. That is, art should
not be based on recording visual reality, nor on expressionistic
or surrealistic irrationality, but rather, through deepening
the sources of reason to include dimensions of existence that
lie beyond even conventional science and thought, art could

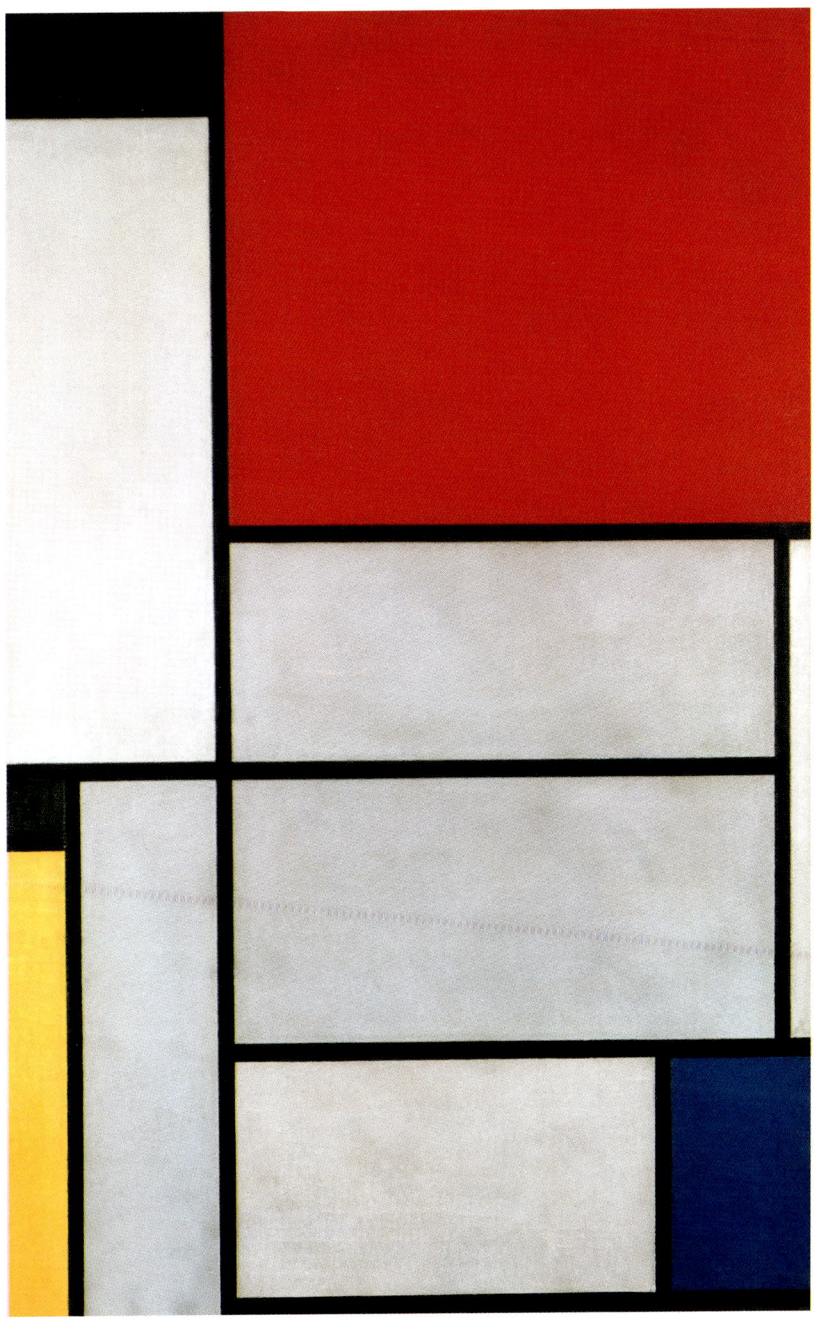

66 Piet Mondrian, *Painting 1*, 1921

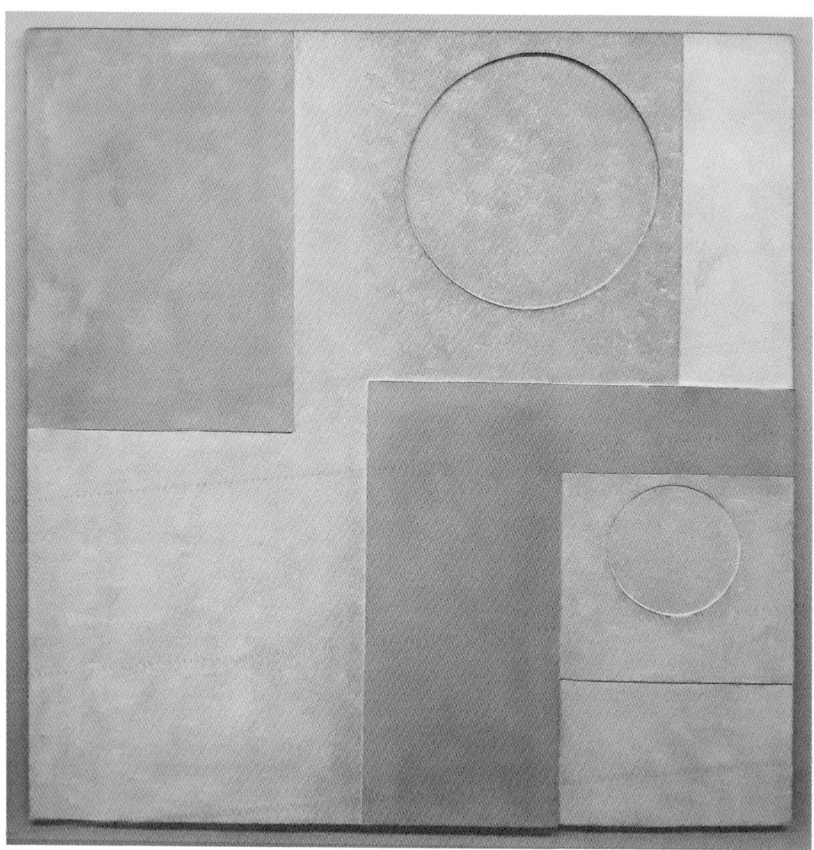

67 Ben Nicholson, *1934 (painted relief)*, 1934

achieve images of a higher absolute reality. As Mondrian stated:
'Non-figurative art brings to an end the ancient culture of art;
at present, therefore, one can review and judge more surely the
whole culture of art. We are now at the turning point of this
culture; the culture of particular forms is approaching its end.
The culture of determined relations has begun.' By 'determined
relations' Mondrian meant non-arbitrary correspondences
based on the simplest rational elements of painting, which
he reduced to the primary colours of red, yellow and blue
with white and black, and the horizontal and vertical line.
Mondrian's agenda also had utopian social implications, for
he believed he was creating painted models or blueprints that
represented a reality characterized by greater social harmony.
Art, Mondrian declared, must be rescued from subservience
to mere perceptual reality, the world 'out there', and also from

Romantic pathos and anecdote, so that its more essential form and value could resonate and its social purpose be revealed.

The goal of purifying painting along geometric lines, and often driven by a utopian social agenda, was pervasive in the 1920s and 1930s. In Paris, in opposition to the growing influence of Surrealism, the principles of geometric abstraction took root through artists associated with the groups Cercle et Carré (Circle and Square) and Abstraction-Création, who published journals and organized exhibitions to disseminate and promote their principles. In Britain, the artist Ben Nicholson (1894–1982) played an especially key role in disseminating this new aesthetic. In 1933 he made the first of his white reliefs, like *1934 (painted relief)* (1934), partly as a result of an inspiring visit to the Paris studio of Mondrian. Nicholson focused on the actual physical properties of the work's surface, building it up into different plains in relief – by cutting shapes in wood – with the result that rather than simulated shadows (as would be the case in realistic painting), *real* shadows are cast. For example, in this particular photograph, we can surmise that this relief was located in a space where light was shining on it from above.

In Poland, Władysław Strzemiński (1893–1952) and his sculptor wife, Katarzyna Kobro (1898–1951), after having studied with Malevich in Russia developed their own interpretation of abstraction – named 'Unism'. This involved turning towards a rigorously literalist interpretation of painting in which the goal was empirical realism grounded in the visual and tactile properties of the medium rather than any external reference point. In his Unist compositions Strzemiński aimed to exemplify this principle by reducing painting to one colour and rhythmic sequences of lines built into low relief. He noted: 'A work of plastic art is not a sign of anything. It is (exists) in itself.' Historically, painting had been split between its status as a surface which is physically made and materially present, and a virtual dimension, by a link to a referent beyond the surface of the painting itself that is materially absent from the actual work and is the site for imaginative transformations and subjective expression. In Strzemiński and Kobro's eyes, even the most innovative of the new art was still too closely bound to this virtual dimension, and so continued to function in relation to extra-pictorial associations and expressive intentions that weakened the power of painting.

These utilitarian, rational and empirical principles within art were perhaps most conscientiously embraced at the Bauhaus, a progressive art school that opened in Weimar, Germany, in 1919. Until its closure in 1933 by the Nazis (whereupon it partially reassembled in the United States), the Bauhaus published

influential texts, organized exhibitions and was host to many of
the major artists, designers and architects of the period, several
of whom taught there, including the painters Kandinsky and
Klee, as well as the Hungarian painter and photographer László
Moholy-Nagy. While the Romantic vision of art inherited by
Symbolism and Expressionism conceived of its role as aiding
escape from the mechanical back to the organic, Bauhaus and
other Constructivist tendencies recognized that modern art
should seek to engage directly with the world as it had become,
raising it to a higher level of perfection. From 1919 to 1928 the
director of the Bauhaus was the architect Walter Gropius, who
announced in 1923: 'The dominant spirit of our epoch is already
recognizable although its form is not yet clearly defined.
The old dualistic world-concept which envisaged the ego in
opposition to the universe is rapidly losing ground. In its place
is rising the idea of the universal unity in which all opposing
forces exist in a state of absolute balance.'

One of the most influential teachers at the Bauhaus was the
German Josef Albers (1888–1976), whose work *Frontal* (*c.* 1927)
clearly reflects Bauhaus ideas. It combines the principle of
geometric abstraction with modern materials and methods –
sandblasted flash glass – to create a work that pushes painting

68 Josef Albers, *Frontal*, c. 1927

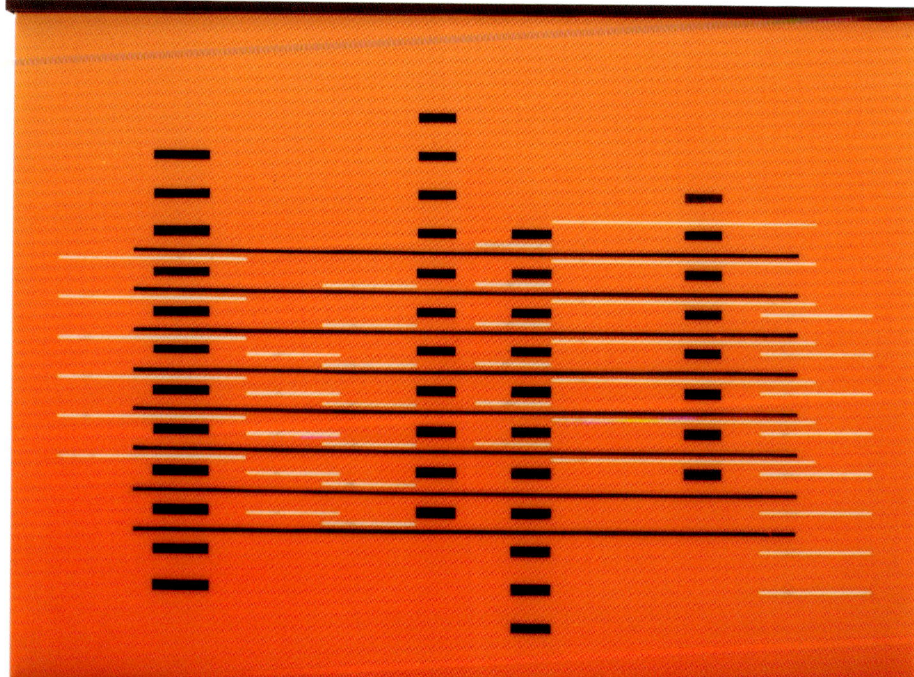

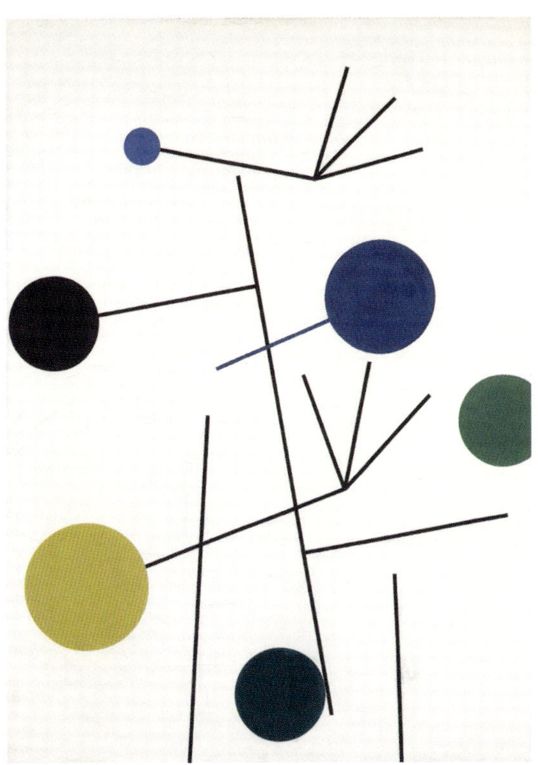

in the direction of the literal and the object-like. Such
works embody the belief, shared by those avant-garde artists
who were dedicated to geometric abstraction, that the various
strategies of reduction, simplification and purification they
employed would serve as models for the rationalistic and
egalitarian attitudes that they hoped to see prevail in the new
urban environment. The goal was not to represent the world
but to transform it.

But the idea that there was a strict polarization of a
Dada-Surrealist avant-garde on the one side and geometric
abstractionists on the other can be overstated. Theo van
Doesburg, founder of the Dutch de Stijl group, maintained close
ties with the Dadaists, for example, and the Swiss artist Sophie
Taeuber-Arp (1889–1943) also moved comfortably between the
two camps, with the result that her work exhibits a welcome
fusion of rigour and playfulness. Her *Rising, Falling, Flying* (1934)
has an exuberant and improvisatory spirit that counterpoints
the structurally ordered and pure nature of the composition's
geometric elements.

Figurative Art Between the Wars

Dwelling on the poles of Surrealism and abstract can also occlude the fact that pre-war expressionist tendencies continued to appeal to many progressive artists who were reluctant to move into full-blown abstraction or an inner psychological world. For example, in Britain, David Bomberg – who as we saw earlier had been a pioneer of geometric abstraction – in part as a result of his wartime experiences as a soldier turned his back on what he had come to see as the dehumanizing tendencies of such art and instead adopted an expressionistic approach to landscape. The Austrian Oskar Kokoschka, based in Berlin, also developed an overtly expressionistic style, painting landscapes and portraits. In Paris, Georges Rouault and Chaïm Soutine made boldly coloured and frenetically painted works that brought Paris-based art closer into line with German Expressionism.

Another French painter of the pre-war generation. Pierre Bonnard (1867–1947) – who had once belonged to the Nabis (see Chapter Three) – was instrumental in pushing Impressionism in a new direction, one that drew more fully on the transformational potential of memory rather than on observation. Bonnard also learned from Matisse, applying more high-pitched colour and, like him, was inspired by Islamic art, in particular by Mughal miniatures of Muslim India. In effect, Bonnard merged impressionistic and expressionistic tendencies to produce a tranquil and sensual art. In *The Open Window* (1921) we see the view from his house in Normandy. The painting exudes a sense of security and peaceful domesticity. Note the woman's face bottom right – his wife, Marthe – and next to her, a black cat. For Bonnard, as also for Matisse, painting was meant to be a sanctuary, a site of resonant harmony in an increasingly violent and alienating world.

Matisse, Derain, Picasso and Braque, who had first come to prominence before the First World War, also evolved styles that in one way or another rejected the lure of both abstraction and Surrealism. Indeed, as the 1920s unfolded, many came to consider Picasso and Matisse the pre-eminent modern artists, and their influence on others was immense. As Wassily Kandinsky put it succinctly: 'In their pursuit of the same supreme end, Matisse and Picasso stand side by side, Matisse representing colour and Picasso form.'

In Germany a confrontational and anguished relationship to the realities of daily life was typically evoked in a style of painting called 'Neue Sachlichkeit' ('New Objectivity' or 'matter-of-factness'). This emerged out of Dada, but backtracked from its more radical implications, becoming the focus for artists

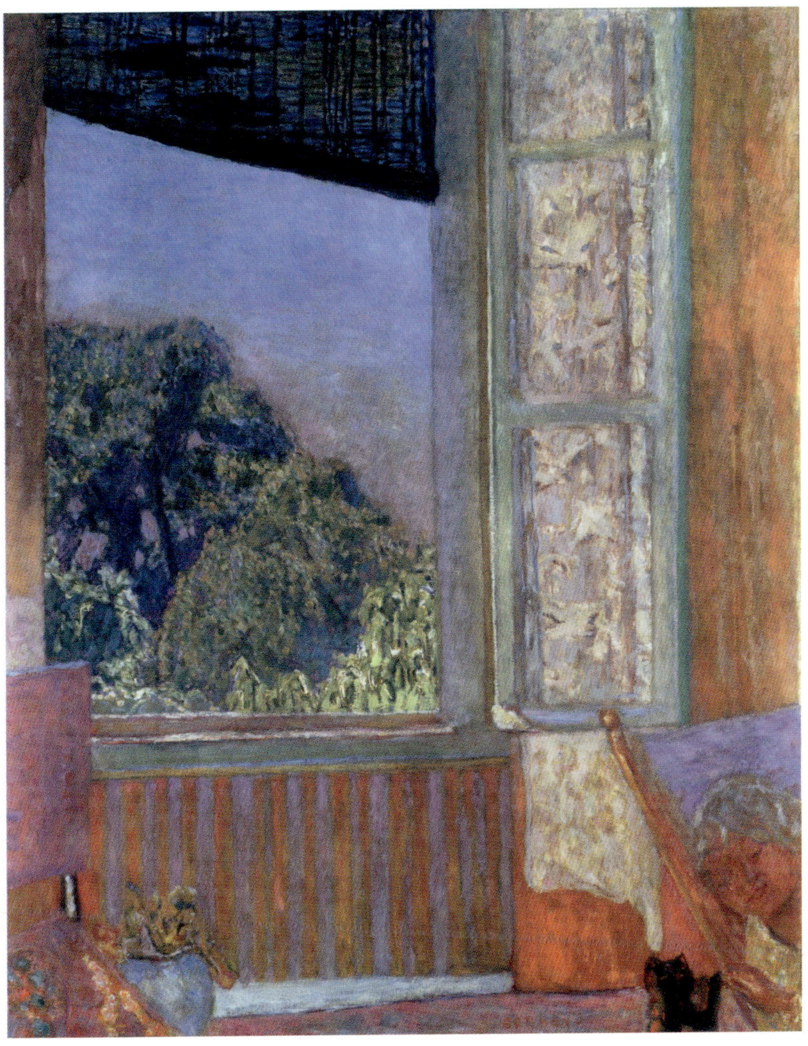

70 Pierre Bonnard, *The Open Window*, 1921

wishing to consolidate forms of optical realism grounded in
a pessimistic and resoundingly de-idealized vision of modern
life. In contrast to pre-war Expressionism, the artists of the
'New Objectivity' confronted the turmoil of the times with
a cool detachment and sense of order similar to that being
pursued by geometric abstract artists. As one of the leading
exponents, another veteran of the First World War and former
Dadaist, Otto Dix (1891–1969), announced: 'Painting is the effort
to produce order; order in yourself. There is much chaos in me,

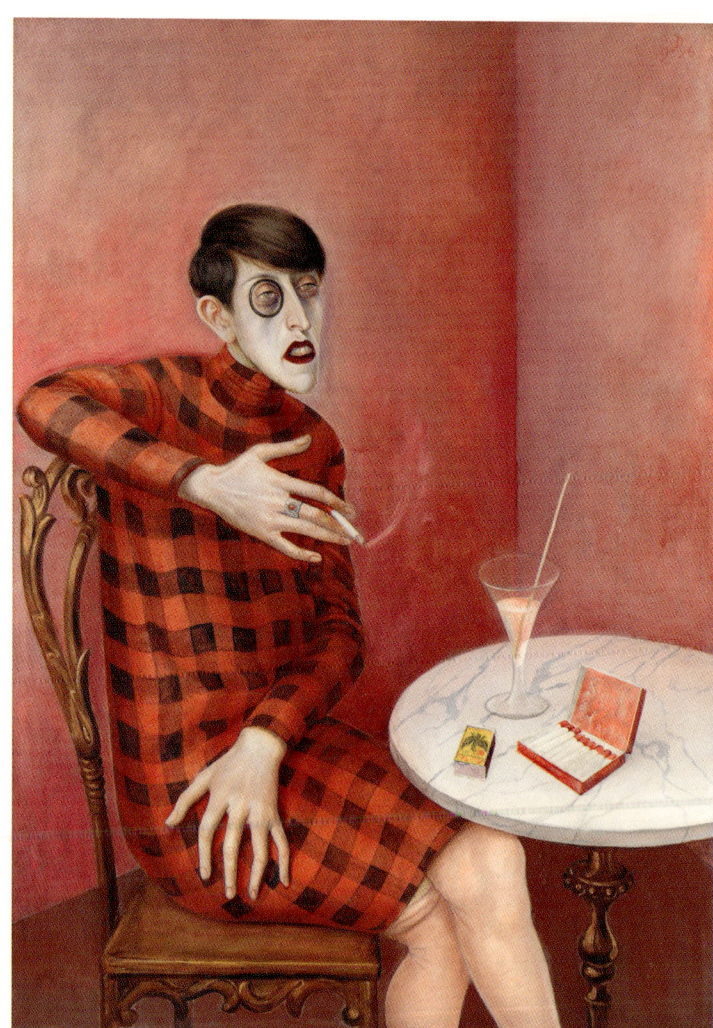

71 Otto Dix,
*Portrait of the
Journalist Sylvia
von Harden*,
1926

much chaos in our time.' To this end, rather than looking to
recent avant-garde trends, such as abstract art or Surrealism,
Dix harked back to German Renaissance masters, such as
Lucas Cranach, reflecting a wider tendency in the figurative art
of this period to seek a return to order through rapprochement
rather than repudiation of the past. In *Portrait of the Journalist
Sylvia von Harden* (1926) Dix painted an unflattering but stylish
portrait of a quintessentially new social type: the independent
woman who has a career and is confident enough to sit alone
in a café and smoke a cigarette.

Art in the United States

The tension between radical modernism and more measured
relationships to the history of art, between outrage and
accommodation, was especially clearly played out in the United
States between the two world wars. On a practical level, the
problem for American artists, like that faced by other non-
Europeans who were drawn to the avant-garde tradition, was
that they were geographically and culturally located far from
the creative 'centre' and knew that – because information about
trends across the Atlantic took a long time to reach them – if
they remained in their homeland their work could be judged
behind the times by the standards of the European avant-garde.
Yet there were also increasing signs that the cultural hierarchy
implicit in the very idea of a 'centre', where all the innovation
occurred, and a 'periphery' that looked to the 'centre' for models
to imitate, was beginning to break down.

American artists became pressingly aware of the difference
of their own cultural perspectives, and the need to find a way
to represent the complexities of the quintessentially *American*
experience. Furthermore, a growing middle class and wealthy
patrons interested in modernized culture were emerging in
the United States, and this also bolstered the confidence and
independence of American artists who could now rely on a
home-grown market for their works. A look at a sample of four
American artists – Edward Hopper, Georgia O'Keeffe, Stuart
Davis and Aaron Douglas – gives some idea of the range of the
paintings made in the United States in the inter-war period,
and a glimpse of the continuities and, more significantly,
discontinuities between Europe and North America.

Edward Hopper (1882–1967) studied in Paris but rejected the
European avant-garde's proclivities in favour of a more moderate
form of painting based on the conventions of linear perspective
and modelling forms in light and dark. This decision in part
reflected Hopper's awareness that the cultural situation in
his homeland was markedly different from Europe's. As he
commented: 'After all, we are not French and never can be, and
any attempt to be so is to deny our inheritance and to try to
impose upon ourselves a character that can be nothing but a
veneer upon the surface.' But while he turned his back on the
most radical tendencies within the European avant-garde, it
would be wrong to interpret Hopper's paintings as inherently
insular and parochial and as simply holding fast to an outmoded
style – a criticism levelled against him by the avant-garde
and its advocates at the time and right up to the present day.
In retrospect, we can recognize that Hopper was aware that
'modern' styles of painting in the United States were developing

not along one single pathway but along several, some of which did not see it as vital to reject illusionistic imitation, and all of which could potentially serve to communicate important truths about modern humanity's relationship to the world. Hopper was keenly aware of how cinema was changing the way people experienced the world, for example, and of the associations viewers brought to his pictures, which are often like stills from movies of the period, and include innovations derived from cinematic cropping and other framing devices. In *Nighthawks* (1942) we seem to be watching characters from a Hollywood film noir – a gangster and his moll, and mysterious lone figure; something is about to happen, and it's probably not good. By co-opting the language of the movies, Hopper effectively renewed the traditional conventions associated with western painting by recasting them in the light of new technology and social practices.

Georgia O'Keeffe (1887–1986) also turned away from more radical experimentation, but having moved from metropolitan New York City to the wilds of New Mexico, she explored the possibilities inherent in the incongruous juxtaposition of recognizable elements within the arid landscape. As *Ram's Head, White Hollyhock-Hills* (1935) demonstrates, O'Keeffe resisted the more fantastical imaginative displacements and juxtapositions essayed by the Surrealists, and this work is comprised of elements familiar from the place she lived. So, while Surrealism demonstrated to O'Keeffe the potential of imaginative transformation, she remained committed to a greater level of commonplace description.

72 BELOW Edward Hopper, *Nighthawks*, 1942
73 OPPOSITE Georgia O'Keeffe, *Ram's Head, White Hollyhock-Hills*, 1935

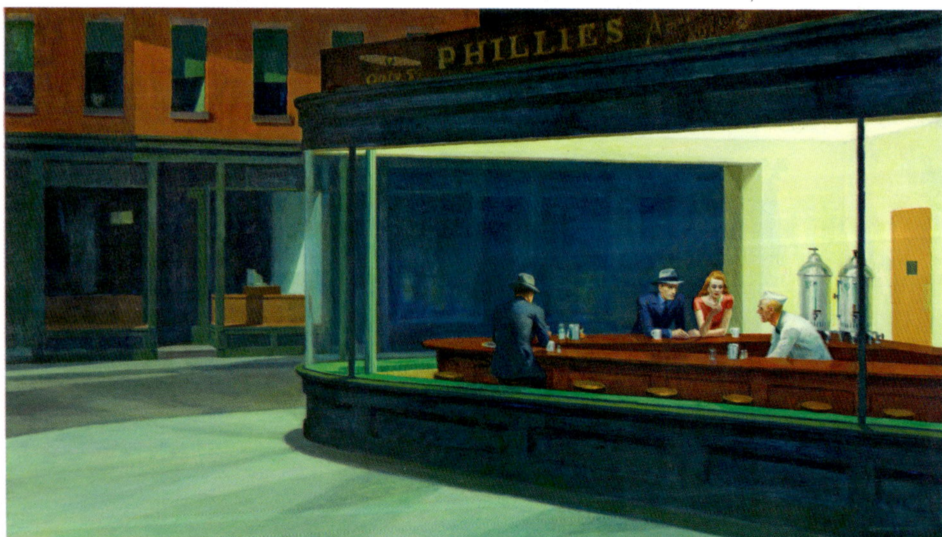

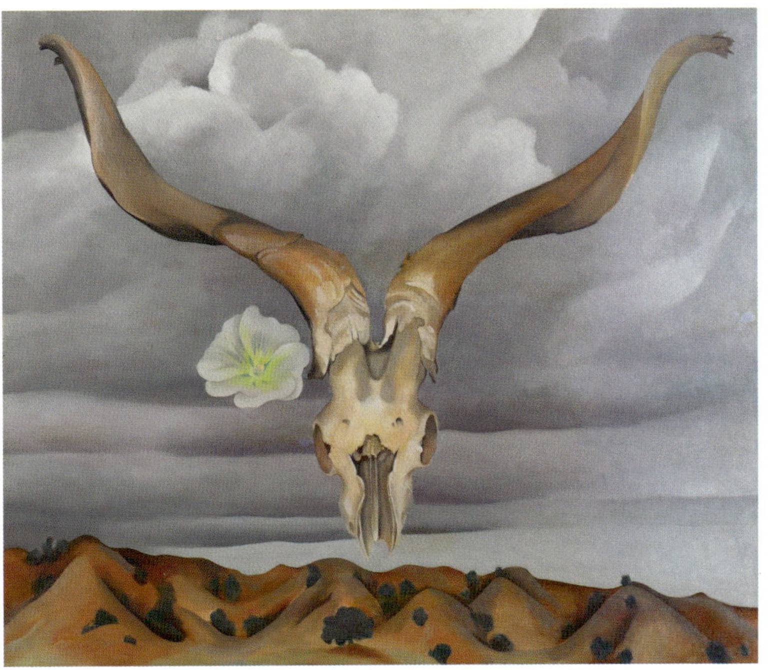

In contrast to both Hopper and O'Keeffe, the huge mural
Swing Landscape (1938) by Stuart Davis (1892–1964), which
was commissioned by the Works Progress Administration
(a government agency set up to support culture and employ
artists in decorating public buildings during the Depression
era), embraces the shallow space of post-Cubist collage and
the bold flat colours of Constructivism to celebrate the
rhythmic dynamism of contemporary America. Amongst the
complex congregation of forms, one can make out buildings,
boats, a bridge, machinery, trees and water. In fact, Davis was
inspired by the waterfront of the fishing village of Gloucester,
Massachusetts. For Davis, the way forward for American art was
to embrace popular culture and to redirect stylistic elements
from European modernism towards specifically American goals.

Aaron Douglas (1899–1979) was part of the so-called Harlem
Renaissance of the 1920s and 1930s, which brought African
American culture to the attention of a wide public. He was also
a beneficiary of the WPA, the first African American artist to be
commissioned, and in 1934 completed a series of four murals of
which *Aspects of Negro Life: Song of the Towers* is the fourth. In
the murals, Douglas aimed to use the innovations of modern art
to reflect the African American experience, and here focused on

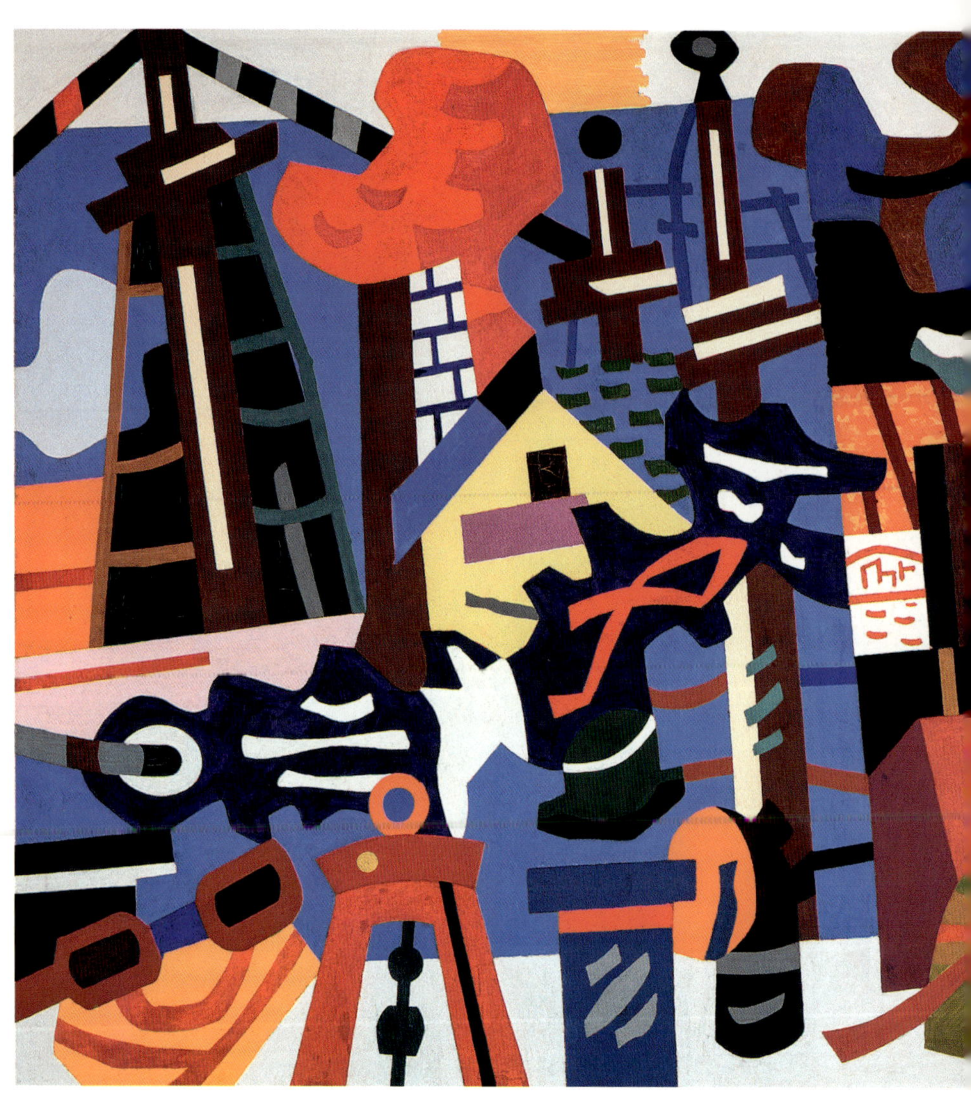

74 Stuart Davis, *Swing Landscape*, 1938

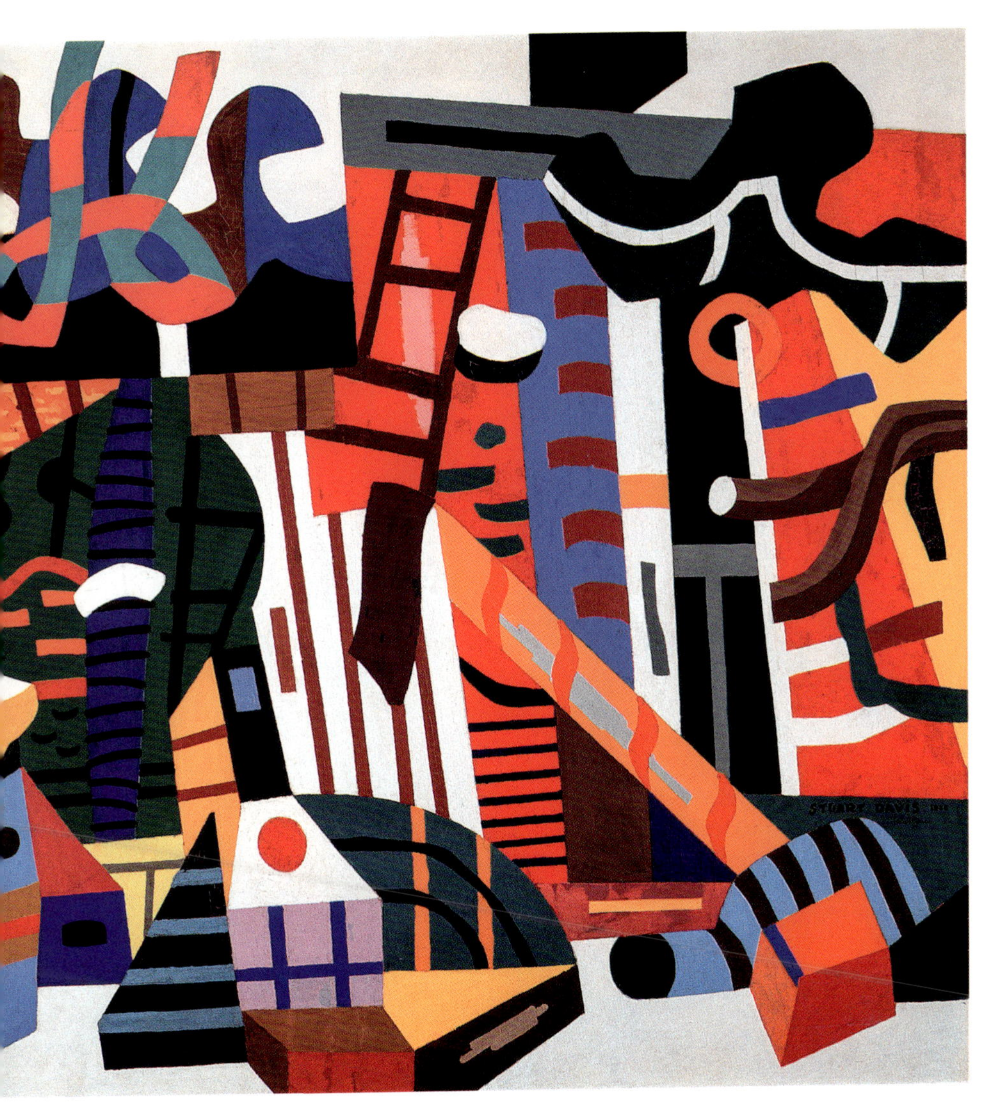

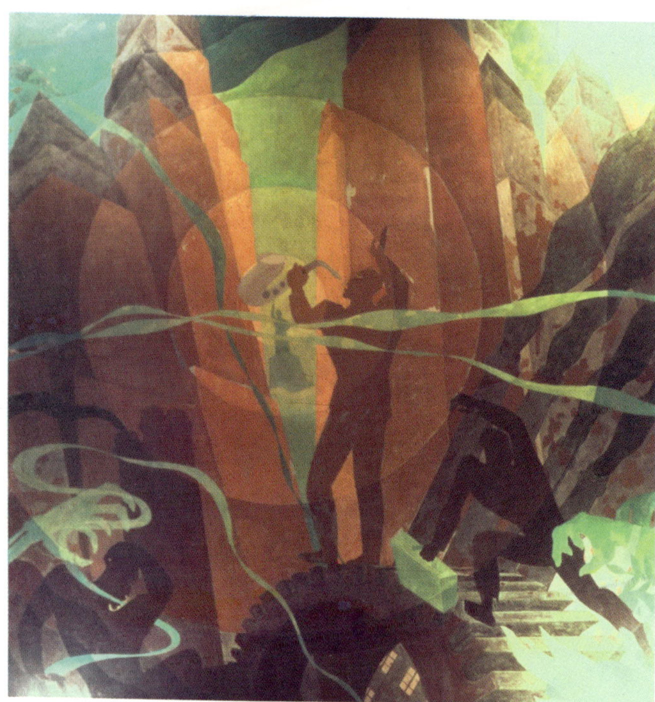

75 Aaron Douglas, *Aspects of Negro Life: Song of the Towers*, 1934

the inspirational power of jazz. In the distance stands the Statue of Liberty surrounded by the skyscrapers of New York City. While his style also owes much to the European avant-garde, it is tempered by Douglas's desire to create a public work with an understandable social narrative.

The Globalization of Painting

Between the two world wars, artists from beyond Europe and North America increasingly found their way to Paris, the capital of art, to study and sometimes to live, and to experience at first-hand the newest developments in art while working in a supportive environment. These non-western artists who embraced modern western painting came from societies in which modernization was already underway, such as Japan, or from the margins of western cultural influence, like South America and India. They mostly were attracted to progressive modern art because it was understood to be representative of the desirable values associated with modernity, signalling their commitment to the ideals of progress and greater freedom.

76 The Argentinian-Italian Leonor Fini (1907–1996) moved to Paris in the early 1930s and chose to remain in Europe, where

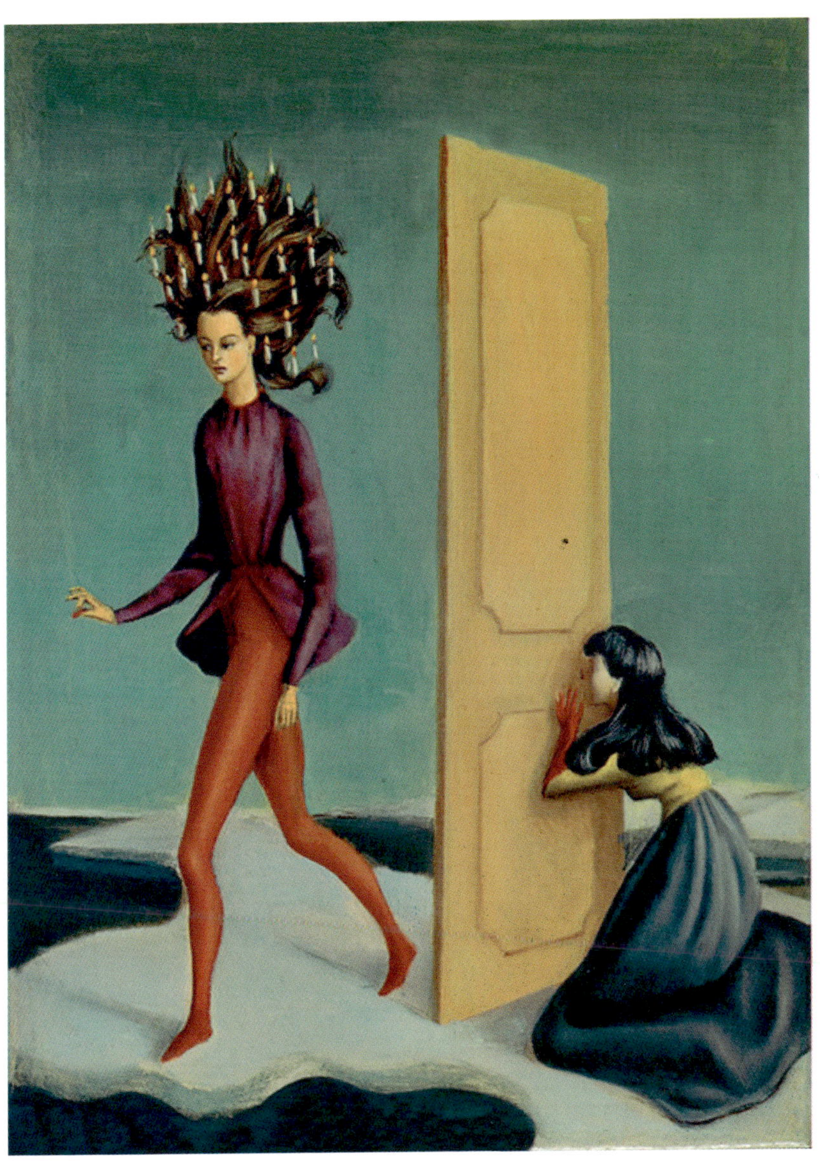

76 Leonor Fini, *Two Women*, 1939

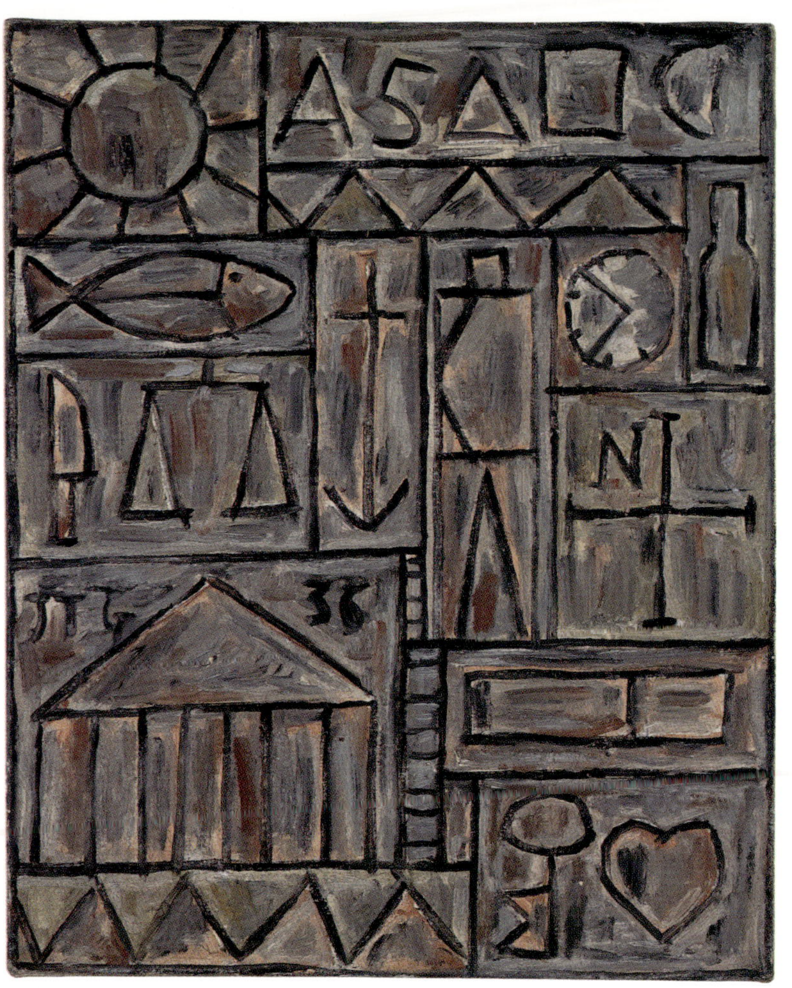

77 Joaquín Torres-García, *Composición constructiva*, 1936

she developed a full-blooded Surrealist style and exhibited regularly with the other Surrealists. Fini added novel dimensions to the 'dream-painting' style that challenged the unexamined prejudices of the self-professed 'liberated' psyches of the male Surrealists, who nevertheless persisted in depicting women as objects of desire and/or muses, and her female protagonists are more active agents – goddesses, medusas, libertines, wise sphinxes. But Fini, who was bisexual, also sought to weaken the binary categorization of gender and described her work as revealing 'a world of non-differentiated, or little differentiated, sexes'.

Increasingly, however, non-Europeans chose to return to their homelands and there they were often instrumental in establishing progressive art scenes. The Uruguayan-Spanish artist Joaquín Torres-García (1874–1949) settled in Paris in 1926, where he began experimenting with Constructivism. But in 1934 he returned to Uruguay, and was the driving force in organizing the local avant-garde scene, proudly declaring that the conventional hierarchy that placed Latin America in a subordinate relationship to Europe should be inverted. In his own work he merged European avant-garde tendencies, bringing together the rational structure of Constructivism and the freedom of Dada and Surrealism, and blending them with elements of traditional Uruguayan folk art.

The Brazilian Tarsila do Amaral studied briefly with Fernand Léger in Paris, but she too returned to her native Brazil, where she was influential in forming a vibrant avant-garde community spanning art, literature and music. Amaral's work strikes a very different and defiantly independent note from the Europeans. One painting, entitled *Abaporu* (1928), takes its title from the Tupi Indian language and means 'the man that eats people'. The overt reference to cannibalism, which was practised by some Amazonian tribes, was intended to signal Amaral's confidence in the possibility of forging a Brazilian cultural identity that, far from being a distant and derivative outpost of Europe, could actively absorb the best of – could 'eat' – the culture of the former colonial masters.

The Mexican artist Diego Rivera (1886–1957) had also moved to Paris in 1911, where he was strongly influenced by Cubism. But in 1921 he moved back to Mexico, and once there, joined the Mexican Communist Party, travelling to the Soviet Union as part of a delegation of Mexican Communist Party officials in 1927. Under the patronage of a supportive Left-leaning government, along with other Mexican artists such as David Alfaro Siqueiros, José Clemente Orozco and Aurora Reyes Flores, Rivera forged a popular political style in murals like

78   *In the Arsenal* (1928), in which he attacked the lingering power over Mexican society of the old elites and the Roman Catholic Church, as well as the new captains of capitalist industry. In this mural, the phrase 'So will be the proletarian revolution' is written in Spanish on the banner at the top. A commitment to a form of propagandist art led Rivera back towards a simplified, monumental and narrative figurative art.

      Frida Kahlo (1907–1954), the wife of Rivera – who had depicted her handing out rifles and bayonets in the centre of his mural – also painted in a figurative style, but eschewed Rivera's propagandist goals in favour of a far more autobiographical art. In 1938 André Breton saw Kahlo's work during a visit to Mexico, and declared it was 'a ribbon around a bomb' that 'blossomed...

79   into pure surreality'. In *The Two Fridas* (1939) we can see what

78 BELOW Diego Rivera, *In the Arsenal*, 1928, mural detail, Court of Fiestas, Level 3, South Wall, Secretaría de Educación Pública, Mexico City
79 OPPOSITE Frida Kahlo, *The Two Fridas*, 1939

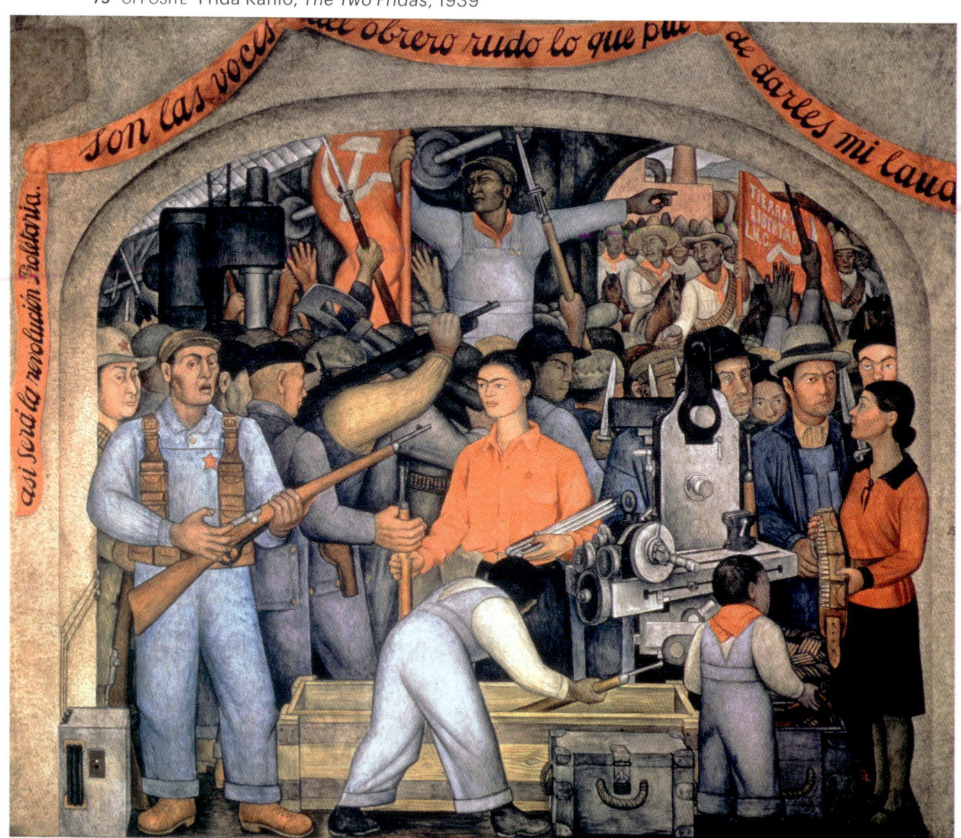

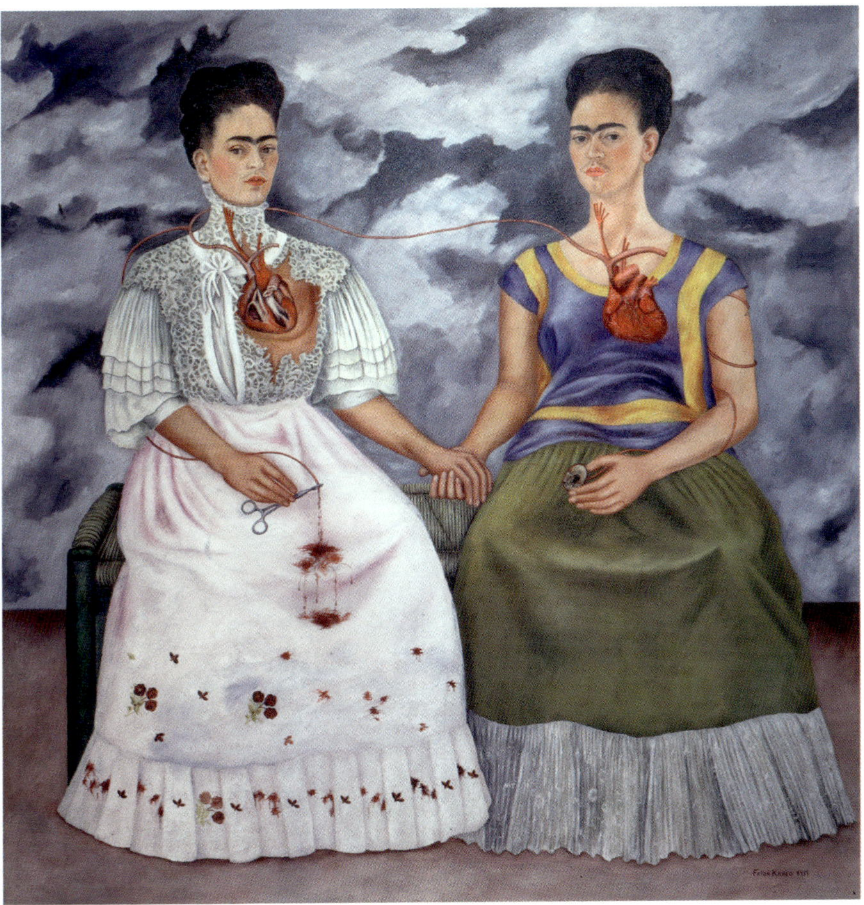

must have appealed to Breton. Kahlo has made a double self-portrait, with hearts visible and an artery joining the two figures; the heart of the Frida on the left is dissected and cut and torn, and a severed artery drips blood. Kahlo explained later that this painting was made soon after her divorce from Rivera and expressed her suffering over the break-up. While, as Breton recognized, her work fits well within the camp of Surrealism, it differs from that of the male Surrealists, as Kahlo focused on her own vulnerability and anxieties. Furthermore, she drew on Mexican folk art, such as the untutored styles evident in the votives left by the faithful in churches.

Indian artists struggling with their country's colonial status within the British Empire were also beginning to respond to modern European art and to treat it not simply as a colonial imposition but as a means of creating a modern and independent Indian culture that could serve to advance the cause of independence. The poet, writer, playwright, composer, philosopher, social reformer and painter Rabindranath Tagore and the artists Jamini Roy and Amrita Sher-Gil were at the forefront of the movement to modernize Indian art. Sher-Gil (1913–1941), who was half Hungarian and another resident of Paris during the early 1930s, in 1934 chose to return to the land of her Indian father. Later, she wrote: 'I began to be haunted by an intense longing to return to India, feeling in some strange inexplicable way that there lay my destiny as a painter.'

Totalitarian Politics and Art

By the mid-1920s in Russia, the attitude of the Bolsheviks towards the avant-garde who had initially openly welcomed them and with whom they joined forces, quickly turned hostile, as it became clear that the totalitarian character of Marxism-Leninism had very different goals. Seeing the writing on the wall, Kandinsky left the Soviet Union in 1921 and began teaching at the Bauhaus in Weimar, Germany. Especially after Lenin's death in 1924, a far narrower and prescriptive interpretation of the role of art within the new 'classless' society was applied when the new leader, Josef Stalin, mandated that a truly 'socialist' art must be wholly in the service of the Communist Party. The avant-garde, but also artists more willing to use forms of realism, were persecuted, and a style of painting that looked back to the nineteenth century was mandated. In pictures like

Isaak Brodsky's (1883–1939) *Lenin in Smolny* (1930) the adoption of the realist style has been used for directly political ends, as the painting celebrates the Soviet Union's first leader planning the destiny of Russia. Works like Brodsky's became the basis for what was known as Socialist Realism, which in 1934 Stalin declared to be the only permitted Communist style for all the arts. Socialist Realism reflected the aggressive rejection of avant-garde art, claiming it was inherently capitalist, excessively dedicated to self-expression, overly pessimistic, and made art incomprehensible to the masses. Painting was instead turned into a narrowly ideological and propagandist tool, and presented in a style that, so it was argued, successfully communicated a more optimistic and 'healthy' vision of society that all could understand.

But the utopian vision of Socialist Realism was increasingly belied by Europe's descent towards another war. In 1924 the Fascists in Italy under Benito Mussolini took power, modelling their authoritarianism in part on the ruthlessness of the Bolsheviks' seizure of power in Russia. It also seemed that,

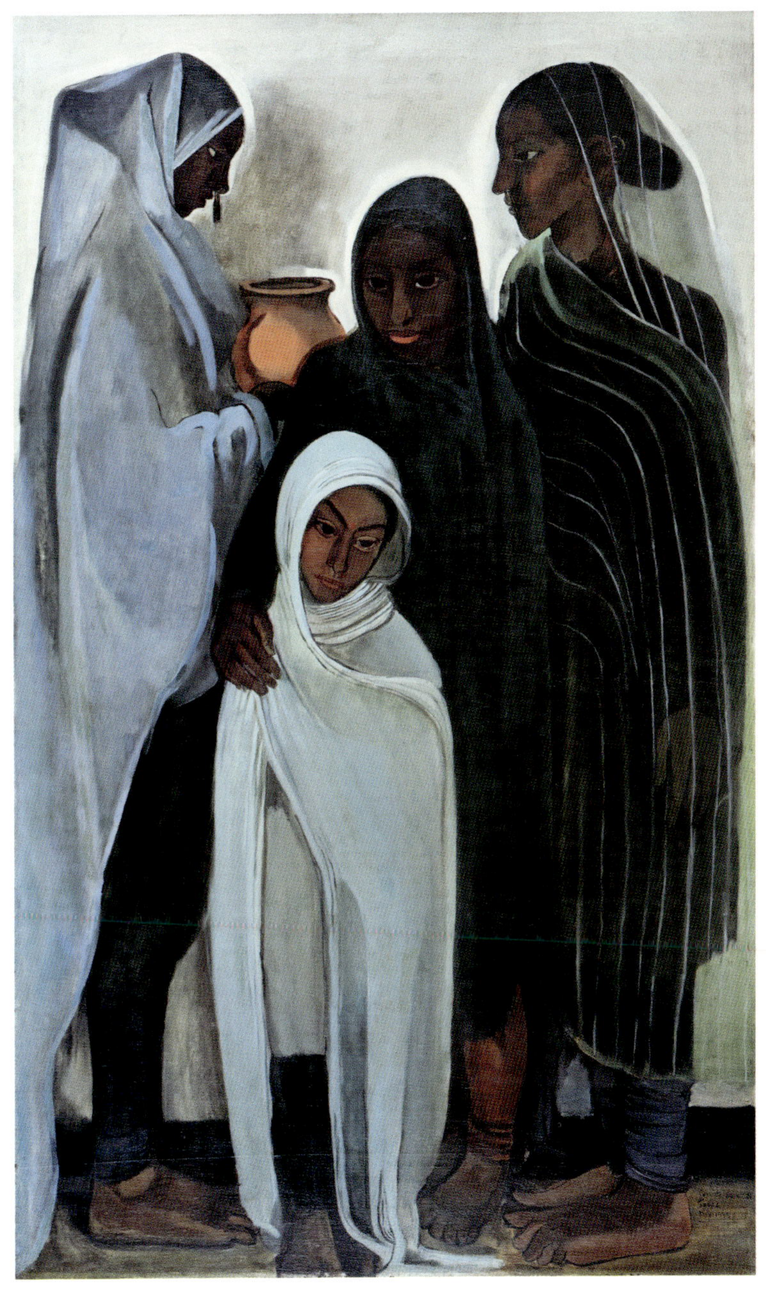

80 Amrita Sher-Gil, *Hill Women*, 1935

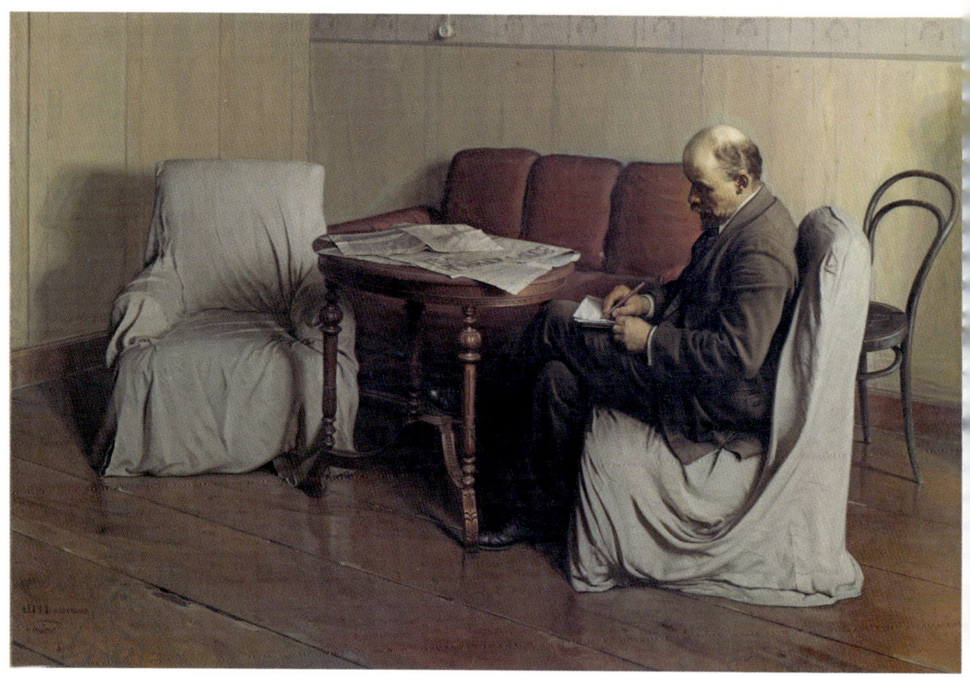

81 Isaak Brodsky, *Lenin in Smolny*, 1930

as the communists predicted, the capitalist world order was in crisis. In 1929, New York's Wall Street Crash led the formerly buoyant economies of the west to suddenly go into free-fall and ushered in the Great Depression. In part as a result of the social unrest caused by the economic crisis, which struck Germany especially hard, Adolf Hitler – also an admirer of Bolshevik *realpolitik* and the leader of the rabidly nationalistic and racist Nazi Party – was elected to power in Germany in 1933, inaugurating what he claimed was a 'Thousand Year Reich' guaranteed through military conquest and persecution of the Jews. Despite their shared animosity towards liberal democracy, the Right-wing authoritarian regimes in Italy and Germany and the Left-wing authoritarian regime in Russia now confronted each other.

Those who supported the radical Right claimed it stood for national or racial strength, purity and eternal values, while those in favour of the radical Left saw their cause as a revolutionary force led by the workers that would usher in a 'classless' society. But both ideologies wanted to sweep away a decadent and materialistic culture as quickly as possible, and along with it the kind of art seen in this book. Artists were forced to take sides politically. Some, like the Futurists, openly welcomed Fascism. In Germany, elements within the Expressionist movement initially found common cause with the Nazis, believing they would rid German society of decadent strains of modernity (Emil Nolde, for example, joined the Nazi Party). But very soon, Hitler, like Stalin, also condemned the avant-garde for making what he termed 'Degenerate Art'; and, in a series of mocking exhibitions, the Nazis even paraded examples of works by most of the artists discussed so far, then sold or burned them. The Nazi preference, too, was for a propagandistic style based on a heroic and idealized form of nineteenth-century realism.

In 1936 civil war erupted in Spain when forces loyal to General Franco, who styled himself the defender of Roman Catholic tradition against the dangerous modernizing and secular tendencies of the Left-leaning Republican government, crossed from Spanish Morocco and marched north. Soon, the Soviet Union had begun supporting the beleaguered Republican government, who allied itself with the Spanish Communist Party, while the Fascists and Nazis aided Franco's Nationalists. Artists everywhere were forced to take political sides. By this period, the Spaniard Pablo Picasso, living in Paris and the most famous living artist, read in a newspaper in April 1937 about the recent aerial bombing by German warplanes of the Spanish town of Guernica during the civil war, and immediately set about making his now famous artistic response to the tragic event: *Guernica* (1937). The use of black and white and the stippling effect that simulates printed type signal the fact that it was via the print media that Picasso experienced the atrocity in Spain. 'Painting is not made to decorate apartments,' Picasso declared defiantly. 'It's an offensive and defensive weapon against the enemy.' His huge mural-size canvas was intended to decorate the pavilion of the Republican government at the World's Fair in Paris.

In 1939 the apparently ideologically opposed communist Soviet Union and Nazi Third Reich made a non-aggression pact, freeing them to join in the invasion and partition of Poland. Another world war soon followed, as Hitler launched his devastating Blitzkrieg. Soon the Germans had occupied most of Europe. Picasso, a neutral Spaniard, remained in Occupied Paris. It is said that on one occasion a German officer visited his studio, held up a postcard of *Guernica* and enquired if Picasso made it. 'No, you did!' the artist is reputed to have answered. But *Guernica* transcends historical context and seems timeless and archetypal. It is undoubtedly the greatest anti-war painting of the modern age, testimony to the capacity of painting to deliver a complex and multi-layered message in ways that are wholly unavailable to photography or film.

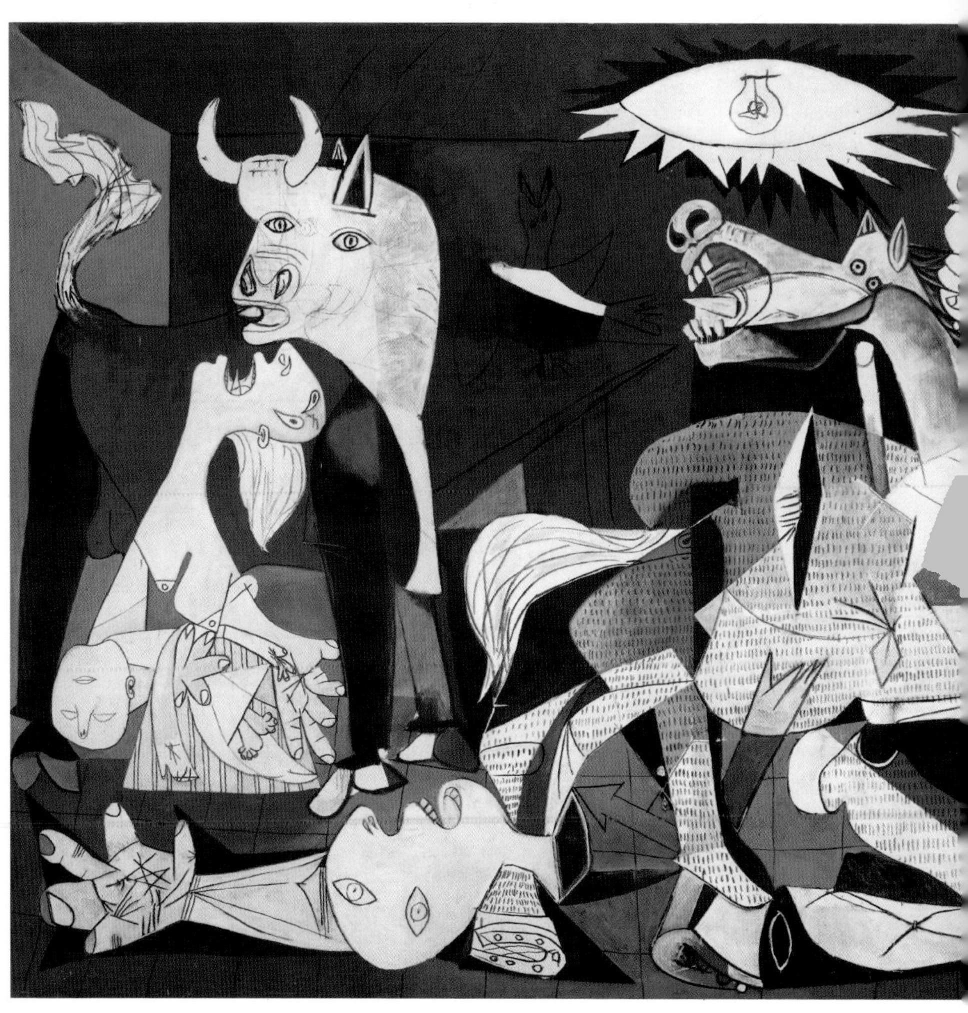

82 Pablo Picasso, *Guernica*, 1937

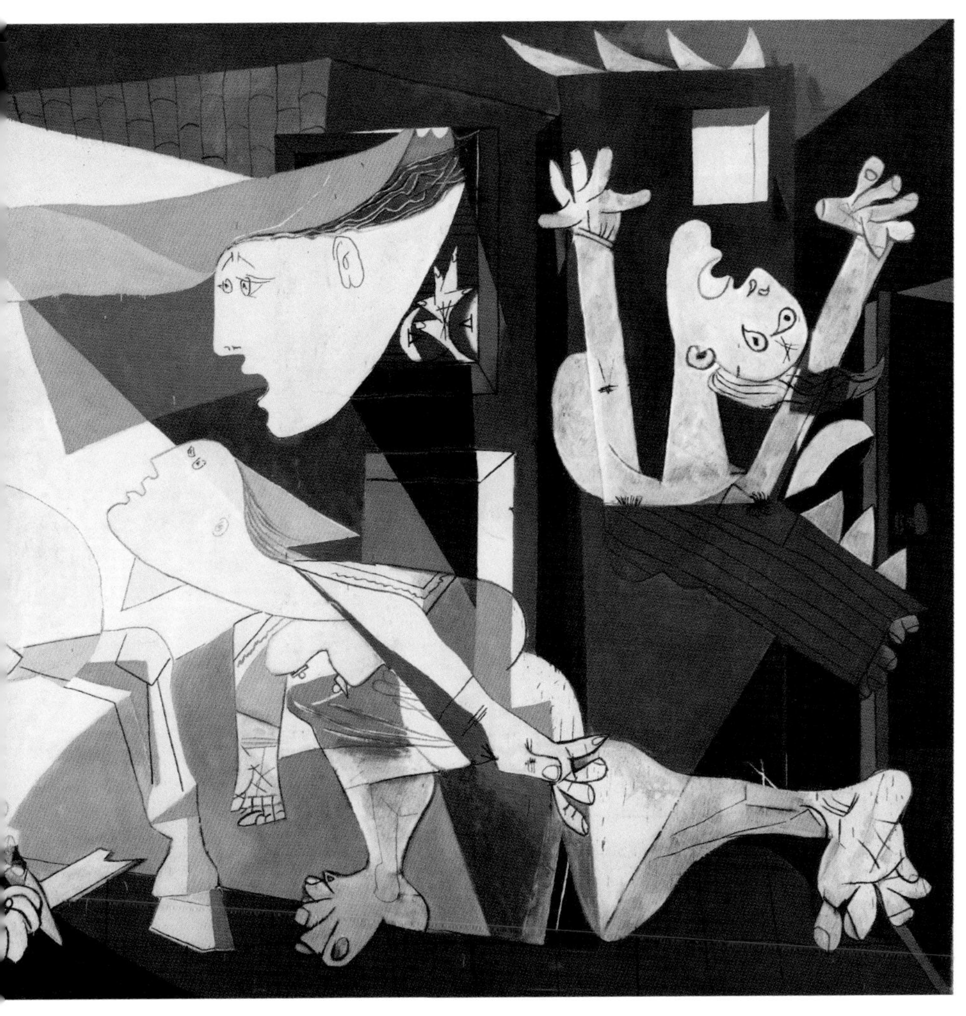

Chapter 6
Post-War Painting
c. 1945–*c.* 1956

Aftermath

The raw materiality of *Head of a Hostage* (1945) by the French
artist Jean Fautrier (1898–1964) conveys the tragic legacy of the
brutality and suffering of the Second World War and vividly
expresses the artist's solidarity with the victims of the Nazi
occupation of France. By the end of hostilities in September
1945, between seventy and eighty-five million worldwide
were dead. Forty to fifty million Europeans were displaced
migrants, there was widespread rationing and famine,
industry was crippled, and ports, bridges and whole cities were
left in ruins – in Düsseldorf, on the Rhine River in the west of
Germany, 93% of houses were uninhabitable. At the cessation
of fighting, Soviet troops stood at the heart Europe, and after
Stalin refused to withdraw and installed repressive pro-Soviet
regimes across the rest of occupied eastern Europe, the whole
continent was transformed into hostile ideological camps. The
Cold War had begun, and the entire world was implicated in
the struggle of rival hegemonic powers that were both soon to
be armed with atom bombs.

In the immediate wake of the genocidal Holocaust in
which six million European Jews, and millions of others
deemed unwelcome in the Nazi's 'Thousand Year Reich', were
exterminated, and following the detonation of atomic bombs
at Hiroshima and Nagasaki, it seemed frighteningly clear that
advanced western society was capable of unspeakable evil and
that techno-science had facilitated the creation of weapons of
mass destruction so terrible that they threatened to obliterate

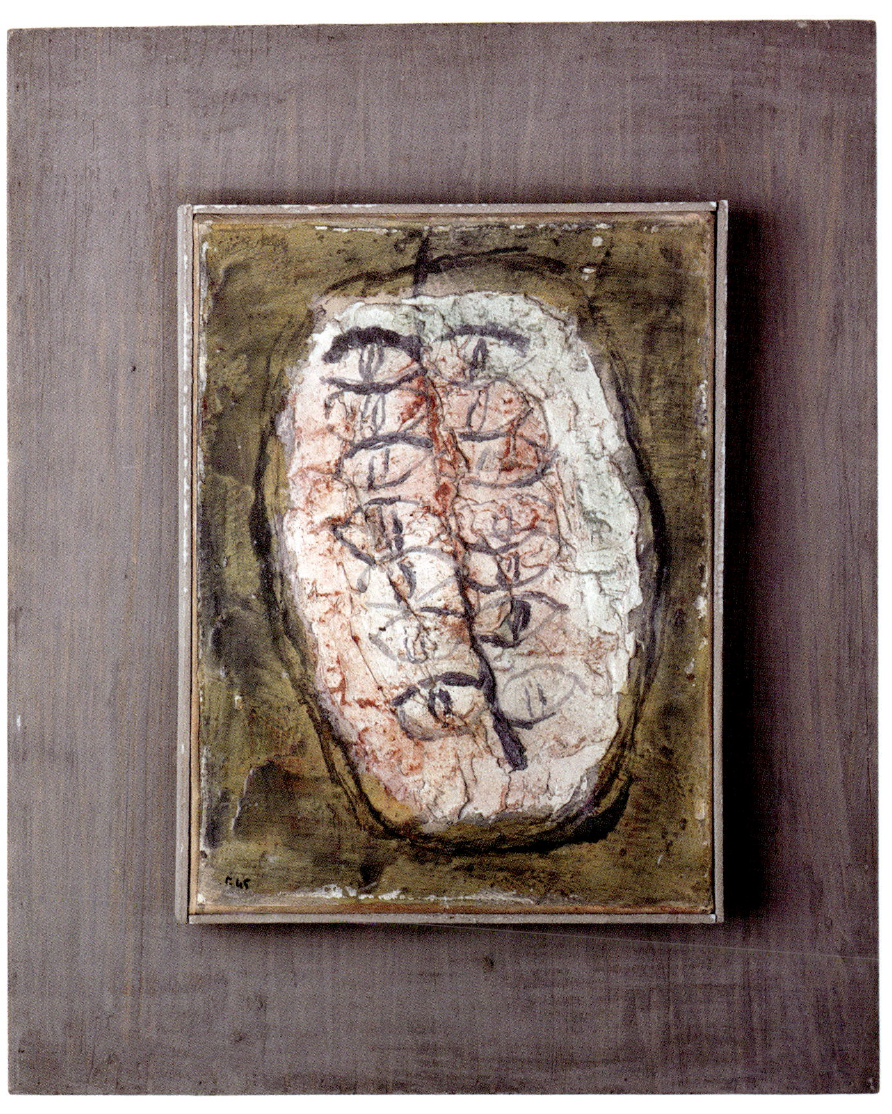

83 Jean Fautrier, *Head of a Hostage*, 1945

all life on earth. As the French writer André Malraux declared
in 1947: 'The Europe of bombed towns is no more ravaged than
the idea Europe has made for itself of man.' That same year,
in an excoriating attack on the whole legacy of the western
Enlightenment, the German-Jewish Marxist critics Theodor
Adorno and Max Horkheimer, who had emigrated to the United
States to escape the Nazis, declared: 'the fully enlightened earth
radiates disaster triumphant.'

But despite such traumatic events, or perhaps because of
them, some of the older generation of French artists, such as
Pierre Bonnard, Henri Matisse, Georges Braque – doyens of the
'School of Paris' – sought to preserve their vision of painting as
a refuge from tragic history and the dangerous and uncertain
present. In Italy, the artist Giorgio Morandi (1890–1964), who
had lived through Mussolini's Fascism and a war that had
raged up and down the length of the peninsula, nevertheless
remained similarly undeterred in the quest to make of painting
a peaceful sanctuary, creating a gently meditative art of the
still-life founded on the patient observation of the bottles and
pots he had accumulated in his Bologna studio.

Politics and Art

But for younger artists this attitude smacked of the ivory
tower and ran the risk of turning even progressive art into an
escapist bourgeois luxury. In fact, making any kind of art in the
name of 'beauty' could seem not only an indulgence but even
a moral outrage. For some, the way to remain optimistic about
the future was to embrace communism, which especially in
France and Italy had been instrumental in defeating Nazism.
In late 1944 Picasso declared: 'the French Communist Party has
opened its arms to me; there I have found that which I most
value.' As Picasso suggests, the allure of communism lay in its
status as a focus of resistance to fascism, but communism also
appealed because it claimed that revolution was historically
inevitable and would immediately bring about greater social
justice. Artistic commitment to communism led some to
repudiate the experimental model of the avant-garde in favour
of Socialist Realism and forms of painting in styles that were
accessible to the 'masses'. They dedicated their practice to
portraying contemporary class struggle, but some also hoped to
avoid the dulling conformity of the Socialist Realism demanded
by the Soviet Communist Party.

The foremost artist associated with the French Communist
Party was André Fougeron (1913–1998), who painted the huge
and ironically titled *Atlantic Civilization* (1953), satirizing in vivid
terms the growing influence of the United States over Europe

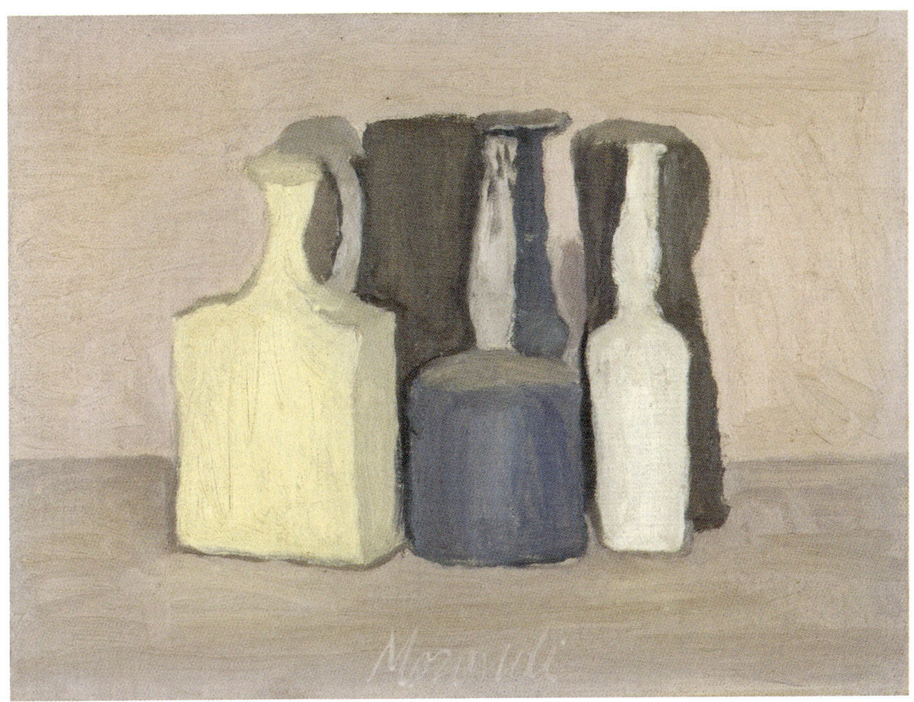

84 Giorgio Morandi, *Still Life*, 1948–49

(note the electric chair stood on a plinth, top centre, which at the time was the characteristically American form of death by execution) – a cultural influence that, as the communists saw it, also included the advocacy of 'bourgeois' avant-garde art. But in the light of knowledge of Stalin's actions within the Soviet Union, such allegiance to communism would prove increasingly difficult to sustain and, especially after the brutal crushing of the Hungarian Uprising in 1956, the political Left in western Europe and the United States sought to reinterpret the Marxist message in ways that insulated it from these crimes while at the same time maintaining the stance of an anti-capitalist and anti-bourgeois opposition.

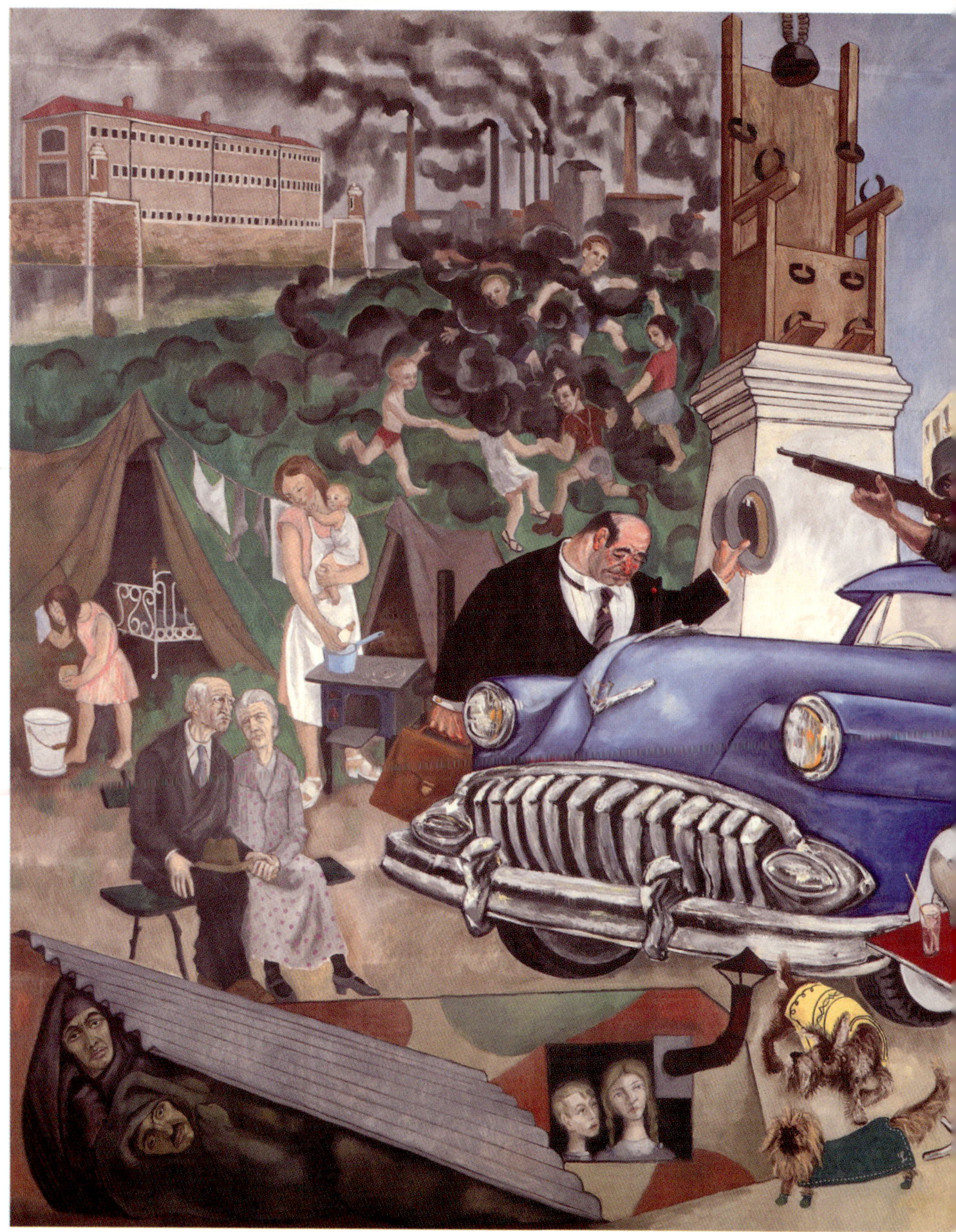

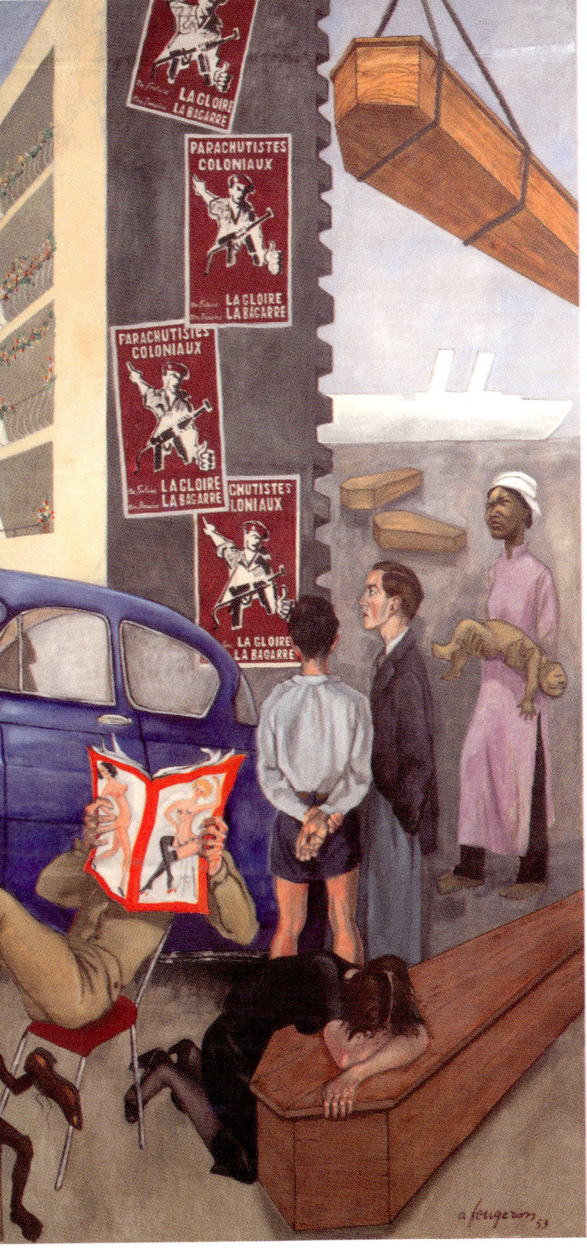

85 André Fougeron, *Atlantic Civilization*, 1953

The 'Age of Anxiety'

Even so, in a period that became known as the 'Age of Anxiety', many artists felt political allegiance of any sort was increasingly irrelevant or had to be of the most uncompromising kind. A new figurative art stripped of the conventions of optical realism and all vestiges of idealism – an art committed to speaking the unalloyed truth – appeared the most appropriate response. This unsettling reality seems to be the motive for the inner psychic landscapes pervaded by fear and uncertainty graphically captured by the London-based Anglo-Irish artist Francis Bacon (1909–1992), who talked of 'returning fact onto the nervous system in a more violent way'. Inspired by the example of Surrealism to reject analysis and reflection, Bacon stated that 'anything I've ever liked at all has been the result of an accident on which I have been able to work.' Yet Bacon claimed not to be a nihilist. 'You can be optimistic and totally without hope,' he declared, suggesting that whatever one might be feeling or thinking concerning the meaning of human existence, the instincts will inherently seek maximum stimulation and resist the inertia of death.

Bacon's work also reflected a new tendency within art of drawing on the wealth of photographic imagery that was now available through the mass media, rather than basing his figurative style on the direct study of phenomena or the creation of dream-imagery. The source for his *Study after Velázquez's Portrait of Pope Innocent X* (1953), for example, was a photographic reproduction of the Spanish artist Diego Velázquez's painting from 1650 (Bacon never actually saw the real work, which is in Rome), which he merged with a now famous still from the Soviet filmmaker Sergei Eisenstein's Soviet epic *Battleship Potemkin*, showing a close-up of the face of a screaming nurse. While Velázquez's masterpiece conveys an air of studied authority and nobility, Bacon's mid-twentieth-century reworking transforms the original to express the horror of post-war existence.

The philosophical tendency known as Existentialism seemed to best express this post-war zeitgeist of disillusionment and fear. Unlike London, which was ravaged by the Nazi's Blitz, Paris – the pre-war 'capital' of modern art – avoided widescale physical destruction, but nevertheless, as the Parisian writer Simone de Beauvoir later reminisced, the wartime period 'remained on our hands like a great, unwanted corpse, and there was no place on earth to bury it'. The Algerian-born French writer Albert Camus observed that 'at any street corner the feeling of absurdity can strike any man in the face' – the inherent meaninglessness of existence was always lying just below the facade of social normality – while the philosopher

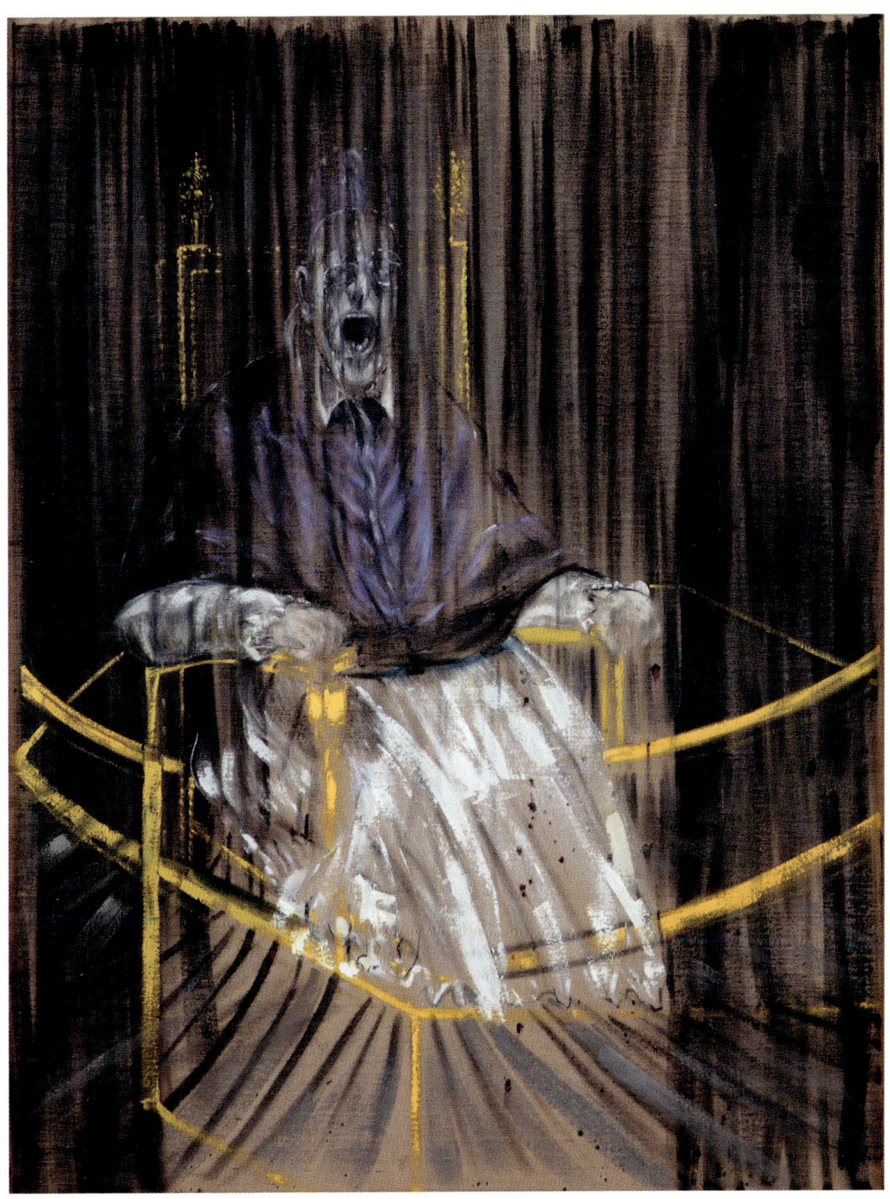

86 Francis Bacon, *Study after Velázquez's Portrait of Pope Innocent X*, 1953

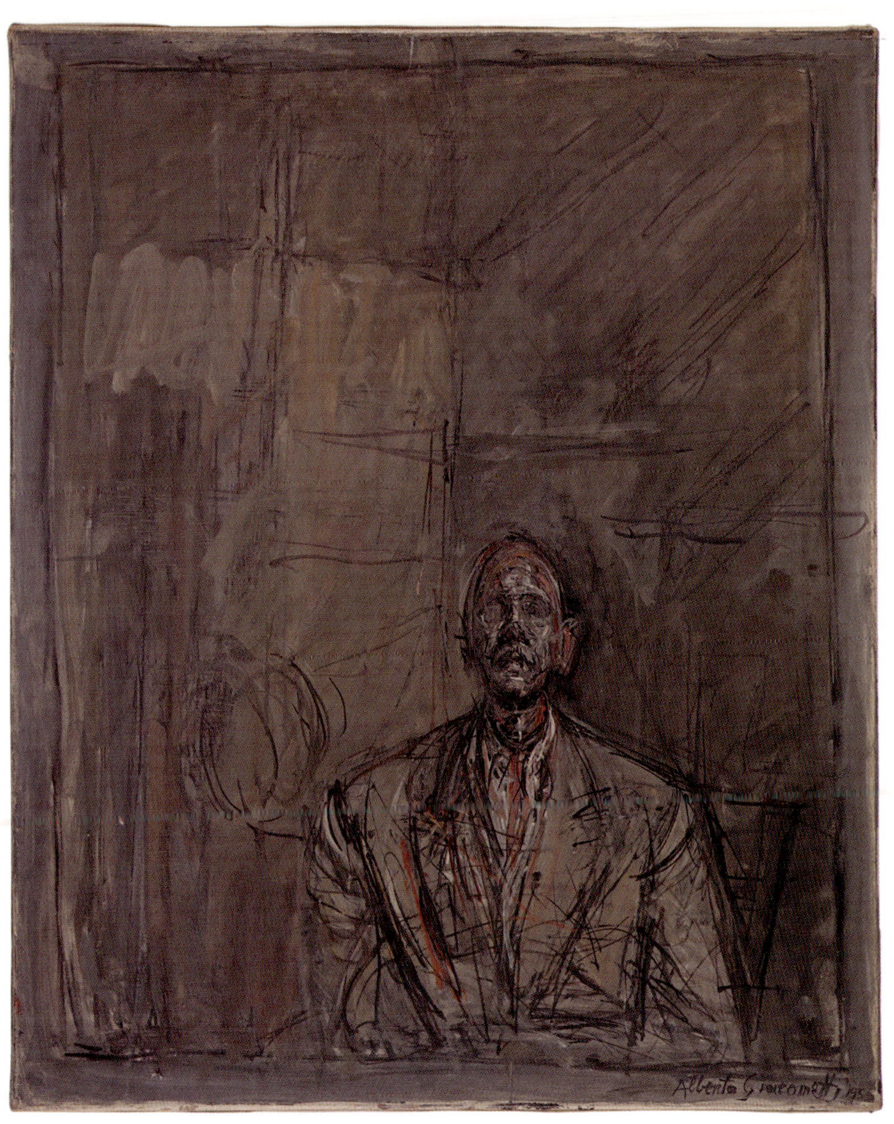

87 Alberto Giacometti, *Jean Genet*, 1954/55

Jean-Paul Sartre, Beauvoir's partner and the most instrumental figure in spreading the new creed through treatises, novels, plays and catalogue essays, declared: 'Man is condemned to be free.'

The artist who for Sartre most fully epitomized the new Existentialist vision was the Swiss sculptor and painter Alberto Giacometti (1901–1966). In the 1930s Giacometti had made a name for himself as *the* Surrealist sculptor, but he pointedly abandoned the art of 'interior reality' to work directly from 'exterior reality'. Giacometti's role-model was Cézanne, who, so he argued, made the impossibility and failure inherent in the task of transcribing visual sensations the essential motive for making art. *Jean Genet* (1954/55) is a portrait of one of Sartre's favourite writers and immediate contemporaries. 'That's the terrible thing: the more one works on a picture, the more impossible it becomes to finish it,' Giacometti observed. Sartre argued that Giacometti's sculptures and paintings showed that, 'Nothing enfolds him [a human being], nothing supports him, nothing contains him: he appears, isolated in the immense frame of the void.' In *Jean Genet* this sensation is graphically communicated by the depiction of a body that barely seems to emerge from the surrounding void and is only tentatively brought into existence by a nervous weaving of brushmarks.

L'Art Brut and CoBrA

In what seemed to be a fallen, morally bankrupt world, many artists felt a desperate need to discover 'innocents', to find those untainted by 'bourgeois' society's pathologies, deceptions and inanities. They looked for new points of origin. In 1945 the French artist Jean Dubuffet (1901–1985) coined the term *l'art brut* ('raw art') – which he also called 'real art' – and said his goal was to overthrow what he called 'cultural art', the official art of the bourgeoisie. He declared that a new beginning could only be made through embracing the values that society deprecated or ignored – for example, the kind of art that was 'always lurking where you don't expect it. Where nobody's thinking about it or mentions it by name', indeed, where imaginative work was made without any conscious intention of being 'art'. Compared to 'cultural art', which only sought beauty and the ideal, *art brut* would inevitably look ugly, raw, shocking – but these were sure signs that it was personal and authentic. In 1947 Dubuffet exhibited his own collection of *art brut* – works by criminals, the dispossessed, the mentally ill and children – and the next year formed the Compagnie de l'Art Brut, with poet and Surrealist leader André Breton as one of the original members. The concept of what in English is called 'Outsider' art emerged to define forms of picture-making that lie outside the mainstream and are made by individuals who live at the margins of society. In *Fautrier spider on the forehead* (1947) – a portrait of the artist Jean Fautrier, who painted the work that begins this chapter – Dubuffet simulated the crude simplicity and directness of children's art; the lines of the figure have partly been made by gouging directly into the thickly painted surface.

Part of the continuing appeal of children's and 'Outsider' art in this period lay in the obvious fact that it was derided by the detested mainstream 'bourgeois' culture. Such art is not based on cultural norms erected around the convention of recording visual observations – the principal central to post-Renaissance art – but rather on what the child or unschooled adult already knows of the world. In other words, this kind of picturing, like non-western art too, is grounded in the recognition that an image is produced not so much by instantaneous seeing but by drawing on a store of personal and cultural memory of what things look like. In the case of children and 'Outsiders', this store consists not of conventional 'cultural' images but of 'rawer', more personal and less orthodox material. 'One must be honest,' Dubuffet stressed. 'No veils! No shams! Naked, all things first reduced to their worst.'

Children's art was also especially appealing to the artists who gathered under the banner of CoBrA, founded in 1948 and including Karel Appel, Constant, Corneille and Asger Jorn. The acronym signalled the fact that these artists were based in Copenhagen, Brussels and Amsterdam, and was intended to show their independence from the dominance of Paris. Like Dubuffet, CoBrA artists revived many of the characteristics of the pre-First World War Expressionist aesthetic, which was now updated through association with the understanding of the human mind proposed by Sigmund Freud and Carl Jung, as well as by Surrealism and Existentialist philosophy. 'Painting is the destruction of what has gone before, the destruction of systems, ideas, logic, routines,' declared Appel. 'It is the dynamic and explosive force of intuition.' CoBrA artists emphasized nonconformity, spontaneity, instinct, the unplanned and the uninhibited. But unlike the mostly dour figurative Parisian paintings of the period, their works tended to embrace a more exuberant spirit of wild, carefree liberation.

Like Dubuffet's work, *Hip, Hip, Hoorah!* (1949) by Karel Appel (1921–2006) mimics the raw directness and untrained look of children's art but with a far more vivid use of colour. Significantly, Appel stressed that the actual process of physically making a painting was in itself generative and inherently meaningful: 'For me the material is the paint itself.

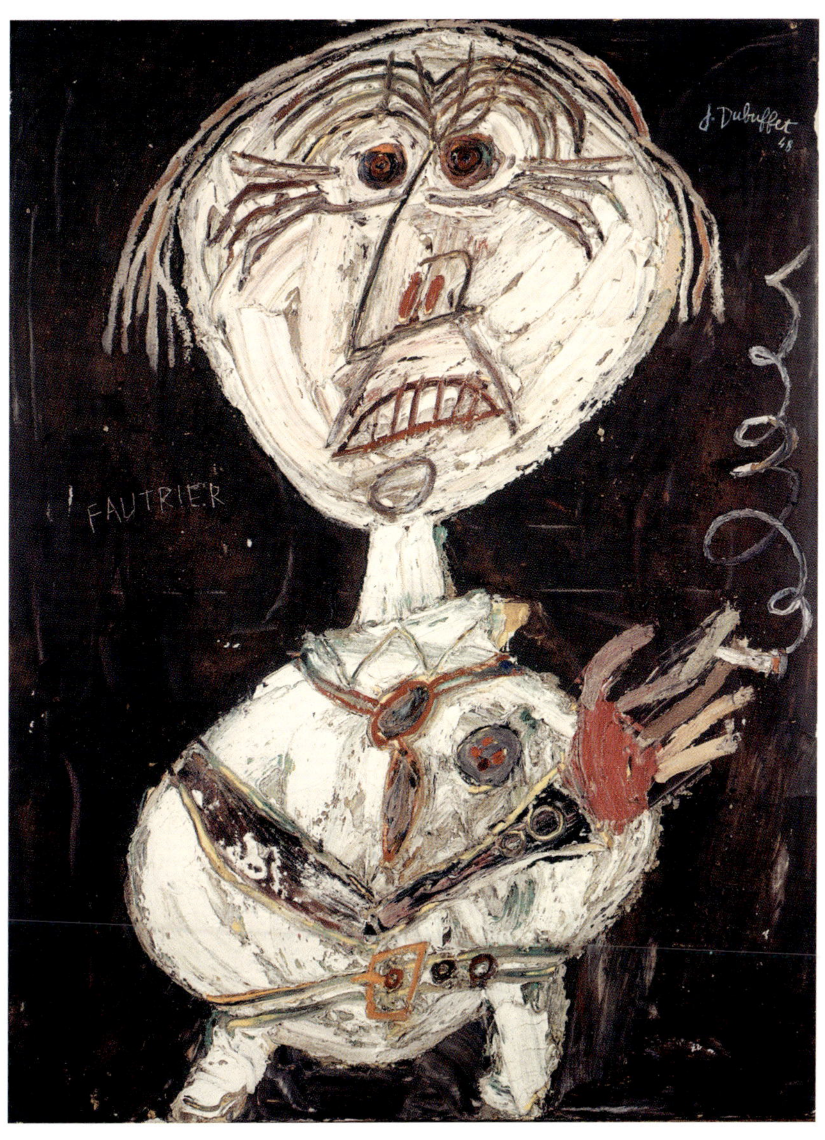

88 Jean Dubuffet, *Fautrier spider on the forehead*, 1947

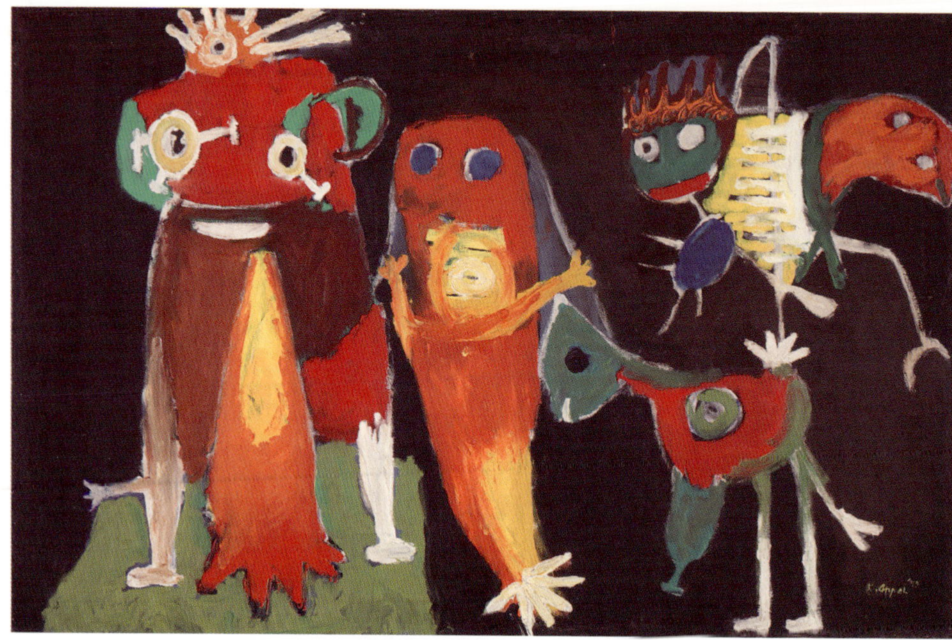

80 Karel Appel, *Hip, Hip, Hoorah!*, 1949

The paint expresses itself. In the midst of paint I find my
imagination and go on to paint it. I paint the imagination
I find in the material I paint with.'

L'Art Informel

For some artists, however, the lingering presence of an image,
however radically de-idealized, was already a fatal concession
to convention and stood in the way of painting being able to
fully 'express itself'. The way forward, it was therefore argued,
was to abandon the whole idea of making an image. But while
Constructivist principles of geometric abstraction continued
to appeal to some artists as a basis for an image-free painting,
increasingly it was assumed that the ideals of purity and faith in
reason such conventions reflected were wholly unsuited to the
messy confusion of the post-war period.

A new kind of abstract art therefore now emerged, one that
was greatly indebted to the Surrealist principle of 'automatism'
and that above all was intended to communicate feelings of
spontaneity, restless process and raw materiality, as well as
embodying a unique 'signature' style manifested through the
original manner in which paint was freely handled *as paint*
rather than as the means used to produce an image. This new

abstract art was slated as part of the ongoing radical critique
of western 'bourgeois' values, and so emphasis was placed
on the paramount importance of individual authenticity. As
the influential French critic and curator Michel Tapié wrote:
'Our interest is not in movements, but in something much
rarer, authentic Individuals.' The *act* of painting was valued
above any preconceived *idea* of painting, and this was a further
conscious reversal of the traditional idea of picture-making in
which an artist first has an idea and then attempts to embody
it in a painting. As we saw in Chapters One and Two, the
importance of the *tache*, the dynamic brushstroke, had become
a key aspect of much nineteenth- and early twentieth-century
progressive painting as it gradually threw off optical realism.
But now, the brushstroke was further unburdened of the task of
representation, as artists explored novel methods of application
and mixed paint with additional textured matter such as sand
and collaged elements.

In continental Europe, the new style became known as *l'art
informel* ('informal' art) or *Tachisme* ('mark-making'); artists
associated with the tendency included Lucio Fontana, Hans
Hartung, Georges Mathieu, Henri Michaux, Pierre Soulages,
Jean-Paul Riopelle, Nicolas de Stäel, Maria Helena Vieira da
Silva and Antoni Tàpies. In Britain, a parallel style was pursued
by such artists as Alan Davie, Patrick Heron, Roger Hilton and
Peter Lanyon.

French artist Georges Mathieu (1921–2012), for example,
squeezed paint straight from the tube onto canvas, emphasizing
the basic activity of applying pigment to a surface, saying, 'What
I love is to act on the canvas. To act? That is to scratch, to tear, to
stain, to invade the canvas with colour, in brief everything which
is not "to paint".' To make *3 April 1954* (1954) another French
artist, Pierre Soulages (1919–2022), used large brushes to rapidly
fashion his composition without any intention of describing
anything in the observable world beyond the canvas. Rather,
he announced that his goal was to explore the act of painting
itself. Instead of laying on paint, Argentinian-Italian artist Lucio
Fontana in 1949 began piercing canvases by making holes in
or slashing their surface with a knife. Fontana described his
works as 'spatial concepts' and 'spatial art', and explained he
was interested in drawing attention to real space rather than
illusionistic space, but a real space that, as he saw it, opened
onto the invisible – to infinity – not the finite space described
by classical physics. Catalan-Spanish painter Antoni Tàpies
(1923–2012) produced encrusted, wall-like surfaces using an
unusual mixture of media. In *Great Painting* (1958) inscriptions
of his presence via graffiti-like marks cover a rough surface

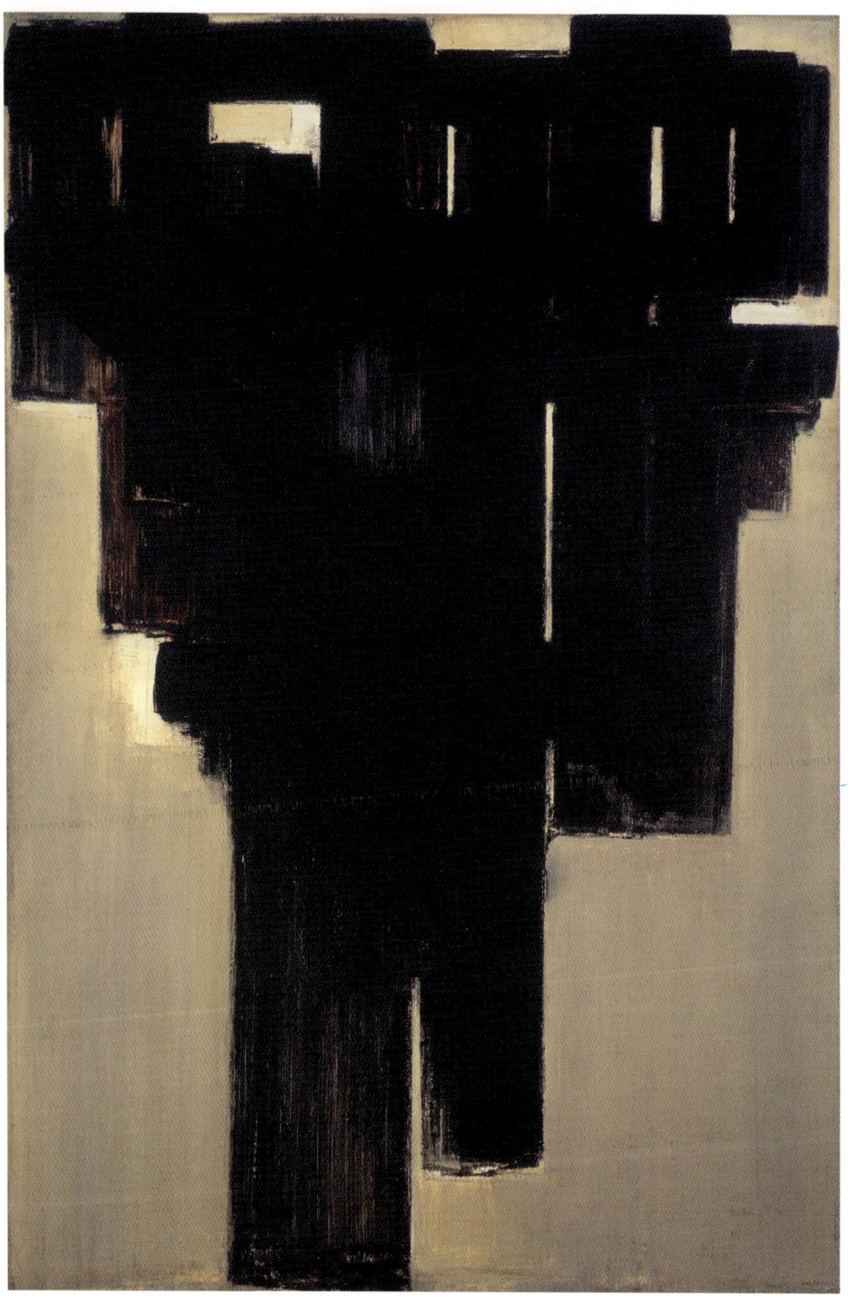

90 ABOVE Pierre Soulages, *3 April 1954*, 1954
91 OPPOSITE Antoni Tàpies, *Great Painting*, 1958

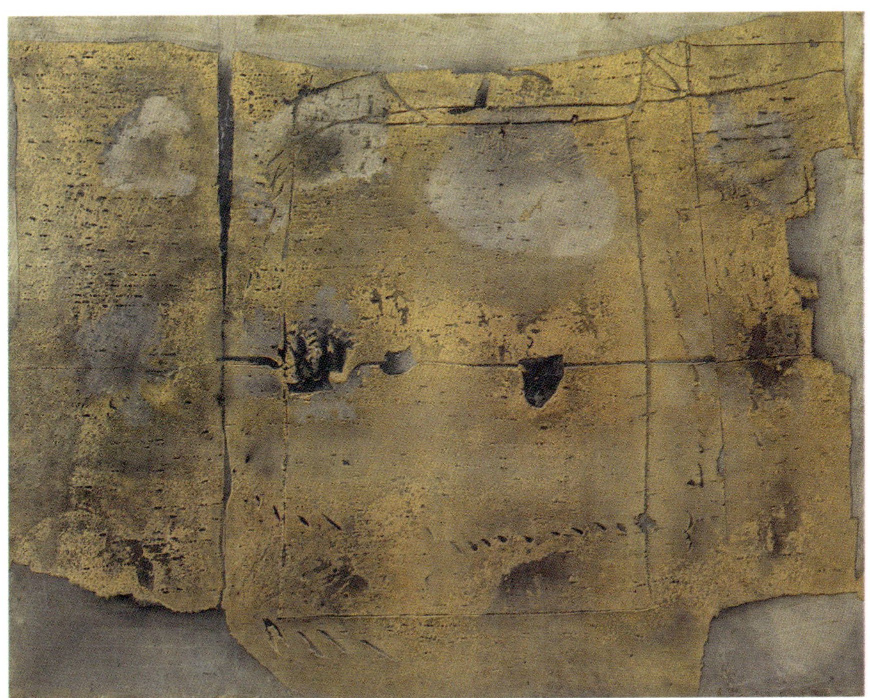

made of oil paint, marble dust and sand on canvas. The
absence of recognizable imagery, the dynamic application
of paint, the lack of clearly defined structure and the
repudiation of obvious skill became intrinsic aspects of a
process-centred, open-ended approach to painting, out of
which unspecifiable meanings would arise. Materiality was
also a dominant concern, and the new 'informal' painting
engaged the sense of touch, supplementing optics by *haptics* –
touch and movement – and drawing attention to the reality
of painting in its most empirical sense, as a material object
with which one physically engages.

American Abstract Expressionism

In the United States a group of artists emerged in the
late 1940s that became known as the New York School
(in comparison to the 'School of Paris') or the Abstract
Expressionists. As with European *art informel*, the new
American art embraced the Surrealist idea of 'automatism'
and focused on the potential of the materials and act of
painting as meaningfully expressive in their own right. But
this new American art was bolstered by a society experiencing

unprecedented economic prosperity and confidently adopting
the role of guardian of the 'free world'. It developed stylistically
along broadly two lines: gestural and dynamic 'action painting',
and more calm and meditative 'Colour Field Painting'. In
the former camp were artists such as Arshile Gorky, Adolph
Gottlieb, Philip Guston, Hans Hofmann, Franz Kline, Elaine de
Kooning, Willem de Kooning, Lee Krasner, Robert Motherwell,
Morris Louis, Jackson Pollock, Clyfford Still and, as part of a
second generation, Helen Frankenthaler, Joan Mitchell, Jules
Olitski and Cy Twombly.

So far in this survey the focus has been on painting in Europe,
and even largely in one city: Paris. But, as a result of the Second
World War, the centre of global political and economic power
shifted across the Atlantic to the United States, and for the next
forty years the future of Europe and the world would be decided
between Washington and Moscow. With the United States' new
global role and sense of purpose also came cultural power,
and the future of modern art would henceforth increasingly be
decided not in Paris but in New York City. Due to the upheavals
of Nazism in Europe, and the war in general, many of the most
important European artists had migrated permanently or
temporarily to the United States: Josef Albers, Marc Chagall,
Fernand Léger, Piet Mondrian and several of the Surrealists,
including André Breton, Salvador Dalí, Max Ernst, Leonora
Carrington and Joan Miró. But modern European art was also
a strong presence due to the growing interest and influence
of American collectors. The abstract paintings of Wassily
Kandinsky were especially visible as they featured prominently
in the Museum of Non-Objective Art in New York (founded in
1939, and later known as the Guggenheim Museum), which along
with the Museum of Modern Art (founded in 1929) indicated that
a vibrant avant-garde art scene was emerging in New York.

Many Americans welcomed the more tangible ties with the
European avant-garde, but they also argued that American art
should nevertheless challenge the universalism of Eurocentric
assumptions. Artists who had largely worked in distant
admiration, contempt or ignorance of European tendencies
suddenly found themselves much closer to the centre of
cultural power and, as a result, as the influential American
critic Clement Greenberg boasted in 1948: 'The main premises
of Western art have at last migrated to the United States.'
But another important American critic of the period, Harold
Rosenberg, talked of a specifically American cultural attitude
which he termed 'Coonskinism', that was to be distinguished
from the 'Redcoat' mentality that kept America tied to the
'Old World'. He described a defiant American individualism

that rejected worn-out European values, and a new American art that reflected 'a dynamic world dominated no longer by things but by the activities of men'. Both Greenberg and Rosenberg reflected the fact that especially strong in America at this time was the conviction that the past – which seemed to be mostly characterized by barbarism and oppression – belonged to Europe, but the present and better future were the responsibility of the 'New World'. This made American artists feel especially committed to innovation, and inclined to disparage or deny the influence of art's past and of Europe on what they were making in the present.

'Action Painting'

'Action Painting' is epitomized by the artist who 'broke the ice', as his friend and fellow artist de Kooning later put it. In the summer of 1949, the thirty-seven-year-old Jackson Pollock (1912–1956) was profiled by the American mass-circulation *Life* magazine under a banner headline asking, 'Is he the greatest living painter in the United States?' The question was meant in part to be facetious, but soon turned out to be answerable in the hyperbolic affirmative, because Pollock's influence over the next two decades and beyond was immense, just as Picasso's had been in the inter-war years. But, like all the soon-to-be dubbed 'Abstract Expressionists', Pollock served a long apprenticeship, working his way through expressionist figuration, Picasso pastiche and Surrealism-inspired work before in 1947 hitting on his trademark practice of laying large rolls of canvas on the floor and in almost dance-like movements covering them with skeins of dripped and poured paint. Pollock explained: 'On the floor I am more at ease. I feel nearer, more a part of the painting, since this way I can walk around it, work from the four sides and literally be in the painting. A painting has a life of its own. I try to let it live.' He also indicated that one of the inspirations for this unusual practise was Navajo Native American sand-painting. In a sense, Pollock found a way to extend the explorations of ambiguous space initiated by 'analytic' Cubism – from which Picasso and the other Cubists turned away when they shifted to 'synthetic' Cubism – where images and signs of things from the familiar world are more clearly restored to pictures. Pollock's paintings, such as *Autumn Rhythm (Number 30)* (1950), possess an unprecedented all over, raw, pulsating energy and vitality in which the last vestiges of perspectival space and modelling have been banished, as well as the compositional control communicated through the organization of a painting around clearly delineated forms and colours.

92

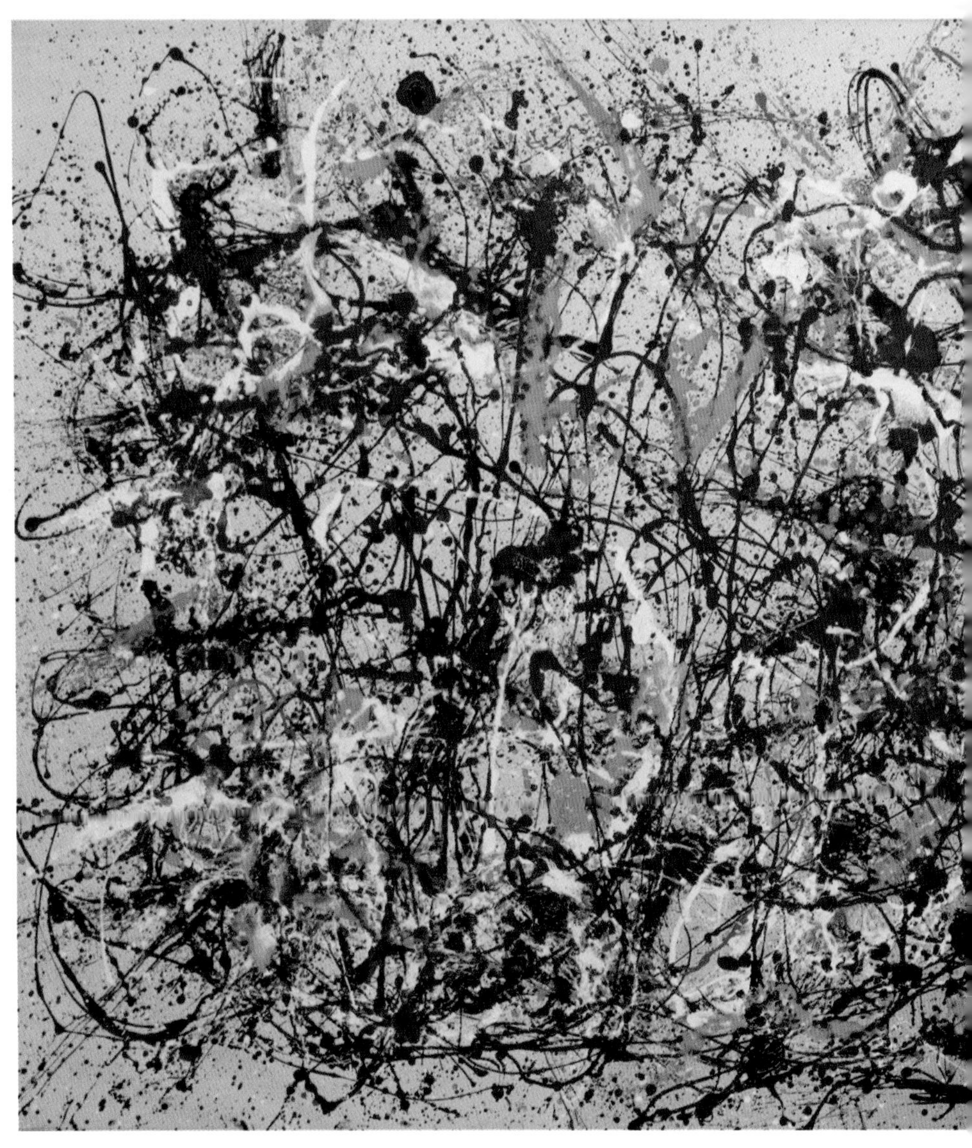

92 Jackson Pollock, *Autumn Rhythm (Number 30)*, 1950

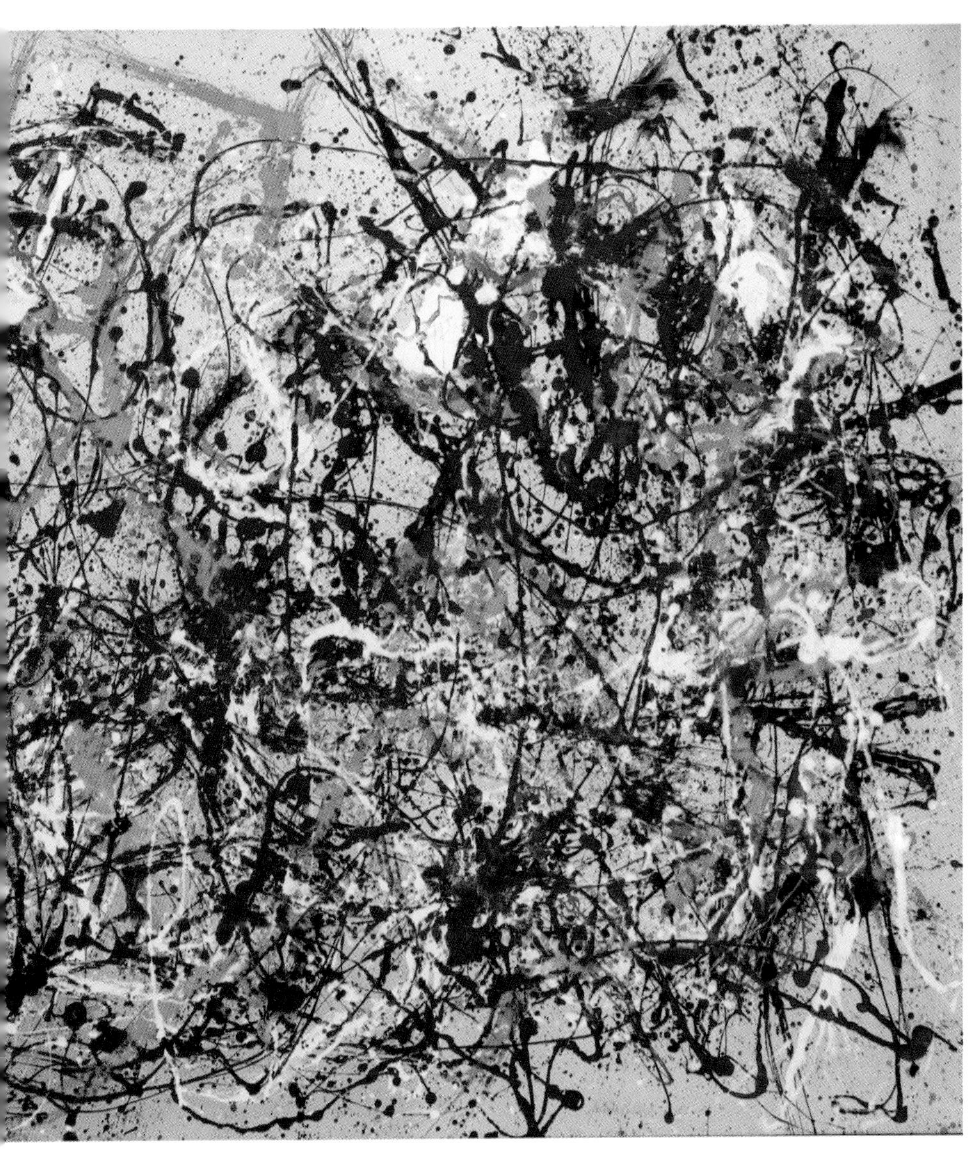

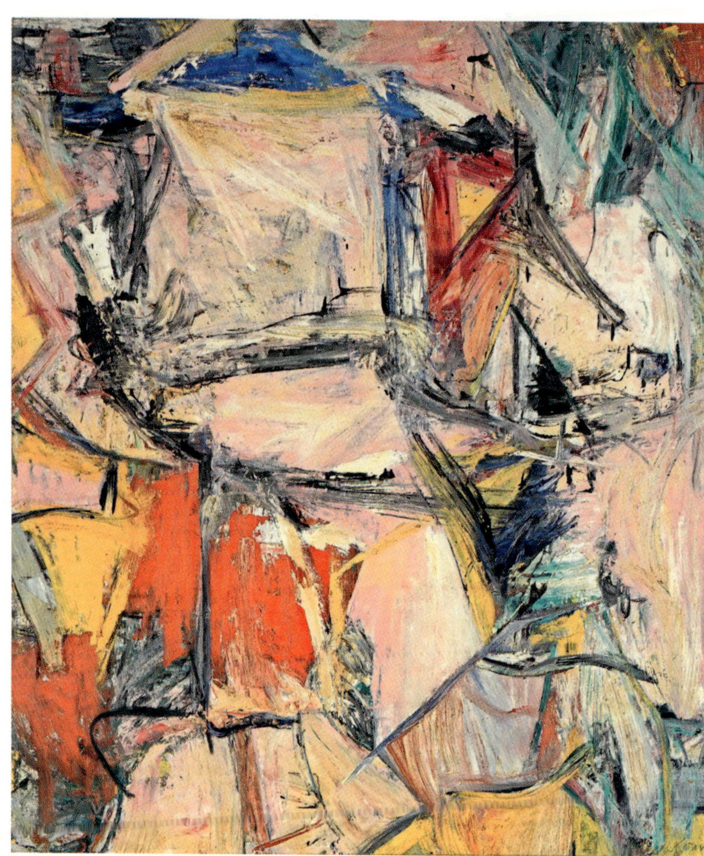

93 LEFT Willem
de Kooning,
Interchanged, 1955
94 OPPOSITE Joan
Mitchell, *Untitled*,
1952

The paintings of the Dutch-born and trained Willem de
Kooning (1904–1997) display even more frenetic dynamism
than Pollock's – even though he still painted with (mostly)
brushes on his canvases while they were upright – and he
therefore perhaps represents most fully the 'Action Painting'
dimension of Abstract Expressionism. One critic described
de Kooning's work as 'a sensual and dissonant cacophony'.
Rather than depicting the lively urban scene alluded to in
93   the title of *Interchanged* (1955), for example, de Kooning
presented the painterly equivalent to the experience. Restless
dynamism in paint also characterizes the work of the younger
Joan Mitchell (1925–1922), who like Pollock and de Kooning,
practised an inherently open-ended, improvisatory method.
In relation to the problem of attributing meaning to works
94   like *Untitled* (1952), Mitchell explained impatiently: 'It seems
very clear what it means. I can't say it but the painting makes

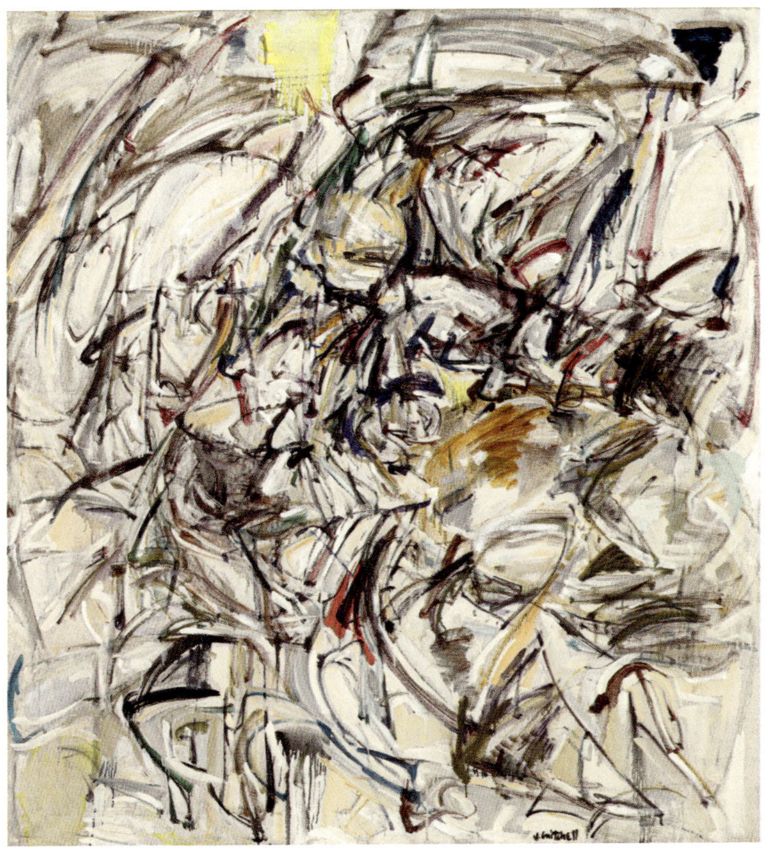

it clear. If I don't know, then it's not working. If it seems right
to me, then it has a meaning, but I can't tell you what meaning.
I can't be more specific than that. It works when it means
something, when I don't question it any more.'

Cy Twombly (1928–2011), of the same generation as Mitchell,
also showcased the liberated gesture, covering his canvas with
wildly calligraphic mark-making, discharges of barely controlled
energy. The manic scribbles in *Untitled* (1955) draw abstraction
towards the realm of graffiti, suggesting a link between
painting, different kinds of inscription, and the movements
of the hand and body. 'Paint is something that I use with my
hands and do all those tactile things,' Twombly explained,
emphasizing the basic processes involved, the importance of
materials and their properties, and knowing how to manipulate
them, rather than any specific goal or concept.

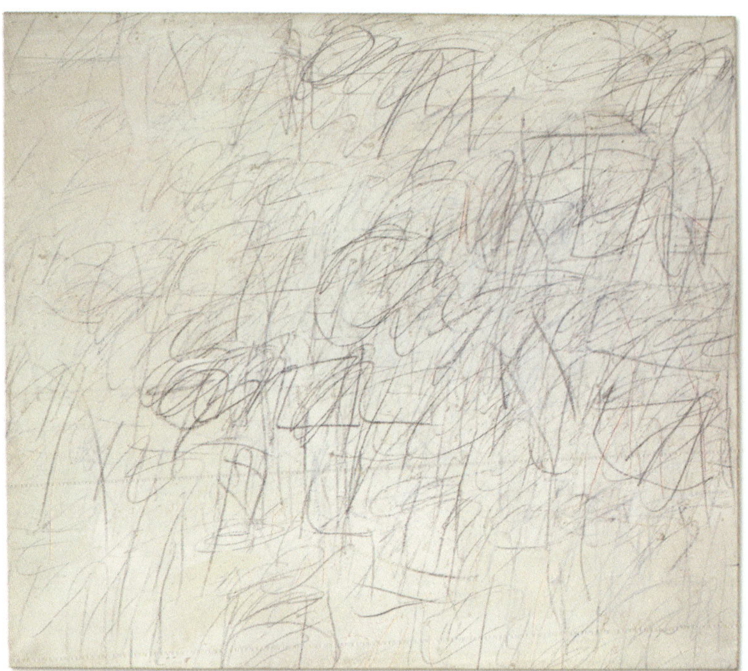

95 Cy Twombly, *Untitled*, 1955

In such works, painting has become a flat surface upon which an artist imposes the tell-tale signs of animated interaction, a surface that is important because it contains the traces of their performance. Like the artists of *art informel* in Europe, the Abstract Expressionists insisted that to perceive a painting as a *painting* rather than as an image, symbol, sign or cultural-historical document, the viewer needed above all to attend to its physical presence, not see it as a cipher of something absent. People do not stand or sit motionless at a fixed distance in front of a real painting. Rather, they will probably move into different viewing positions, and these unscripted movements (in the sense of not being predetermined according to a strictly formalized itinerary) allow them to gather valuable information about surface, colour, detail and mode of making, and to become emotionally affected in ways that go beyond the experience of painting as only a sign or representation. These dimensions were enhanced because the Americans' works were also on an imposing physical scale: Pollock's *Autumn Rhythm (Number 30)* is over five metres across. Such paintings suddenly made even the new expressive abstract paintings produced in Europe look tame by comparison.

'Colour Field Painting'

While the Abstract Expressionists discussed above were primarily interested in exploiting the dynamic properties of paint and in using the canvas surface as a receptacle for the accumulation of expressive gestures, others treated it as a fabric substrate for covering or staining with colour. This style became known as 'Colour Field Painting'. Morris Louis (1912–1962), for example, developed a staining technique by folding unstretched canvas and using the newly available water-based synthetic polymer paint called acrylic, which offered exciting new possibilities as it preserved the pigmented intensity of oil paint but made dilution more stable and quick-drying. Helen Frankenthaler (1928–2011) also adopted Pollock's procedure of laying unstretched canvas on the floor. To make *Mountains and Sea* (1952) she mixed oil colour with paint thinner, pouring and applying the fluid liquid onto the horizontal canvas to create delicate flowing and merging forms that, in an effect reminiscent of watercolour, she described as the 'soak-stain' technique. The title of this particular work indicates that landscape is alluded to, though more in the sense of mood or feeling than a description of the topography of a specific place, but thereby directing the viewer's interpretation of the picture beyond strictly formal or decorative properties.

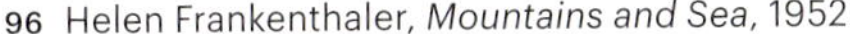

96 Helen Frankenthaler, *Mountains and Sea*, 1952

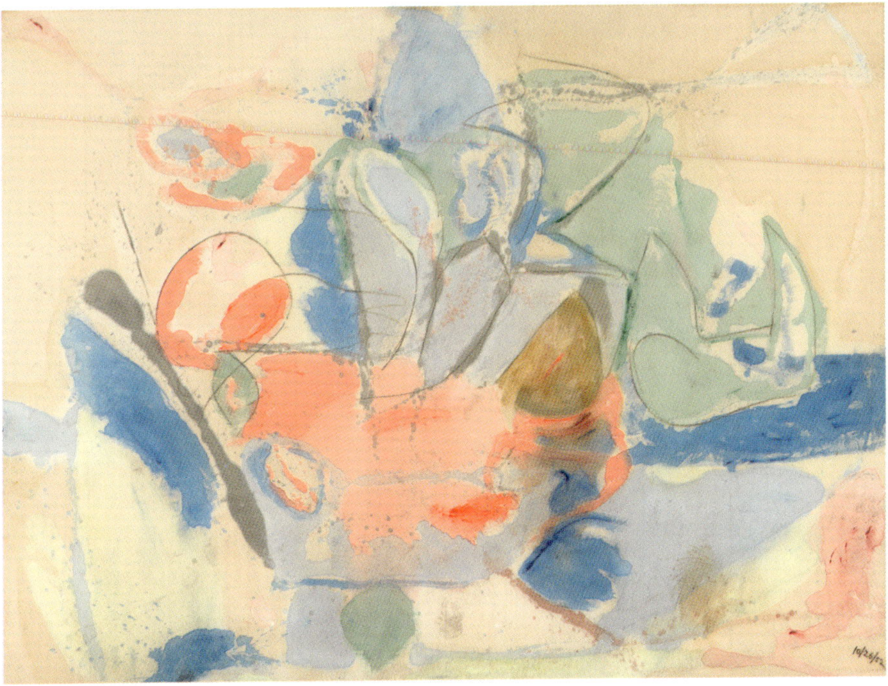

Mark Rothko (1903–1970), a Russian Jew who migrated to the United States (Portland, Oregon) when he was ten years old, developed a technique that emphasized the absorptive and emotional capacity of simple colour relations, stacking up fuzzy-edged coloured rectangles. Rothko was acutely aware that the minimalism or simplicity of his works made them dependent to a much greater extent than is usual on the viewer's willingness to engage with paintings that by conventional standards looked unfinished or uninteresting. He noted: 'A picture lives by companionship, expanding and quickening in the eyes of the sensitive observer. It dies by the same token.' Rothko also explained that the overt simplicity of his work was actually 'clarity' and that he desired 'the elimination of all obstacles between the painter and the idea, and between the idea and the observer. As examples of such obstacles, I give (among others) memory, history or geometry.... To achieve clarity is, inevitably, to be understood.' Many of Rothko's paintings involved delicate arrangements of different colours, but to those who considered that his work expressed his pleasure in aesthetic colour relations – like Matisse's art, for example – Rothko angrily replied: 'my paintings are intimate and intense, and are the opposite of what is decorative.' Indeed, he preferred to describe them as 'tragic' and 'sublime', in that he believed they were addressing fundamental human existential concerns, not just providing aesthetic pleasure. Here, too, the attitude of the viewer was crucial, for the sparce visual evidence of the works themselves made interpretation of their meaning intrinsically open-ended, obliging one to work to give it significance...or not.

The work of New York-born Jewish artist Barnett Newman (1905–1970) is still more challenging. Newman also invoked the sublime in discussing his paintings, even naming one vast work *Vir Heroicus Sublimis* (1950–51). Compared to Rothko's paintings, Newman's are far less 'expressive', in the sense that they lack the dynamic brushwork of Rothko's, which keeps his paintings within an interpretative field that might, for example, include the possibility that they are atmospheres or landscapes. Newman's paintings, by contrast, are comprised of large zones of colour laid on using a flat-ended house-painter's brush to produce areas of smooth untextured paint, divided by usually vertical lines marked off using masking-tape. These chromatic fields visually interact and resonate, and take on scale though the insertion of the vertical bands – which Newman called 'zips' – bisecting the canvas. Newman

97 OPPOSITE Mark Rothko, *Green and Maroon*, 1953

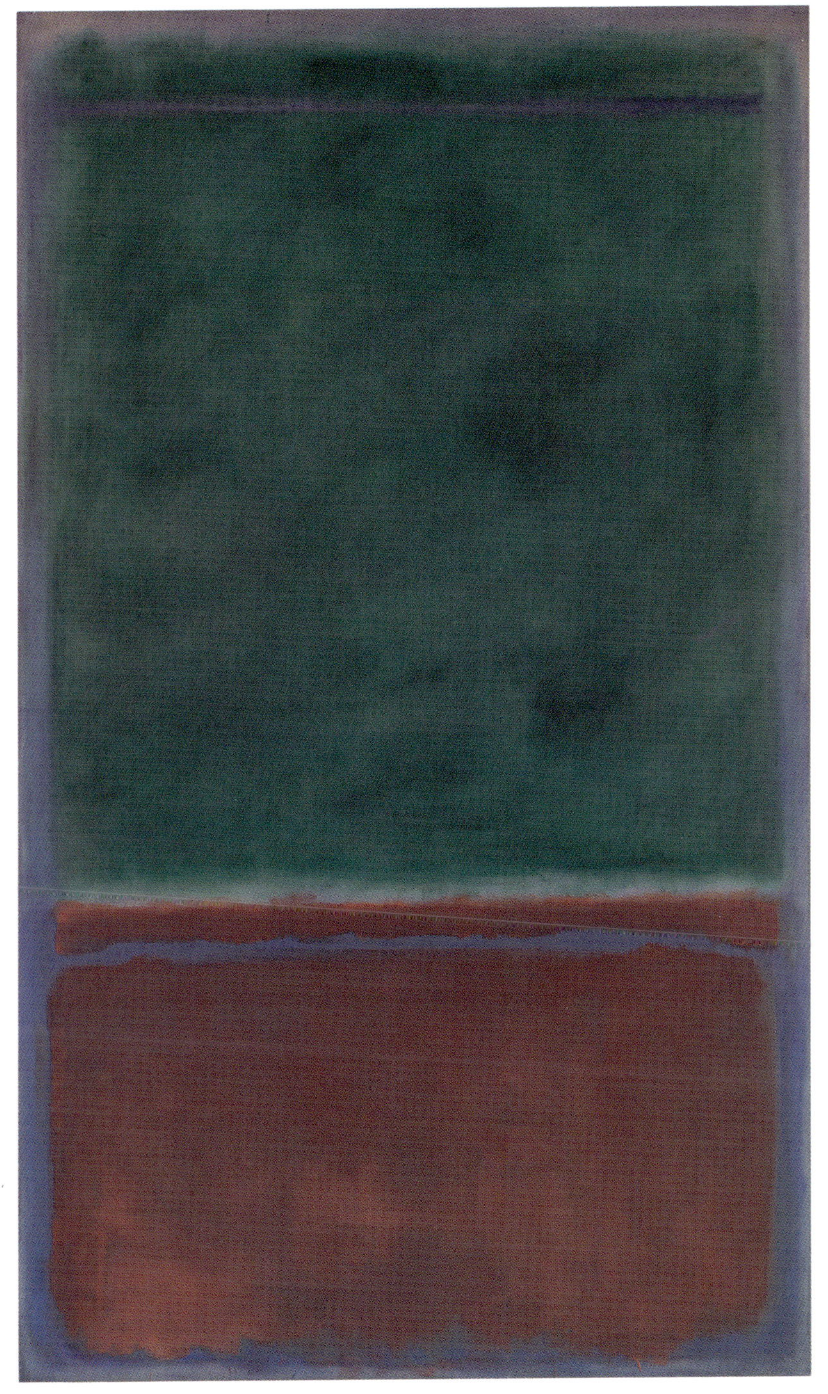

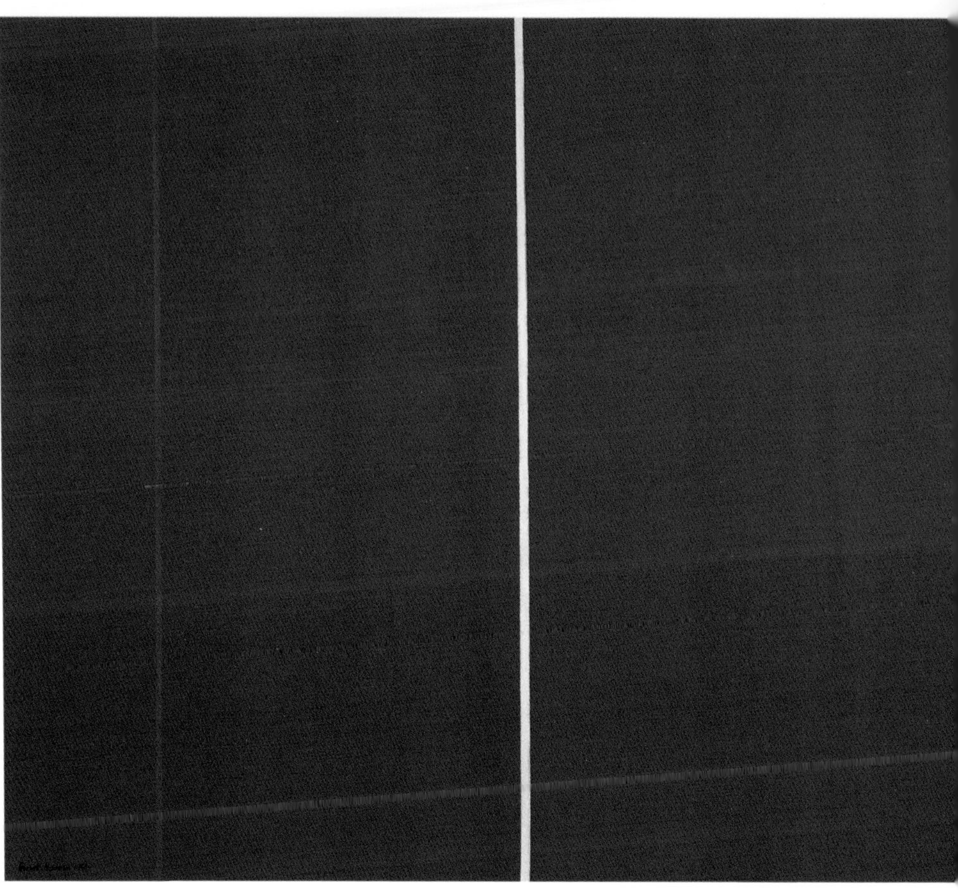

explained that his paintings were 'sublime' because they were pictorial equivalents to a primordial scene of creation, to the moment when something emerges from nothing. The lingering association with landscape that persists in the works of Rothko and other Abstract Expressionists, providing the viewer with some kind of link to more traditional art, is thereby more fully expunged; and the viewer is confronted emphatically by the actual presence of the painting as an experience in itself, shorn of all familiar points of reference. Like the other Abstract Expressionists, Newman was convinced that what he was doing had to be fundamentally distinguished from European art, declaring: 'I believe that here in America some of us, free from the weight of European culture, are finding the answer, by completely denying that art has any concern with the problem of beauty and where to find it.'

Abstract Art and Meaning

Critics in this period were split over how best to talk about
the new art. In America, Harold Rosenberg adopted a broadly
Existentialist approach, and it was him who dubbed the new
work 'Action Painting', arguing in 1952: 'The gesture on the
canvas was a gesture of liberation, from value – political,
esthetic, moral.' Henceforth, a painting was an 'arena in
which to act. Rather than a space in which to reproduce,
redesign, analyze, or "express" an object, actual or imagined,
what was to go on the canvas was not a picture but an event.'
Like Michel Tapié – the advocate of *art informel* – in Europe,
what Rosenberg recognized was that the new painting was
a practice of the present moment – that the artists assumed
that the 'real' or 'true' is what is experienceable *now*, free from
memory and tradition.

Another influential American critic, Clement Greenberg, agreed, but he had a more rational and methodical understanding of what was at stake. Greenberg perceived links with the School of Paris, but only because he believed Americans had succeeded where Europeans failed. The 'American-Type' painting, as Greenberg termed it, was above all concerned to fulfil the 'law of modernism' formulated in Europe: 'that the conventions not essential to the viability of a medium be discarded as soon as they are recognized.' Greenberg observed that the attention paid by the American painters to animating the surfaces of their works meant they were paring painting back to its unique, formal characteristic: flatness. All other uses and meanings of painting, averred Greenberg, were therefore failing to fully embody the zeitgeist. This 'formalist' reading, which Greenberg dubbed 'Modernist', propounded a reductive concept of the 'modern' in painting as an emphasis on its autonomy. Within the context of the mass technological society emerging in the post-war world, this idea was especially appealing and influential, as it suggested that some art was maintaining its cultural value through its refusal to be of obvious – and inevitably corrupt – social utility.

Meanwhile, other American critics, such as Dore Ashton and Robert Rosenblum, argued that both Rosenberg's and Greenberg's interpretations failed to take into consideration the obvious links between Abstract Expressionism and the deeper history of European painting, and most especially, with Romanticism. For Rothko and other American painters were making works of the 'abstract sublime', as Rosenblum termed it, and their close affinities with the paintings of the Hudson River School (discussed in Chapter One), for example, meant they had little in common with 'School of Paris' aestheticism and modernist formalism, nor were they quite so wholly liberated from the past. The views of such critics all converge, however, on the belief that avant-garde art functioned as the only truly authentic art in contrast to what Greenberg termed the 'kitsch' – commercialized and superficial art being produced for the masses. The avant-garde stood for resistance to the economic and political forces that were alienating the masses and draining modern life of value and meaning. So a commitment to abstraction in particular was interpreted as involving a process of deliberate distancing, a refusal and disdain for popular taste, and thereby successfully not producing artworks for the shallow bourgeois mentality and the marketplace.

There was a tendency to establish hard-and-fast ideological distinctions that aligned certain kinds of painting with clearly defined and intransigent positions that ignored the extent to which the lines between present and past art, and avant-garde and 'kitsch', were often blurred. Arch-Abstract Expressionist Willem de Kooning, for example, shocked his more dogmatic supporters when, between 1950 and 1953, he painted a series of works entitled *Woman* in which, amidst the frenetic flurry of paint, can be made out big-breasted and big-buttocked women sporting red lipstick – like movie stars of the period, but also simultaneously invoking such 'high art' references as the work of the Baroque painter Peter-Paul Rubens. But even if the more overtly abstract of Abstract Expressionist works drew attention to the material and visual dimensions of painting, their makers did not necessarily seek to close their art off wholly from reference to the world. As we have seen, several abstract artists titled their works to draw attention to landscape or environment. But the connection to some subject matter that took a painting well beyond its formal properties could also be more attenuated – more abstract. The series of paintings by another Abstract Expressionist, Robert Motherwell (1915–1991) entitled *Elegies to the Spanish Republic* (1948–67), for example, do not correspond to any recognizable image associated with the civil war in Spain (1936–39), the event that Motherwell intended his work to conjure up memories of as a powerful symbol of the struggle of the free and open society against tyranny. He described the wedged black pillars and lozenges silhouetted against light backgrounds that characterize the series as 'general metaphors of the contrast between life and death, and their interrelation'. Similarly, in Europe, Antoni Tàpies, who was working in Barcelona during the repressive rule of General Franco, emphasized abstract art's power to encourage political, social and personal transformation, declaring that for him abstract art's role was 'to promote reflection, reveal, attract attention, throw light on reality and, in brief, to exalt everything that makes us freer and more perfect as human beings'.

Yet by no means all avant-garde artists agreed with the capacity of abstract art to deliver profoundly transformational or culturally defiant messages. Those who remained committed to the depiction of the figure, however disrupted and distorted, were often implacably critical. In Britain, Francis Bacon noted in an interview: 'One of the reasons I don't like abstract painting, or why it doesn't interest me, is that I think painting is a duality [both an image of something and an aesthetic object], and that abstract painting is an entirely aesthetic thing. It always remains on one level. It is only really interesting in the beauty of its patterns or its shape.'

Post-War Globalization

In this period, modern western art in all its rich and unsettling variety began to be known far more widely across the world, at least within those nations beyond the control of communism, and became inextricably linked to the implementation and contesting of westernizing cultural politics and its programme of economic development. After the Second World War the many countries that had been colonized by European nations clamoured for independence, often resorting to armed rebellion in order to achieve freedom. Wars of independence broke out, for example against the French in Algeria and Indochina, while the British granted independence to India in 1947. These struggles were acted out within the wider context of the Cold War, in which the two hegemonic powers of the Soviet Union and the United States moved to assert their control over the newly independent nations. In 1949 China ended its civil war and the Chinese Communist Party assumed power. In 1950 war broke out in Korea after the peninsula was divided between rival Soviet- and American-backed states, and the Soviets and China moved to support the North, while an American-led United Nations force supported the South. At the same time, the rapid development of trade and mass communications during this period, brought real advances in science, technology, medical knowledge, educational standards and economic prosperity. In those regions open to American influence, this also meant the introduction to the Christian religion, democratic values and the quintessentially modern western ideal of individualism. But such contact also demanded subordination to the global aims and interests of the dominant superpower.

While it was still common for ambitious (and financially able) non-western artists to gravitate to Paris to study or live, increasingly their preference was for New York, the new capital of modern art. But, more and more frequently, non-western artists returned to their homeland after their studies, or indeed never left at all, recognizing that it was now necessary and possible to forge there their own interpretations of 'modern painting' without fear of being merely derivative or stranded at the inconsequential peripheral margins. A new generation of non-European and non-North American artists began exploring ways to both assimilate, emulate and, more significantly, contest the impact of western culture upon their own.

In the late 1930s there were a number of international recruits to Surrealism, such as the Chilean Roberto Matta (1911–2002), who spent the war years in New York and had an influence on the development of Abstract Expressionism. Another was the Cuban Wifredo Lam (1902–1982), who was

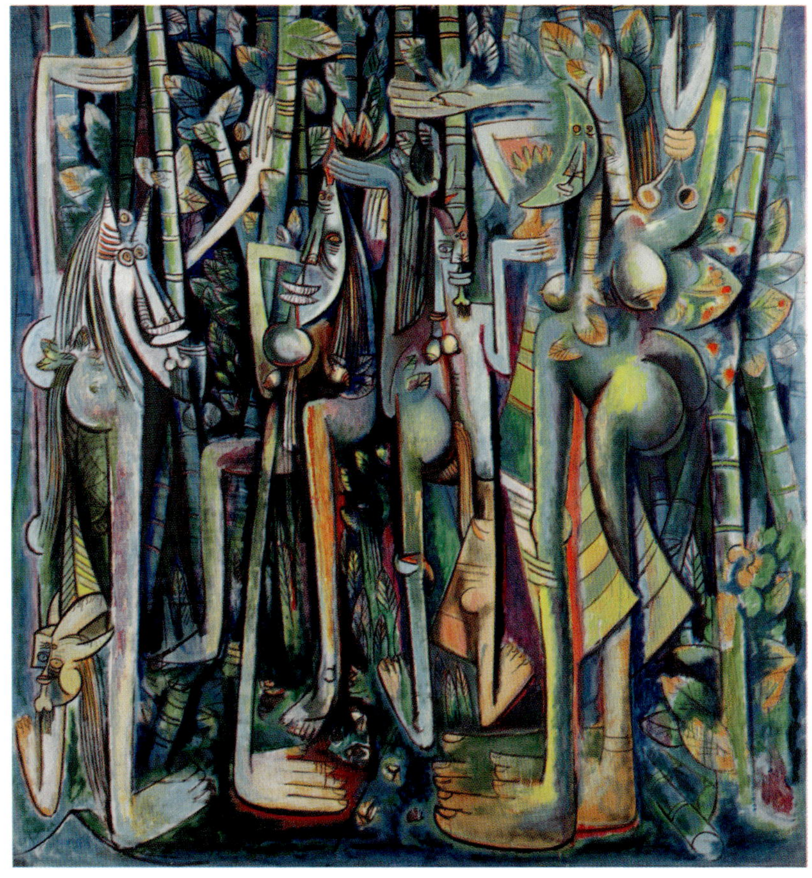

99 Wifredo Lam, *The Jungle*, 1943

of enslaved African descent. Lam moved to Paris in 1938 but returned to Cuba in 1943 due to the war and, in works like *The Jungle* (1943), adopted a style that fused elements drawn from his Afro-Cuban roots, such as tribal masks and voodoo symbols, with the distorted forms and fantastical imagery of European Surrealist aesthetics. Rather than producing a personalized 'dreamscape', Lam chose to evoke the era of slavery and colonialism in Cuba, which had only finally been abolished in 1886, paying homage to those working in the sugar cane plantations who were forcibly brought to Cuba by the Spanish as part of the Atlantic slave trade.

Some non-western artists embraced more formal styles of abstraction, finding within the geometric rigour pursued by westerners direct parallels with their own local traditions.

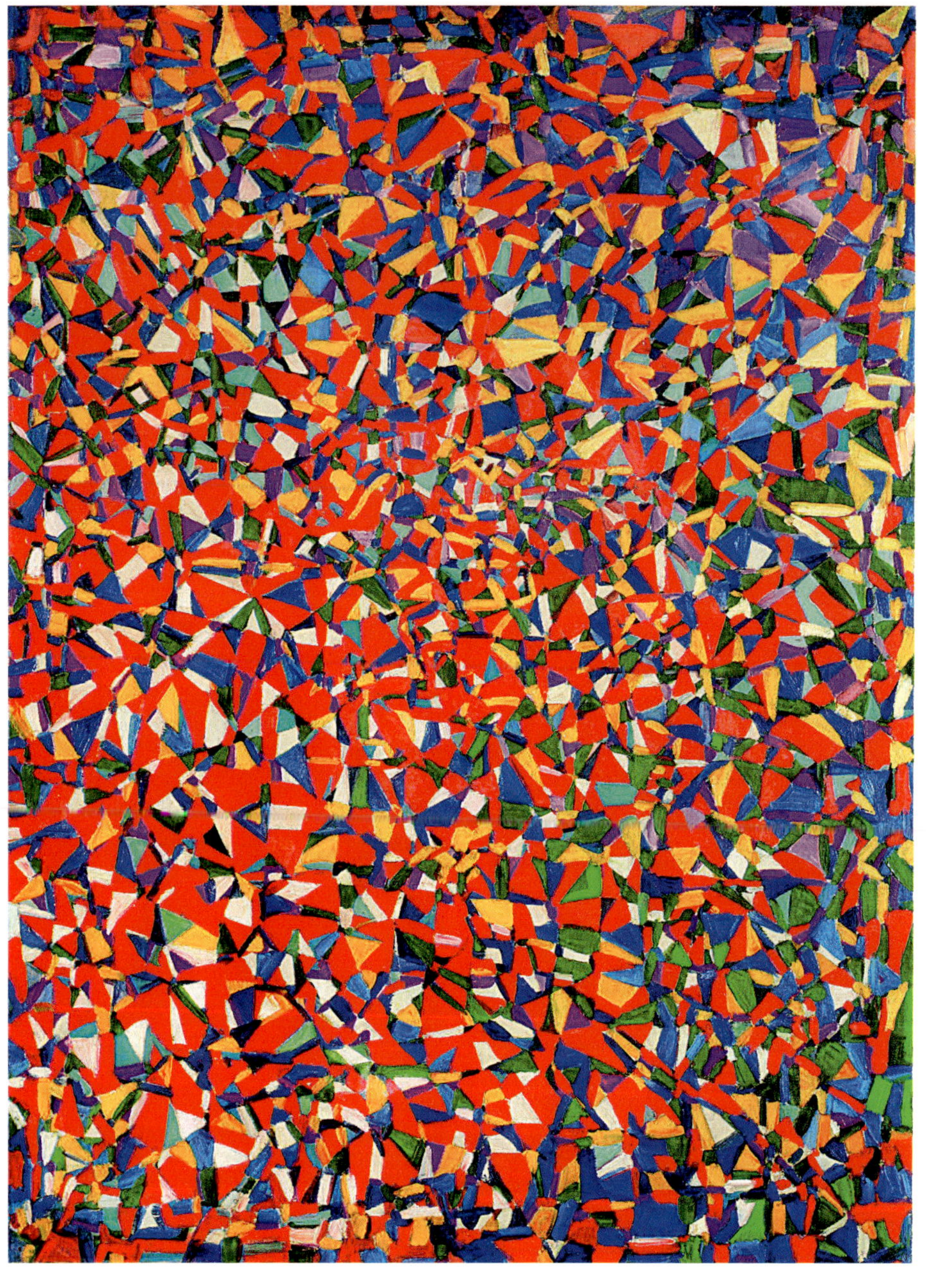

100 Fahrelnissa Zeid, *Resolved Problems*, 1948

The Turkish artist Fahrelnissa Zeid (1901–1991), for example, studied in Paris but returned to Istanbul in the 1930s, where she was instrumental in creating an avant-garde art scene. After the Second World War, Zeid relocated to London and Paris, before moving to Jordan for the rest of her life. In her work, she sought to blend western abstraction with local Byzantine, Islamic and Persian influences. Zeid's use of colour and geometry in *Resolved Problems* (1948), for example, draws on the traditions of the Near East, most notably Persian miniature painting and Islamic geometric design, and is a reminder that the formal principles that became important in western non-objective art or abstraction have long been central to traditional Near Eastern culture – in part because of the influence of Islam's prescriptions concerning the representation of the divine, which meant that as a result much Islamic art is inherently geometric in form and often uses elaborately designed calligraphy. Seen in this context, Zeid brought to geometric abstraction a much wider range of potential associations than those inherent in its initial western origins, and she also transformed the implications of geometric design within the society from which she came, creating a bridge to the democratic values of the west.

As noted in Chapter Five, Japan was the first East Asian nation to embrace westernization, and it would also be the first to nurture an influential home-grown avant-garde art movement, known as Gutai, which was active throughout the 1950s and early 1960s. Gutai included the artists Kazuo Shiraga, Saburo Murakami, Atsuko Tanaka and Toshio Yoshida, as well as the group's founder, the artist and curator Jiro Yoshihara, who between them engaged in painting, sculpture, printmaking, performance, installation and theatrical events. Kasuo Shiraga (1924–2008), for example, placed a canvas on the floor and suspended his body from a rope hung from the ceiling, and then, while swinging back and forth, applied dynamic brushstrokes to the surface of his canvases. Yoshihara urged artists to 'do what has never been done before', thereby demonstrating a basic allegiance to a fundamental principal of the western avant-garde: innovation. But Gutai artists were also dedicated to transforming western individualism and its cult of the 'new' by merging these values with what they saw as intrinsically Japanese features. The word 'Gutai' means 'concreteness' in Japanese, and as the name suggests, materiality and the spontaneous physical encounter were especially significant and, in part, were a reflection of the spirit of Japanese Zen Buddhism and its emphasis on escaping 'brain-centred' thought. A sense of openness and responsiveness to the 'immediate' was encouraged – the unstructured 'wildness' of direct empirical experience – as evidenced, for example, in *Sumi-e* (traditional calligraphy), a form of painting-writing in dynamic brushstrokes that was inspired by Zen.

But transcultural exchange was now happening dynamically in both directions, and several western artists in this period revitalized links between western painting and 'Oriental' art and culture. A new wave of influence from Japan swept over western art. Pierre Soulages, for example, visited Japan and met calligraphers skilled in the traditional practice of *Sumi-e*, which he felt echoed his own interest in painting as based on bodily rhythm. The critic and curator Michel Tapié travelled to Japan in 1958, and subsequently forged links between Gutai and European *art informel*, drawing attention to the converging interests of east and west – the shared commitment to a counter-cultural movement that challenged the dominant values of western capitalist society. Zen Buddhism proved an especially fruitful point of reference, a new reformative model which was understood to call for the suspension of analysis, to welcome indeterminacy and prioritize non-conceptual knowing. The influential Japanese philosopher D. T. Suzuki, resident in the United States, emphasized that Zen was fundamentally illogical, non-cognitive and irrational, and the spirit of Zen would be especially significant in forging visions of painting as the expression of radical openness and a direct experience of the here-and-now. The heightened interest shown by western artists in reduction and simplification, the concrete and the material, the mark, trait and gesture, as well as in the link between drawing and writing (graphism), were also to a significant degree the result of western exposure to Zen – which also impacted on the exploration of such themes as emptiness and nothingness, gesturalism and dynamism, seriality, and reflective and meditative practices.

Chapter 7
Pop Art to Conceptual Painting *c.* 1956–*c.* 1975

Neo-Dada and the Affichistes

In the mid-1950s the American Robert Rauschenberg (1925–2008) came to epitomize an important shift within painting through merging the conventions of abstract art with the imagery and symbols that abstract art had thrown out as culturally debased. He claimed to be working in the 'gap' between art and life. In the aptly entitled work *Collection* (1954/55), the first of what would become known as Rauschenberg's 'Combine' paintings, a bewildering mishmash of materials – fabric, metal, paper, wood – has been collaged onto the surface of three joined panels, while attached along the top of the canvas are bits of furniture. This was also a new kind of pictorial space, one that had first been explored in Cubist collage, what the art historian Leo Steinberg termed a 'receptor surface' that was inherently open and accepting of all kinds of visual sources. In this sense, Rauschenberg's work was symptomatic of a wider development in which artists increasingly treated the surface of a painting like a 'flatbed' that alluded to other flat, hard surfaces, such as 'tabletops, studio floors, charts, bulletin boards', as Steinberg wrote. These were surfaces for the inscription of diverse codes, not for the transcription of an illusion of three-dimensional depth or expressive arrangement of shape and colour. Rauschenberg said that, for him, 'anything was material' for art, and because of the irreverent pick-and-mix aesthetic that pervaded these new works, the term Neo-Dada was often used to describe them. This reference to an earlier art movement also signalled the emergence of Marcel Duchamp (who died in 1968) as an important influence on the new generation of artists. Duchamp said he developed his more conceptually oriented practice because he wanted to break free of what he termed 'retinal art' – art to do with naive seeing rather than thinking *and* seeing – to put art more solidly at the service of the trans-visual and the exploration of the mind's depths.

One of the reasons for this shift within art was the recognition that by the mid-1950s the older avant-garde's boast that it was inherently 'anti-bourgeois' and resistant to commodification and co-option by the status quo was being belied by three developments. Firstly, the new painting rapidly became a market success, with works by Jackson Pollock and the rest of the New York School selling for considerable sums to avid collectors. Secondly, it has since been revealed that Abstract Expressionism was covertly deployed by American 'Cold Warriors' as part of the cultural struggle against communism, and was actively promoted internationally by the CIA, who used it to represent the values of the 'American way of life'. After all, it is hard to imagine a greater difference in painting style than Pollock's all-over drip painting and a work of Socialist Realism depicting smiling factory workers or collective farm labourers. Thirdly, it was clear that the older generation of progressive abstractionist and figurative artists were failing to come to grips with the new, technology-driven, commercialized but vibrant mass culture that was emerging all around them.

For the avant-garde of the first half of the century had believed that they were pitting their work against hypocritical governments, arid conformity and the trivial media enjoyed by the masses. They looked on with disdain as a new kind of commercial popular culture consolidated around the new information and communication technologies such as newspapers, photographic magazines, cheap paperback fiction, advertising, radio and cinema, which were profiting from a literate populace with disposable incomes and leisure time. This mass culture, which intellectuals viewed as 'low art', 'lowbrow' or the 'culture industry' and Clement Greenberg dubbed 'kitsch', was believed to do little more than manipulate people's shallow desire for sentimental emotions and consumer products, and as such, the true avant-gardists believed their role was to decry and defy it on every level. Pablo Picasso belonged in a wholly different and elevated cultural space to Walt Disney.

But much deeper changes were also taking place. Up until the 1950s, western economies were based on a carbon-economy and industrial power geared towards overcoming material scarcity and austerity. Within this system, people's identity and social status were closely linked to the character of their

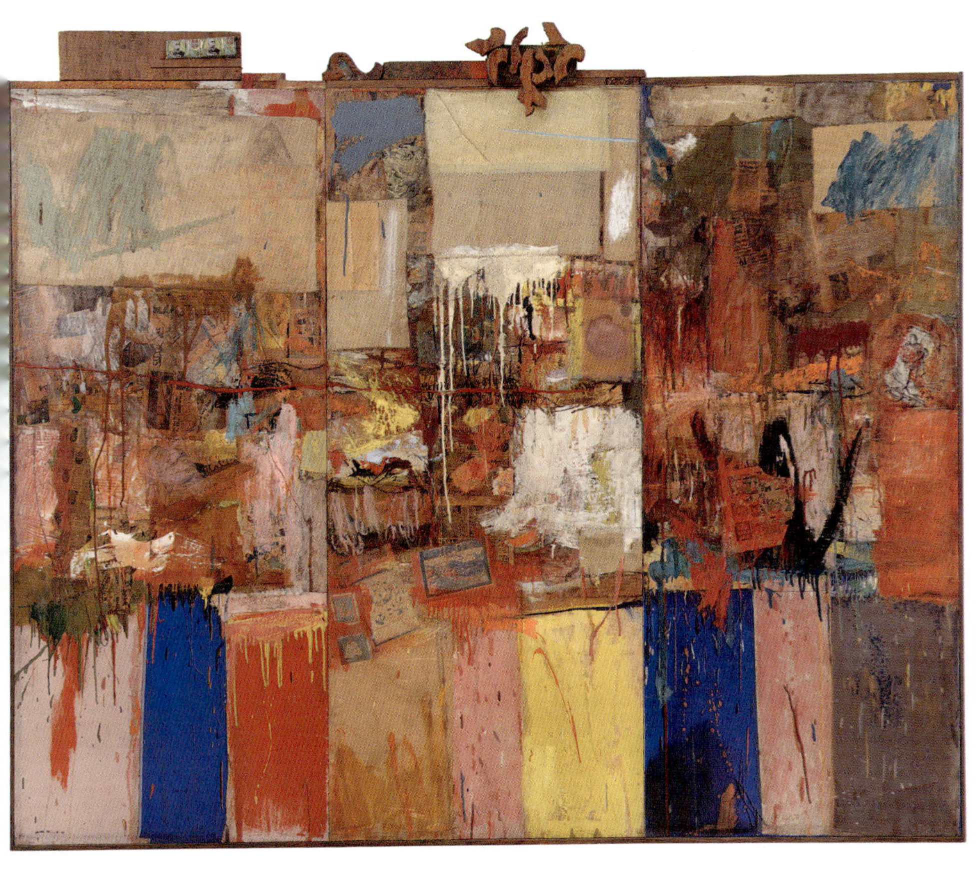

101 Robert Rauschenberg, *Collection*, 1954/55

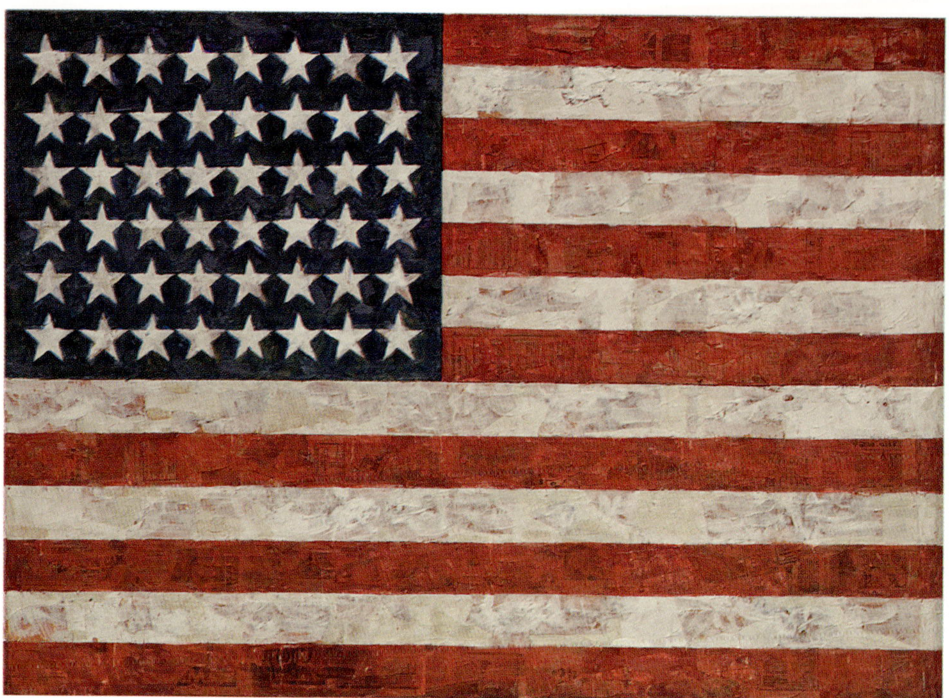

102 Jasper Johns, *Flag*, 1954–55

employment, and the traditional hierarchies of 'high' and
'low' culture persisted. But in the new phase that was now
beginning – which has been called 'The Great Acceleration' –
a capitalist society founded on apparent abundance was
rapidly emerging, which linked the economy to higher
standards of living, expendable incomes, the exploration
of identity, and achieving social status through consuming
goods and leisure activities. This new kind of consumerist
culture was also emerging at the height of the Cold War,
when the two rival powers of the United States and the Soviet
Union confronted each other armed with thermonuclear
warheads, and so the rapid development of this new affluent
society in the 'free world' threw into even starker contrast the
differences between those nations who adopted capitalist or
communist ideologies.

As a result, the 'elitist' assumption behind the idea of
a sacrosanct distinction between an 'authentic' 'high' and
'inauthentic' 'low' art was collapsing. The newer technological
mass media, especially television – which became
ubiquitous in the 1960s – undermined this hierarchy by:

'de-territorializing' images, wresting them from their relative positions within culture. On the common denominator surface of the screen, all manner of images could be brought together. It therefore seemed increasingly clear that the old hierarchies had to be abandoned and replaced by alternative ways of understanding culture. Progressive art had to proceed as part of a continuum of what the British critic Lawrence Alloway, writing in the late 1950s, termed 'the long front of culture', one that placed 'high' art in direct competition with 'low' popular culture.

In 1958 Rauschenberg's friend Jasper Johns (b. 1930) delivered an even more shocking challenge to the principles of the dominant avant-garde in the New York artworld when he exhibited *Flag* (1954–55) for the first time: a painting of an American flag made of collaged and thickly encrusted paint. Johns also painted other iconic signs – targets, maps, letters, numbers – and as a result, the every-day returned to avant-garde painting, embedding it in non-aesthetic, utilitarian sources. Although it was not his primary intention, Johns had also chosen a symbol with unavoidably political, jingoistic and patriotic connotations, thereby overtly bringing painting back into contact with these aspects of social life that were suppressed in abstract art. For Johns, as he explained, the point of painting a flag and other signs was that they were ready-made designs that can be easily measured and transferred, and as such, were a way of limiting what he saw as the arbitrary inventiveness or capriciousness of Abstract Expressionism. The image had returned, not as an expressionistic representation but as a prosaic sign, and one that shares basic formal properties with painting itself – flatness, rectilinearity, compositional organization. In fact, Johns's painting is more complex and layered than it seems in this illustrated reproduction. We cannot really see that it is not just a hand-made version of a famous icon and, like Rauschenberg's work, that the painted image covers up numerous printed fragments – advertisements, cartoons and news headlines which can read by the naked eye.

Pop Art

In Europe, there were similar tendencies away from the unbridled subjectivity and expressiveness of abstract art, but also from the angst-ridden deformations of post-war figurative art. A group calling themselves '*Affichistes*' ('poster-artists'), including Jacques Villeglé, Raymond Hains and Mimmo Rotella, also 'sullied' the pure and hallowed arena of abstraction by developing their own Dada-inspired

collage style, which they termed *décollage* ('unsticking').
They collected torn and defaced posters from billboards
around Paris and other cities and glued the ripped pieces
onto canvas or wooden supports, thereby removing themselves
from the direct activity of painting and appropriating
ready-made fragments that had accumulated by chance.
Like Johns and Rauschenberg, the *Affichistes* had not so
much rejected abstract art as allowed the sanctuary to be
invaded by the unruly public sphere of advertisements,
signs and political slogans.

'Popular (designed for a mass audience), Transient
(short-term solution), Expendable (easily forgotten), Low-
cost, Mass-produced, Young (aimed at youth), Witty, Sexy,
Gimmicky, Glamorous, Big-Business.' This was how the
British artist Richard Hamilton (1922–2011) described the new
Americanized popular 'admass' culture he observed evolving
around him in the mid-1950s. Hamilton's list describes more
or less everything the Existentialists (and the artists they
endorsed, figurative and abstract) and 'high-brow' critics
found culturally reprehensible. But Hamilton was doing no
more than acknowledging the fact that progressive artists
could not afford to ignore the abundance of communication
that characterized mass-media culture, or the impact of
technology on art. In his own paintings of the period,
Hamilton adopted the collage principle and married it
to a detached and ironic style that borrowed from advertising.
In *$he* (1958–61), for example, Hamilton explored the intimate
connection between modern ideas of female glamour
and the latest 'mod cons' – modern conveniences like the
refrigerator, vacuum cleaner and toaster that were then
being imported to Britain from America and revolutionizing
the domestic sphere.

The question Hamilton and other progressive artists
increasingly asked themselves in the late 1950s was what
purpose art could serve within this newly emergent consumer
culture. Should it continue to emphasize the individual's
struggle for self-expression in a world characterized by
the alienatingly banal and inauthentically commonplace?
Hamilton and others believed not. Rather, they envisaged
art as a tool in the hands of individuals who accepted the
inescapable conventionality of their vision, and who realized
they were wholly saturated in mass-media images, words and
sounds – as part of the 'long front of culture'.

Part of this transformation involved recognizing that the
United States was now not only guardian of this 'free world'
but also its banker and tastemaker, and it oversaw the birth

103

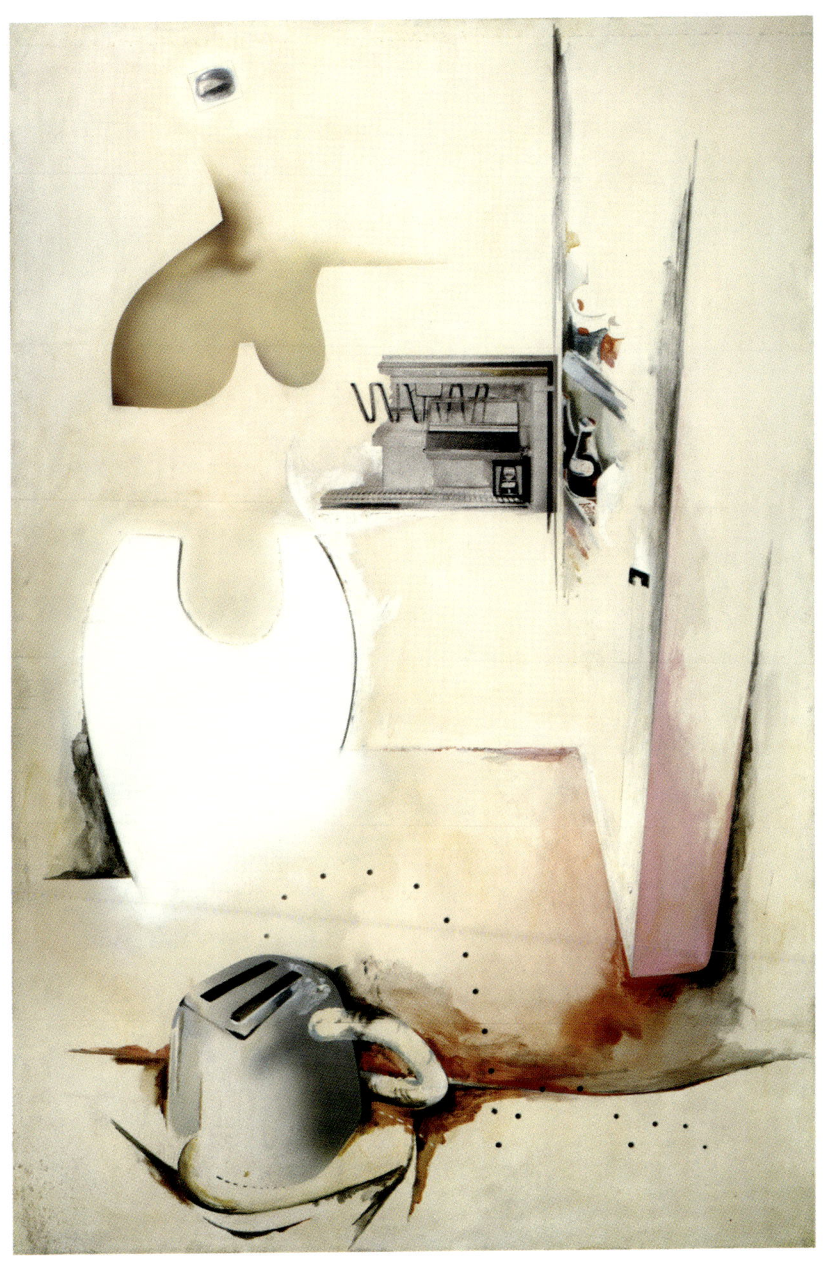

103 Richard Hamilton, *$he*, 1958–61

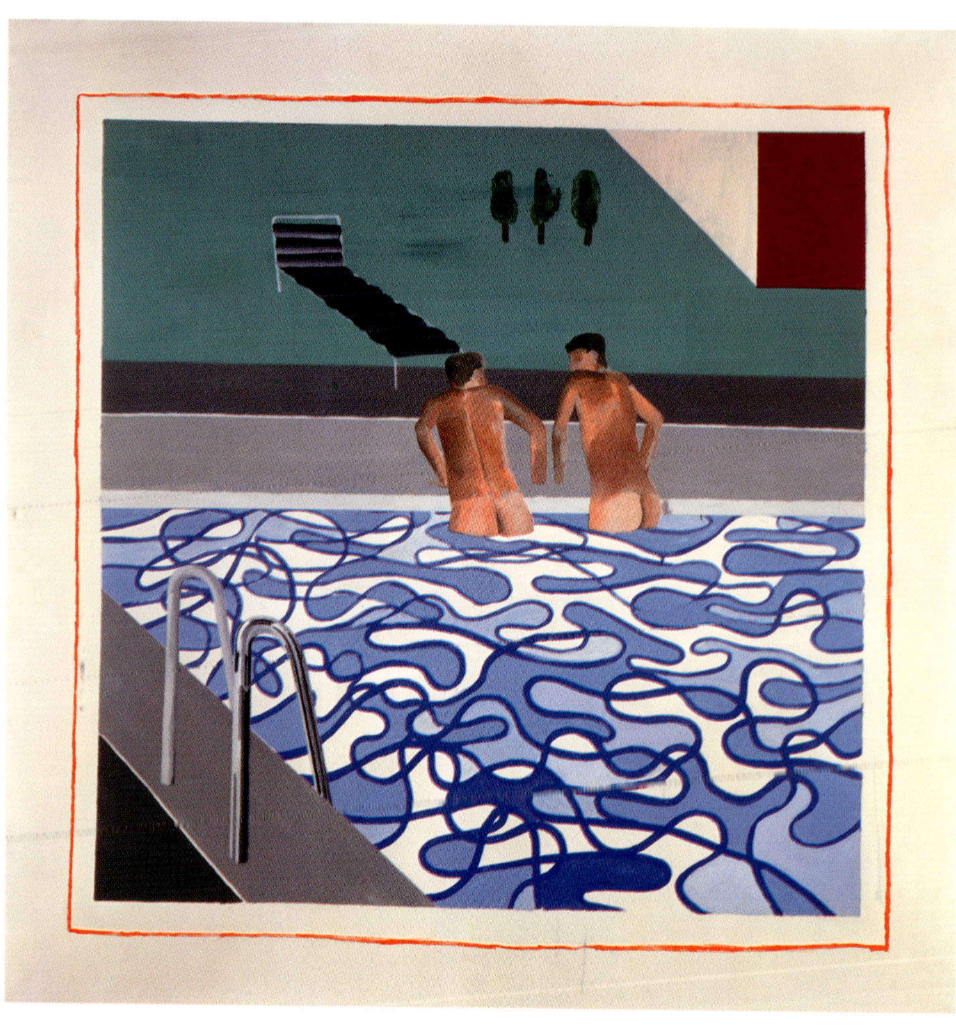

104 David Hockney, *Two Boys in a Pool, Hollywood*, 1965

of a consumer society that was increasingly reliant on the
mass media, such as television, to interpret the world. Because
of its historical ties and shared language with the United
States, Britain experienced Americanization much more
directly than the rest of Europe, and consequently became
a dynamic centre for the creative absorption of the new
consumer culture, forging a symbiotic relationship that is
most famously epitomized by the pop group the Beatles,
who adopted American rock'n'roll but created a unique
sound with massive appeal.

British artists of the same generation as the Beatles were
associated with what became known as Pop Art, amongst
them Peter Blake, Pauline Boty, Patrick Caulfield, David
Hockney, Allen Jones and Joe Tilson. Even more acutely aware
than the older Hamilton that the expressionistic and mass-
media deriding stance of post-war art failed to engage with
the lived realities of contemporary 'admass' culture, these
younger British artists therefore adopted a more open and
playful relationship to this new reality.

David Hockney (b. 1937) proved especially precocious
in engaging coolly and humorously with the glamour of
Americanized consumer culture. As a gay man, he was also
especially keen to celebrate the freedom from the oppressive
and backward-looking morality that still prevailed in 'Auntie
Britain', as he called it, and when he moved to southern
California Hockney's work became a eulogy to its hedonistic
lifestyle. In *Two Boys in a Pool, Hollywood* (1965) he struck a
decidedly contemporary note by blending photographically
derived homoerotic imagery, advertising design, abstract
decoration and flat fields of 'abstract art'-style colour. Note
that the space within the painting is not constructed using
the conventional western model of linear perspective, in
which orthogonal lines converge at a single vanishing-point.
Rather, Hockney used the alternative model common in East
Asian painting called 'axonometry', mentioned in Chapter
Two. As a result, the edges of the sun lounger in his painting
remain parallel.

Today, Hockney is one the most admired living artists.
Over more than fifty years he has practised his art in a variety
of styles and media in ways that the label 'Pop' artist fails to
adequately reveal, just as, indeed, labelling Picasso a 'Cubist'
also belies his protean output. Hockney is an influential
advocate of art as being fundamentally involved with the
history of image-making, but also with the exploration of the
complex interplay between convention and direct experience
within visual perception. But the playfulness, inventiveness

104

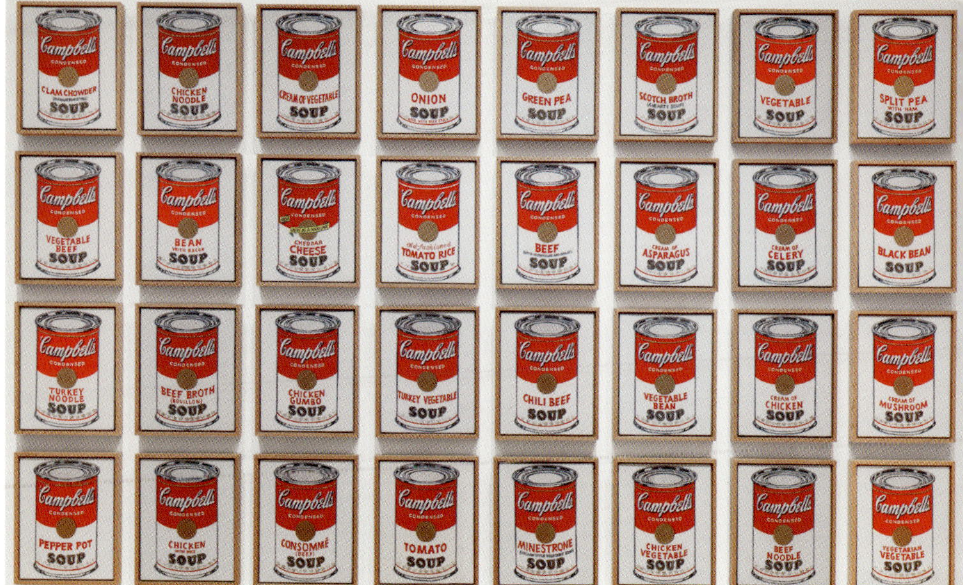

105 Andy Warhol, *Campbell Soup Cans*, 1962

and the accessibility of his art have guaranteed him a high level of popularity with a wide audience.

In New York in the early 1960s, a former commercial graphic designer named Andy Warhol (1928–1987) came to epitomize the new Pop Art aesthetic most fully, and he too subsequently went on to exert immense influence. Indeed, for some, Warhol is credited as being the definitive American, even *contemporary*, artist. Warhol began exhibiting works such as *Campbell Soup Cans* (1962) – at the time, such humble consumer products were certainly not considered worthy subjects for art. But Warhol argued that it was precisely the fact that they were an unextraordinary aspect of daily life, a humble and useful part of modern existence, that made them artistically significant. Furthermore, he adopted the silk-screening technique (which Robert Rauschenberg also began using around the same time), a low-tech method for mass producing images that distanced his working methods from the conventional physical process of making a painting, setting up a very different relationship to the activity from both traditional 'easel' painting and the more expressive gesturalism of the Abstract Expressionists. In *Campbell Soup Cans* Warhol produced a set of thirty-two individually silk-screened panels, one for each of the brand's soup flavours, and they were originally installed on shelves in the gallery, accentuating the relationship of art to commodity.

Warhol's style and technique deliberately courted the banal. He divested painting of the obvious signatures of expressive power and, in place of the artist as a creative hero, substituted the artist as cultural operator. This, in its turn, reflected the dominance within American society of technological and mechanical apparatuses in manufacture, transportation and entertainment. Warhol said in 1963: 'The reason I'm painting this way is that I want to be a machine, and I feel that whatever I do and do machine-like is what I want to do.' He proudly admitted he was 'a deeply superficial person', meaning to directly challenge the rhetoric of authenticity espoused by the Abstract Expressionists and offer a very different ideal for the artist's persona.

In addition to Warhol, other important American 'Pop' artists include Robert Indiana, Roy Lichtenstein, Claes Oldenburg, James Rosenquist and Ed Ruscha. In an interview, Roy Lichtenstein (1923–1997) said: 'Pop Art looks out into the world; it appears to accept its environment, which is not good or bad, but different – another state of mind.' In Lichtenstein's paintings the primary source was the 'lowly' visual art of the comic book, and he even simulated in oil and acrylic paint the Ben-Day dot printing technique employed in the originals. But importantly, Lichtenstein enlarged the original source many times, so it took on the proportions of a 'fine art' painting. His goal was to bring art down to earth, in order to revitalize it.

Out in California, Ed Ruscha (b. 1937) began exploring the brash landscape of commercialized words and images that were proliferating in the wake of the expansion of the advertising industry, especially focusing on the overtly visual dimension of the giant slogans to be seen on billboards that aimed to capture the attention of the hungry consumer as they drove by in their automobiles. Living near Hollywood, he was naturally drawn to the world of the movies, and in *Large Trademark with Eight Spotlights* (1962) employed the slick techniques of graphic design to render the iconic Twentieth Century Fox logo. The unusually elongated horizontal format of the painting also suggests a movie screen and, as such, explicitly indicates the latent affinity between painting and cinema, both in terms of their shared rectangular, flat format and their capacity to contain imagery or forms. Like Warhol and the other Pop artists, Ruscha – who became one of the most influential painters of the late twentieth and early twenty-first centuries – noted that he was interested in 'taking something that's not subject matter and making it subject matter'.

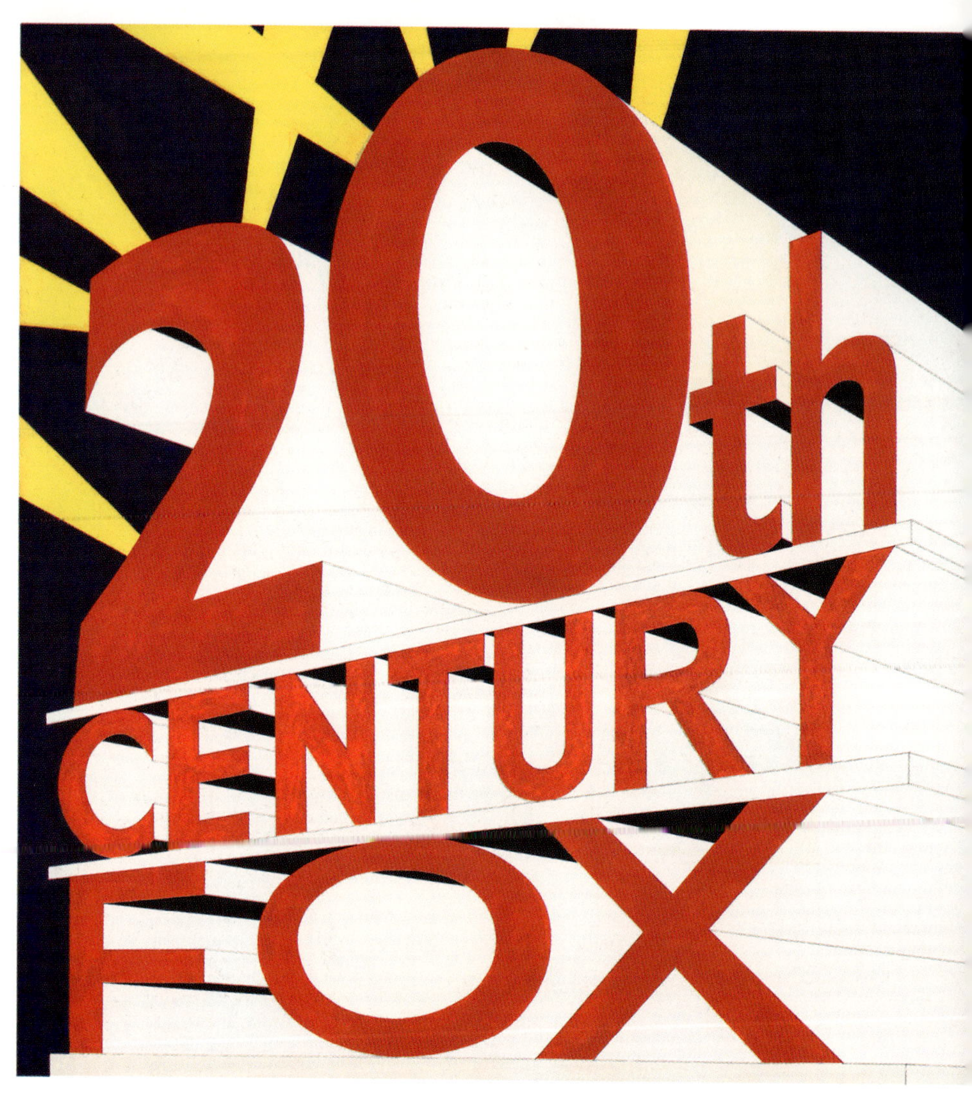

106 Ed Ruscha, *Large Trademark with Eight Spotlights*, 1962

The renewed interest in the image displayed by Pop Art, albeit now thoroughly mediated through technological apparatuses, was also evident in the short-lived trend known as Photorealism. As the term suggests, Photorealist painters, such as the Latvian-born American Vija Celmins and the Americans Chuck Close, Richard Estes and Audrey Flack, painstakingly duplicated in paint the look of photographs – often city views and automobiles – even to the degree that in reproduction it can be impossible to tell the difference. Between 1968 and 1970 Chuck Close (1940–2021) produced a series of large-scale black and white portraits of his friends and acquaintances in acrylic paint, based on eight by ten-inch photographs which he exponentially scaled-up onto gessoed canvas. *Phil* (1969) is a portrait of the American composer Philip Glass and, technically, the work conveys the same cool, slick air characteristic of Pop Art in general. Photorealism implicitly acknowledged the omnipresence of the photograph and its ability to convey what seems to be a direct trace of the real, while at the same time defying its dominance through a virtuoso display of technical painting skill.

The appropriation of photography was also central to the work of the German artist Gerhard Richter (b. 1932). Richter was born and studied in Communist East Germany, where he received training in the mandatory Socialist Realist style, but in 1961 he escaped to West Germany. Once there, Richter was struck by the unexpected parallels between the culture he left behind and the one he had now joined, noting that although under the yoke of communism art was overtly forced to conform to a political ideology, in the apparently 'free' world art was still subservient to mass popular culture and yoked to an ideology that celebrated material wealth and consumerism. He also observed that 'high' art – including avant-garde art – was increasingly becoming a luxury item or investment for the fashionable ruling elite. Richter therefore asked himself what the role of a truly independent artist could be under such conditions and answered the question with what he dubbed parodically 'Capitalist Realism', an ironic counterpoint to the style he had studied in the East Germany he had left behind.

Unlike the American Photorealists, the paintings Richter produced, such as *Uncle Rudi* (1965), are not meant to be realistic replicas of the photographic sources he selected, and instead are clearly made by hand in oil paint that has been blurred with a dry paintbrush, as if the artist had struggled and failed to produce a tangible record of the real subject. For Richter, it was the attempt to paint that was significant, the act of painting.

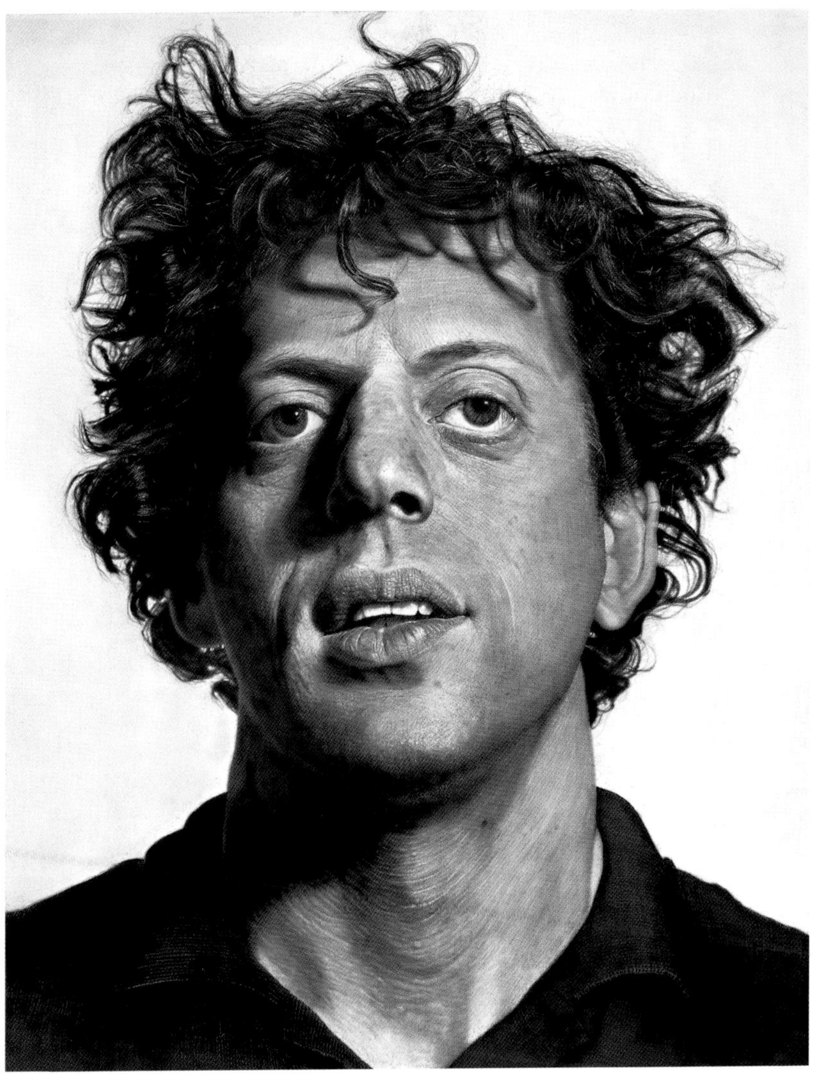

107 Chuck Close, *Phil*, 1969

Here, the result is an image haunted by death: Richter's source
was a family snapshot of his favourite uncle in the uniform
of the German army during the Second World War; Rudi was
killed in action soon after the photograph was taken. Although
Richter saw parallels between his work and Pop Art – and later
to Photorealism – unlike the mostly affirmative tone of British
and American art, he adopted an approach that is ultimately
more in line with the Existentialists' sense of social alienation.

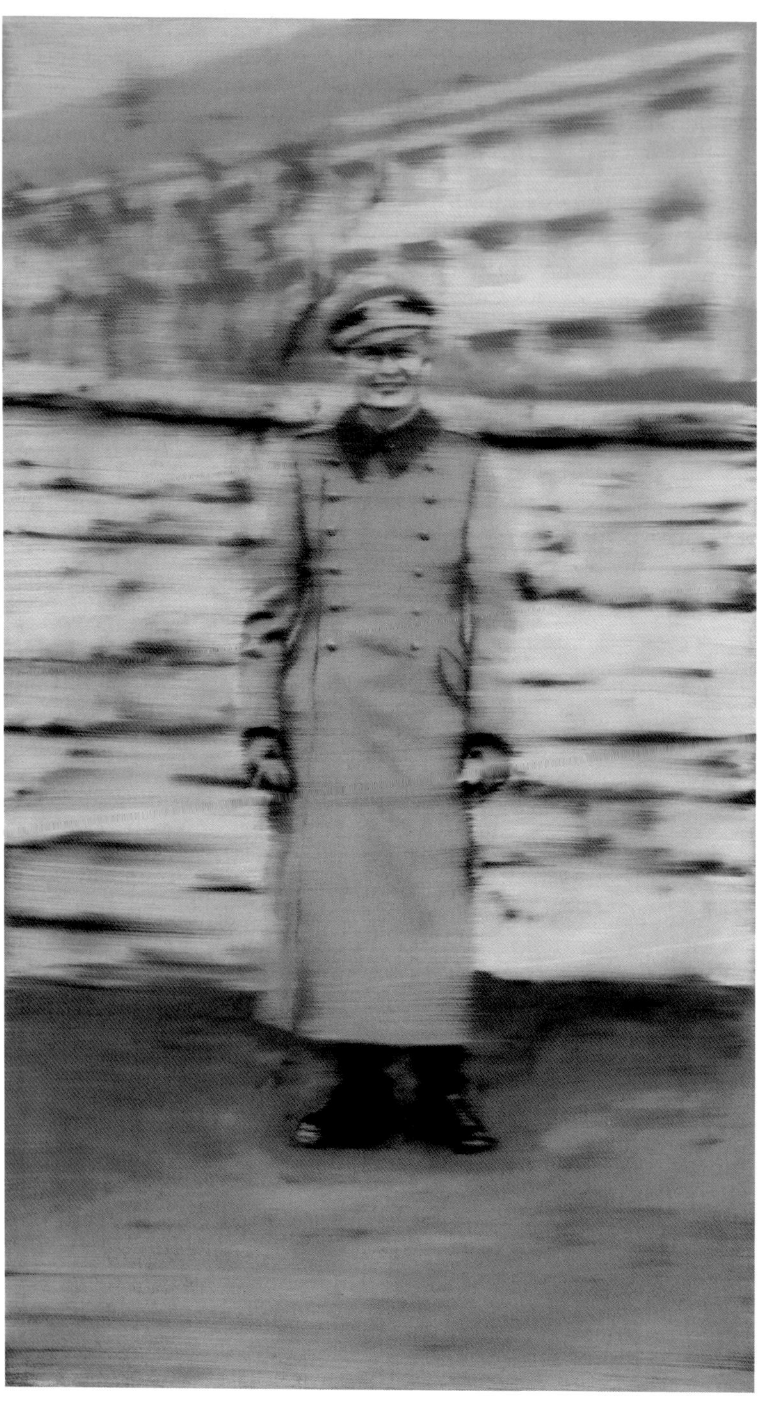

108 Gerhard Richter, *Uncle Rudi*, 1965

Minimalist Painting

Despite the emergence of Pop Art and Photorealism, the embrace of the 'long front of culture', and the confident reintroduction into art of the now highly mediated and commercialized image, this period was also one in which many radical artists continued a pre-war tendency by turning inward towards the resources of painting itself, which were judged to be independent of any external reference point and thereby relieved it from the risk of becoming merely illustrational or propagandist. During the 1960s there emerged alongside Pop Art forms of painting that were sometimes dubbed 'hard-edge'; these gravitated towards the overtly minimal, the reductive and exclusionary, towards what the critic Susan Sontag described at the time as an 'aesthetics of silence'. Out of the pre-war drive towards abstract purity and determined independence from the mass media, and in reaction against the overt expressiveness of post-war developments in abstraction, more austere forms of abstract painting developed in the work of such artists as the Americans Jo Baer, Ellsworth Kelly, Brice Marden, Robert Mangold, Agnes Martin, Kenneth Noland, Ad Reinhardt, Robert Ryman, Leon Polk Smith, Larry Poons, Frank Stella and the Cuban-American Carmen Herrera.

Ellsworth Kelly (1923–2015) was an especially important proponent of the direction in abstract art towards an anti-expressionistic exploration of colour and geometric form. The sharply contrasting colours in *Green Blue Red* (1963) are divided by hard-edged, linear boundaries, and the paint is applied smoothly and uniformly to avoid the tell-tale signs of the expressive gesture. Between 1948 and 1954 Kelly lived in Paris, which explains why his early development as an artist was largely free from the influence of New York and of Abstract Expressionism; but Kelly also rejected the dynamic brushwork of continental *art informel* in favour of the more detached qualities of pre-war geometric abstraction (see Chapter Five). Kelly advised that the viewer should not look beyond the four edges of the canvas for decisive points of reference, but rather experience the self-sufficient properties of the work itself. 'The painting is the subject rather than the subject, the painting,' he wrote. In other words, it was the shapes and colours of the painting itself, severed from any external reference point, that were the source of sufficient visual pleasure and meaning.

While some artists, like Kelly, explored pure painting as a realm of aesthetic pleasure, an 'oasis' within a world increasingly characterized by brash and alienating complexity and image-overload, others were more interested in making painting a space of resistance through negation and erasure.

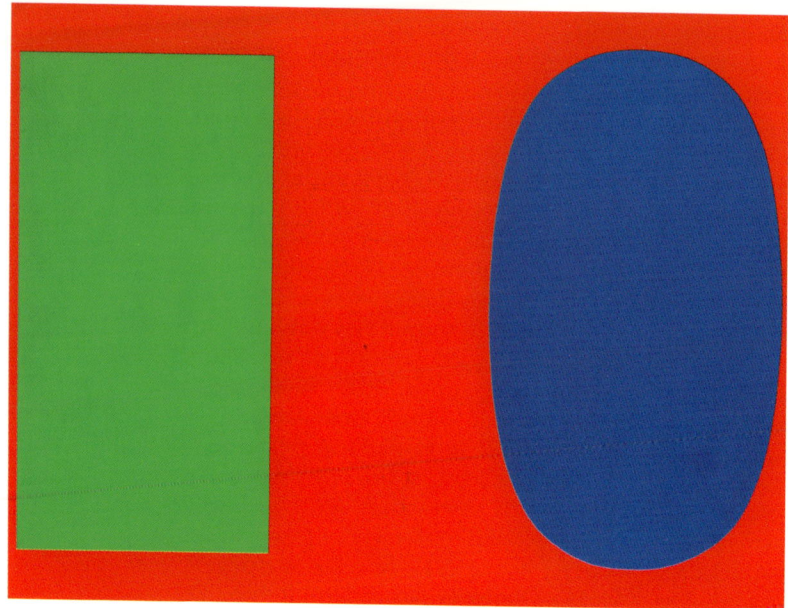

109 ABOVE Ellsworth Kelly, *Green Blue Red*, 1963
110 OPPOSITE Ad Reinhardt, *Abstract Painting*, 1962

110 In 1962 the American Ad Reinhardt (1913–1967), one of the most important and devoted practitioners of the more austere wing of the new geometric, hard-edged and often monochromatic Minimalism – one series of Reinhardt's paintings was comprised of grids of nine almost identical black coloured squares – announced uncompromisingly: 'The one object of fifty years of abstract art is to present art-as-art and as nothing else, to make it into the one thing it is only, separating and defining it more and more, making it purer and emptier, more absolute and more exclusive – non-objective, non-representational, non-figurative, non-imagist, non-expressionist, non-subjective.'

In this period monochrome painting became an especially important idea. A painting covered in a single colour may be *visually* simple, but can be *cognitively* very complicated. For some artists, a monochrome meant seeing painting as an object, while for others it took on the status of a spiritual icon. It may be physically flat but also potentially infinitely deep, empty of imagery but full of coloured paint. The many artists who have made monochrome art have claimed to be concerned with the experiences of emptiness, nothingness, absence, silence, spiritual and intellectual transcendence, immateriality, infinity, purity, origins, essences or iconoclastic destruction. But they could also be interested in more tangible and empirical things like autonomy, absoluteness, specificity, materiality, repetition and seriality. Through the monochrome, artists explored limits and limitlessness, the bounded and boundless, form and formlessness, being and nothingness, meaning and meaninglessness, hope and despair,

Frank Stella (b. 1936), for example, pushed the idea of monochromatic, hard-edged minimal painting in a pragmatic direction that was shorn of any metaphysical or psychological intentions. He adopted a deliberately anti-heroic, anti-spiritual and anti-individualistic stance to painting, embracing instead a mechanical, repetitious, predetermined and circumscribed methodology that at the time was more readily associated with the laboratory and the factory than the artist's studio. Indeed, the sober descriptions Stella gave of his methodology suggest the procedures of the technician bent on ensuring his machine functions optimally – anyone following instructions could do the same. The hand was reduced to the role of maintaining the smooth running of a mechanical process, and this was painting as a rationally imposed system that explicitly abandoned the metaphysics of Romantic expressionism.

In essence, what Stella was proposing was a new, more empirical definition of 'realism': painting was in itself the

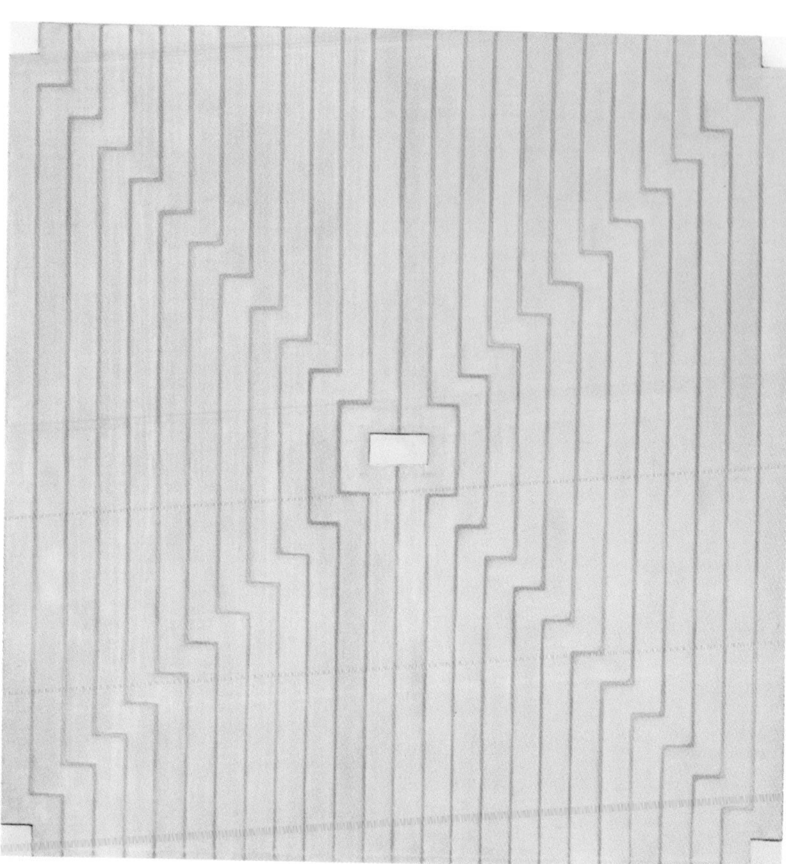

111 Frank Stella, *Avicenna*, 1960

real thing – stripped of illusion, and sufficiently interesting and culturally valuable as such. This was a radical idea. As Stella complained: 'I always get into arguments with people who want to retain the old values in painting – the humanistic values that they…find on the canvas. If you pin them down, they always end up asserting that there is something there besides the paint on the canvas. My painting is based on the fact that only what can be seen there *is* there….What you see is what you get.' The logic of Stella's thought led him to abandon the conventional rectangular format of painting, which he reasoned was a residual anachronism, a device intended to mimic a window. In the new 'realism' any shape could serve and, as a result, a viewer's inclination to see *into* a painting's surface, or to explore possible associations, would be resoundingly countered. Thus, in *Avicenna* (1960) grey aluminium paint sits obdurately on the

112 Robert Ryman, *Untitled*, 1969

surface, reflecting the light, and the four right-angled edges of
the traditional canvas are replaced by right-angled incisions,
while a rectangular hole has been inserted in the middle of the
canvas where customarily, in a representational work, we would
expect to see something significant.

Fellow American Robert Ryman (1930–2019) also explored
the implications of the monochrome as a robustly empirical
entity – painting as something physically 'real'. *Untitled* (1969)
was part of a series in which Ryman used only white paint
applied to different supports, such as canvas, card and, in this
case, fibreglass, attached directly to the wall while he worked;
the ochre-coloured marks at the top and bottom were caused
by the sticky tape used to hold the sheet in place. Ryman
argued in defence of his work that most so-called 'abstract'
art still referred to something outside itself. While in the

case of the old notion of 'realism', this fact was obvious – it
represented an image of a person, a landscape, a story from
mythology – Ryman's point was that even most 'abstract' art
drew on symbols and expressive associations to gain meaning.
He asserted that the more rigorous, new empirical 'realism'
he practised began from the premise that there was no point
any longer in making paintings that claimed to be about
something that wasn't actually *there*. For him, the purpose of
the artist in making a painting was to help the viewer to see
not what is absent but more acutely what *is* physically there
in front of them. 'With Realism the aesthetic is an outward
aesthetic instead of an inward aesthetic, since there is not a
picture, there's no story,' Ryman explained. 'And there's no
myth. And there's no illusion, above all. The lines are real, the
space is real, the surface is real, and there's interaction between
the painting and the wall plane unlike in abstraction and
representation.' Ryman's practice aimed to lead one to consider
aspects of painting that would otherwise go unnoticed.
Painting's 'reality' is now all on the surface. Recalling the
windscreen analogy introduced in Chapter Two, one could say
that attention is now being focused wholly on the glass screen
and not what lies beyond it.

Over in Europe, similarly reductive or minimalistic
tendencies were also much in evidence. Italian artist Piero
Manzoni, German artist Blinky Palermo and artists associated
with the 'Zero' group in Germany and beyond, such as Heinz
Mack, Otto Piene and Günter Uecker, pursued forms of painting
that emphasized the medium's capacity to be a self-sufficient
and stimulating visual experience – its status as an object
rather than an image.

In Britain, artists such as Robyn Denny, John Hoyland,
Bob Law and Bridget Riley developed strategies for reducing
painting to its constituent visual elements. Riley (b. 1931)
focused on painting as a source of extreme optical stimulation,
and her work became known as Op (or Optical) Art. This
was part of a wider tendency that also included such artists
as the Hungarian-French artist Victor Vasarely. Riley
believed a painting should deliver a visceral, physiologically
transformative impact, and a work like *Movement in Squares*
(1961) has the capacity to 'disturb', as Riley put it. She also
noted that her emphasis on painting as having a direct
impact on the senses of the viewer had affinities with other
developments in art occurring beyond painting, in particular
'Happenings' – impromptu actions involving the audience –
in other words, artforms in which the viewer was no longer a
passive observer.

113

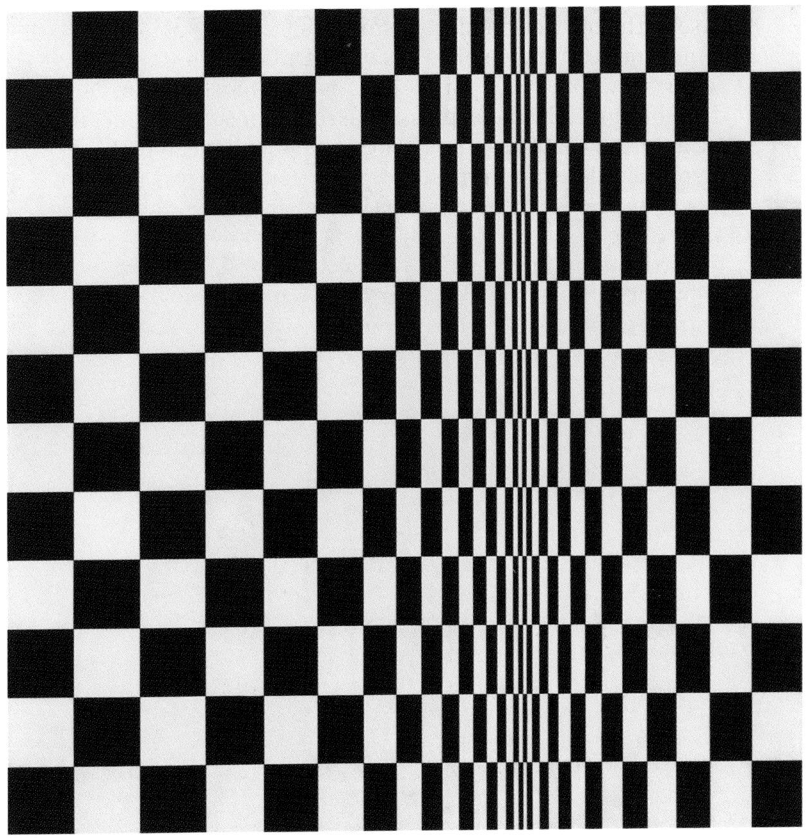

113 Bridget Riley, *Movement in Squares*, 1961

On both sides of the Atlantic artists were also seeking ways to break free of the constraints imposed by the convention of the stretched canvas hung on a wall, turning painting into an object rather than a surface for a representation. In Paris, the Hungarian-born artist Simon Hantaï (1922–2008) developed a technique in which he randomly folded fabric, which when unfurled served as the surfaces for his paintings, before being folded and knotted again. In this way, unpredictable compositional structures would emerge. In the late 1960s the French 'Support/Surface' group, which included the artists Louis Cane, Daniel Dezeuze and Claude Viallat, further systematically deconstructed what they saw as the constitutive elements of painting: the 'support' (the wooden stretcher holding the canvas) and the 'surface' (the canvas itself). They hung, draped, rolled and interlaced unstretched lengths of

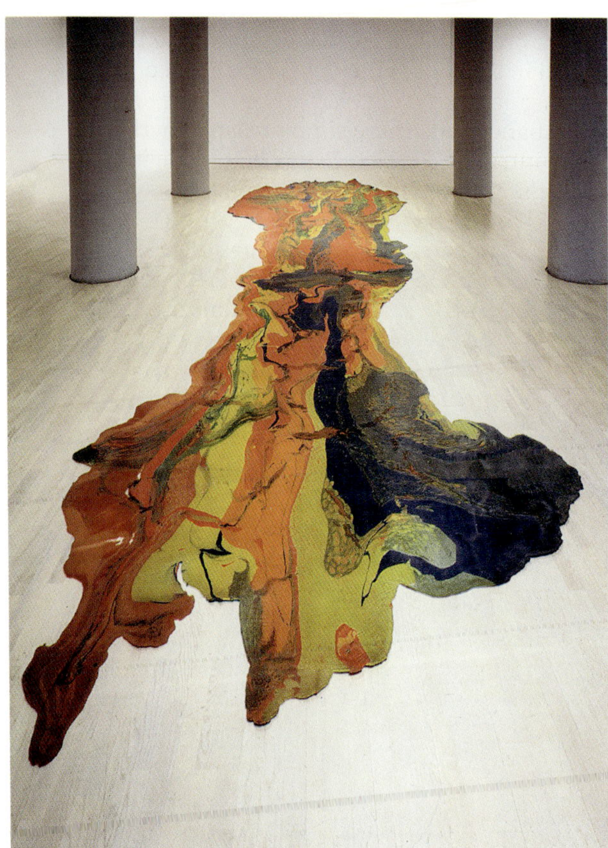

material, experimenting with what painting could be when
many of the assumptions about what it was were jettisoned.
In the United States, Sam Gilliam (1933–2022) also liberated
the canvas from its rigid support, draping and suspending
stained rolls of canvas from the ceiling and walls, while in
works like *Contraband* (1969), Lynda Benglis (b. 1941) went even
further, focusing on paint applied without the customary
support of either a textile or a wooden frame, pouring and
throwing buckets of pigmented liquid rubber latex directly
onto the floor. In part, Benglis was consciously taking Pollock's
dynamic 'action' painting style in another direction – literally
– by presenting the resulting work horizontally and unframed,
rather than stretching it on a rectangular frame and hanging
it on the wall. Calling her works 'poured' or 'fallen' paintings,
Benglis remarked: 'I realized that the idea of directing matter
logically was absurd. Matter can and will take its own form.'

But for some younger progressive artists it was painting itself
as a medium that stood in the way of the dynamic and free
evolution of art. Painting, it was argued, had reached a dead-
end and needed to be abandoned. There simply wasn't anything
left to do. But it was its intrinsic characteristics that made it
no longer relevant. 'The main thing wrong with painting is
that it is a rectangular plane placed against a wall,' wrote the
influential American artist and critic Donald Judd (1928–1994),
arguing that 'Actual space is intrinsically more powerful and
specific than paint on a flat surface. Three dimensions are
real space. That gets rid of the problem of illusionism and of
literal space, space in and around marks and colours – which is
riddance of one of the salient and most objectionable relics of
European art.' For Judd, therefore, as for several other artists,
the logical step must be to abandon painting in favour of more
tangible forms – what Judd termed 'specific objects'.

Abstract Painting in the Global Frame

In this period some western artists continued to explore non-
western cultural traditions in search of new possibilities. The
Canadian-American Agnes Martin (1912–2004) saw her highly
reductive, quasi-monochromatic paintings as being in line
with the aesthetic vision of Abstract Expressionists like Mark
Rothko, and claimed she wanted her work to be as detached

116 Yves Klein, *Untitled Blue Monochrome (IKB 47)*, 1956

as possible from the changing and unpredictable world so it
could evoke a benign and untroubled level of consciousness.
In one of the texts she wrote to supplement and contextualize
her paintings, she quoted the Chinese Taoist philosopher
Chuang Tzu's aim of 'free and easy wandering', adding: 'In
free and easy wandering there is only freshness and adventure.
It is really awareness of perfection within the mind.' When
Martin declared more generally that 'These paintings are about
freedom from the cares of this world', she was also implicitly
drawing on the wisdom of a worldview in which learning how to
achieve such detachment from 'the cares of the world' – to
be 'enlightened' in the eastern cultural sense – was a primary
goal. Her status as a woman artist seeking to forge a different

artistic identity to that of 'macho' male painters was surely one reason why she chose to emphasize not bravura paint-work and performance but the importance of self-effacement and 'humility' within her painting.

The Frenchman Yves Klein (1928–1962) lived in Japan between 1952 and 1953 (having gone there to continue his studies in judo), and his experiences led him to reduce his paintings to a monochromatic finish – he dubbed himself '*Yves le monochrome*' and talked about embarking on the 'monochrome adventure'. He commissioned a specially mixed blue acrylic colour which he applied uniformly with a house-painter's roller across the entire surface of a canvas. From a western point of view, as noted earlier, his work evolved from a reductive tendency that began life in the second decade of the twentieth century with the work of Malevich and fellow Russian Alexander Rodchenko, where monochromism signified the most minimal or most extreme possibility in painting (see Chapter Five).

Klein's interest in the monochrome derived from his study of Zen Buddhism, which emphasizes the importance of freeing oneself from the illusory world revealed by the senses – of 'cleansing the mirror' or clearing the mind – so as to come into contact with a deeper reality. The true essence of art, and the most important trait possessed by the artist, so Klein announced, was a wholly intangible 'pictorial sensibility'. In a lecture of 1959, he explained: 'What is sensibility? It is what exists beyond our being yet belongs to us always. Life itself does not belong to us. It is with our sensibility that we can purchase life. Sensibility is the currency of the universe, of space, of Nature. It allows us to purchase life in the first material state. Imagination is the vehicle of sensibility. Transported by imagination we attain life, life itself, which is absolute art.' In practice, this faith meant that, for Klein, it was possible to conceive of two visually identical paintings, only one of which possessed the vital invisible substance that made it truly art, a quality that only a sensitive viewer was able to distinguish. Ultimately, for Klein, the medium of painting was valuable only when it somehow materially marked the threshold at which art could take flight and be released from the fetters of the phenomenal world. 'My works are the ashes of my art,' he declared on more than one occasion, and in 1958 Klein staged an exhibition entitled 'Le Vide' (The Void), for which the Parisian Iris Clert Gallery was completely empty of objects. In this context, monochrome painting became the work of art in its most attenuated material form, pointing towards spiritual dematerialization.

As knowledge of and access to western progressive art
became more universally available in countries outside
Communist control and influence, styles of painting continued
to evolve in the hands of non-Euromerican artists drawn
to modern art as a symbol of westernization, progress,
liberalization and creative freedom. But they often also
recognized how the specificity of their local cultural, social and
political conditions inevitably meant that western painting's
value and meaning should be interpreted differently and
critically. As a result, many of the assumptions of western
artists were challenged, rejected and redirected towards other
goals, as non-western artists sought ways to bridge the gap
between the freedom that was afforded by the radical modern
art coming out of Europe and America and the realities of their
own local culture and social conditions. They used their art to
understand where and who they were in the present, and where
they and their society might be heading. They also believed
that as artists they could be instrumental in directing how
their societies evolved, in particular how they responded to
the impact of westernization.

117 Yayoi Kusama,
Infinity Nets (2), 1958

118 Kim Whanki, *10-VIII-70 #185*, 1970

In 1957 the Japanese artist Yayoi Kusama (b. 1929) left her homeland for the United States, moving to New York where she lived until 1973. Here, she began making what she called *Infinity Net* paintings, in which she covered the surfaces of her canvases with intricate meshes of repetitive monochromatic paint-marks. In *Infinity Nets (2)* (1958) Kusama spread off-white impastoed circles of paint over a dark ground, creating a reiterative all-over pattern that produces an effect reminiscent of a faded, roughly woven net. Kusama's personal psychological preoccupations (she suffered from mental psychosis, although she continues – at the time of writing – to work prolifically in a variety of media), and the influence of Japanese traditional culture, had the effect of transposing the conventions of western abstract painting into a form in which emptiness is experienced not as absence or lack but as plenitude of consciousness.

For the Korean artist Kim Whanki (1913–1974), initial encounters with western modern art had come via his country's then colonial master, Japan (Korea was colonized between 1910 and 1945). After the division of Korea in 1945 and the Korean War (1950–53), South Korea experienced a troubled period of military dictatorship, but also rapid westernization and modernization. The local artworld was small and constrained by political and economic limitations, so many artists sought to forge their careers abroad. Kim moved first to Paris, but while living in New York City developed a form of abstract painting characterized by an all-over covering of thin, repetitive smudges of paint that can be related to the kinds of minimalistic paintings discussed above, but that also possesses specifically personal and cultural aspects. Like Kusama's, the slow, measured and accumulative character of *10-VIII-70 #185* (1970) reflects Kim's interest in painting as an infinite space of restrained contemplation, a role he associated with an essentially East Asian tradition that was at odds with the more inherently extreme character of a western art dedicated to perpetual progress and the liberating values of post-religious modernity.

In Morocco, which gained independence from France and Spain in 1956, Mohamed Melehi (1936–2020) strove to reinterpret western geometric abstraction according to local cultural conditions in his homeland. After studies and travel in Europe, and residence in the United States, in 1964 Melehi returned to Morocco and became an influential teacher at the Casablanca Art School – which also included the artists Farid Belkahia and Mohammed Chabâa – seeking there to nurture a specifically Moroccan version of modernism, drawing, amongst other things, on indigenous architecture and Berber crafts. In relation to such works as *Pink Flame* (1972), Melehi observed: 'Hard-edge painting made me rediscover the abstraction inherent in Islamic art. Moroccan art was always hard-edged.'

In Brazil, artists associated with the *Neoconcretismo* (Neo-Concrete) movement pushed beyond the confines of the conventional painting format. Lygia Clark (1920–1988) emphasized that the defining properties of painting – its planar rectangularity and siting against a wall, and what Frank Stella termed its 'relational' composition – were fundamental obstacles in the way of making relevant art: 'before the artist situated himself in front of the rectangle, he projected himself onto it and in that projection, he filled the surface with transcendent meaning. To demolish the plane as the support for expression is to become aware of unity as an alive and organic whole.' In his 'Bilateral' series, another Brazilian, Hélio Oiticica (1937–1980), sought to actively engage the viewer through opening his work onto their surroundings by cutting the support into irregular shapes and hanging it in space away from the wall. In *Spatial Relief* (1960) differently oriented planes

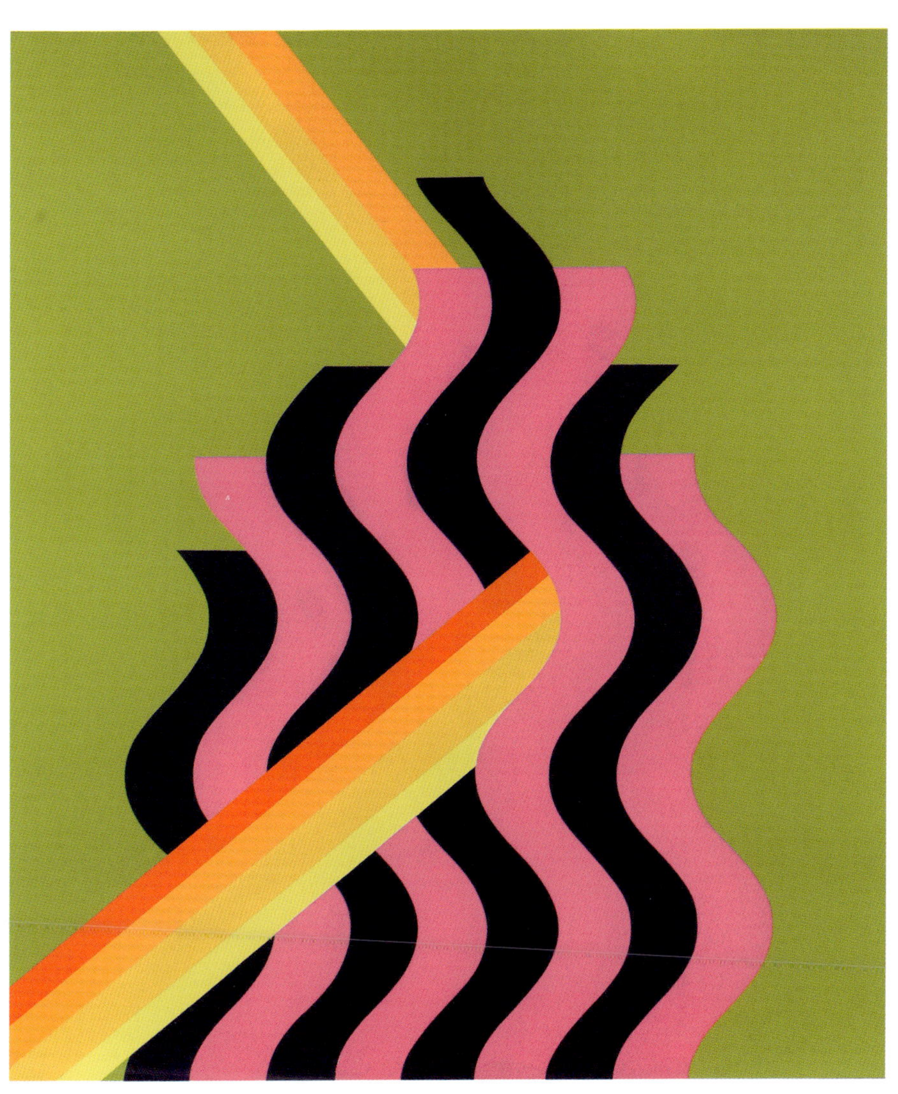

119 Mohamed Melehi, *Pink Flame*, 1972

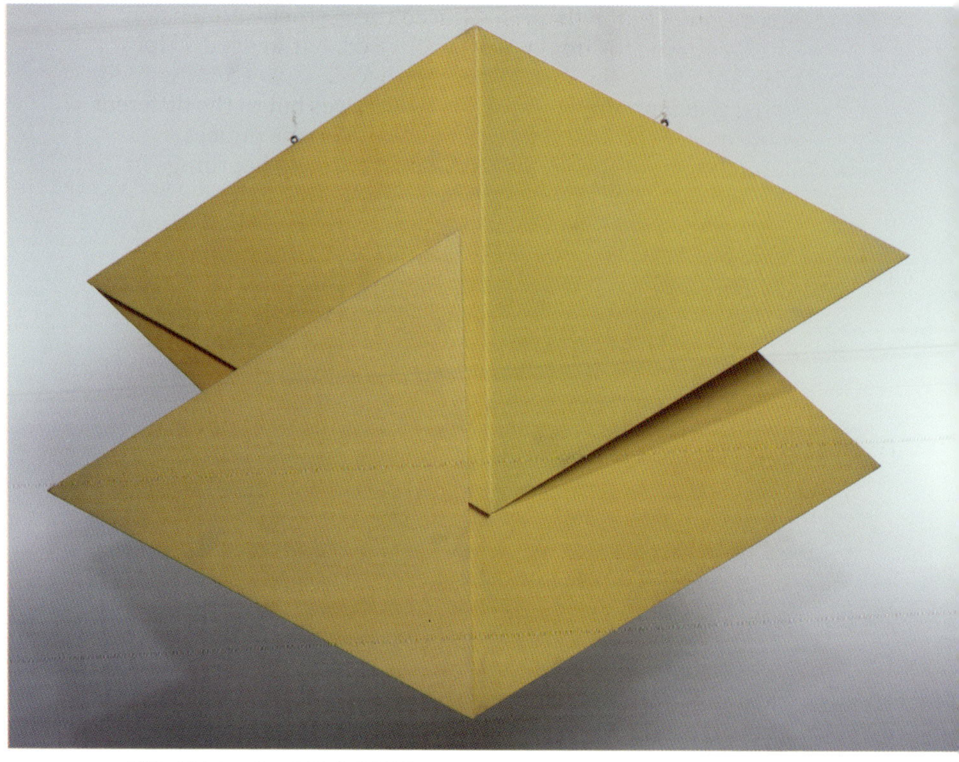

120 Hélio Oiticica, *Spatial Relief*, 1960

are suspended freely within space, thereby inviting the viewer
to interact more directly not only with the art object itself but
with the area around and within it. Oiticica spoke of such works
as creating a new sense of time in art – a 'sense of colour-time'
or 'time-structure', in which duration is extended through
engagement with the multiple facets of the work distributed in
space. Eventually, Oiticica's interest in 'time-structure' would
lead him to abandon painting in favour of what would later
become known as 'Installation Art': works that aim to animate
the spaces of the gallery through expanding the frame to
incorporate real space.

Conceptual Painting

In the 1960s the belief that painting as an aesthetic
experience – figurative or abstract – was inextricably tied to
outdated and socially and politically compromised ideas grew
increasingly influential. Pressure was especially exerted on
the conventions of painting by an aggressively anti-aesthetic
tendency that became known as Conceptual art. The French

artist Daniel Buren (b. 1938) reduced the aesthetic dimension of his painting to simple, single-coloured, hard-edged stripes with no symbolic or formal significance, to draw attention not to the visual nature of the works themselves but to the different contexts of their exhibition and display. For one project, Buren pasted his printed stripes on advertising hoardings in Paris Métro stations, while for *Hommes/Sandwichs* (1968) he appropriated the commercial format of the sandwich board poster, thereby inserting his works into the everyday world while also setting them in motion. Buren expanded the 'frame' of the work beyond the physical rectangle to incorporate the institutional and social 'frames' – the structures that enclose or surround – within which a painting is encountered, but that usually go unnoticed.

The new conceptually oriented art often focused on the written word, because texts automatically encourage a more intellectual and conscious engagement with the visible, literally making a work of art something to be read. The American John Baldessari (1931–2020), for example, detoured and parodied the ideal of making painting about painting, and the idea of the artist's unique and authentic 'touch', which was central to Abstract Expressionism, making these hallowed and in his opinion now hackneyed values ironically explicit by hiring a commercial sign painter to paint texts purloined from amateur

121 Photo Souvenir: Daniel Buren, *Hommes/Sandwichs, work in situ*, Paris (detail), April 1968

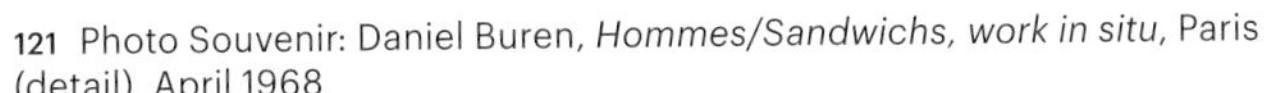

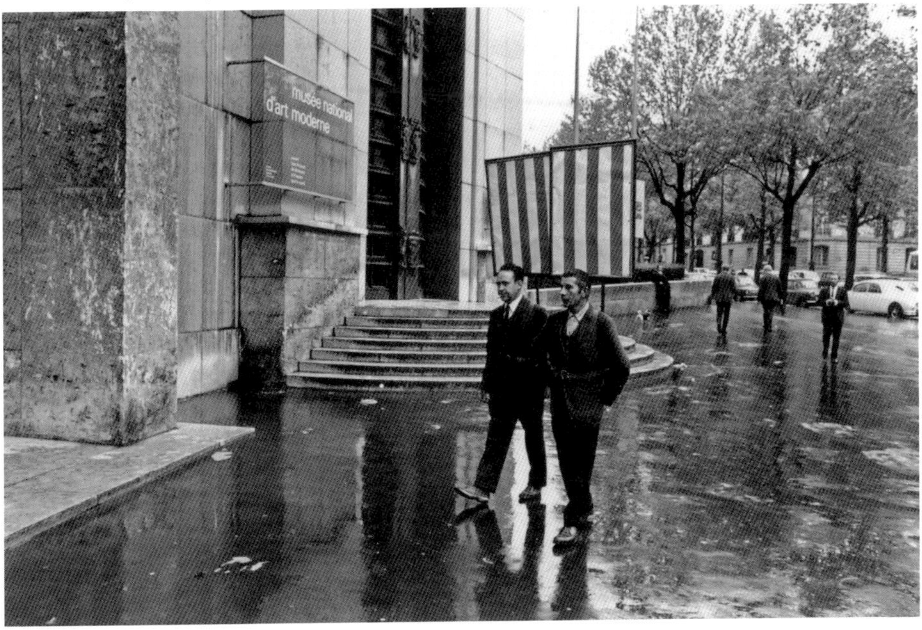

'how to' instructional manuals. One of these paintings from 1966–68 carried the following text in black on a white ground:

What is painting
Do you sense how all the parts of a good
Picture are involved with each other, not
Just placed side by side? Art is creation
For the eye and can only be hinted at with
Words.

The Anglo-American art collective Art & Language also placed words as carriers of explicit meaning at the centre of their multi-media practice, in order to expose what they saw as the spurious claims of abstract art. In *Secret Painting* (1967–68), by the British artist Mel Ramsden (b. 1944), who was part of Art & Language, a square black monochrome canvas is placed next to a framed text printed in black on white paper that reads: 'The content of this painting is invisible; the character and dimension of the content are to be kept permanently secret, known only to the artist.' Ironic reference was thereby made to the concept of monochrome painting specifically, but also to the whole Romantic tradition in which a painting becomes a vehicle for the spirit, the invisible and the mysterious, embodying an essence knowable only to the initiated – like Yves Klein's 'pictorial sensibility'.

Words could also be used to import the messy realities of contemporary geo-politics directly into the 'hallowed' space of minimalistic-style painting. In *Title* (1965) the America-based Japanese artist On Kawara (1932–2014) cited the then escalating conflict in Vietnam in a coolly detached and meditative manner that undermined attempts by Minimalist-inclined abstractionists to turn painting into a purified, quarantined aesthetic space. Kawara insinuates historical time (1965), war and politics (VIET-NAM) and verbal concepts central to current ideas about painting (ONE THING) into the pure world of the monochrome (the three red painted canvases).

Conceptually oriented painting shifted the focus of the medium to what is going on *in front* of a work. The traditional conventions associated with painting placed the content 'behind' it in the perceived world that is represented. The artists of the second half of the nineteenth and first half of the twentieth centuries challenged this convention by increasingly treating the content as what lay *on the surface* of a painting – in the material traces and visual properties of the work itself. But the new conceptual practices now shifted attention again to what was going on around the painting in the social

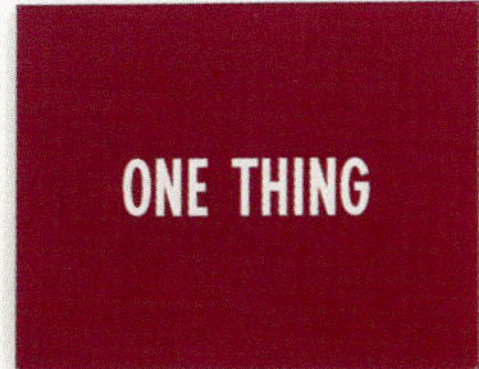
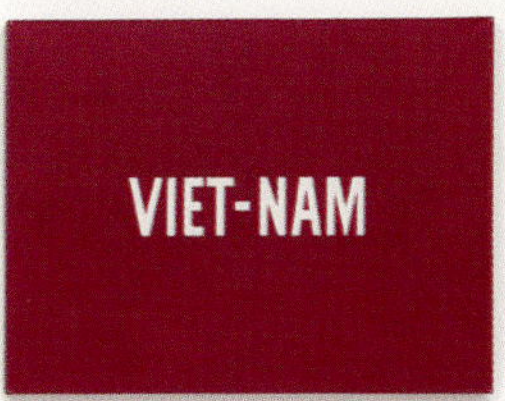

122 On Kawara, *Title*, 1965

world, amidst the institutions and interest groups involved in conditioning how a work of art was interpreted and valued.

By the mid-1970s, then, many avant-gardists had concluded that painting's long and illustrious history condemned it to necessary extinction. Painting was just an ornament of conspicuous consumption. It was complicit in perpetuating oppression, a 'patriarchal' and imperialist tool. Artists argued that the whole idea of the 'aesthetic' – issues of beauty and taste – with which painting was concerned, however novel and challenging, was essentially 'bourgeois', and stood in the way of critical engagement with society. Instead they advocated an 'anti-aesthetic' art.

Thanks to conceptually based art the idea became paramount that the material form taken by an artwork was now a secondary consideration; avant-garde art had progressed towards what one important American critic of the period, Lucy Lippard, termed the 'dematerialization of the art object'. Many artists considered the gallery space as constrained by convention and began making often temporary works out in nature. New media such as photography, video, installation and performance expanded the field of art far beyond painting. Henceforth, whatever style of painting was pursued now existed alongside art practices with which it likely had very little in common, and which, furthermore, seemed to render it hopelessly limited and old-fashioned.

Chapter 8
Postmodernism
c. 1975–*c.* 2000

Postmodernity

In a series of dislocated stencilled text-paintings, of which
Apocalypse Now (1988) is a typical example, the American artist
Christopher Wool (b. 1955) draws sardonic attention to the
fragility of conventional social values, to a culture unwilling
to acknowledge that it was teetering on the brink of disaster.
During the 1970s, the west transitioned to what became known
as 'postmodernity', the prefix indicating that advanced capitalist
society was exiting from the specific conditions associated with
'modernity', which in one way or another had informed the
work of the artists discussed up to this point. There was a shift
within advanced economies from the earlier model of production
rooted in heavy industry towards new means of production
and consumption, and new information and transportation
technologies. These changes had many positive repercussions –
richer, better educated, healthier and technologically empowered
societies where war, famine and disease were proportionately
much rarer than in any previous period. Thanks to the
globalization that was part of postmodernity, many non-western
nations were developing prosperous economies and democratic
institutions, and pursuing conciliatory foreign policies. But at
first, these transformations occurred within a polarized world in
which two hegemonic powers – the United States and the Soviet
Union – confronted each other armed with nuclear weapons. After
the dissolution of the Soviet Union in 1991 and the end of the
Cold War, however, the ideology of neoliberalism, with its avowed
celebration of democracy married to capitalism and a particular
ideal of material progress, emerged in apparent triumph. While

123

123 OPPOSITE Christopher Wool, *Apocalypse Now*, 1988

SELL THE
HOUSE S
ELL THE C
AR SELL
THE KIDS

the threat of thermonuclear war was still present, it now receded
into the background. In these ways, the ingredients were present
for what seemed like a new age of transnational prosperity.

But as social critics stressed – and Wool's painting coolly
suggests – such positive developments co-existed alongside other
worrying tendencies that reflected deep and troubling upheavals,
and that portended badly for the future. In particular, as the
political Left's dream of social revolution waned after the failure
of the protest movements of the late 1960s and early 1970s to bring
about radical change, and when the collapse of the Soviet Union
seemed to definitively signal the triumph of American-style
capitalism, it appeared there was now no exit from the 'iron cage'
of the reigning social system. It was also becoming increasingly
evident that the relentless developmental logic of this system
was causing profound and irreversible damage not just to the
fabric of the traditional societies with which it had contact but
also to the natural world upon which it relied for the fossil fuels

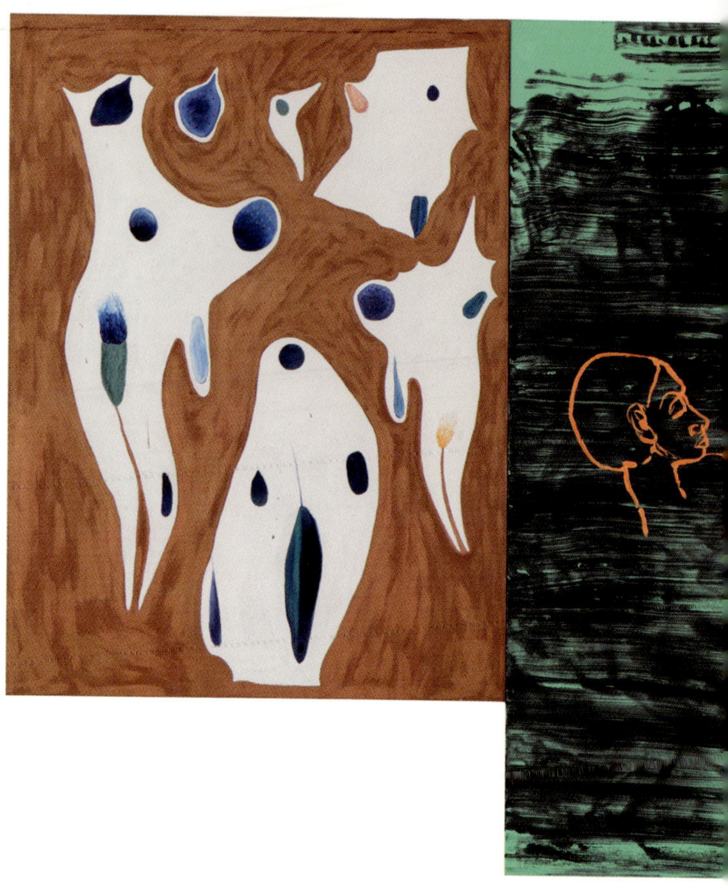

that sustained development. While the Civil Rights movement
in the United States, and the struggle to end racial prejudice
elsewhere, had had notable successes, it was obvious that racism
remained pervasive. The struggle for women's rights had also
been remarkably successful in reducing the inequities of the
'patriarchal', male-dominated social system, but here too it was
obvious that much still needed changing. Likewise, for minorities
such as the gay community, great strides had been made towards
removing legal and social obstacles, but these positive changes
only made the continuing injustices more difficult to accept.

Faith in the dynamic nature of modernity, in the equation of
progress with growth, was being replaced by the awareness that
resources were marshalled simply to maintain the status quo
rather than increase the freedom and equality of people. Thanks
to the mass media, most social relationships within developed

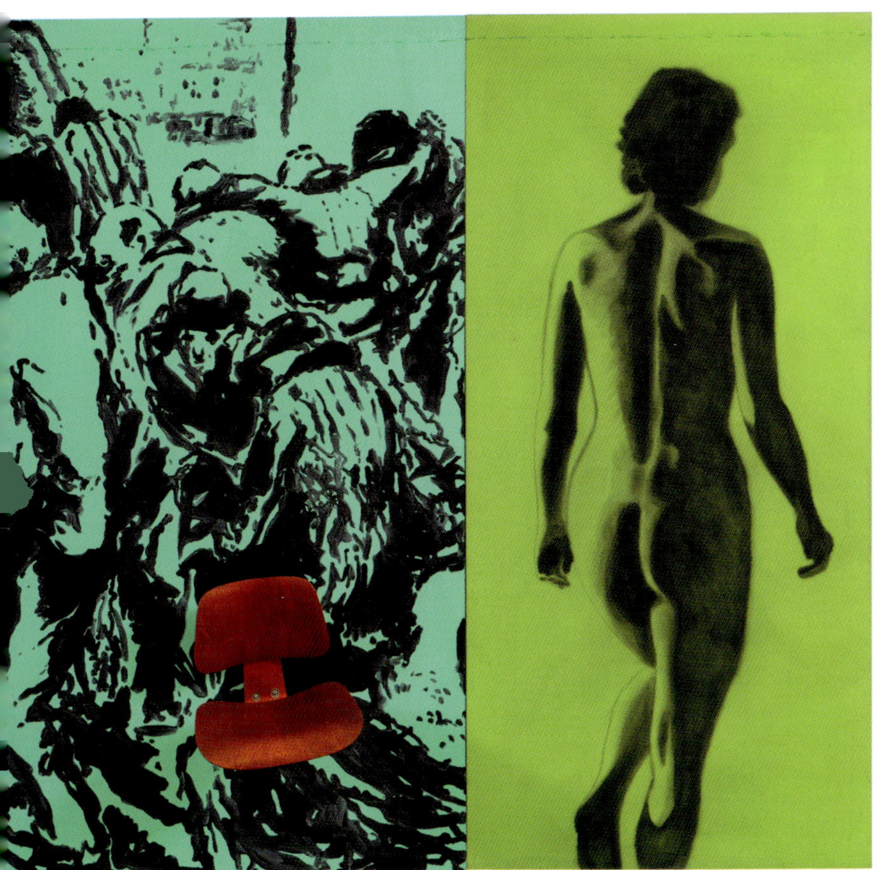

countries were increasingly being carried out via images, and
in this 'society of the spectacle', as the French philosopher
Guy Debord termed it, there was growing confusion between
material 'real life' and the false, represented one – the 'spectacle'
whose capacity for domination lay in the fact that it was aimed
at nothing other than itself. So, despite all the positive signs,
to many progressives western society meant blind domination
of nature by humanity, and the domination of the majority of
humanity by the powerful few, and the reduction of people to
mere consumers.

Postmodernism of 'Resistance' in the United States
David Salle's (b. 1952) *Poverty Is No Disgrace* (1982) responds to
these conditions by casting the 'postmodern' artist as a *curator*
of images rather than a *creator*, signalling the fact that the

medium of painting was now geared towards the appropriation
of the vast spectrum of readily available visual information – a
spectrum that, thanks to digitalization and the invention of the
Internet, would expand exponentially over the next two decades.
Salle described painting as 'dead', not in the sense that it was
finished, but because most of the values that once endowed it
with admired cultural status were withering away, and it was
precisely this situation that needed to be reflected within the
medium. Salle's relationship to his plethora of sources is parodic
– he imitates or appropriates the styles of others – and is suavely
detached and non-expressive. Note the plastic chair attached
to the central panel, which adds a glossy three-dimensional
consumer product to the colourful collage of media, styles and
images culled from 'high' and 'low' culture.

The avant-garde art of the 1980s and 1990s assumed that
establishing meaningful, resonant relationships to the world
within this capitalist society was virtually impossible. It was no
longer possible to use art to give form to the yearning for release
from social oppression, alienation and 'false consciousness'. It
was pointed out that as part of the production process central
to capitalism, the arts are inevitably implicated and participate
in the injustices of the social and economic divisions. Works of
modern art, especially paintings, were increasingly turning into
valuable commodities, and artists into commercialized 'brands'
with marketable identities. The arts now functioned in a culture
glutted with other attention-capturing visual media, most of
which were mass-produced and short-lived. Indeed, of all the
visual arts, painting was judged especially inadequate, as it was
too intrinsically aesthetic, bound to tradition and commodifiable.
Art as a cultural practice had become complicit in 'aestheticizing'
life, that is, turning the world into something to view passively,
keeping it at bay and thereby ensuring it had no claim on people
beyond aesthetic value. Art was as much a symptom or even a
cause of social problems as any kind of solution. It was part of
a culture that encouraged spectators rather than actors.

It was judged naive to believe art could be involved with
the expression of authentic feelings or address the ineffable,
and it was misleading to think in terms of genius, inspiration,
creativity, or any other transcendental or non-material, non-
socially determined quality that resided in the personality or
soul of a creator. As the influential American art critic and
historian Hal Foster wrote in the early 1980s, what was needed
was 'a resistant postmodernism', one 'concerned with a critical
deconstruction of tradition...with a critique of origins....it seeks
to question rather than exploit cultural codes, to explore rather
than conceal social and political affiliations.' This 'resistant'

postmodernism was inherently 'anti-aesthetic' – in the sense of not being about art as a source of visual pleasure or arousal – and emphasized instead that art must engage in rigorous critique of its institutions and of social norms.

In the event, this essentially pessimistic vision of culture as a prison-like social construct provided surprisingly firm foundations from which to launch a powerful critique of all systems of values (except those of 'resistant' postmodernism itself). Especially productive was the task of bringing the struggle against sexism and racism into the art arena, exposing the fact that the social role of women was not 'natural', that the concepts of 'gender' and 'patriarchy' are inbuilt and inherently repressive and unequal aspects of advanced capitalist society. In the United States, Barbara Kruger's (b. 1945) works were not made using conventional painting materials or even by hand, but they nevertheless deconstructed painting – and the culture that holds it sacred – from within, by exploiting the large-format and installation protocols of the artworld. Kruger also used text, employing the techniques of advertising in combining words and photographic images on an often large scale. She was especially influenced by feminism, believing that what passes for reality is a false consciousness imposed by the ruling phallocratic – male-centred – elite and drawing attention to the fact that in patriarchal social systems a woman's body is controlled, exploited and suppressed. 'My work has always been about power and control and bodies and money,' Kruger explained. 'Who is granting power? Who's withholding power? What are the systems of absence, presence, seen, unseen, heard, unheard?' One work from 1989 shows a woman's face split down the middle into a positive and negative photograph. Across the face is written the slogan 'Your body is a battleground.'

While text and the newer media such as photography, video and installation art, which were unburdened with painting's compromised attributes, continued to be adopted by the conceptually oriented, 'anti-aesthetic' postmodernists, at times, painting could also be co-opted as part of this art of 'resistance'. One possibility was, like Christopher Wool, to use text to undermine the aesthetic purity sought by modernist painting. Jessica Diamond (b. 1957) painted provocative texts directly on the wall. One says: 'EAT SUGAR SPEND MONEY'. In his 'Monochrome Joke' painting series, Richard Prince (b. 1949) 'polluted' the purity of the modernist monochrome by incorporating slogans that were decidedly 'kitsch': a two-panel blue monochrome from 1988 carries the following joke: 'I never had a penny to my name, so I changed my name.' Prince's art practice, which involves a wide variety of media of

which painting is only one component, also signalled a more general tendency – that began in earnest in the 1990s – away from medium specificity towards employing whatever medium seemed best suited to presenting an idea or concept. As Prince noted: 'the subject comes first, the medium second.' A painting in this context was an object whose meaning people inferred intellectually, not something that carried meanings that bypassed conscious inference.

Another option was to foreground the relationship between painting and the mass production of objects central to modern societies. Allan McCollum (b. 1944) produced a series entitled 'Surrogates' that consisted of variously sized casts of flat, black-

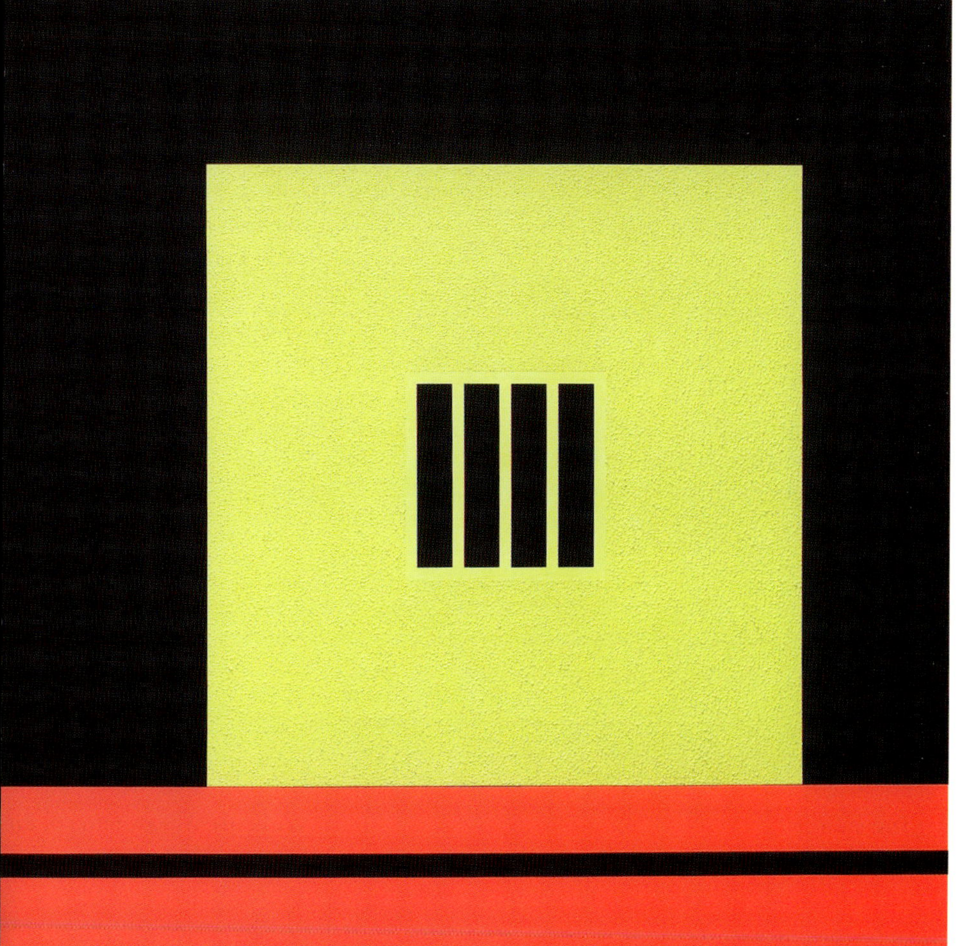

coloured and framed 'paintings'. As one critic put it, they were
'false pictures, pseudo-artifacts', painting as an empty sign of
a society dominated by the sameness of mass duplication and
production. In works like *Prison with Conduit* (1986), Peter Halley
(b. 1953) aimed to make a direct link between the language of
geometric abstraction and the reality of social confinement,
between the utopianism of modernist art and the exercise of
power under capitalism. 'Where once geometry provided a sign
of stability, order, and proportion, today it offers an array of
shifting signifiers and images of confinement and deterrence,'
Halley opined. New technologies, and particularly information
technology, were having a detrimental effect on human

consciousness. Citing the influential French theorist Jean Baudrillard, Halley declared that his work 'emphasizes the role of the model within the simulacrum....The simulacrum is a place "where the real is confused with the model"; it is a "total universe of the norm", a "digital space", a "luminous field of the code".'

Black artists born in the west and working in a predominantly white artworld were especially acutely aware of society's injustices, and many saw their role as to confront the hidden prejudices within art, so that what for white people were the unknown experiences of Black people could be incorporated. At first, *White #13* (1994) by Glenn Ligon (b. 1960) looks like a black monochrome painting, but it is in fact entirely made out of text drawn through letter stencils with an oil stick. The obliterated text came from an essay entitled 'White' by Richard Dyer about the representation of whiteness that questioned the relative visibility and invisibility of race within American culture.

'Resistant' postmodernists also sought to address the legacy of western colonialism, drawing attention to the fact that people assess the qualities of other cultures through the eyes of their own, and fail to recognize the true nature of the unfamiliar 'other'. The 'universalism' central to the vision of the Enlightenment, and that had informed the earlier avant-garde's conviction that the values it embodied were valid for all, was exposed as nothing more than the colonization of the world by western values, and therefore very far from truly global. In its place, multiculturalism was advocated, which within art aimed to broaden the range of cultures incorporated into the official narrative and to critique narrowly western-centred approaches that considered the greatest cultural accomplishments to have been made almost exclusively by males of European descent. The very notion of 'art history', the idea of giving the past a recognizable shape, was criticized as a narrowly western idea. Instead, one should strive to see modernity as unfolding at different speeds and in different manifestations that relate to specific geographic conditions and cultural forces.

The Shock of the Old

But other, very different, interpretations of the meaning of 'postmodernity' were also surfacing. The 'anti-aesthetic' art of critical resistance was especially opposed to what its proponents perceived as a reactionary turn towards 'tradition' within western culture during the 1980s, involving the reprising of cultural and political forms. Hal Foster described this tendency as 'an instrumental pastiche of pop or pseudo-historical forms' and 'a return to origins' that concealed dubious social and political affiliations. But the advocates of the new pluralism

126 Glenn Ligon, *White #13*, 1994

saw it very differently: it was a refreshing indication that contemporary art could justifiably be many things. They pointed out that the 'resistant' postmodernists still believed in a version of artistic progress as exclusionary, a vision tacitly founded on an idea of artistic obsolescence that mirrored the logic of perpetual innovation dominating modernity in which the outmoded was continuously replaced by a newer 'model'. By contrast, the ideal of pluralism in culture granted that the present could accommodate numerous stylistic tendencies, none of which was inherently tied to a specific moment or set of values, and so artists could engage with the past not only in a spirit of critique but also of recuperation and repositioning. This reflected a new cultural openness, inclusivity and permissiveness. Art need no longer be dominated by the idea that one '-ism' at a time was the sole bearer of the zeitgeist, because the 'postmodern' present was broad enough to accommodate a wide variety of different styles, some of which were indeed revivals of what the 'avant-garde' judged moribund.

The British painter Lucian Freud (1922–2011) rose to critical prominence during the 1980s, although he had been working since the 1950s in what had increasingly seemed an anachronistically realistic figurative style that consciously turned its back on the innovations of modernist art. Freud approached his task in a spirit that recalled Gustave Courbet's mid-nineteenth-century declaration that representational art must be totally unidealized. In particular, Freud devoted himself to portraiture, and almost exclusively portraits of the people he knew – *Esther* (1980) is a portrait of one of his daughters.

Another London-based artist, Frank Auerbach (b. 1931), had also bucked the dominant trend by devoting himself since the 1950s to painting portraits and cityscapes. But unlike Freud, Auerbach engaged more directly with the earlier modernists' preoccupation with the process of painting as an end in itself, struggling over long sessions to bring into existence a barely legible image of a chosen subject through massive accumulations of oil paint. For the critical avant-garde, artists like Freud and Auerbach seemed motivated by a retrograde and eccentric conviction that painting's primary task was to use the outdated technique of optical realism to depict the visible world as seen and experienced by the artist.

In America, Alice Neel (1900–1984) had also long been dedicating herself to the traditional subject of portraiture, choosing as her subjects the members of the New York scene of which she was a part – art historians, critics, students and transvestites, as in *Jackie Curtis and Ritta Redd* (1970). For Neel, the formal experimentation characteristic of the avant-garde

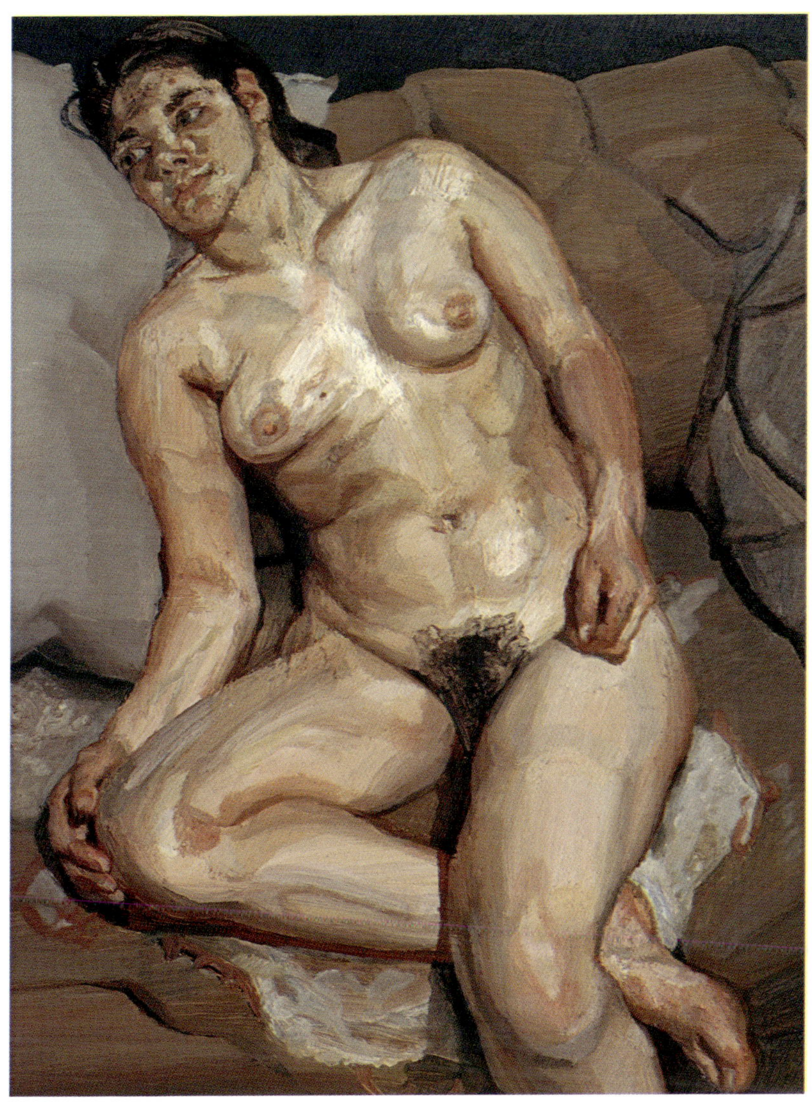

127 Lucian Freud, Esther, 1980

was less important than painting's more traditional role as a hand-made image-making process capable of communicating empathy and intimacy. She observed: 'Whether I'm painting or not, I have this overweening interest in humanity. Even if I'm not working, I'm still analyzing people.'

Another American, Alex Katz (b. 1927), bucked the avant-garde trend by developing a cool and suave form of figuration that seemed to capture perfectly the affluent lifestyles of the fashionable American middle class. For Katz, the modern world was an endless source of aesthetic pleasure, and the more traditional role of painting as a record of the perceived world using linear perspective and modelling of forms was exploited to communicate an essentially optimistic vision of middle-class life in America. 'So many things can be great subject matter,' Katz observed. 'I could be looking at Nefertiti, and that could be something I see today. But it also could be movies and billboards and TV. I think everything in our culture is potential subject matter.'

The African American Faith Ringgold (b. 1930) also considered that the painted (and sometimes quilted) image was a primary and accessible means through which to confront the familiar realities of contemporary life in America, noting: 'I became fascinated with the ability of art to document the time, place, and cultural identity of the artist.' However, her status as a woman and African American led her to a more questioning attitude. She asked: 'How could I, as an African American woman artist, document what was happening around me?' In practice, this meant at times the obligation to address troubling dimensions of contemporary American society. In *The American People Series #18: The Flag is Bleeding* (1967), in a clear and uncompromisingly representational style, Ringgold confronted head-on the racial, Anti-Vietnam War or just random violence irrupting throughout the United States in the 1960s and early 1970s. The iconic symbol of America, and also, perhaps, Jasper Johns's iconic painting of the American flag (see Chapter Seven) are stained by the uncomfortable realities of contemporary American life.

The dark side of American meddling in global politics was also central to the work of Leon Golub (1922–2004), who since the 1970s had been grappling with what he saw as the failure of the radical art of his time to confront the terrible political injustices and violence of contemporary life. In characteristic works such as *Mercenaries I* (1979) Golub culled images from the news media, choosing to paint assassins, interrogators and mercenaries, and working in a crudely expressionistic figurative style on large, unframed rolls of unprimed canvas. Golub described himself as a 'reporter', and the events that drew his attention

128 RIGHT Alice Neel, *Jackie Curtis and Ritta Redd*, 1970
129 BELOW Alex Katz, *Islesboro Ferry Slip*, 1975

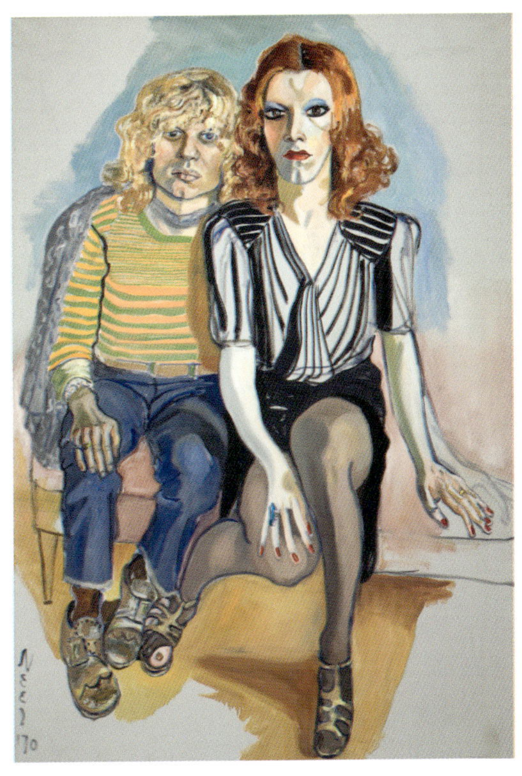

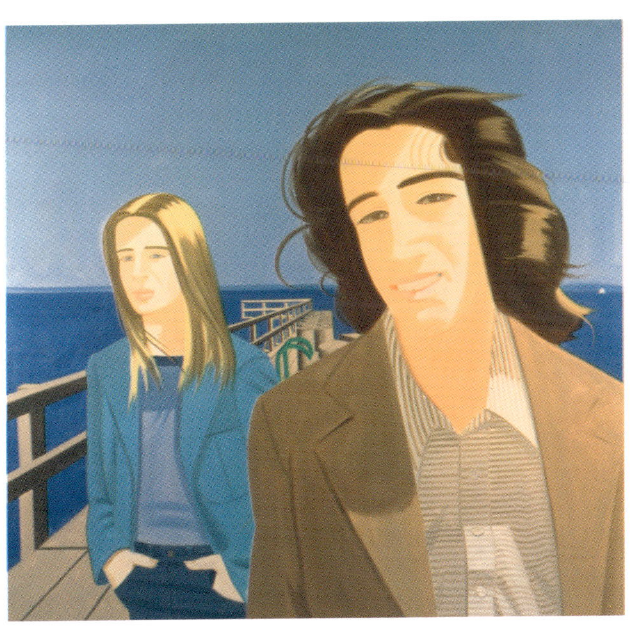

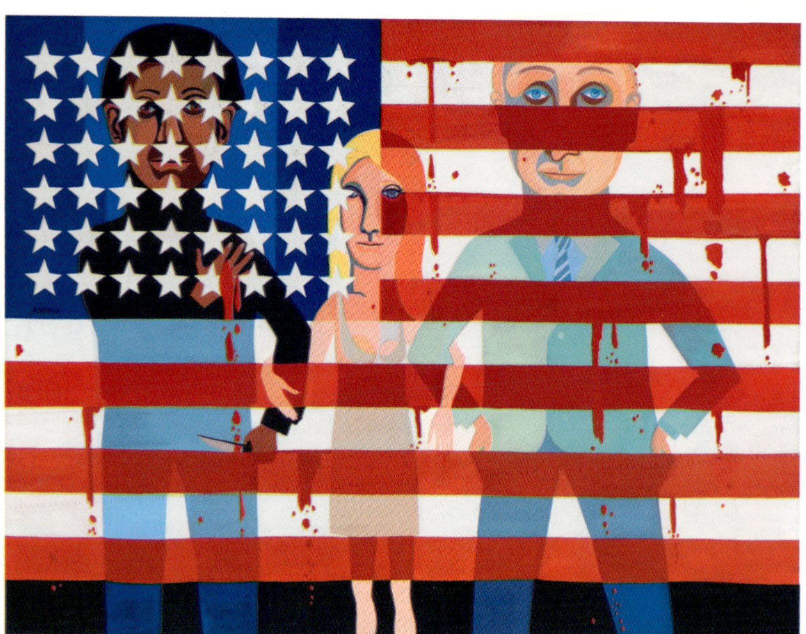

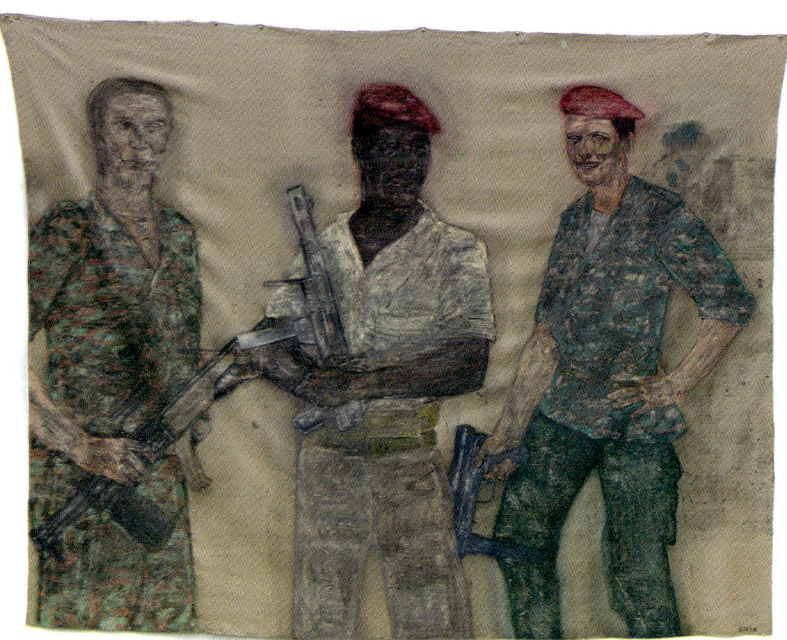

130 TOP Faith Ringgold, *The American People Series #18: The Flag is Bleeding,* 1967
131 ABOVE Leon Golub, *Mercenaries I,* 1979
132 OPPOSITE Eric Fischl, *Bad Boy,* 1981

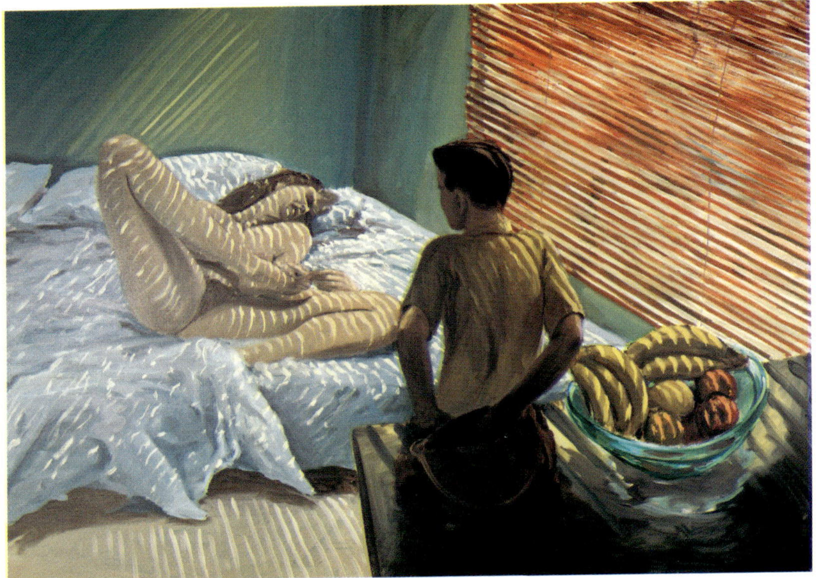

were invariably terrible – indictments of the brutality of white supremacy, damning evidence in an artistic case against the west's malign influence.

Amongst the younger generation of American artists, Eric Fischl (b. 1948) became known in the early 1980s as the 'postmodern Hopper'. But, unlike the older artist's work, Fischl's paintings focused not on loneliness and yearning but on the taboo and sleazy underside of middle-class America – incest, alcoholism, drug abuse and suicide (all of which Fischl had himself experienced at first hand). Fischl deftly composed his works so the viewer becomes complicitly voyeuristic. In *Bad Boy* (1981), described by the artist as his 'most famous and notorious painting', we seem to be witness to a boy's sexual abuse or consensual complicity, and his theft of the woman's (his own *mother*?) money from her handbag. In direct opposition to the deliberate obscurity of much modern art, Fischl noted: 'My whole career I've been trying to make paintings that people can relate to, respond to emotionally – not stand in front of scratching their heads.'

132

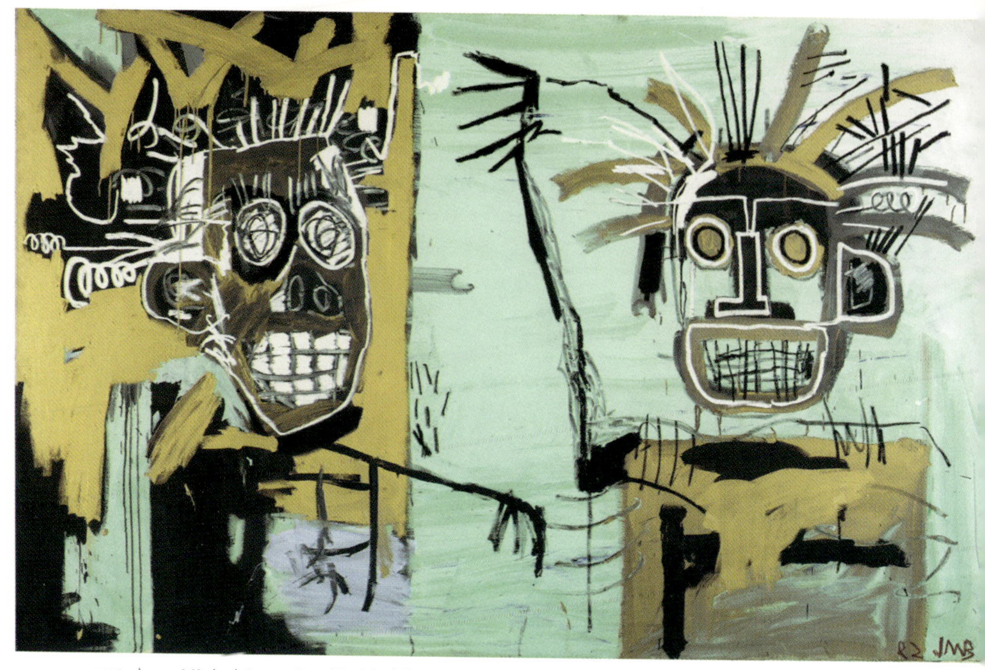

133 Jean-Michel Basquiat, *Untitled (Two Heads in Gold)*, 1982

Graffiti Art

The 'post' in postmodernism could also describe a new aesthetic openness and populism, signalling the breaking down of the boundaries between high art and popular culture – a general widening of the scope and character of aesthetic experience. This was especially evident in the emergence of Graffiti Art in the United States. Using the cheap and readily available spray-can aerosol and ink-marker, usually working-class urban youths had started 'tagging' surfaces ranging from subway cars to the walls of apartment buildings. In what became known as 'wildstyle', the distinction between writing and imaging broke down, while the term 'bombing' – used to describe the marking-up of graffiti – reflected the fact that graffiti was an intended assault on the anonymous and uncaring surfaces of the city.

In the late 1970s, graffiti crossed over into the commercial gallery system in New York, where it was seen to reinvigorate – aesthetically and economically – a contemporary art that had become overly intellectual and focused on new media. A popular figure in this cross-over was the white American artist Keith Haring (1958–1990), whose simple, black-outlined figures danced and cavorted across any surface he could find. Another important newcomer was Jean-Michel Basquiat (1960–1988), who at the age of fifteen had left his family home in Brooklyn and taken to the streets, where he used a Magic Marker to graffiti slogans throughout downtown Manhattan under the name SAMO. In 1981 Basquiat began painting and, encouraged by art dealers and a receptive artworld, worked prolifically until his early, drug-related death. Using charcoal, pen, oil stick, synthetic polymer paint and collage, Basquiat developed a highly energized and expressive improvisatory style. He manically drew on images and codes culled from 'high' and 'low' culture, while knowingly staging the signs of the 'primitive' in relation to his identity as a young Black artist in a predominantly white artworld. *Untitled (Two Heads in Gold)* (1982) is a typical example of his work, in this case evoking a powerful sense of threat and unease.

Neo-Expressionism

The artworld's interest in Basquiat's work was also part of a wider development in painting that became dubbed Neo-Expressionism, Transavantgarde, Bad Painting or *Neue Wilden* (German for the 'New Wild Ones'). A key older figure in the United States in the context of this general reassessment of figurative expressionism was the Canadian-American artist Philip Guston (1913–1980), who had made a name for himself in the 1950s as an Abstract Expressionist but became disillusioned with the movement's failure to deal directly with social, political and psychological realities, especially the pervasiveness of racism and violence within American society. Guston's solution was to drop abstraction and embrace his own form of figurative expressionism, and his work from the 1970s onwards until his death can be linked to the pre-war Expressionism discussed in Chapter Four, but also to Surrealism (especially de Chirico), as discussed in Chapter Five.

In the 1980s and beyond, Guston's turn away from Abstract Expressionism to expressive figuration was to prove especially instrumental in reintroducing the idea of painting as an 'image-ridden' form. In terms that echo Francis Bacon's critique of abstract art, Guston stressed that, for him, a painter was above all an 'image-maker', someone who responds to the fact that humanity itself is inherently 'image-ridden'. In *Tears* (1977) two giant eyeballs pivot upwards, shedding one tear each. It is as if Guston wanted to convey his anguished recognition that seeing – the essential activity of artists – inevitably exposes them to scenes of sorrow and violence, making them complicit in society's barbarism but also obliging them to record what they see. The simple, childlike or cartoonish style, unappealing colouration and loose, viscous brushwork of Guston's works conspire to imbue them with a raw and uncompromising authenticity – signalled by a clear rejection of obvious technical skill and attention to aesthetic values – which was rooted in the artist's struggle to produce images that conveyed his often distraught and anguished experiences.

Influenced by Guston, the much younger Julian Schnabel (b. 1951) self-consciously applied an aesthetics of expressive excess to his practice – trumping the minimalism of the previous decade with overt 'maximalism', even in one phase attaching broken crockery to the laden surfaces of his paintings. *Hope* (1982) is an early work painted on luscious velvet and carries a plethora of appropriated references to recent and ancient art historical styles, and to the kind of religious symbolism that was anathema to the conceptually oriented postmodernists. Indeed, when compared to the works illustrated in the previous chapter and the beginning of this one, it is evident that American artists such as Basquiat and Schnabel were setting out to redirect painting towards a greater acceptance of its connection to history and images, revelling in the inherently pleasurable dimensions of working in the medium and of using it as a vehicle for self-expression, despite their choice of often challenging and grotesque subject matter. However, this connection to the past could often seem

135

134 BELOW Philip Guston, *Tears*, 1977
135 OPPOSITE Julian Schnabel, *Hope*, 1982

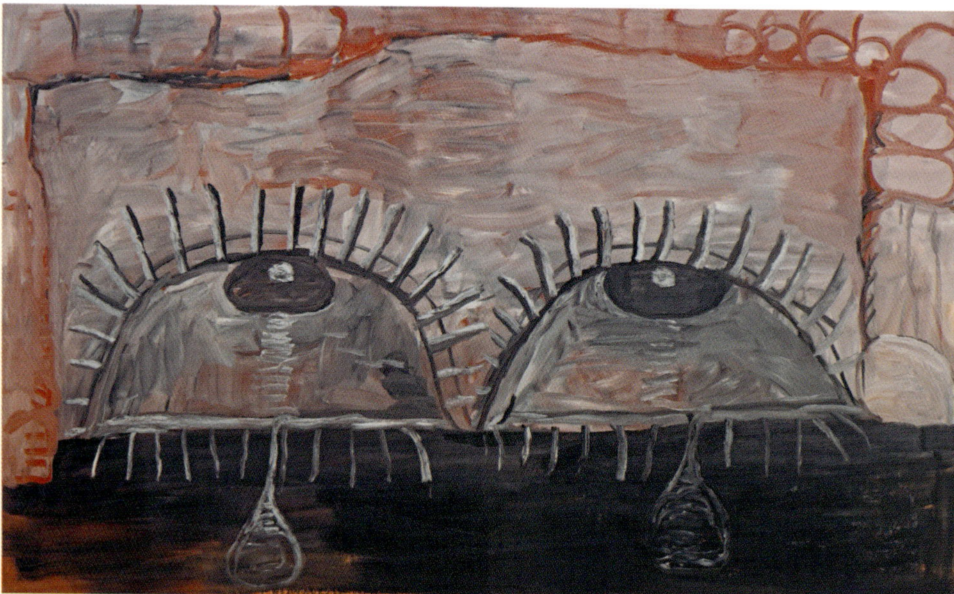

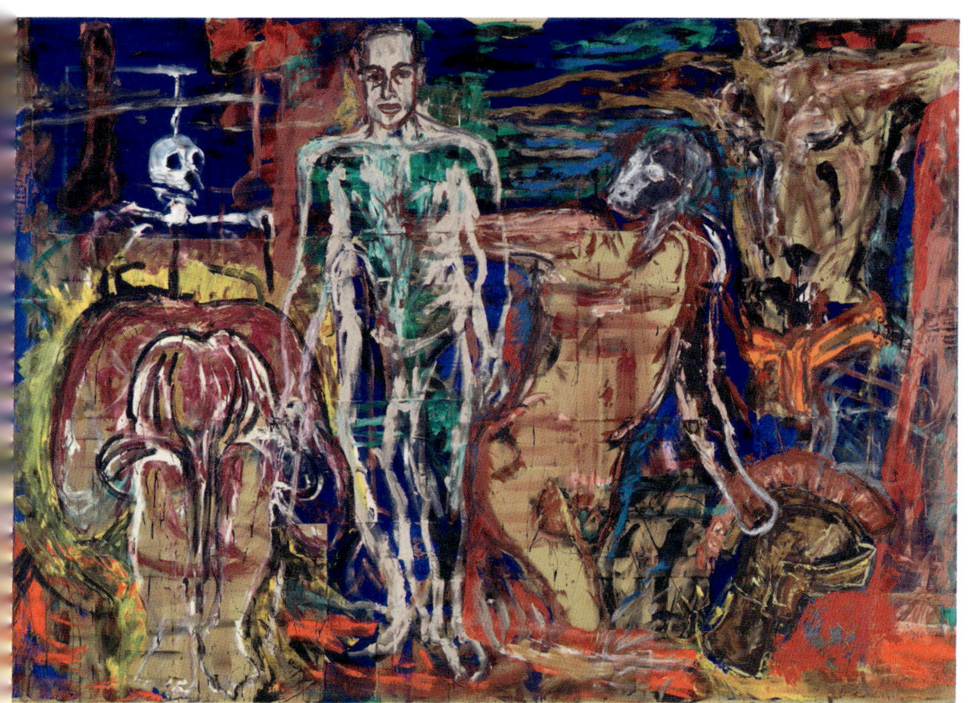

merely parodic, in the sense that – in imitating others' styles – ambiguity regarding the expressive intentions of artists in relation to their appropriations was introduced. Indeed, the term 'appropriation' was commonly used to discuss the new 'postmodern' art. For artists now took and used what already existed – in the mass media or history – and often without permission (leading to some awkward legal cases in which artists, including Salle, were accused of 'stealing' others' creative property). However, the notion of appropriation was intended to reflect the reality of a culture in which relationships to the world were overwhelmingly mediated by images, and where notions of authentic self-expression were deeply compromised.

Neo-Expressionism as a trend also signalled the broadening out of the art scene after a period in which, as this survey attests, it was largely dominated by American artists, and by their critic and curator advocates and collectors. Italians such as Sandro Chia, Francesco Clemente, Enzo Cucchi and Mimmo Paladino were especially significant in overtly dedicating themselves to painting as an expressive medium in which the image played a central role, and in seeking to evoke a living

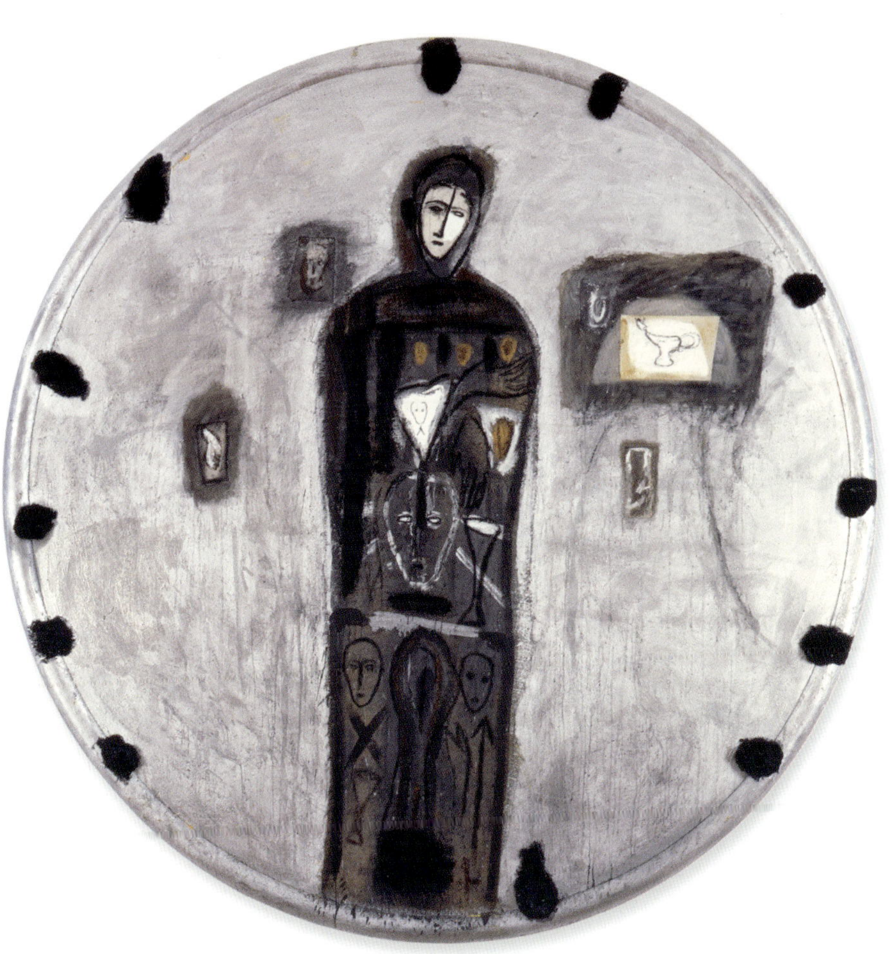

136 Mimmo Paladino, *Baal*, 1986

connection to the illustrious history of painting, a past that was especially evident to artists from a nation that felt close cultural ties to Classicism and the Renaissance. Paladino (b. 1948), for example, began his career as a Conceptual artist, using mostly photographs, but switched to painting and carved sculpture in the late 1970s. His works are replete with symbols appropriated from or evoking ancient civilizations, and consciously associate painting with its history, and especially with a history linked to the Romantic yearning for origins. Like many of the artists who now turned to painting, Paladino saw it as a space within which to pursue his impulses freed from the limitations imposed by more conceptually oriented practices, which, while accessing a great variety of new media, were constrained by the dominance of an intellectualizing mindset.

But the most dramatic expansion in the possibilities of expressionist painting involved West German artists. They were working in a nation deeply scarred by a dark Nazi past and now divided between the spheres of influence of rival superpowers. As we have seen, figurative expressionism was an especially significant dimension of German art in the late nineteenth and early twentieth centuries, and in the late 1970s and early 1980s it was revived again in the works of such artists as Georg Baselitz, Rainer Fetting, Jörg Immendorff, Anselm Kiefer, Markus Lüpertz, A. R. Penck and Sigmar Polke. Baselitz (b. 1938), for example, employed a style that overtly evoked early twentieth-century German Expressionism, but artfully distanced himself from the earlier painting by working on the monumental scale that Abstract Expressionism had introduced and, most significantly, inverting the canvas, so the viewer first engages with his work as a physical trace of dynamic paint application and only subsequently interprets the representational dimension. Baselitz thereby blurred the boundary between abstraction and figuration, a tendency we will see repeatedly explored in the works of the artists in this and the next chapter.

Anselm Kiefer (b. 1945) adopted a stridently painterly, expressionistic style and, like Baselitz, also made sculptures and sometimes installations. Kiefer cast his work as a struggle to reconcile his country's recent Nazi history with the myths of Germanic legend, and the realities of Germany in the present day, and his work emerged from the emotional trauma of growing up in a defeated, ruined, impoverished and divided nation, a situation that was complicated by its universally reviled Nazi past. Between 1980 and 1983, Kiefer made paintings such as *Innenraum* (1981) that drew on photographs of Hitler's monumental architecture, as well as on Norse

folklore, Wagnerian motifs and German Romanticism. As his
work evolved, and he became one of the most influential and
admired contemporary artists, Kiefer opted for increasingly
monumental proportions, producing works loaded up with
thick layers of paint, shellac, sand, earth, lead, clay and other
organic and inorganic material like straw and flowers, as
well as such things as computer motherboards and electrical
cabling. Enigmatic inscriptions were also often scrawled over
these heavily encrusted surfaces, which consistently evoke
apocalyptic events. As Kiefer observed: 'If I do something that
depresses, it's not because I'm depressed, but because political
life and history is depressing.'

Another German, Sigmar Polke (1941–2010), in works such
as *Watchtower* (1984) – one of a series of paintings focusing
on the motif of a border lookout post – was also struggling

137 BELOW Anselm Kiefer, *Innenraum*, 1981
138 OPPOSITE Sigmar Polke, *Watchtower*, 1984

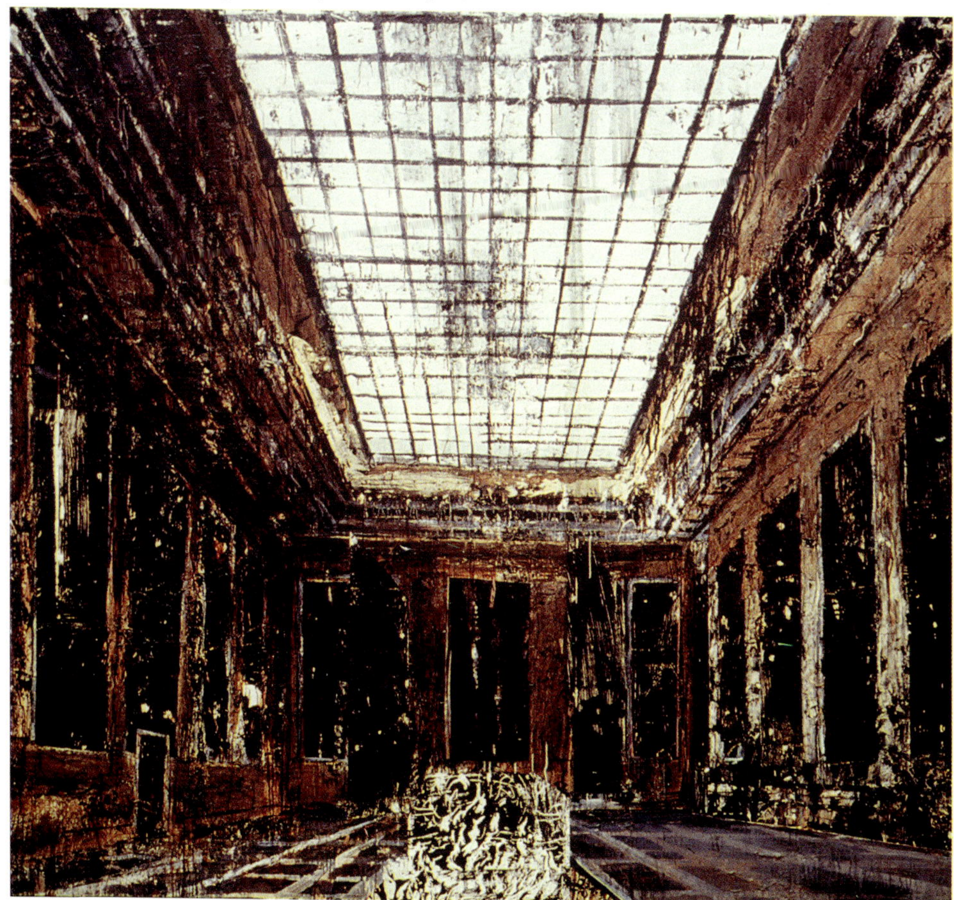

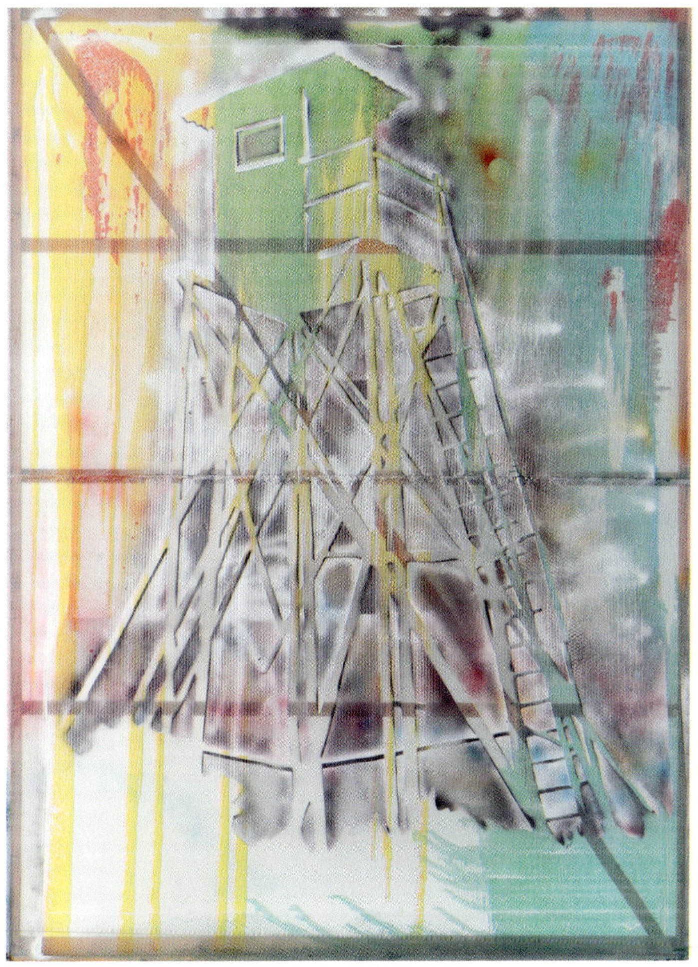

to banish the demons of Nazism, to address the continuing
forced division of his country, and on a personal level to seek
a mode of existence less constrained by social convention.
For Polke, nothing was sacred. 'The conventional definition
of reality, and the idea of "normal life", mean nothing,' he
declared. Like Kiefer, Polke accumulated an unusual range
of media in his paintings, but he was far more irreverent
in bringing together unusual colour combinations, paint
applications, and 'high' and 'low' cultural refences and
materials. In the case of the work illustrated, Polke used
enamel paint on transparent bubble wrap, so that the stretcher
bars of the canvas are evident as a ghostly geometric grid.

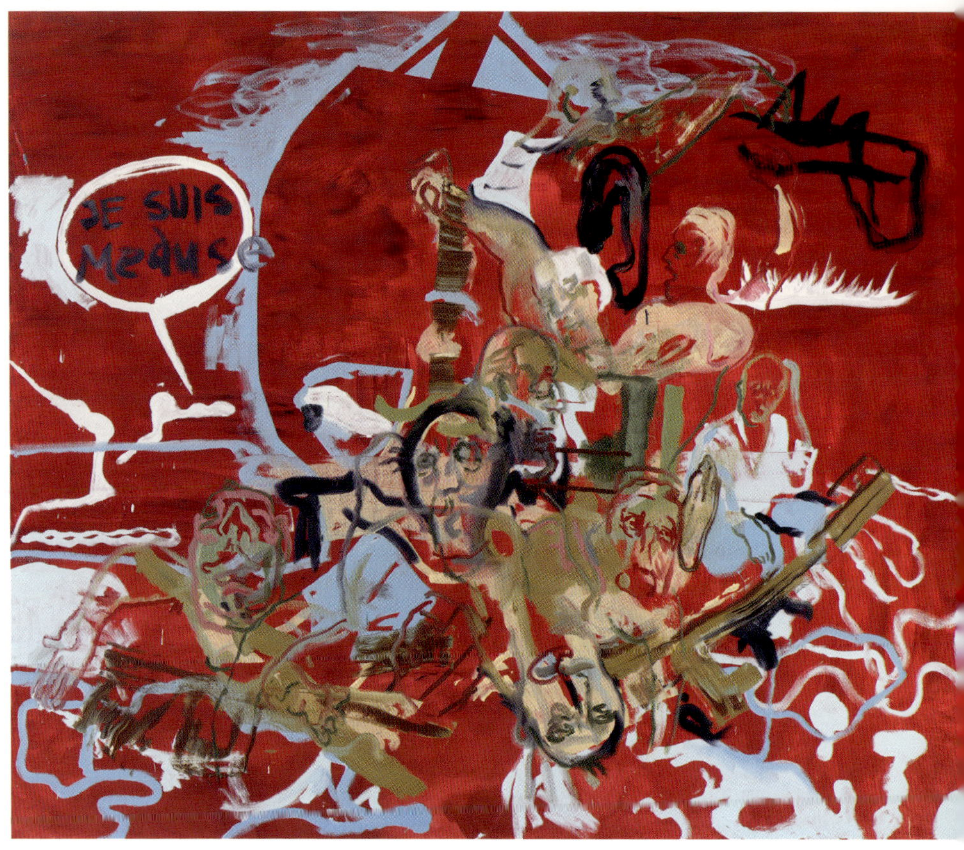

139 Martin Kippenberger, *Untitled (from the series The Raft of Medusa)*, 1996

Beyond Neo-Expressionism in the 1990s

As is evident from the work of Kiefer and Polke, the kind of images upon which artists were now drawing often derived from photographic sources or the history of art rather than from direct observation of the visible world. In other words, artists now used the media as a vast storehouse of available imagery, and no longer considered it necessary to choose between an 'abstract' or 'figurative' style, or a 'high' or 'low' cultural source. Painting now incorporated all kinds of visual properties, and within its spaces there could co-exist an often bewildering variety of formal, symbolic and expressive dimensions and techniques.

But images were often motivated by the artist's overriding desire to create an unsettling and uncanny mood of latent violence or impending disaster, which reflected the pervasive belief amongst progressives that the world was heading into a deepening crisis. Another German, Martin Kippenberger (1953–1997), developed a prolific practice involving painting, performance and collaborations with other artists, using biting satire to challenge the viewer, confronting them with confusing and uncomfortable juxtapositions of styles, imagery and forms. One critic aptly described Kippenberger as a 'moralist in despair'. *Untitled* (1996), which is from a series of works based on Théodore Géricault's masterpiece of Romantic art, *The Raft of the Medusa*, includes a speech bubble carrying the French words 'Je suis Meduse' – 'I am Medusa'. Kippenberger seems to be drawing a parallel between himself and the shipwrecked sailors, who are torn between despair and hope. Or perhaps Kippenberger was referring to the Medusa of Greek mythology, one of the three monstrous Gorgons with a head of hair consisting of snakes, who turned men to stone if they looked at her.

The new figurative painting was unashamedly based on appropriation, but the ironic and parodic qualities central to the painting of the 1980s were increasingly replaced by renewed faith in painting as a vehicle for the melancholy expression of anxiety and alienation. The South African-born, Netherlands-based artist Marlene Dumas (b. 1953) evolved a stark, sketchy, unfinished style to convey the ambiguity of her subject matter, especially focusing on the exploitation of women, and using images culled from the mass media concerning violence and persecution. For *The Painter* (1994), however, she used an innocuous snapshot of her daughter taken while finger-painting. But Dumas transformed the source into a disturbing evocation of the relationship between innocence, sexuality, creativity and malevolence.

Painting seemed haunted by an awareness of tragic history that compelled artists to deny themselves both aesthetic pleasure *and* the luxury of detached parody, and that was pitted against the indifference and hypocrisy of society. *Gas Chamber* (1986), by the Belgian Luc Tuymans (b. 1958), for example, used as its source image a photograph relating to the Holocaust – and an uneasy and morbid sense of an incomplete, washed-out, barely existent and fundamentally de-idealized reality pervades his work in general. As a form of self-imposed discipline, Tuymans also restricted himself to finishing each of his paintings in one sitting. For Tuymans, painting was inevitably implicated in addressing events in the wider world. He declared: 'Life is politics, basically, but you don't just go to a gallery and put the words "art" and "politics" on the wall.'

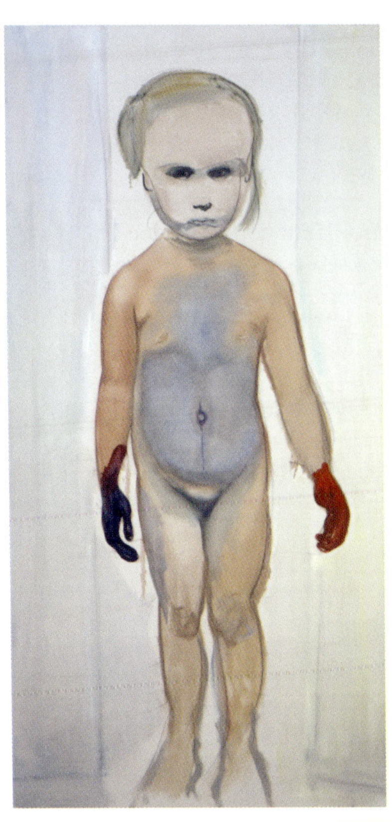

140 LEFT Marlene Dumas,
The Painter, 1994
141 BELOW Luc Tuymans,
Gas Chamber, 1986

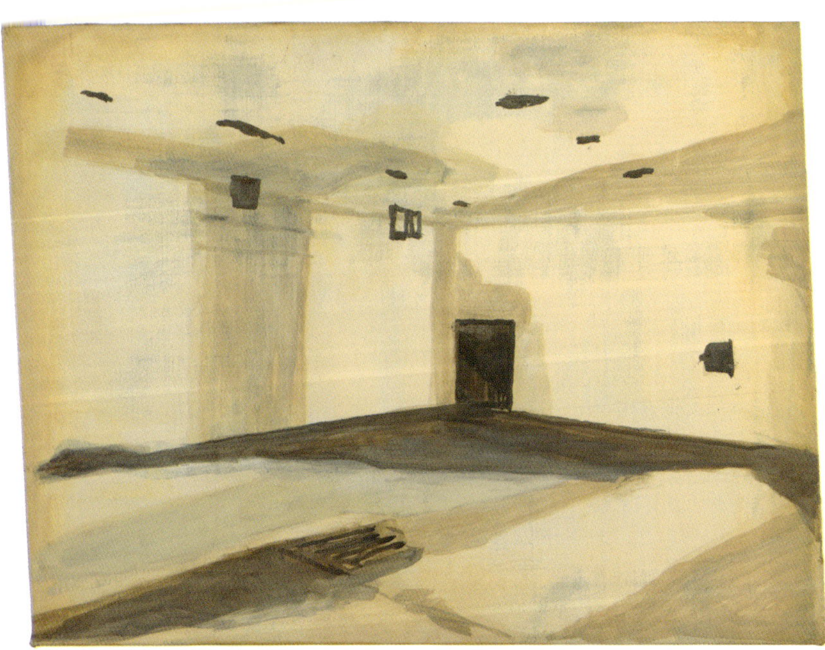

Abstract Painting in the 1990s

By the 1990s, the inherent pluralism of the 'postmodern' turn had served to rehabilitate painting in general. The old polarities, such as 'figurative' and 'abstract', and the idea that an artist must remain loyal to one 'signature' style, were no longer relevant. Paintings of all sorts now existed within the expanded field of diverse art practices, and an important consequence of this was that a painting had more in common with another painting – of whatever sort – than they had differences. They shared a limited range of common characteristics. Within painting practices themselves there was also much greater willingness to blur the boundaries of style, either within a single painting or within an artist's practice. For example, Christopher Wool, whose text-based work is illustrated at the start of this chapter, also developed a parallel practice involving the making of black and white, gestural abstract works; Richard Prince, mentioned earlier, made paintings in a wide variety of styles, but also produced photographs in which he appropriated already existing images and re-presented them as his own works; the German artist Gerhard Richter, whose photorealist work was discussed in Chapter Seven, and who by the 1990s was being considered by many to be the pre-eminent living painter – the exemplary 'postmodern' artist – developed a significant body of overtly titled 'abstract' paintings alongside his photo-based work in the mid-1980s. Richter applied and removed layers of paint on large canvases, scraping their surfaces with a squeegee (a tool with a long blade usually used in silkscreen printing), then adding spatters and brushstrokes, creating works that have been described as elegant palimpsests bearing the traces of the successive stages that went into their production.

In addition to the resurgence of figurative painting, the blurring of old distinctions and the pluralization of styles, more obviously abstract kinds of painting also continued to evolve during this period. There were several artists internationally – including, for example, the German artist Imi Knoebel, Alan Charlton in England, the Irish-born New York-based Sean Scully, and Americans such as Marcia Hafif, Jonathan Lasker, David Reed, Peter Schuyff, Pat Steir and Philip Taaffe – who in one way or another sought to maintain a connection with earlier modernist ideas about the value of the self-sufficiency of painting, and explored what they considered unexhausted possibilities or still unrealized potential.

The paintings of the French artist Bernard Frize (b. 1949) demonstrate an especially varied repertoire of painterly effects, almost an inventory of what is possible in paint while avoiding the production of a recognizable image. Rather than establishing one dominant 'signature' style, what was interesting for Frize was working models that tested what abstract painting in general could do. 'Painting is a way of exploring ideas and embodying them, so that they can be seen and shared,' Frize noted. *Pacifique* (1991), for example, is a practical demonstration of the effects of the rhythmic movement of the brush across the work's surface while tracing a loosely symmetrical pattern.

The much younger British artist Gary Hume (b. 1962) explored the ambiguous border line between the image and abstract form, and produced works with sleek, glossy paint that removed all signs of expressionistic brushstrokes, thereby associating his practice with the industrial surfaces of modern urban life and the computer screen. In some of his paintings, the simplified shape of a human figure, a plant or an animal is evident, but in *Close-Up (Green)* (1999) Hume has ensured his painting is read, at least at first glance, as just flat blocks of colour. On closer examination, and with reference to the title, a relationship to an external referent – a detail of an object or person – is suggested.

Several artists mined the possibilities already opened up by moving painting away from the constraints imposed by limiting

142 BELOW Bernard Frize, *Pacifique*, 1991
143 OPPOSITE Gary Hume, *Close-Up (Green)*, 1999

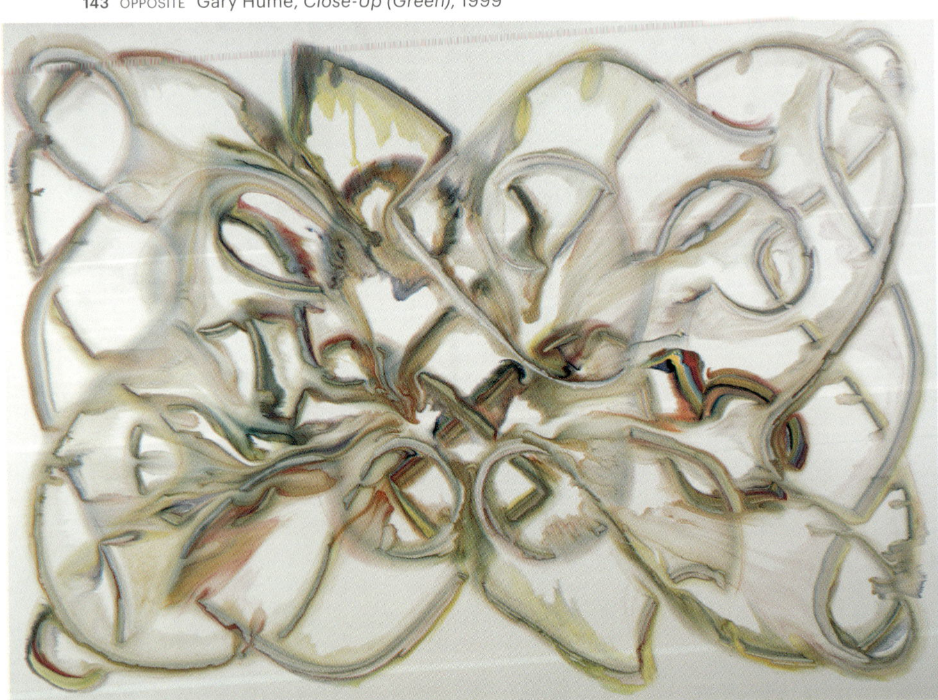

it to a flat surface hanging on a wall. In improvised, free-form installations the American Jessica Stockholder (b. 1959) broke down the boundaries between painting and sculpture, the work and the audience. In *Your Skin in this Weather Bourne Eye-Threads & Swollen Perfume* (1995–96), Stockholder employed the vivid flat colours of abstract painting but dramatically moved beyond the wall into the surrounding space to create a dislocated, animated and immersive environment.

144

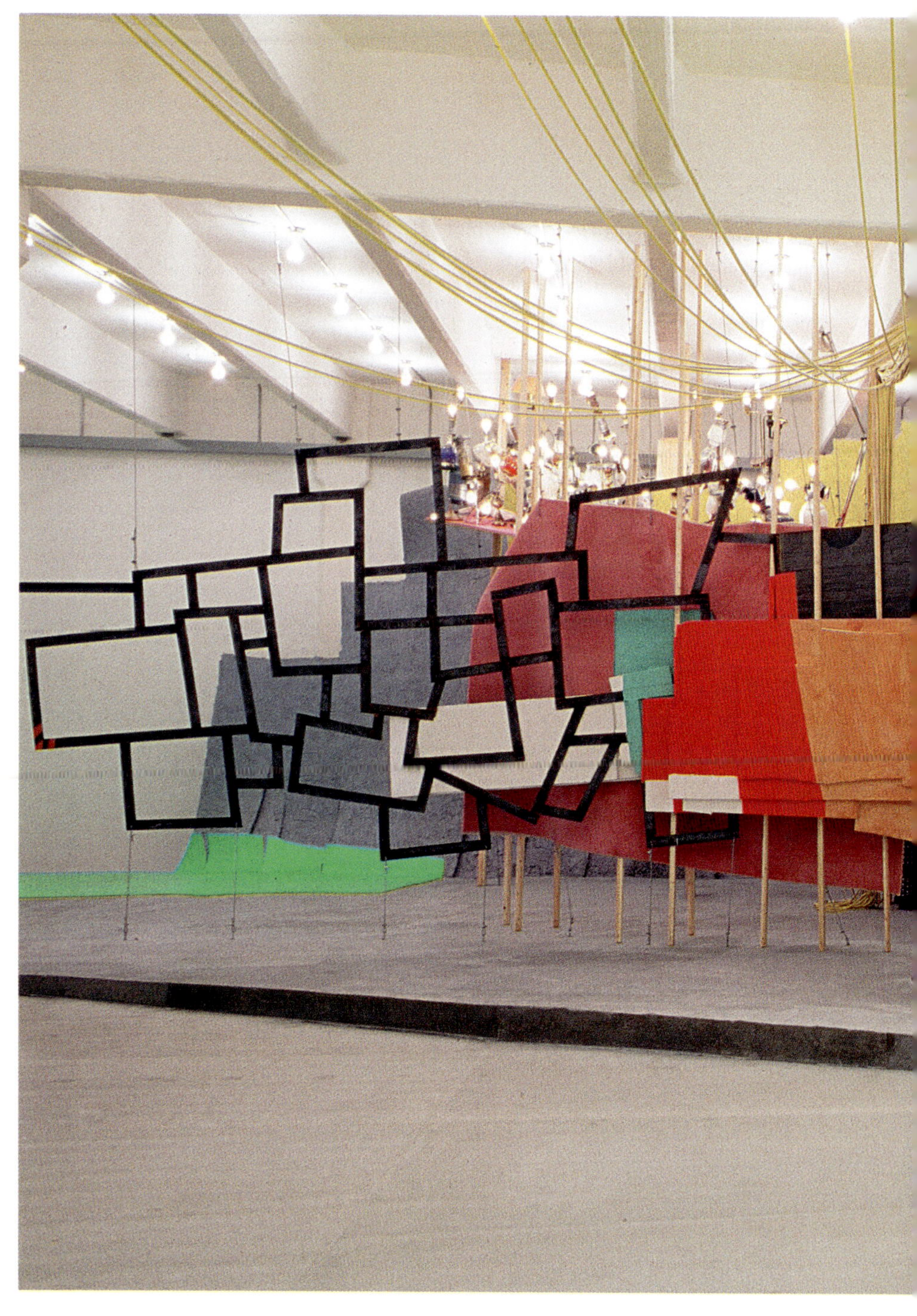

144 Jessica Stockholder, *Your Skin in this Weather Bourne Eye-Threads & Swollen Perfume*, 1995–96

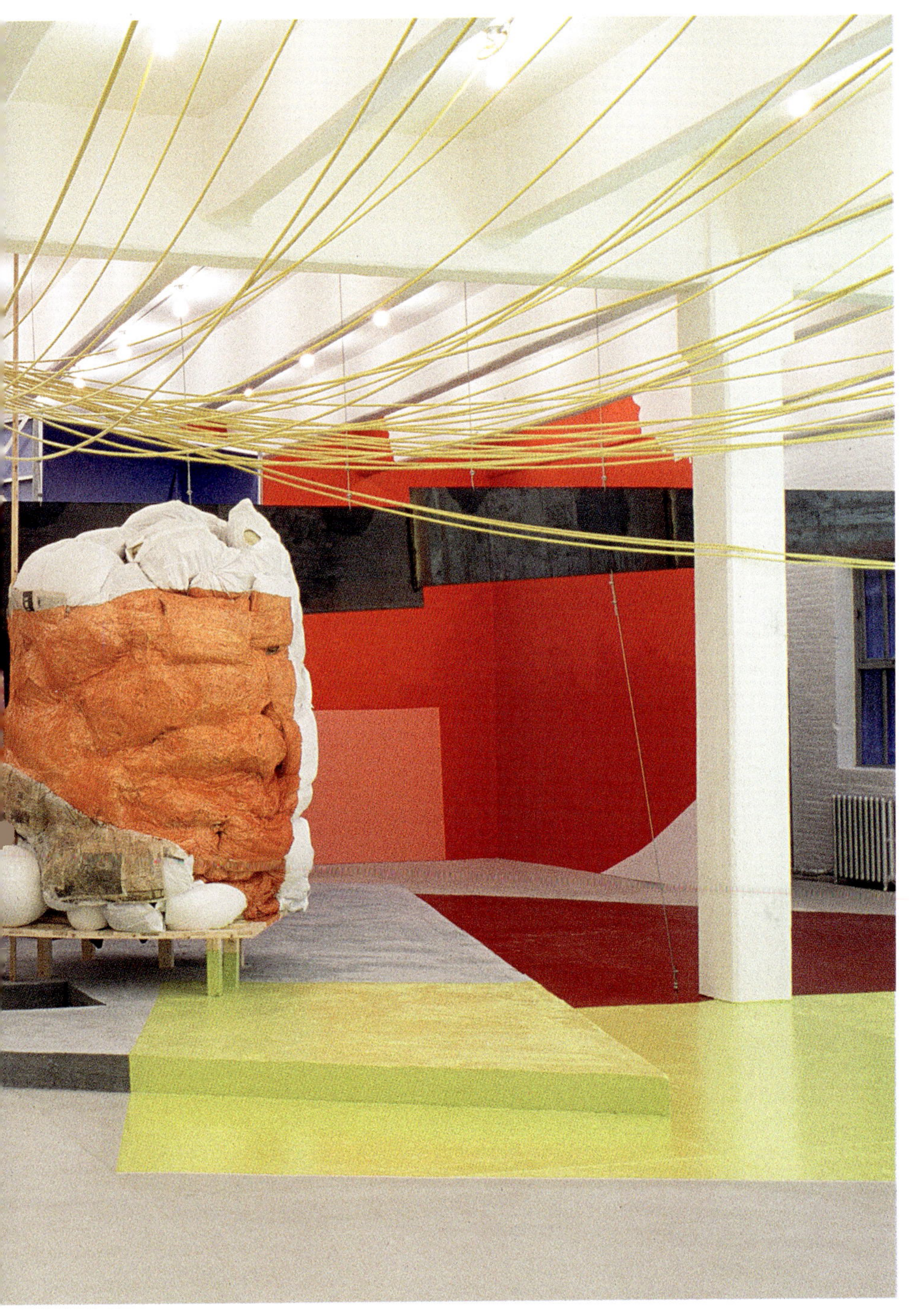

Postcolonial Painting

Postmodernity also involved a process of globalization, which drew once-distant cultures closer together, while also leading to western societies becoming increasingly multicultural. Many varieties of painting emerged from cultural contexts beyond Europe and North America which made their way to western art centres via important exhibitions. In 1989 an especially influential exhibition was staged at the Centre Georges Pompidou in Paris, entitled 'Les Magiciens de la terre' ('Magicians of the Earth'). In part, it was a critical response to a blockbuster exhibition held at the Museum of Modern Art, New York in 1984–85, entitled '"Primitivism" in Twentieth Century Art: The Affinity of the Tribal and the Modern', which had largely displayed non-western art and artefacts only as they related to western practice. 'Les Magiciens de la terre' marked an important shift in perceptions by showing works made outside the European and North American mainstream on an equal footing. This reflected a radical rethinking of knowledge and social identities from the perspective of the post-colonial era, as notions of non-western cultures as inherently 'timeless', 'pure' and 'original' were dismissed as western myths. Globalization was creating an international culture based neither on 'otherness' nor on simple multiculturalism grounded in the diversity of cultures, and was undoing visions of 'Eurocentrism' to promote postmodern cultural 'hybridity' – new fluid transcultural forms being created within the contact zones initially produced by colonization.

The Congolese artist Chéri Samba (b. 1956) was one of the artists featured in 'Les Magiciens de la terre'. Samba had taken to signing his paintings 'Chéri Samba: Artiste Populaire' and set out to document in a clear and colourful figurative style the social, political, economic and cultural realities of what at the time was Zaire and is now the Democratic Republic of the Congo, addressing the many dimensions of everyday life in the capital city of Kinshasa. In *The Officials of Black Africa* (1994) Samba satirized the civil servants running the country, whose sole incentive seemed to be to take bribes. For Samba, the crucial function of the artist was to communicate to the people directly, and thereby to signal solidarity with the oppressed; thanks to the new pluralistic and global perspectives of postmodernism, his work was now assimilated into the expanded field of contemporary painting practices.

Another artist who participated in 'Les Magiciens de la terre' was the Australian Aboriginal Clifford Possum Tjapaltjarri (1932–2002). In the 1950s Tjapaltjarri had begun making carved wood sculptures, but in the 1970s he was introduced

145

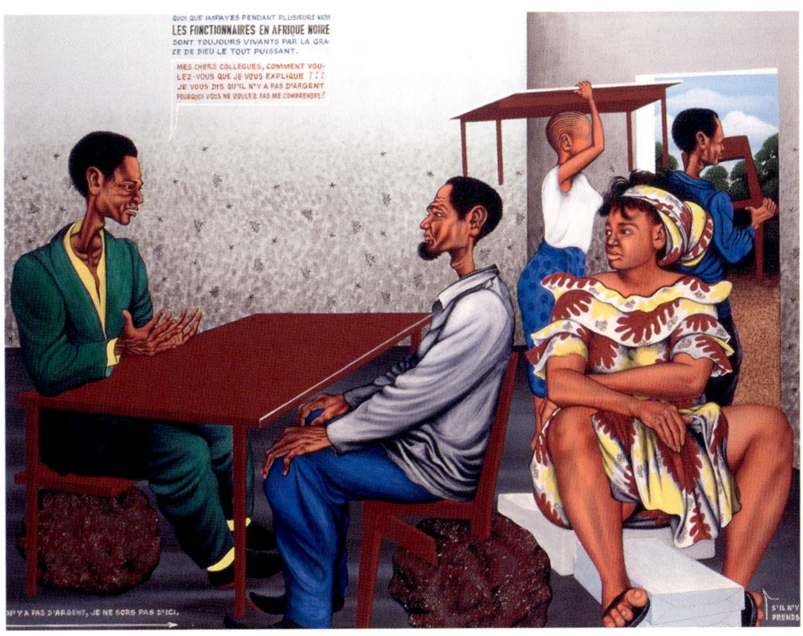

145 Chéri Samba, *The Officials of Black Africa*, 1994

to the western media of acrylic paints and stretched canvas and, as part of what became known as the Aboriginal Art Movement, developed a uniquely 'hybrid' form of painting that blended western materials with Aboriginal content and style. The colour, composition and stippling technique appear 'abstract' to the untrained eye, but for Tjapaltjarri and his fellow Aboriginals, paintings such as *Spirit Dreaming through Napperby Country* (1980), which was made in collaboration with the artist's older brother Tim Leura Tjapaltjarri (1930–1984), are full of symbolic mythological detail – visual codes expressing the reality of their 'Dreamtime'. When asked why he became an artist, Clifford Possum Tjapaltjarra explained: 'That Dreaming been all the time. From our early days, before European people came up. That Dreaming carry on.' Other Indigenous Australian artists, such as Emily Kame Kngwarreye, Dorothy Napangardi and John Mawurndjul, also became internationally celebrated.

'Les Magiciens de la terre' also showcased the work of several Chinese artists for the first time in the west. As part and parcel of the thawing of the authoritarian political situation that nevertheless led up to the Tiananmen Square demonstrations of 1989, a relatively open art scene developed in China, and even after the violent repression of the protests

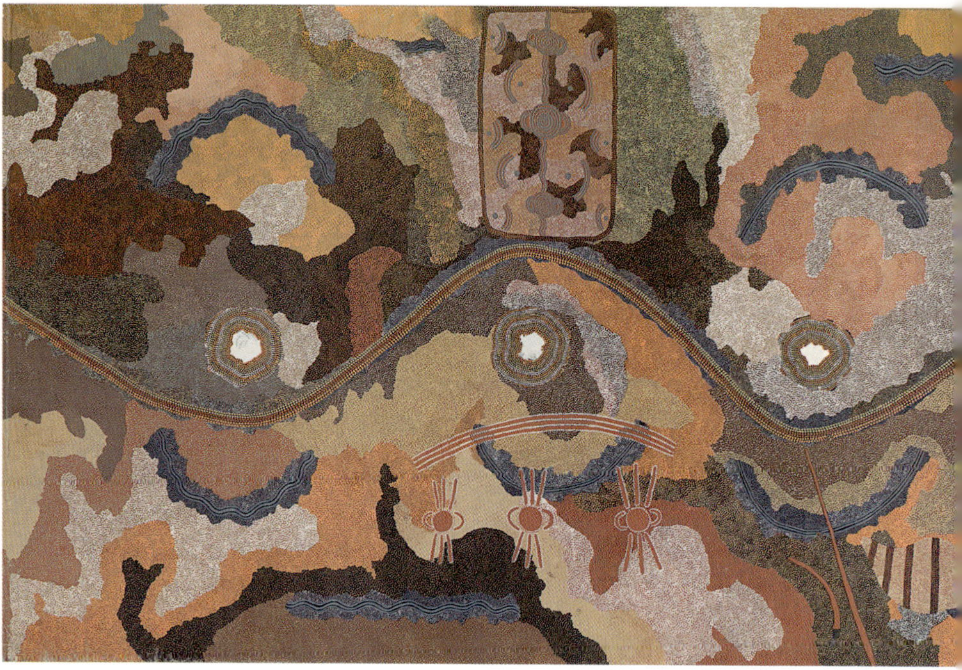

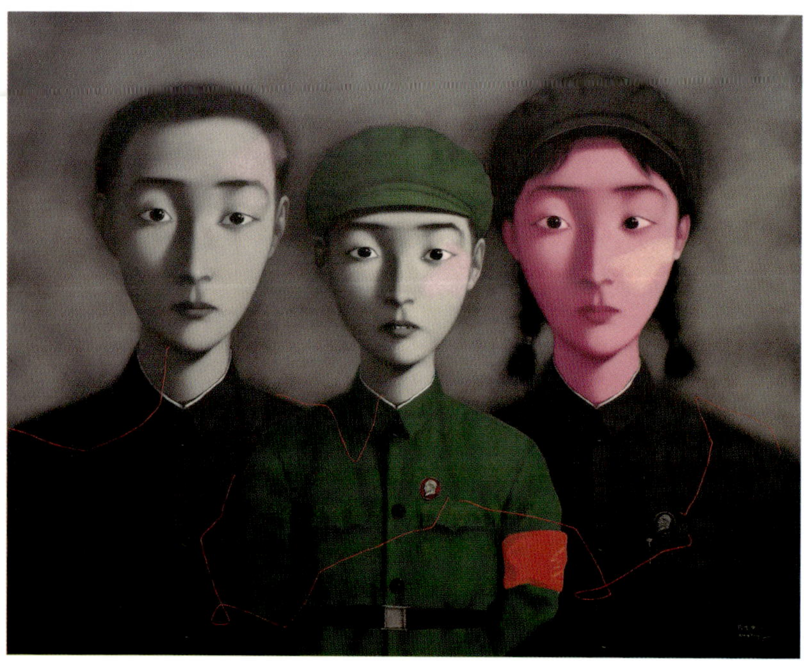

146 TOP Tim Leura Tjapaltjarri and Clifford Possum Tjapaltjarri, *Spirit Dreaming through Napperby Country,* 1980
147 ABOVE Zhang Xiaogang, *Bloodline – Big Family No. 3,* 1995

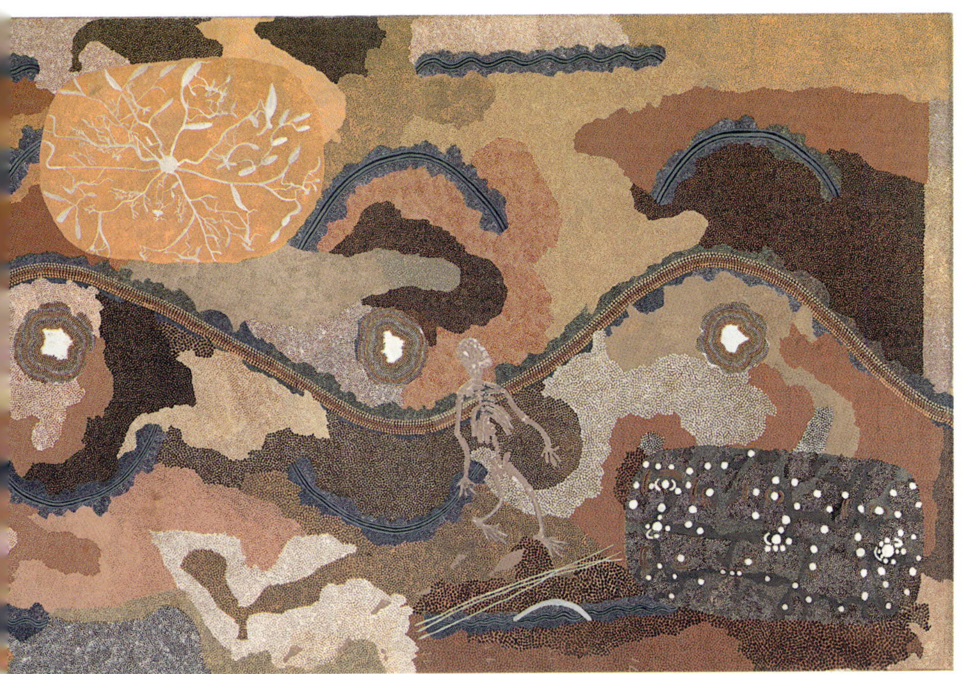

Chinese art continued to evolve in unique dialogue with western art. The imposition of communism in China from 1949 onwards had three main effects on Chinese artists. It stigmatized traditional Chinese art because it was associated with the old order. Following the model of the Soviet Union, the Chinese Communist Party rejected progressive western art as 'bourgeois' and instead mandated a Chinese variant of Socialist Realism, which as we saw in Chapter Five, was based on nineteenth-century conventions of optical realism, harnessed by the Party to serve as propaganda. Thirdly, and as a result, Chinese artists growing up in communist China, especially during the Cultural Revolution (1966–76), were shielded from the influence of western modernism. But after the end of the Cultural Revolution, some, such as Yue Minjun, Zeng Fanzhi and Zhang Xiaogang, chose to employ the skills learned in order to practise Socialist Realism in decidedly non-doctrinaire fashion. Zhang (b. 1958), for example, in 1993 began to paint family portrait themes, as in *Bloodline – Big Family No. 3* (1995), in which figures stare directly at the viewer, wide-eyed and inert, reflecting the Chinese people's traumatic experience of the Cultural Revolution and the intense pressure put on them to conform to the ideological norms of their society.

147

The Art Market

The development of Chinese painting as an increasingly globalized artworld phenomenon was encouraged by a buoyant art market hungry for signs of innovation and the exotically unfamiliar. Indeed, by the 1990s, modern and contemporary painting had become big business. A key sign of things to come was the 1973 auction by Robert C. Scull (a New York taxicab impresario and collector of contemporary American art) of fifty of his best paintings at Sotheby Parke-Bernet in New York. The sale raised prices for living artists to unprecedented levels. A painting by Cy Twombly sold for $40,000, over fifty times the $750 that Scull had paid for it, while one by Jasper Johns, which Scull had bought for $10,200, went for $240,000. These were record sales for living artists, and represented very healthy returns on the original investment. But the Scull auction indicated more than simply that modern and contemporary painting could be a major source of profit; the hype around it also showed that modern art was ripe for exploitation by marketing and publicity interests, and that artists had now become celebrities. In 1985 Jean-Michel Basquiat, mentioned earlier in this chapter, was featured on the cover of *The New York Times Magazine*, and an accompanying article discussed the dynamic international art market in which the works of the still very young Basquiat were much sought-after prizes. In the 1990s the London-based advertising executive Charles Saatchi amassed a huge collection, often of young up-and-coming artists, but also promoted his holdings, displaying them in a grand manner once reserved only for museums, before then often selling them on at a healthy profit.

Saatchi helped brand and promote the 'Young British Artists' (YBAs), the most famous of whom is the now multi-millionaire mega-artist Damien Hirst (b. 1965). Hirst's practice from the beginning was prolific, involving almost the whole gamut of contemporary art media – painting included. This inclusivity is more evidence that artists no longer felt constrained by the premise that they had to pursue one 'essential' style that embodied their unique 'truth'. The fact that Hirst used studio assistants to make his paintings also highlighted that, for him, the idea that a painting was somehow a direct expression of the artist's psyche communicated through the body's unique and meaningful interactions with materials and a work's surface was no longer deemed either very challenging, interesting or culturally significant. Artists like Hirst increasingly adopted whatever medium seemed to suit the specific idea or project at hand.

Often, this meant that painting was used as a medium precisely for the reasons that had made it suspect for artists

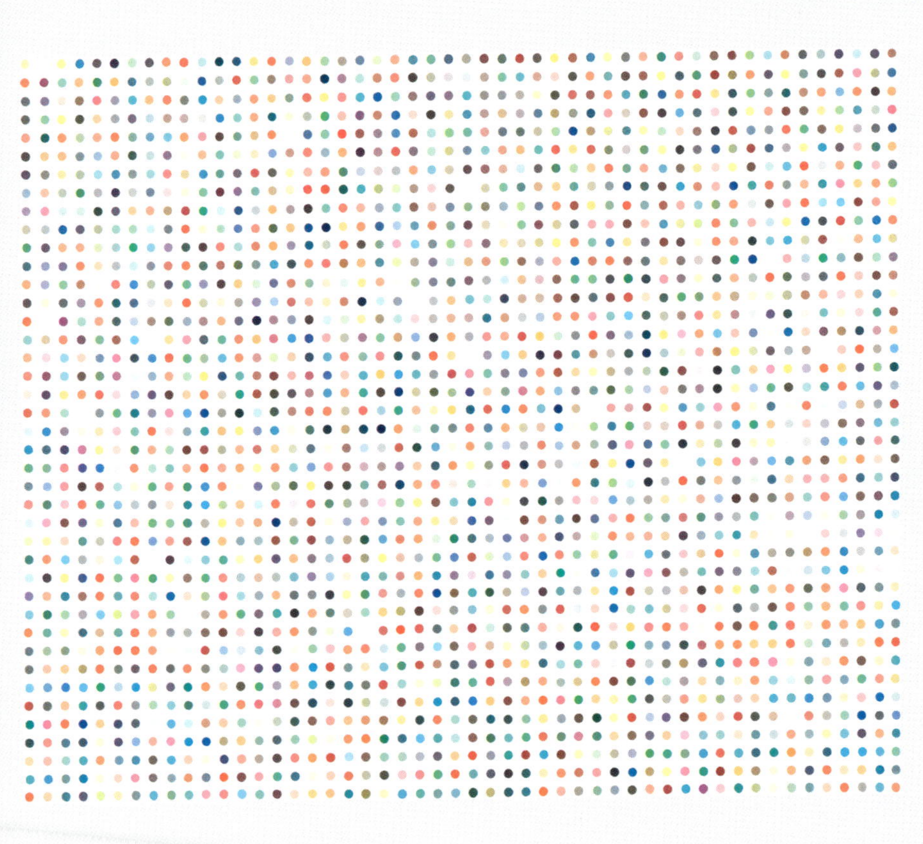

 Damien Hirst, *Anthraquinone-1-Diazonium Chloride*, 1994

of the 1960s to the 1980s: because of its aesthetic appeal and ease of marketing. *Anthraquinone-1-Diazonium Chloride* (1994) is an example of a series made by Hirst and his studio assistants entitled the 'Spot Paintings', the early examples of which were named after pharmaceutical medications, and thus are a gesture towards the critical postmodern strategies of deconstruction as practised, for example, by artists such as Peter Halley. But Hirst explained that his goal was to produce a purely aesthetic experience for his audience: 'It was just a way of pinning down the joy of colour.' By 2012 Hirst had already produced almost 1,500 such 'Spot Paintings'. The minimal language of modernism had become a means of establishing a lucrative brand identity.

Painting and the People

But who was this kind of painting really for? In 1995 the dissident Russian Conceptual artists Vitaly Komar (b. 1943) and Alex Melamid (b. 1945), who were living in the United States, set out to learn what a genuinely 'people's art' looked like. Informed by their training in Socialist Realist propaganda art in the Soviet Union, they wanted to know what ordinary people in different countries wanted to see in a picture and then to paint the results of their research. The project began in their adopted country with the goal of painting America's 'Most Wanted' and 'Least Wanted' paintings. Through a professional marketing firm, they conducted market research; the questions were straightforwardly visual and, armed with the data, they amalgamated the 'most/least wanted' traits into two pictures,

America's Most Wanted and *America's Least Wanted* (1994). In the end, Komar and Melamid polled people in fourteen countries and discovered that, despite being rival superpowers, Russia and China's most-wanted paintings were remarkably like those of the United States – minus George Washington but still with children playing beside a lake, and a predominantly blue colouration. In fact, they discovered that in every country they polled – from China and Kenya to Iceland and Ukraine, but with the curious exception of Holland – people seemed to want more or less the same anodyne picture.

Komar and Melamid's project was essentially parody in the service of social critique. It confirms that a secure, socially uncontroversial and optimistic message is what most people seek from a painting, and that in the modern world these consoling values are still best understood through a style of painting that employs optical realism. As we have seen, in the modern period progressive painters sought multiple strategies for exposing the conventional, culturally constructed,

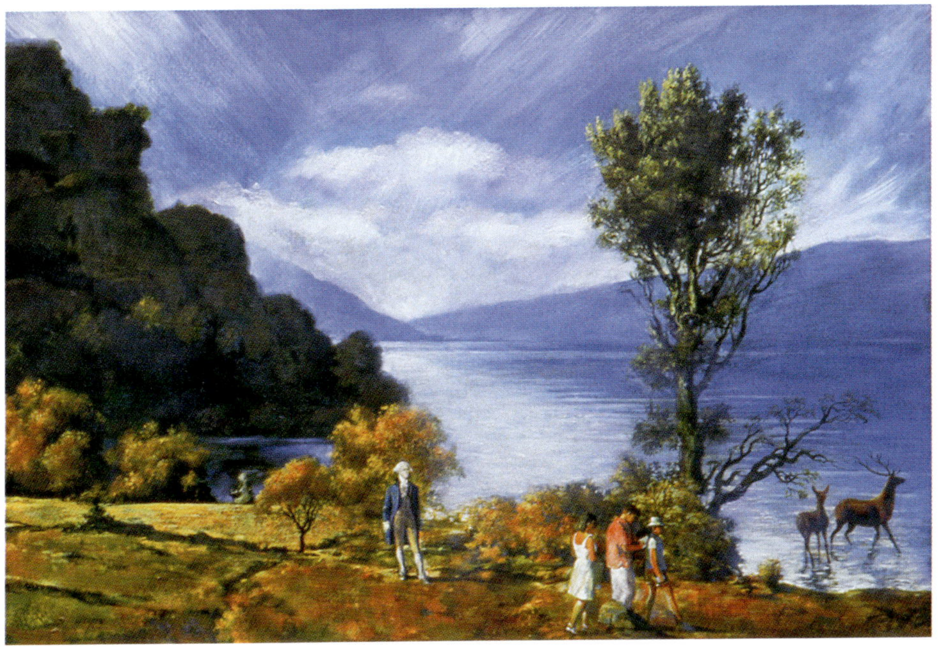

149 Komar and Melamid, *America's Most Wanted*, from 'The People's Choice' series, 1994

expressively limited status of this idea, emphasizing the fact that it is very far from producing a replica of reality. Even when they persisted in the use of this convention, they used it to address the confusing and usually dark dimensions of human existence – those that people naturally prefer to ignore or forget. Within popular culture, however, the convention in which a fictional three-dimensional space is created using linear perspective and modelling in light and dark clearly still dominates.

It might seem strange that modern people prefer in particular to look at realistic representations of landscapes with stretches of water – that is, environments in which they are unlikely actually to live, but that are likely to be where people of today wish to take their vacations. Evolutionary biologists have a hypothetical answer, however. They postulate that this near-universal association of happiness with blue skies, water, open prospect and distant mountains is a deep unconscious memory of humanity's origins on the savannahs of Africa that was long ago imprinted on the human brain. Even though most people in the developed world are city dwellers and their everyday experiences certainly do not include such idyllic vistas, images of such environments remain the 'most-wanted' subject for pictures to this day because across thousands of years they still engender universally positive emotions.

You have probably already guessed what the 'People's Least Wanted' painting was: abstract art of the geometric, monochromatic and roughly textured variety – works not unlike some of those populating these pages. In this sense, Komar and Melamid's parody wittily revealed the fact that the ambitious social projects of modern art – to bridge the gap between art and life, to be an ally in the struggle for social justice, to fill the void left by the loss of religious devotion – have largely failed, at least for the majority of people. Progressive painting remains the marginal concern of a select few. But we should not be surprised. Such specialism or elitism in relation to culture is surely inevitable. Most great art demands of its audience a level of education and commitment that will render its specialized language and complex messages accessible, comprehensible and potentially transformative. This is especially true of unfamiliar new visual art, because we assume that we have not had to learn to look at paintings, like we have learned to read and write, and that images are somehow 'natural'. As photography mechanically replicates the optical effects first produced using optical realism, and this technological device is now the dominant means of recording visual experiences, we also assume it is a copy of reality, and that this is still the primary function of painting.

For many reasons, the majority of people cannot, or do not wish to, devote their attention to 'difficult' or sometimes deliberately repellent art. They want familiar and therefore reassuring style and content. Above all, Komar and Melamid's findings show that in most people's lives paintings play a limited and specific role, one in which they are meant to give uncomplicated visual pleasure, encourage reverie and reaffirm values. They are not, as the progressive artists and their supporters of the modern period insist they should, meant to challenge and question, disturb and repulse, and thereby to potentially transform our relationships to the world.

Chapter 9
Painting Today
c. 2000–*c.* 2022

Painting and the Digital

The Ethiopian-born American painter Julie Mehretu (b. 1970) creates vertiginous screen-like spaces which are often monumentally sized, some stretching more than seven metres wide. Mehretu includes what she calls 'DNA' traces of the real world encountered via the mass media in her paintings, often using multiple collaged news photographs blurred in Photoshop, which are first projected onto her canvases and then drawn or painted on – images of a world of racial injustice, violence and oppression. In *Retopistics: A Renegade Excavation* (2001), which measures over five metres across, an important source for her composition was the study of aviation flightpaths.

Mehretu's paintings suggest spatial relations and states of affairs that seem to arise from the loss of the familiar coordinates of time and space caused by digitalization, depicting radically different networks that evoke a weightless dynamism that releases objects from the force of gravity. The vast pictorial spaces she creates specifically evoke the Internet, which is comprised of infinite numbers of 'rhizomic' nodes or networks – complex links that extend less like organized geometric structures and more like developmental vectors or organic-synthetic hybrid entities. The goal, Mehretu declares, is to create an 'immersive experience', so the viewer feels an 'aspect of dislocation inside the painting'. The viewer becomes physically and mentally mobile, actively garnering different kinds of information and experience from the spatial and cognitive positions they inhabit. 'From a distance, you can see the whole thing. But as you come close to it, to really see it – because it's made up of all these small parts – you don't

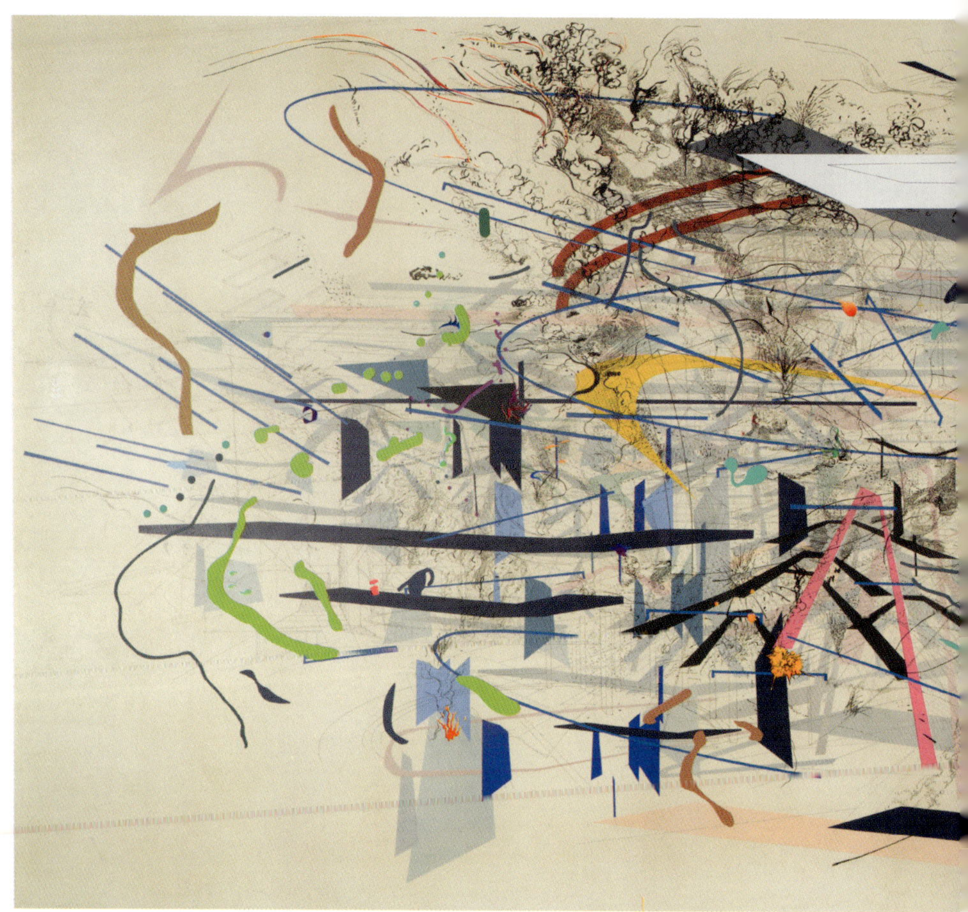

have a sense of the whole,' Mehretu observes. 'You're immersed in what you can see and can only make sense of it from that place. I'm constantly negotiating and thinking about how these paintings are viewed and experienced [in relation to] how I make them.' Mehretu's pictorial structure is therefore radically different from the kind produced by linear perspective, but also from the static grid of artists like Piet Mondrian, whose works mirrored the rational geometric structures of what at the time were new models of architectural planning.

Like Mehretu, many contemporary artists merge the codes of painting with present forms of data-processing and organization by relating the framed-off space of painting to the digital screen, the dominant data-viewing format of the contemporary world. Their work reflects the fact that through

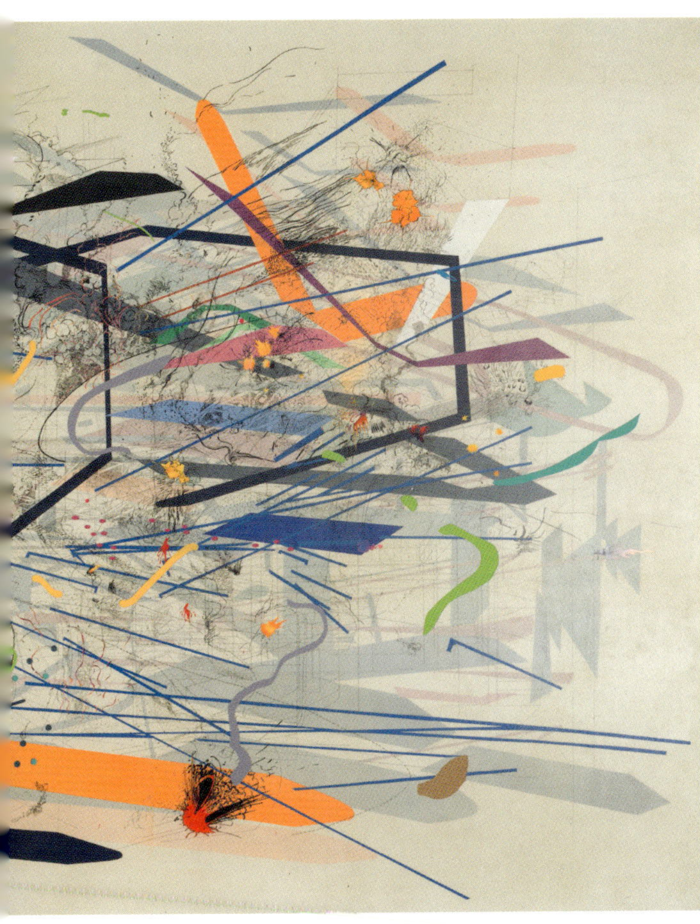

the exponential extension of digital networks across time and space facilitated by the Internet, mass participation in the creation and dissemination of information is now possible, cheap and easy. People today are linked via search engines and social media networks which create unprecedented levels of interconnectedness, and information has been emancipated from its attachment to the material forms that once incurred expensive production and distribution costs and made it easy to control by an elite few. Important and valued public and private interactions with the world now take place 'on-line' rather than 'off-line' (in the actual world of time and space).

With the development of high-resolution digital cameras and large inkjet printers, photographs can be presented in dazzling colour and on the imposing scale formerly reserved for paintings alone. These technological developments allowed artists to merge the conventions of painting with photography. The German artist Andreas Gursky (b. 1955), for example, actively draws on the conventions and history of painting but makes large-scale photographic prints, manipulating the digital image on the computer so as to engage in the kinds of transformations that were formerly the preserve of painting. Today, the realm of the image is populated by mechanically produced and hand-made fabrications that share the capacity to be manipulated in order to produce specific effects and meanings. But despite this significant transformation, within mass and social media the photograph continues to be treated as if it is an authentic picture of reality, a belief that 'deep fakes' (convincingly real images produced using computer software) are inevitably going to make increasingly unsustainable.

Inevitably, painters sought to incorporate these new aspects of the contemporary world into their practices. The American artist Amy Sillman (b. 1955), who makes expressive semi-abstract paintings and often works in series, noted that in addition to responding to the physical world around her, 'My palette is also infected by Apple, my work with animation on iPads and iPhones, and the polychromatic effortlessness of weightless colour options one can change in an instant across a screen by the mere drag of a finger'. Fellow American Wade Guyton (b. 1972) uses the inkjet printer and embraces the anonymity of the computer. He remarks: 'We all use a computer these days, we all have phone and a camera in hand, I use wifi like everybody else. I love AirDrop, it really speeds things up!.... The process is simple; technology is now part of our physicality. We all get the same hand cramps with these stupid iPhones.' But while the digital is characterized by immaculate rendering and surfaces, Guyon actively scuffs and dirties the surfaces of his works by rolling them on the floor of his studio often for weeks or months before attaching them to stretchers. In this sense, Guyton enlists painting in a struggle to incorporate the imperfect, random detritus of what we are coming to think of as 'off-line' life into the smooth, perfect social spaces dominated by protocols of digital 'on-line' existence.

German artist Alfred Oehlen (b. 1954) creates dissonant compositions combining figurative elements, collage, silkscreen and inkjet printing with wild gestural paintwork, much of which seems like a haphazard inventory of the history of abstract painting. In *More Fire and Ice* (2001) the rectangular support of the painting is analogous to the space behind the

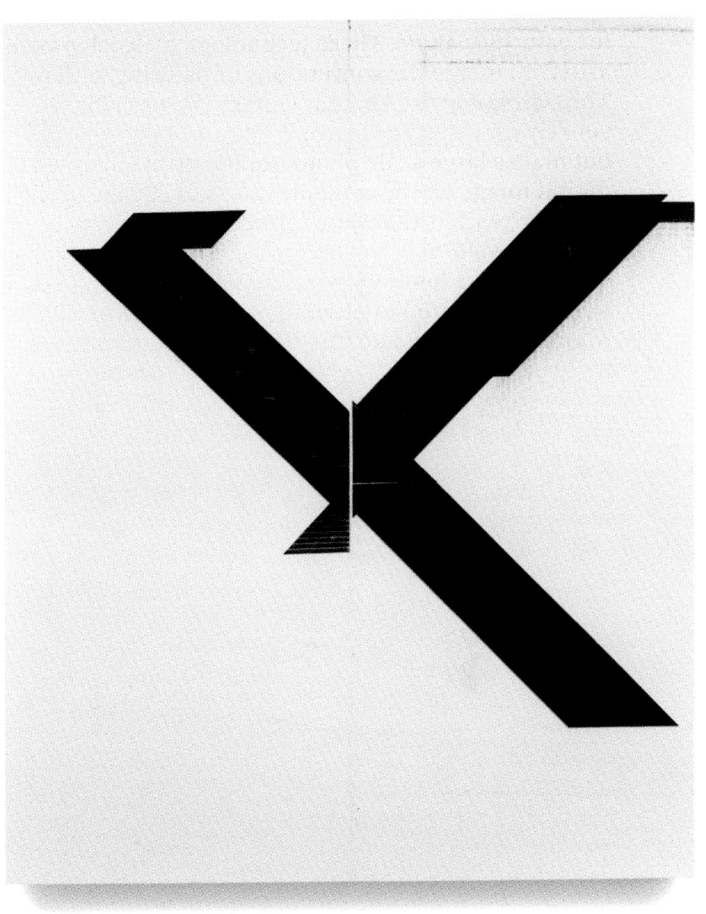

glass of the computer screen, where artificial light illumines a sea of information and data. Several artists evoke complex spaces overflowing with visual data of different kinds, and sometimes, as in the work of British painter Matthew Ritchie (b. 1964) or German painter Franz Ackermann (b. 1963), they literally overflow the boundaries of the painting rectangle, blurring the relationship between virtual and real space, embracing the idea that the digital world encourages a maximalist principle – painting as a generative event, a space for continual dynamic evolution. Artists create spaces within which to envisage and plot alternative possible worlds, using multiple visual codes to convey knowledge, to explore the new modes of social existence and psychic reality spawned by digital technologies.

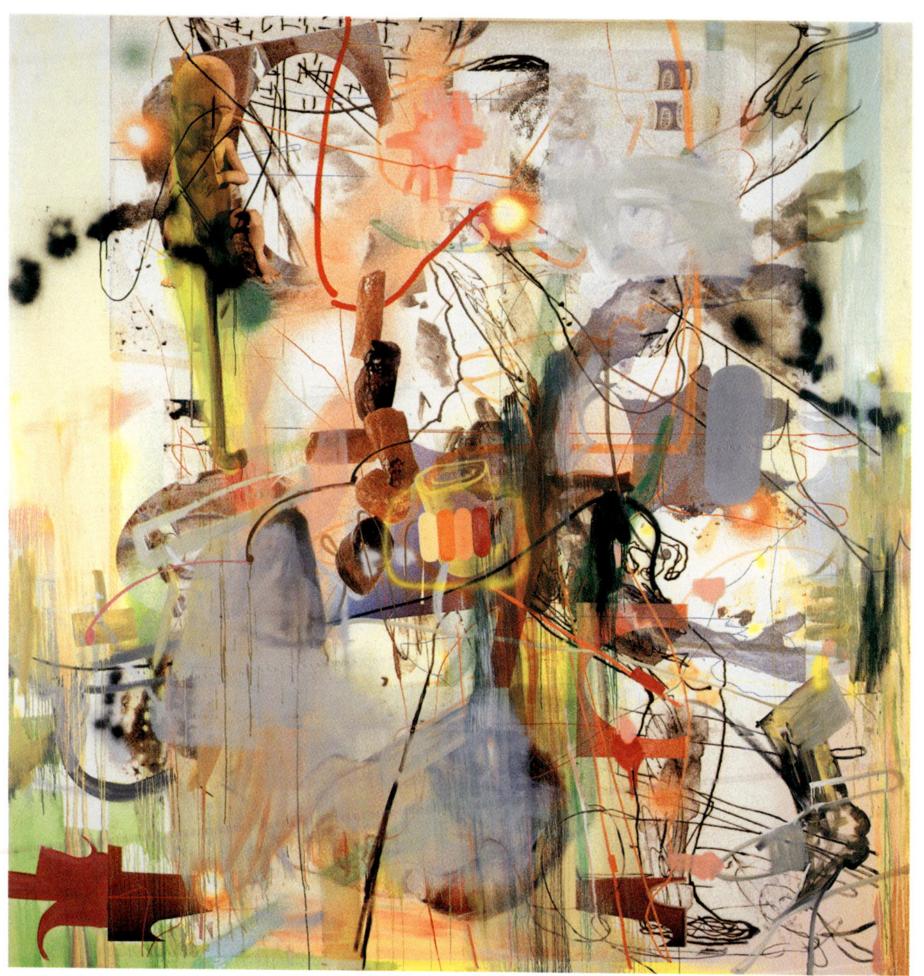

152 Albert Oehlen, *More Fire and Ice*, 2001

The chaotic quality of Oehlen's work seems to reflect the fact that because of the innovations associated with the digital, many people are being overloaded with information, which they cannot process, and find it increasingly difficult to distinguish fact-based information from spurious conspiracy theories. Furthermore, people are also becoming habituated to primary relationships with the mechanical and synthetic, which involve a high degree of physical detachment and passivity, and withdrawal from physical presence, from a world of human intimacy. The exigencies of 'social distancing' during the global Covid-19 pandemic only accelerated the development of a mode of lived experience that is increasingly independent

of the location occupied by the human body. The smartphone
screen, for example, is a portable surface via which to access
a vast range of data, from the weather to the news, consumer
products to social media contacts. When people are not looking
at their smartphones, they are likely fixated by their computer
or plasma television screens. Indeed, as never before, people
relate to the world via a geometrically shaped frame, which
severs the focus of vision from the periphery, thereby producing
a radical disjunction between the world the body inhabits and
the one attended to through a screen. Meanwhile, programmed
algorithms have reached such sophistication that they often
seem to know us better than we know ourselves, and as a
result authority is shifting from the self to outside databases
produced technologically. These technical innovations are
immensely liberating but they also challenge basic assumptions
about human nature, such as the belief that the individual and
their feelings are a sacrosanct source of authority.

Painting in the 'Expanded Field'

In the 1960s the American critic Rosalind Krauss identified
an important tendency within art to exist within an 'expanded
field', one in which the old distinctions between painting,
sculpture, architecture and other media break down. When
she surveyed art at the turn of the new millennium, she used
the term the 'post-medium condition'; specific practices are no
longer what count, and ideas and attitudes and less material
and stable forms of engagement abound. Painting now
co-exists with a bewildering variety of different kinds of art
practice, many of which have almost nothing in common
with painting – except that they are displayed in the same
cultural institutions.

Some contemporary painters seek to draw painting into
line with notions of the 'expanded field' through engaging
with more porous ideas of the 'frame' and through
incorporating new technology. In *Point de Gaze, Chapter 23*
(2011) by R. H. Quaytman (b. 1961), stylistically and materially
diverse elements – in this case silkscreen prints and different
material surfaces such as a protruding shelf (on the left) –
are unified by a preference for a melancholy palette of
whites, blacks and half-tones. Quaytman's works are always
conceived as series and relate to the location where they were
first exhibited – in this case Gladstone Gallery in Brussels – and
invariably involve the elaborate intertwining of themes linking
the personal and the public, past and present, memory and
aesthetic principles that reference art history. Quaytman's
use of the literary convention of the 'Chapter' in the naming

153

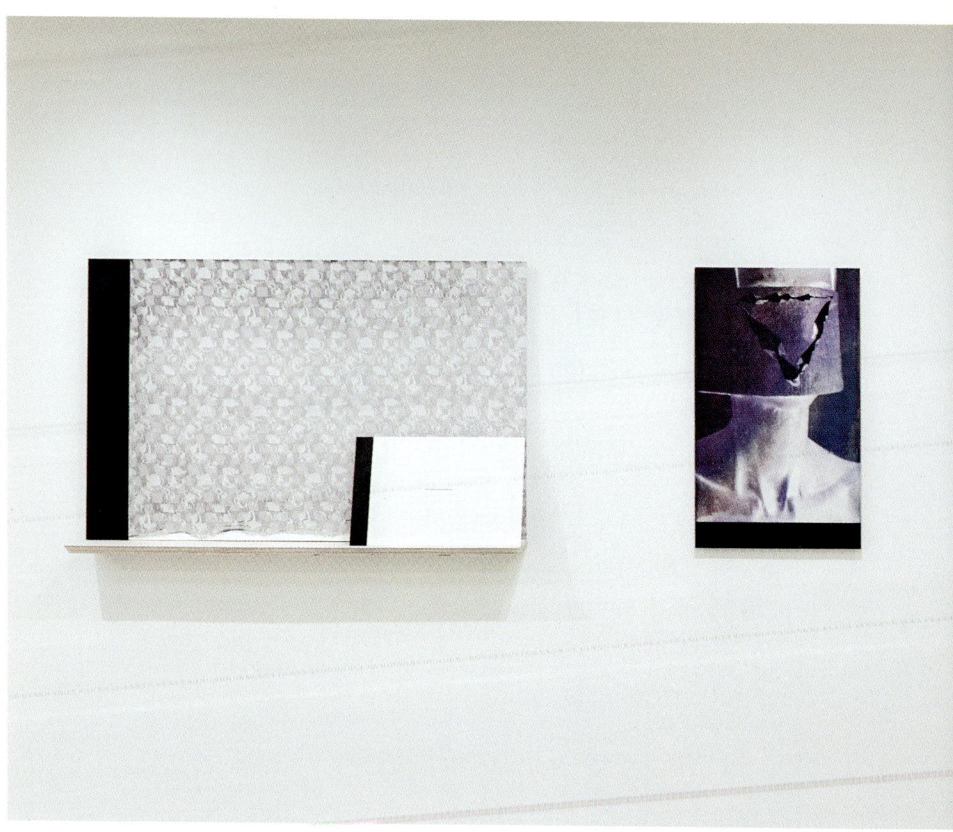

of her interconnected works also draws attention to her interest in extending the 'frame' of painting in the direction of unspecifiable but evocative serial narrative content – telling a story but in ways that literary forms cannot.

The American duo Mary Reid Kelley (b. 1979) and Patrick Kelley (b. 1969) push the notion of painting well outside familiar territory by employing digital media to challenge its status as a stationary rectangle on the wall. Mary studied painting and her husband Pat, photography, so they see their work as combining their skills in analogue and digital media. In their black and white videos, history, mythology, poetry, literature and sheer unbridled fantasy converge. A central goal of their practice is to give imaginative voice to women who have been historically marginalized. *The Syphilis of Sisyphus* (2011), for example, is set in 1852 and tells the story of a young pregnant Parisian woman named Sisyphus, who wanders the bohemian *demimonde* meeting such varied personages as Jesus and Karl

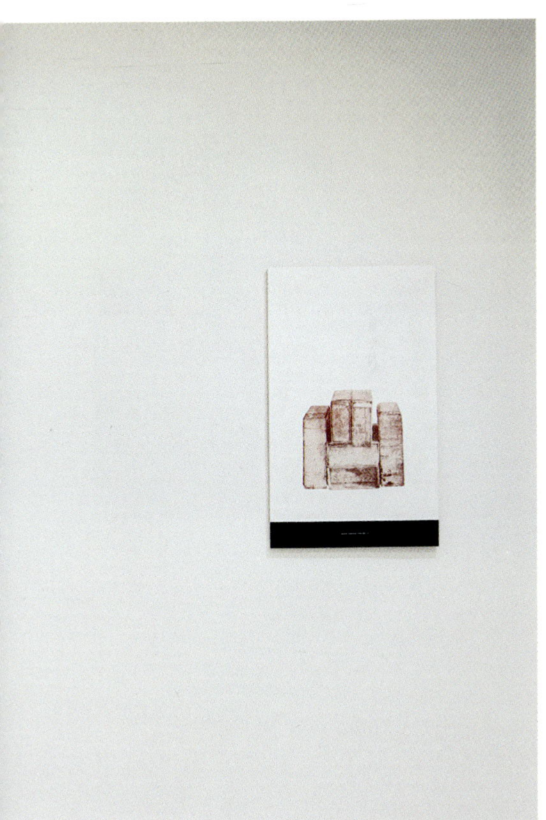

Marx. The artists merge analogue and digital media in video films that include face- and body-painting, costume- and scene-painting, rhyming verse recitation, text slogans, burlesque and theatrical performance. Mary Kelley herself – painted, costumed and bewigged in black and white – plays almost all the roles in the stories (others are usually taken by family members). The sets are hand-painted, but also digitally manipulated in post-production, blurring two- and three-dimensions and disrupting orientation in space.

The work of the Kelleys reflects the fact that the mediations made possible by digital still and video photography, and mass-disseminated via the Internet, are increasingly the primary tools for presenting works of art to audiences. As a result, people are becoming less familiar with the complex meanings gleanable from actual paintings through animated explorations of their surfaces, and more habituated to passive contact with a static image. This has the effect of distancing the

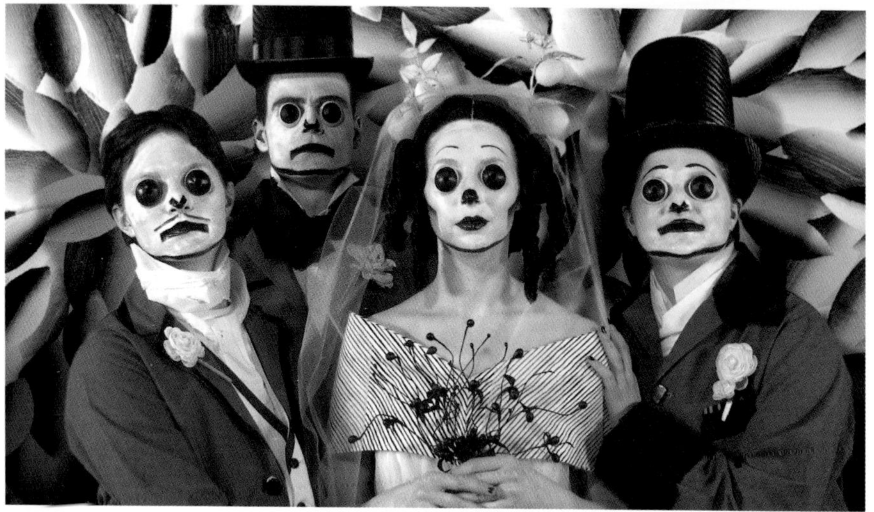

154 Mary Reid Kelley with Patrick Kelley, Still from *The Syphilis of Sisyphus*, 2011

viewer from physical and emotional engagement with a painting in the space in which it is actually displayed, and tends to bias interpretation towards a relationship of detached analysis which draws on the theoretical and the intellectual aspects of the mind rather than the emotional and the physically engaged.

Contemporary Narrative Figurative Painting

But many artists no longer feel so obliged to burn bridges and look to the future. This shift in relationship to history and in attitudes to the role of art in society is a reflection of much wider cultural changes which are the result of the recognition that the faith in limitless progress and development that characterized modernity is now being challenged by the manifold signs of social, political, economic and ecological crisis, thereby demanding a move to consideration of the collective 'commons' – the whole community – and of sustainability. As a result, questions relating to conservation and rejuvenation are now far more pressing than how to deliver the next 'shock of the new'. This reframing of the relationship of the art of the present to that of the past has meant that artists increasingly work as if they exist not so much within the rigid linear geometry of past, present and future, but in a more amorphous, indeterminate and personalized 'then' and 'now', where it is not a question of rejecting the past (like the avant-garde) or of rebirthing the past (like the traditionalists and reactionaries), but of living with powerful historical residues.

While almost all the artists discussed in the previous chapters
were in one way or another haunted by the anxiety of influence
– that is, were preoccupied with being new and original –
many of the younger painters at work since the start of the
new millennium have shown more willingness to acknowledge
the inevitability of their embeddedness in the history of the
medium, and even actively invoke it through drawing on the
styles and themes of admired predecessors as an important
and valuable dimension of what they do.

Today, many artists committed to painting also feel freed
from the censure of the intellectualizing, academic language-
based theories associated with much radical art theory that
had done much to discredit painting, and figurative painting in
particular, as a viable 'critical' or 'resistant' modern medium.
Indeed, an important strength of painting as a contemporary
medium is now perceived to be its capacity to work in dialogue
with its own history, reconfiguring themes and styles from the
past to make new and provocative connections in the present.
For those wedded to the critical logic of the avant-garde, the
resurgence in the new millennium of what they saw as the
'outdated' and 'reactionary' genres of narrative figurative
painting, and especially of landscape – which was in part a
reflection of the new awareness of the natural world and our
place in it provoked by the climate change crisis – proved
particularly controversial. But this renaissance in narrative
figurative painting is a sign that many contemporary artists
are looking back to the roots of modern art in Romanticism
and beyond – to the whole history of painting. For example,
the frequent association made by the feminists of the 1960s
and 1970s of painting with specifically 'patriarchal' values,
most obviously evident in the genre of the sexualized female
nude – but also, it was argued, in the very activity of painting
itself (Renoir, who painted a good many female nudes, is said
to have explained that he painted with his penis) – has been
resoundingly challenged by such woman artists as Jenny Saville
(British, b. 1970), who paints monumentally scaled female
portraits and female nudes in a bold and brash style.

Even more dynamic and challenging of stereotypes are the
paintings of the British artist Cecily Brown (b. 1969). At first
glance, Brown's paintings appear 'abstract', in the sense of
being devoid of recognizable imagery, but as one looks more
closely, figures emerge from the maelstrom of paint. Brown also
makes a direct connection between sex and painting, which, as
a woman, also has the effect of wresting this connection from
its historical association with male bravado. In *When this kiss
is over* (2020) one can make out two naked bodies locked

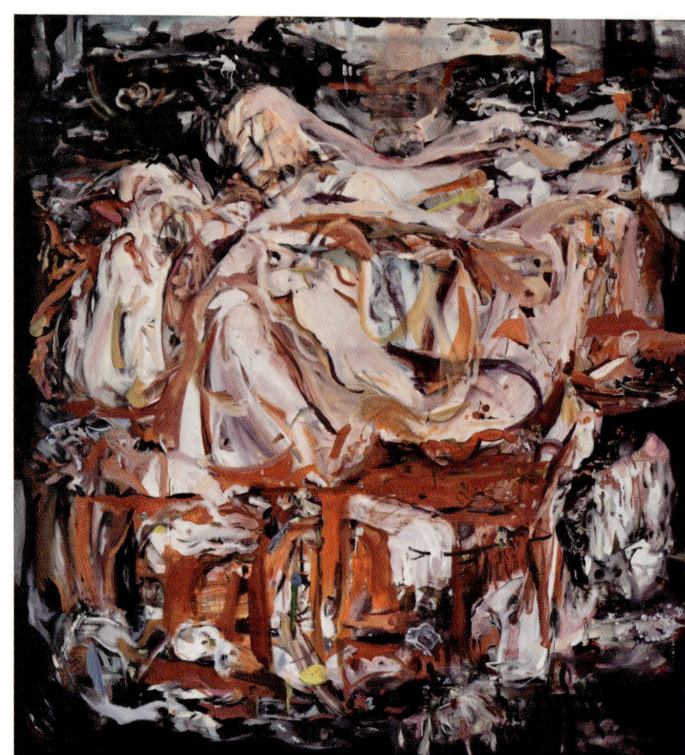

155 LEFT Cecily Brown, *When this kiss is over*, 2020
156 OPPOSITE Dana Schutz, *Bound*, 2019

In an embrace (their heads are at upper left), perched on chairs or a bed (perhaps). Brown's practice is strongly process-oriented, drawing attention to the dynamic act of painting using the medium of oil paint. In this, she is influenced by the brushwork of earlier expressionists such as Francis Bacon, Willem de Kooning and Joan Mitchell, as well as by those Old Masters who display in their work an overtly sensual engagement with painting as an activity – such as the Dutch painters Peter-Paul Rubens and Rembrandt van Rijn.

In the work of the American Dana Schutz (b. 1976), some form of narrative is implied, but as is evident in *Bound* (2019), Schutz rejects the conventions of optical realism and confounds to an even greater extent the viewer's desire for a clear message. Her cartoony, deliberately slap-dash style is especially inspired by the example of Philip Guston. 'More than any other artist, Guston renders the messy contradictions and heart-breaking ambiguity it is to be a person,' she remarks. In Schutz's paintings, the exuberant accumulation of images often seems pervaded by a sense of anxiety and

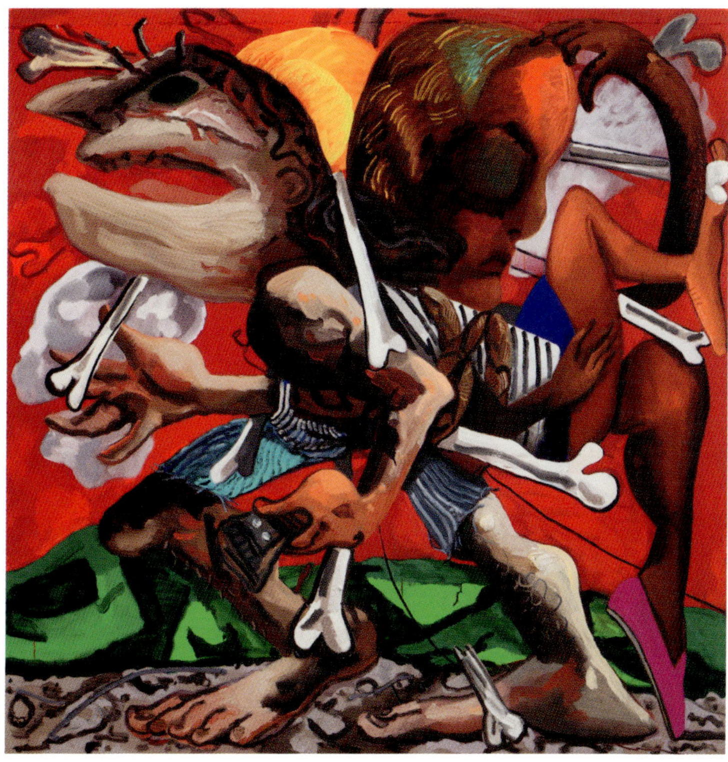

fear, and to amount to a searing critique of modern America. But as Schutz has noted: 'I think paintings always have a second subject; there's the painting with a subject you can write down, or title, but I think the actual subject is way more open or diffuse or nebulous, or something that is not quite nameable. And I think that that may be painting's power.' Schutz's reference to paintings' deeper, non-linguistic, 'not quite nameable' something is a reminder that they are far from simply inert objects upon which articulated meanings can be inscribed (by an artist, art historian, curator or critic) and have their own unpredictable agency and capacity to generate a field of feelings and associations.

Canadian-British artist Peter Doig (b. 1959) exuberantly embraced western painting's history, referencing the work of landscape artists such as Caspar David Friedrich and J. M. W. Turner, alongside that of Expressionists like Edvard Munch and realist painters like Edward Hopper, while the uncanny, dreamlike quality of his work owes much to Surrealism's quest for the painting of 'interior reality' (see Chapter Five).

157

As had already become increasingly typical in the 1980s, Doig draws inspiration not so much from direct observation of the world but from found images, such as film stills, newspaper clippings, personal photo albums and record covers. In *Gasthof zur Muldentalsperre* (2000–2) the two figures were appropriated from an antique postcard showing a view from the old German tavern after which the painting is entitled. Doig has said of this painting: 'If you look at the two costumed figures represented in Gasthof, they are the gatekeepers to the world of painting. These are the people who allow you to disband your disbelief, like an entrance to a dream. For me they are dressed up like the Byrds [the 1960s pop group], pretending to be from another time, although this could lead to a much too specific background, musically as well as historically. In the end, they are at the center [*sic.*] of attraction while equally being out of time.'

German artist Daniel Richter (b. 1962) also makes full use of painting's history and its material properties, and, like Doig, is drawn to art historical referents like James Ensor and Munch, while promiscuously sourcing imagery culled from high and low culture, such as photographs of street protests. But Richter takes more jarring liberties than Doig, both with representational language and the use of extreme colour relations. Like many contemporary painters, Doig and Richter manipulate found images using Photoshop or similar computer programs, employing digital software as a tool in the generative

157 BELOW Peter Doig, *Gasthof zur Muldentalsperre*, 2000–2
158 OPPOSITE Neo Rauch, *Der Blaue Fisch*, 2014

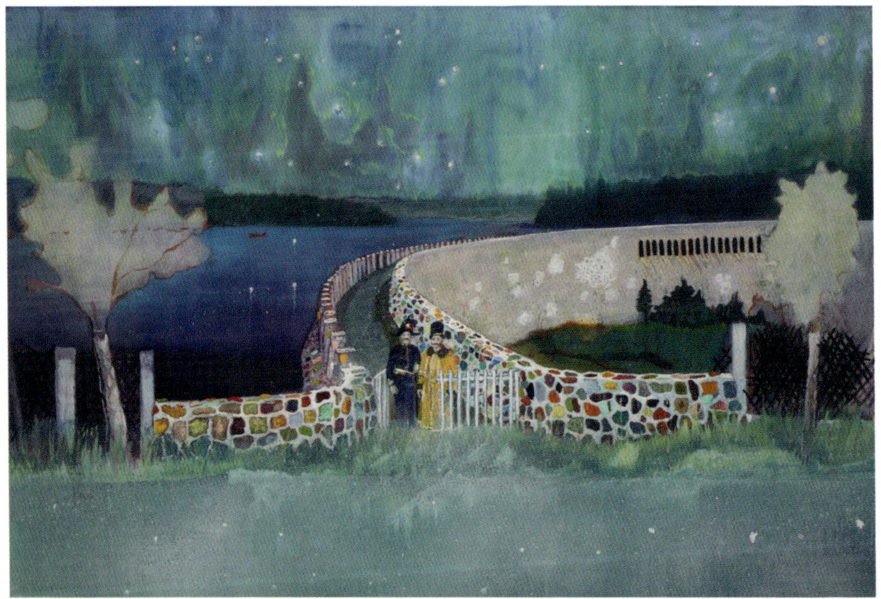

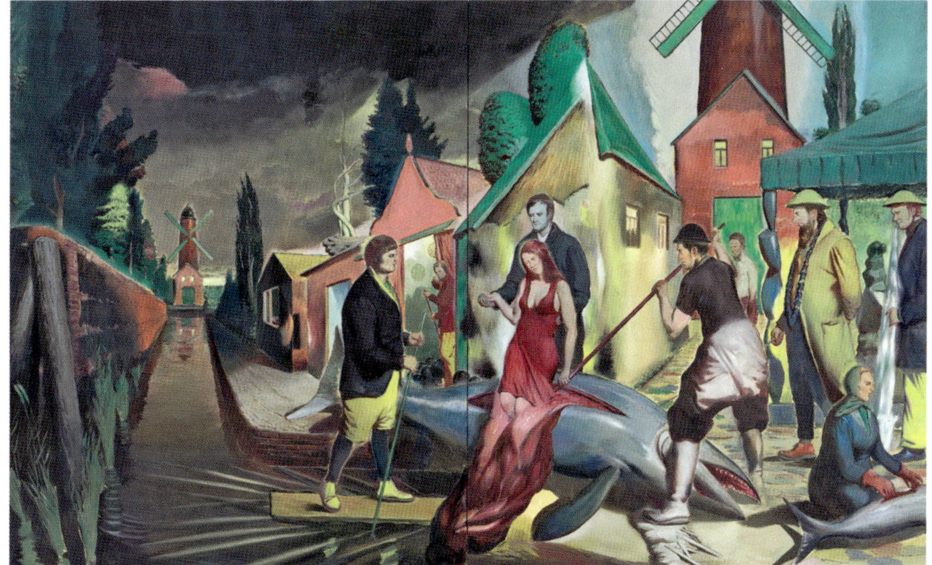

stages of the creation of their works, which freely blend the languages of 'abstraction' and 'figuration', and amount to an exuberant celebration of painting's technical as well as representational possibilities.

Another German artist, Neo Rauch (b. 1960), also draws on a rich and varied archive of images, using an obviously Surrealism-inspired style to create disjunctive landscapes peopled by bizarre casts of characters; he has observed: 'For me, painting means the continuation of dreaming by other means.' Rauch studied in the former Communist East Germany and was therefore trained in the mandatory Socialist Realist style, but he redirected his skills in figurative painting towards the creation – as in *Der Blaue Fisch* (2014) – of fictional worlds or ominous historical narratives. In this work, a man helps an elegantly dressed woman out of a wound in a large, freshly caught blue-coloured fish. The multiple perspectives, mix of historical periods and powerful mythological dimension conspire to give Rauch's pictures an uncanny and oracular air, earning their description as 'postmodern history paintings'.

158

Painting and Social Identity

A key aspect of contemporary social transformation reflected in much painting is the question of social identity. Artists from ethnic minorities in particular employ painting to confront how social prejudices function as especially limiting 'frames'

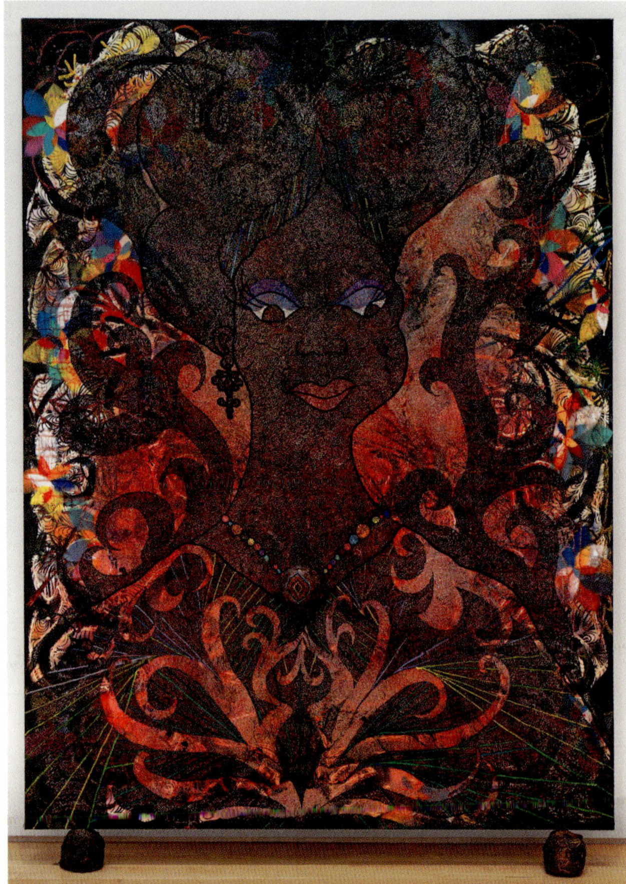

159 LEFT Chris Ofili, *Princess of the Posse*, 1999
160 OPPOSITE Hurvin Anderson, *Is it OK to be black?*, 2016

in dire need of critical interrogation. In his early paintings the British artist Chris Ofili (b. 1968), whose parents migrated from Nigeria to England before he was born, drew on and parodied western ideas about African culture: he often applied real elephant dung to his pictures in the form of dried spherical lumps, and used them as decorated and varnished foot-like supports for paintings such as *Princess of the Posse* (1999), which are displayed casually leaning against the wall. In this particular work, the title comes from the pop song of the same name by Queen Latifah.

For several Black British artists working in the multicultural milieu of postcolonial Britain, such as Hurvin Anderson, Sonia Boyce, Lubaina Himid and Lynette Yiadom-Boakye, painting became a medium through which to celebrate and make visible

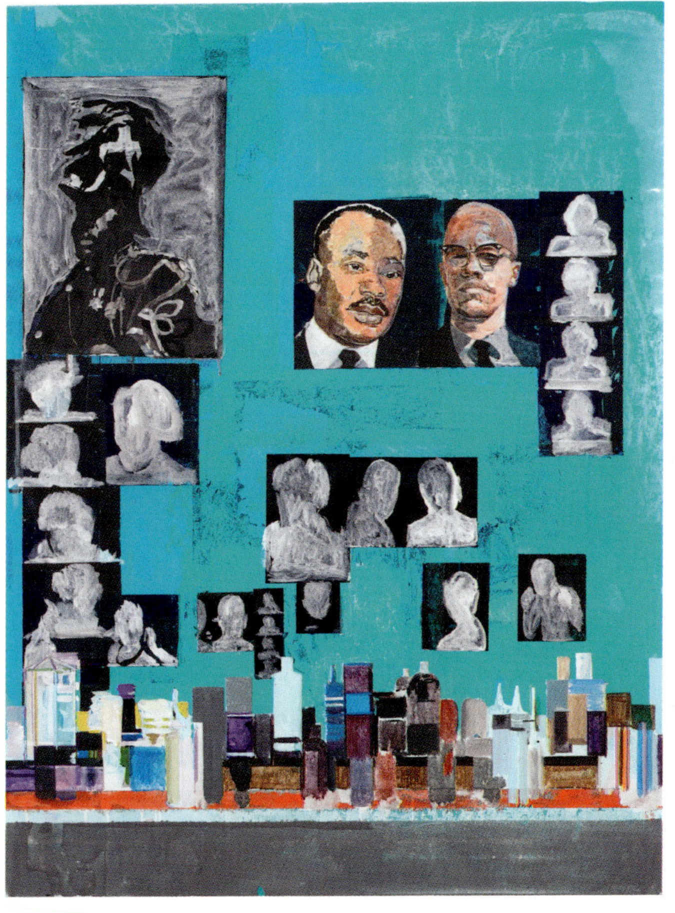

their own cultural identity. Hurvin Anderson's (b. 1965) parents were Caribbean migrants to Britain – members of the so-called 'Windrush Generation' – and he explains that his paintings aim to 'create a new space', one in which diverse elements intentionally coexist in unfamiliar ways that he believes reflect the reality of the Afro-Caribbean diaspora. *Is it OK to be black?* (2016) is from Anderson's series of 'barbershop paintings' and was made as a specific response to the heightened awareness of racism provoked by police brutality in the United Kingdom and the United States. 'I was trying to make a painting about figures that were seen as influential to the black community in Britain,' Anderson has stated. 'There was a sense that there was a side to take – either of Malcolm X or Martin Luther King – and I wanted to bring the two of them together.'

160

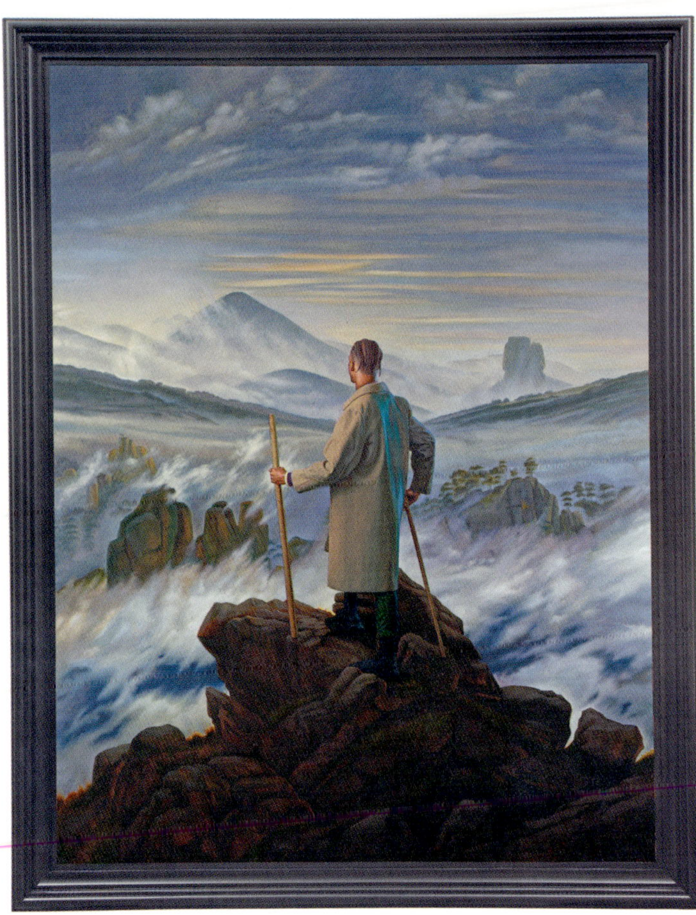

161 LEFT Kehinde Wiley, *The Prelude (Babacar Mané)*, 2021
162 OPPOSITE Salman Toor, *The Bar on East 13th*, 2019

Across the Atlantic, several artists expressly adopted figurative painting styles in order to explore and foreground Black culture in a manner that questioned the dominance of the cultural stock associated with the white elite. In often monumentally sized paintings, Kerry James Marshall (b. 1955) mines the historical genres of landscape, portraiture, still-life and history painting, and sees an especially compelling reason to paint figuratively so that Black history can be chronicled in pictures and memorialized in museums. Kehinde Wiley (b. 1977) also adopts a realistic figurative approach to painting, but one that more overtly appropriates the styles of, as well actual paintings by, white Old Masters, making portraits of Black people – including former US president Barack Obama but, more commonly, of ordinary people from the streets of Harlem.

Wiley's painting *The Prelude (Babacar Mané)* (2021) was made specifically as part of Wiley's exhibition as artist-in-residence at London's National Gallery. An African man stands proudly atop the mountain in the place of the artist Caspar David Friedrich in his masterpiece of Romantic art (illustrated in Chapter One). For the project, Wiley also appropriated the dramatic themes of the landscape pictures of the Romantic period for his own paintings, as well as making a video. His version of Friedrich's painting is monumental, much larger than the original, which adds further impact to his assertive repurposing, in which hierarchies are upset and the presence of unresolved social injustices exposed. Wiley notes that the explicit citation of Friedrich's work is not intended as mere parody, however, but rather is a homage and a call for inclusion: 'if you look at the paintings that I love in art history, these are the paintings where great, powerful men are being celebrated on the big walls of museums throughout the world. What feels really strange is not to be able to see a reflection of myself in that world.'

The works of such artists demonstrated that figurative painting continues to have potential as a space within which to represent and celebrate cultures whose invisibility or marginality have been enforced by mainstream society. Another dimension of this social inclusivity, whereby painting's history is re-presented through new eyes so as to empower people in the present, is the work of Salman Toor (b. 1983), a Muslim born in Pakistan and now living in New York City. Toor depicts his community of genderqueer people in ways that

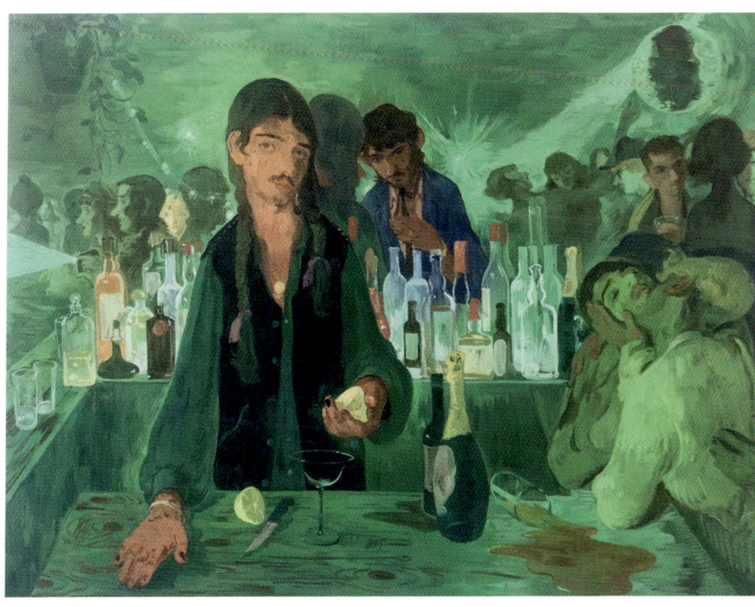

accommodate them within the history of western painting. In *The Bar on East 13th* (2019) Toor consciously evokes Edouard Manet's celebrated painting *A Bar at the Folies-Bergère* (1882, Courtauld Institute, London). In Manet's work a female bartender blankly stares directly out of the picture into the space occupied by the viewer. Toor's bartender, by contrast, looks back with coy confidence at the man dressed in a blue shirt who is reflected in the mirror, and also at us, the viewers of his painting.

Contemporary Painting Between Figuration and Abstraction

In a world in which digital images have become infinitely manipulable, duplicable, communicable and omnipresent, interest in visual worlds that cannot be photographed – or aspects of the visible world that are overlooked due to sensory overload – have become more important and have contributed to a resurgence of interest in various forms of abstract or semi-abstract painting. These evolved in styles that have been grouped together under such monikers as 'Modest Abstraction', 'Zombie Formalism' or 'Crapstraction'.

'Modest Abstraction' is a good stylistic label for the works of the London-based German artist Tomma Abts (b. 1967), who creates intimate small-scaled paintings that uniformly measure 48 by 38 centimetres. She has said that works such as *Lüür* (2015) feel to her 'like objects or things', and that there is a 'virtual' dimension to the space she creates that produces a recognizable connection between her paintings and the familiar but often overlooked dimensions of the perceptual world. We are asked to pay unusually close attention to mundane visual experience, to contemplate spatial relations as arresting in their own right. While in ordinary life, looking at a serpentine line casting a shadow would be interpreted primarily in terms of its potential practical interest and context, or probably be dismissed as uninteresting, in Abts's work this effect is presented as an intrinsically significant visual experience.

The New York-based German artist Charline von Heyl (b. 1960) also explores a distilled world composed of lines, shapes, colours, textures and volumes. She is interested in the fact that such formal properties can suggest three-dimensional and two-dimensional occupations of spaces that make her paintings seem involved in more than their underlying and ostensibly 'abstract' formally material properties. In *Slow Tramp* (2012), for example, the grey patterned shape in the centre could be a curtain or a vase, while the vertical stripe pattern could be wallpaper or a reference to geometric abstract art. The black

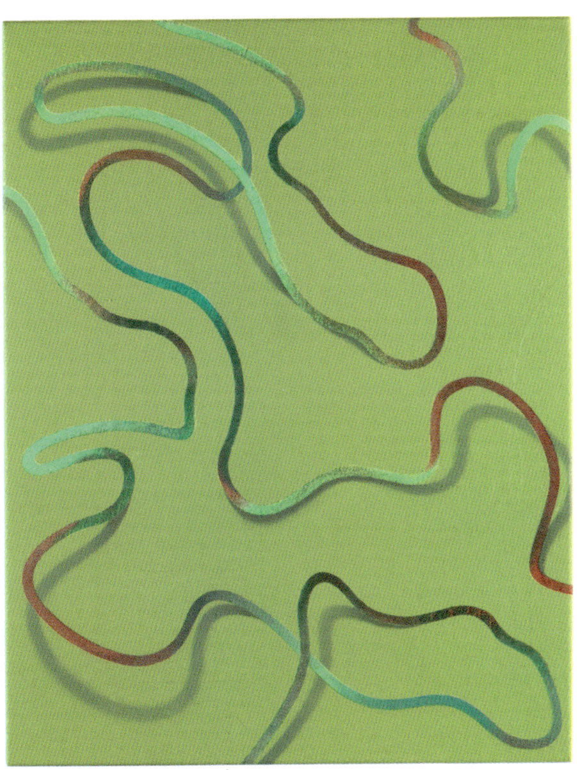

shape could be a reclining figure or, if the painterly horizontal band at the top is read as the sky, a pathway. None of these readings seems definitive, and none is necessarily right or wrong. Von Heyl's work suggests that despite what had been claimed by an earlier generation of more strictly formalist abstract artists, a shape in a painting is never just a shape. It always affords us something, that is, it means something in terms of possible use, or as a memory trigger. Both Abts's and Von Heyl's work also reminds us that what is now most salient for many painters is not whether a painting is 'abstract' or 'figurative', or what particular style characterizes it. Rather, the key point is that it is a *painting* – any kind of painting – rather than a video, installation, performance or digital art, or any of the other forms taken by contemporary art.

The potential of abstract art to serve as a way of mapping actual social worlds in ways that reveal dimensions that more overt forms of figurative art cannot address is also central to the work of the American artist Mark Bradford (b. 1961), albeit used to very different ends. Bradford dubs his work 'social

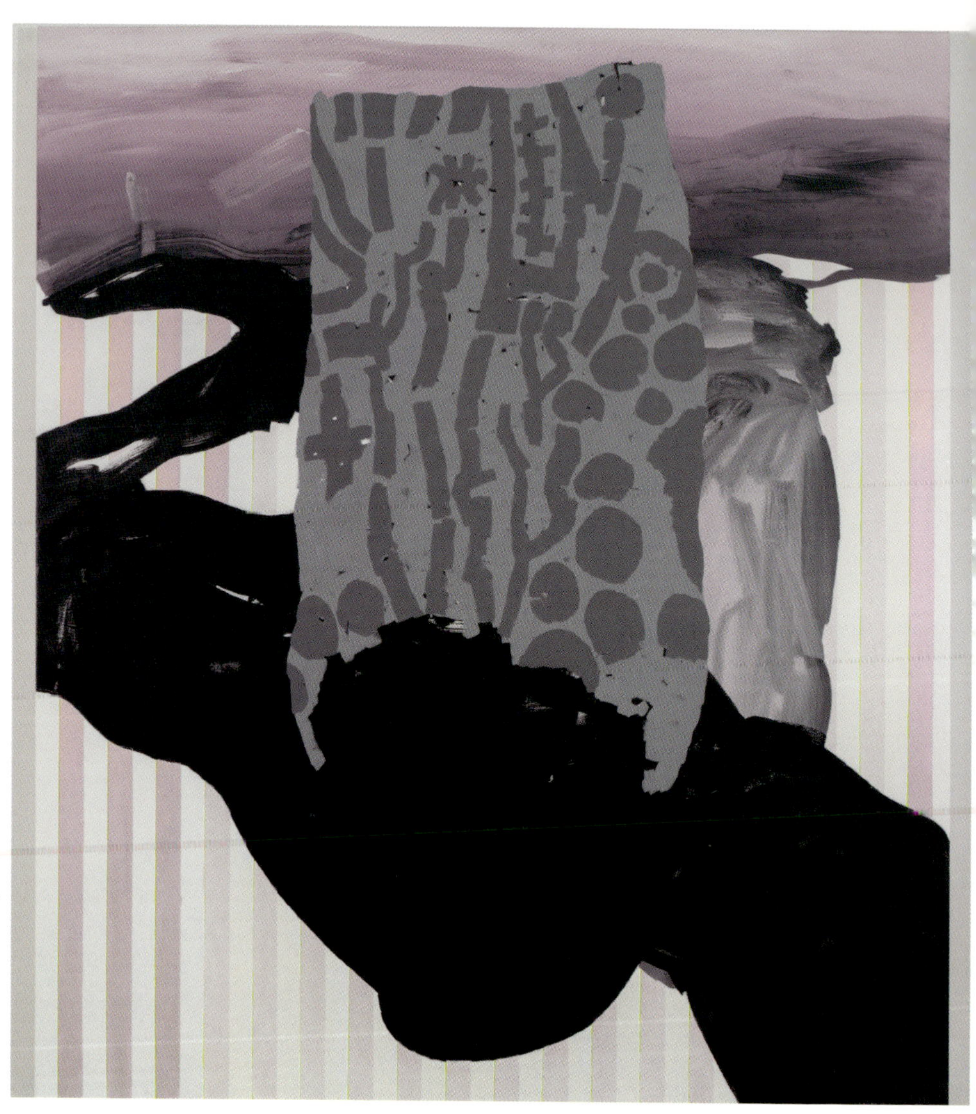

164 Charline von Heyl, *Slow Tramp*, 2012

abstraction', and says: 'Abstraction for me, I get it – you go internal, you turn off the world, you're hermetic, you channel something. No. I'm not interested in that type of abstraction. I'm interested in the type of abstraction where you look out at the world, see the horror – sometimes it is horror – and you drag that horror kicking and screaming into your studio and you wrestle with it and you find something beautiful in it. That's what I was always determined to do. I have never turned away.' This social engagement, especially in relation to the experience of African Americans, underlies works such as *Tomorrow Is Another Day* (2016), which are the result of the accumulation of materials and traces – bleach, caulking and paper taken from advertising hoardings – sourced from the streets of Los Angeles. Bradford softens the paper in water until it is a malleable pulp which is then layered onto the canvas and sanded down. The finished painting is comparable to the scarred and pitted surface of the city itself, a personalized mapping.

Another African American, Torkwase Dyson (b. 1973), also adopted an inherently critical stance in relation to the history of abstract art, invoking a complex and oppressive social context through the shapes, colours and textures in her paintings. Inspired by what she terms 'Black spatial history', Dyson has developed an austere abstract vocabulary comprising design systems of architecture, water infrastructure, the oil and gas industry and the physical impact of global warming. Dyson applies what she calls 'Black Compositional Thought' to her cartographic paintings, linking the black abstract forms in her art to the networks of power that shape the political landscape, in particular the histories of racial and spatial segregation in her country, the United States.

Globalized Painting

While the initial interactions between western and non-western artists took place in terms of a centre and a periphery, a hierarchy of leader and follower, we have seen how increased globalization led to a process of de-territorialization in which art comes to function independently of, or in novel relationships with, specific geographical or cultural locations. Encouraged by ease of international travel and access to the Internet, and by the emergence of a homogenized global culture dedicated to the perpetually new, severance of social, political and cultural practices from native places and populations brought new freedoms, but also new forms of alienation. As the Internet, world trade and the values of consumerism drew once far-flung and isolated cultures together, the voices of those who

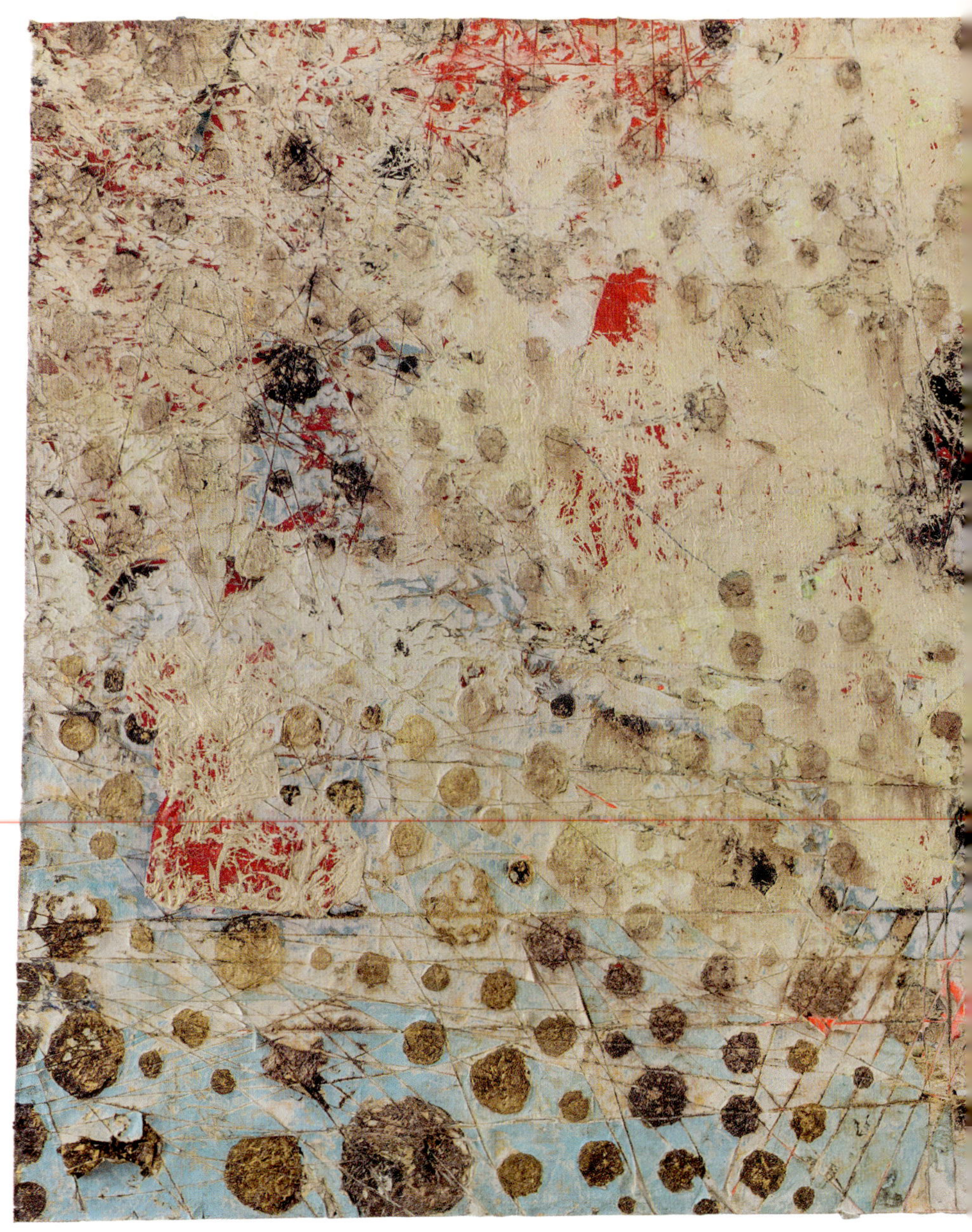

165 Mark Bradford, *Tomorrow Is Another Day*, 2016

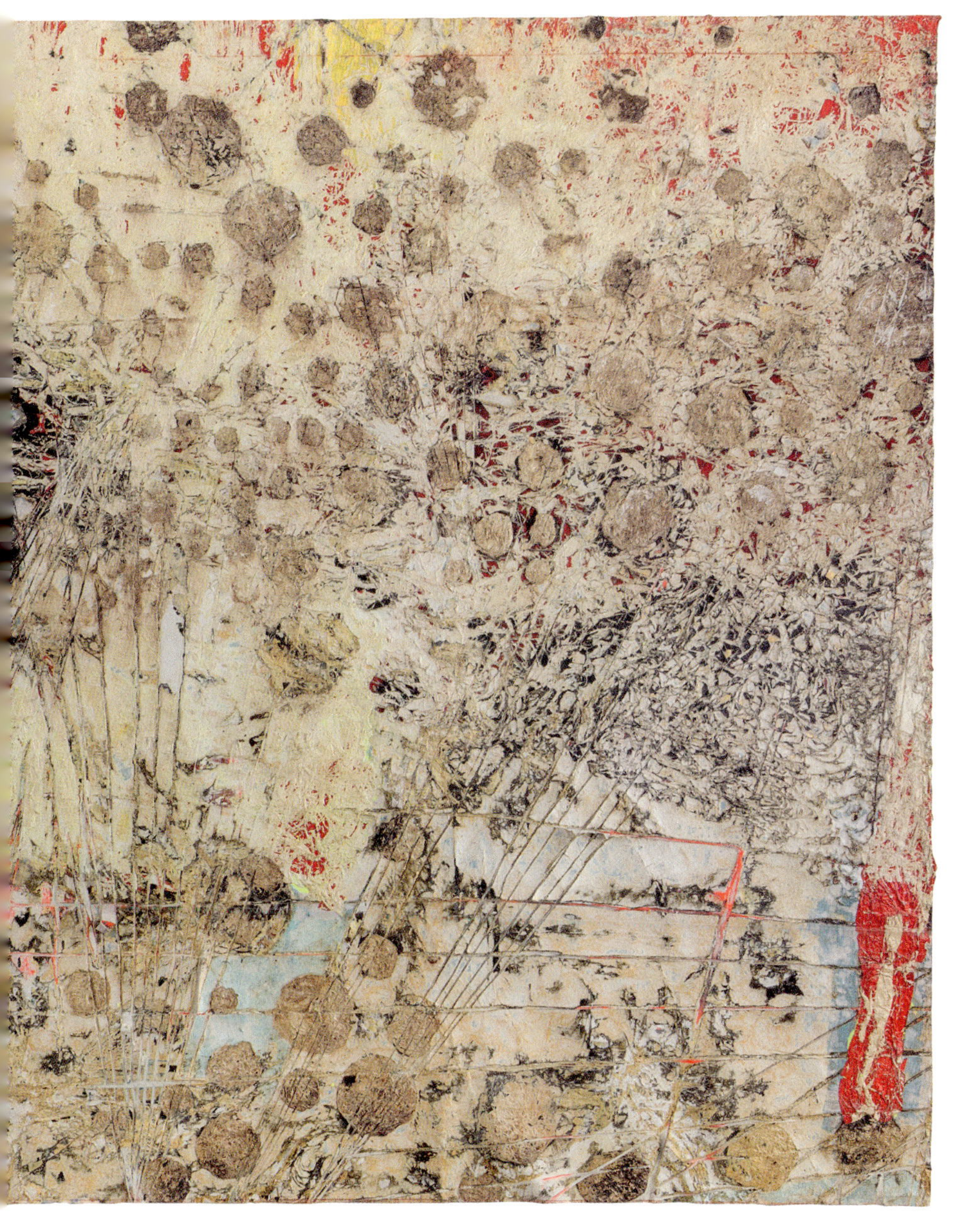

felt excluded or who despised the values of the new globalism
sometimes turned to violent expediencies. Islamicist terrorism
and internecine warfare reflected deep-seated grievances and
exposed seemingly unresolvable differences in worldviews.
The defenders of liberal humanism were forced to question
the universality of their convictions, and this could lead to
the posing of uncomfortable questions concerning the true
motivation and goals behind western modernization, and
to an increasing sense that the values espoused by the west
concealed unexamined prejudices and injustices.

As we saw in Chapters Seven and Eight, principles
associated with the development of abstract art in the
west often corresponded in interesting and, to westerners,
unexpected ways with traditions elsewhere in the world which,
on converging within the mainstream artworld, created
new styles, experiences and values, and alternative models
of interpretation. Thus, for example, the exploration of the
traditions of the Islamic art of his native Iran, and of the
affinities or differences between it and modern western art,
lies at the heart of the practice of New York-based artist Y. Z.
Kami (b. 1956). Working across painting, collage, photography,
prints and site-specific sculpture, Kami is best known for
exhibitions in which he juxtaposes 'abstract' works with large-
scale figurative oil paintings based on blurred photographs,
especially of faces or, as in *Daya's Hands II* (2015–16), of palms
pressed together as if in prayer. Like another Iranian, London-
based artist, Shirazeh Houshiary (b. 1955), Kami is particularly
inspired by the thirteenth-century Persian mystic and Sufi
poet Rumi, and paintings such as *White Dome 1* (2014) evoke
celestial cupolas built out of tessellated concentric circles.
For Kami, the most important function of painting within the
contemporary world is to offer a space of silent contemplation
and presence, an island in an ocean of internecine conflicts and
restless data. Kami's work is especially provocative because, by
working in what in the west were once considered aesthetically
incompatible and historically distanced styles, he indicates
that painting today can no longer be understood in terms of
a succession of innovative '-isms', or associated only with the
interests of western culture. Kami's works do not just bring into
contact two radically different languages of western painting –
one that, by coincidence, is conducive to the tenets of Islam and
linked to its traditions, while the other is inimical – but also
two worldviews. He implies that both are valid ways to evoke the
ineffable dimension of human experience through painting.

But the sense of crisis is now felt at much deeper levels
than just within human society. From the year 2000 the term

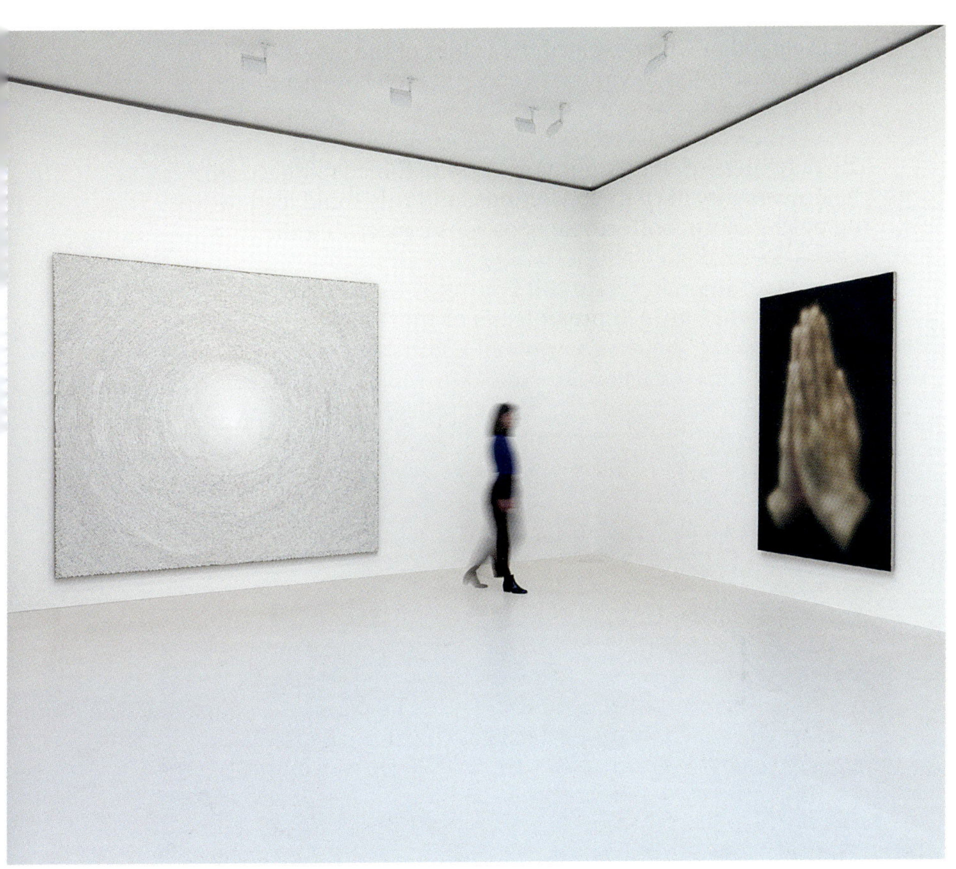

166 Y. Z. Kami, *White Dome 1*, 2014 (LEFT) and *Daya's Hands II*, 2015–16 (RIGHT)

'Anthropocene' – the 'Age of Humans' – began to be used to describe the radical and profound impact of humanity on the earth's ecosystem caused by the transformations facilitated by new technologies, the burning of fossil fuels such as coal, gas and oil, colonial expansion and contraction, and the exponential growth of the human population that occurred during the period covered by this book. These specific and distinctive transformations extend to include non-human deep history and the very future of all life on the planet. Humans are now cast as geological agents with the power to change the most fundamental physical processes. One significant consequence of this situation is that in order to confront and navigate this complex and multi-faceted new reality, it is necessary to think not just in terms of the global but of the planetary. It is in the light of the 'Anthropocene' that we approach artists from regions of the world who, in one way or another, have felt the impact of the forces unleashed by the west over the past two hundred years.

The Kenyan-born American artist Wangechi Mutu (b. 1972) uses painting to capture the unprecedented character of today's world culture in which the local and the global – the 'glocal' – merge unstably, and the human, technological, non-human, geological and meteorological fuse to create new realities. In one of her characteristic works, the diptych *Double Fuse* (2003), Mutu combines painting with photographic collage, creating imaginary hybrid creatures, part-human, part-animal, made by combining found materials and sampling sources drawn from her own African tradition, world politics, fashion, pornography and science fiction. She sees and parodies western ideas of the exotic 'other', while also playing into these same fantasies.

Like several artists from beyond the Euro-American region, Mutu sees globalization as an ongoing creative mutation involving the unstable blending of dangerous and mysterious but also exciting and liberating forces that transcend terrestrial coordinates. Her work reflects the fact that the process of globalization has involved multiple feedback loops in which western artists are positively influenced by – and have appropriated – non-western art and artefacts, and in their turn non-western artists are influenced by westerners.

167 BELOW Wangechi Mutu, *Double Fuse*, 2003
168 OPPOSITE Beatriz Milhazes, *Banho de Rio*, 2017

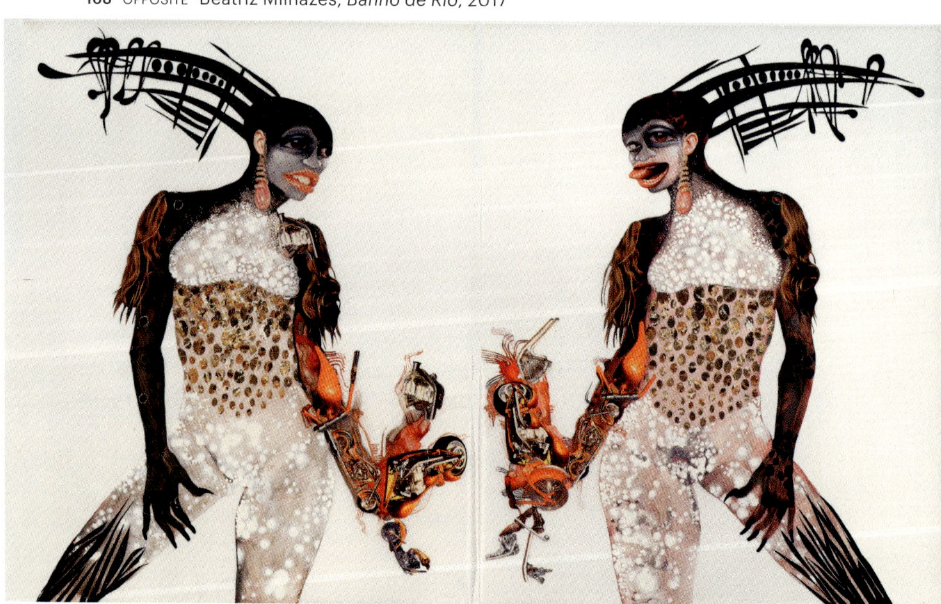

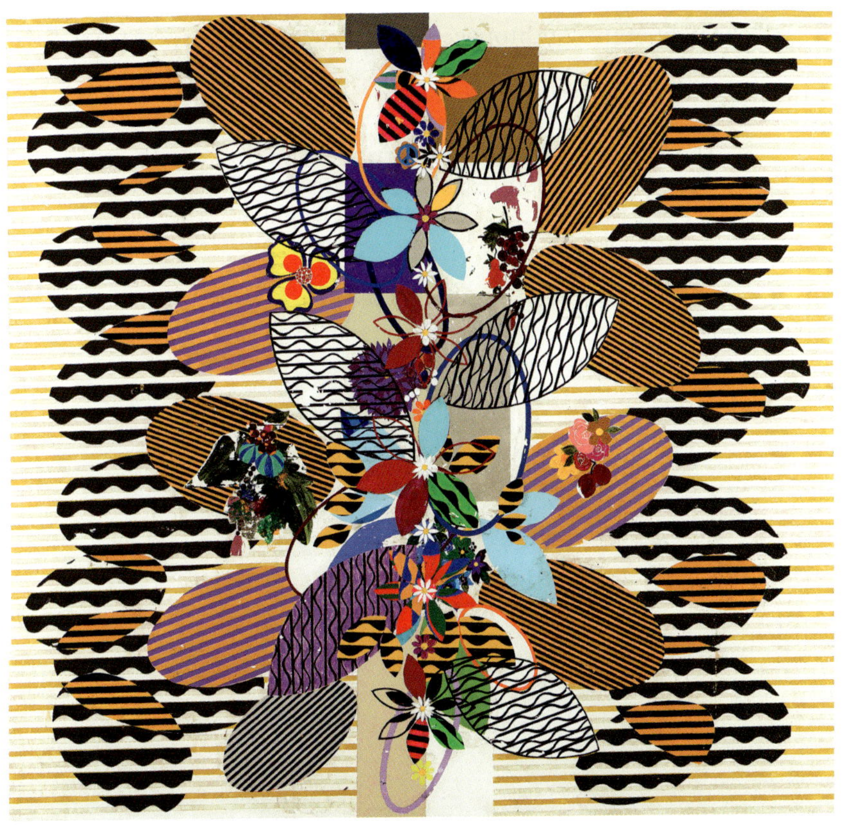

Eventually, these exchanges lead to forms of modern art linked to western examples but embodying unique and independent characteristics that have developed beyond the domineering gaze of the west.

The Brazilian artist Beatriz Milhazes (b. 1960) adopts a more geographically focused approach to the intersection between the global and the local in her painting, basing her practice on her intimate knowledge of geographical, ecological and historical location – the botanical gardens, the Tijuca Forest near her studio in Rio de Janeiro, the ocean front – along with childhood memories and the cultural motifs of Brazil. Her works blend European abstract art with early twentieth-century Brazilian modernism (such as that practised by Hélio Oiticica) and the legacy of the Baroque in South America. Some critics have also associated Milhazes's interest in pattern, collage and craft techniques with traditional 'feminine' qualities, and therefore with an underlying critique of patriarchal society.

168

Whatever the case, for Milhazes, painting is clearly an arena within which to explore cultural identity in relation to the experience of place and global perspectives, alongside pure aesthetic qualities; visually, her art is festively decorative and affirmative, and painting becomes an expression of the sensual, a celebration of pleasure and creative freedom.

From the 1960s onwards, the Korean-born but Japan-domiciled artist Lee Ufan (b. 1936) dedicated himself to integrating western concepts of modern abstract art with those of East Asia. Lee is especially critical of unexamined parallels between even progressive western art and western attitudes more generally. He remarked that western artists fill their canvases 'with their thoughts as if they were managing a colony'. To counter this tacitly 'imperialistic' relationship he proposed reinterpreting his own East Asian traditions, in which taking into account the 'untouched' or the 'blank' within painting was deemed important. As we already saw in relation to the work of the Japanese artist Yayoi Kusama and fellow Korean Kim Whanki, the emptiness or 'voids' – the untouched areas – of Lee's paintings reflect the fact that within the traditional East Asian aesthetic abridged, suggested, invisible worlds and elusive states of mind that lie beyond human control were highly valued. An important goal was to convey immersion in the dynamic openness or continuum of an infinite and uncontrollable nature. In Lee's *Dialogue* (2014), for example, one solitary brushstroke sits in, floats on, or perhaps slips in or out of a large empty ground. This brushstroke initially suggests the trace of a sudden dynamic gesture, but in fact it is the result of careful and methodical planning governed by the duration of Lee's held breath. He first placed a piece of paper the size of the brushstroke on top on the canvas, exploring positions, then painted in the brushstroke with a methodical, controlled gesture that was subsequently repeated to consolidate the stroke.

Lee is associated with a group of South Koreans, including Park Seo-Bo, Chung Sang-Hwa, Chung Chang-Sup and Yun Hyong-Keun, who developed forms of monochrome painting in the 1970s and 1980s that later became known collectively as Dansaekhwa ('One-colour-painting'), but who only became internationally celebrated during the 2010s. The appeal of such reductive abstract art within the context of South Korea lay not so much in confronting the problem of representation and in the iconoclastic rejection of figuration, however, but in how it could facilitate the transformation or updating into modern times of traditional indigenous ideas that centred on the value of painting as a receptive surface upon which, through ritualized action, an artist can articulate the experience of harmonious integration of mind, body and world in the present moment.

In Japan, Takashi Murakami (b. 1962) rejected the principles of western modernism in favour of what he termed the 'Superflat' style, an aesthetic programme that emerged from the interest of a number of Japanese artists, such as Yoshitomo Nara (b. 1959), in their nation's contemporary popular culture – in *anime*, *manga*, video games, fashion and graphic design. But Murakami's concept also threw down a challenge to what he argued is an artificially imported 'western' distinction between 'high' and 'low' art, and he looked back to the period when Japan first began to westernize in the mid-nineteenth century.

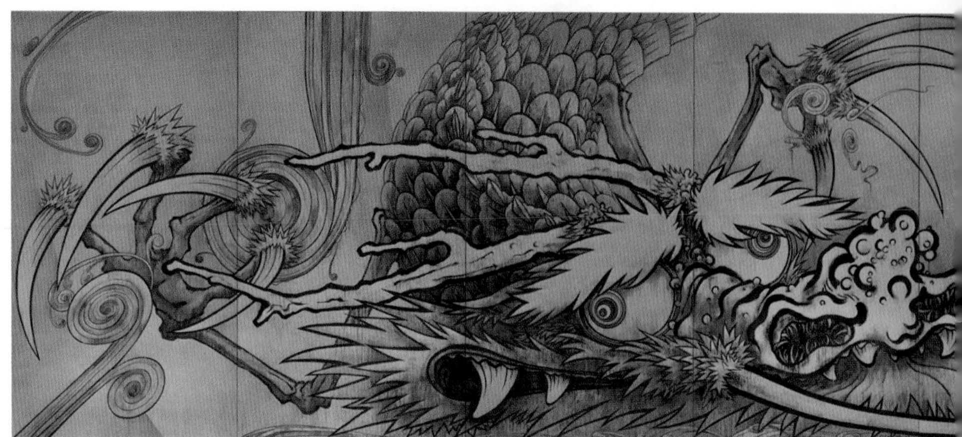

170 Takashi Murakami, *Dragon in Clouds – Indigo Blue*, 2010

At the same time, however, while exposing the inherent contradictions in concepts of the local and the international, Murakami knowingly enlisted the west's received ideas about Japanese culture in order to appeal to a global audience. Birthed in Japan but owing much to western Pop art influences, Murakami's use of 'Superflat' aimed to appropriate the western perception of Japan and repackage it for the same audience. Technically, the 'Superflat' style appropriated traditional Japanese painting techniques to depict pop culture subjects within a flattened representational picture-plane like that used in classical Japanese art. Murakami's huge mural-sized painting *Dragon in Clouds – Indigo Blue* (2010) comprises nine panels and was originally installed facing an equally big painting of a red dragon. Cloud-and-dragon paintings were a common theme in traditional Japanese art, where the dragon is a symbol of good fortune and hope, but Murakami mixed this inspiration with motifs from popular culture.

In China, which, as we saw, was segregated from progressive modern art by the cultural programme of the Chinese Communist Party, some artists were able in the new millennium to look more consciously backwards to traditional pre-western and pre-communist traditions to create forms of painting that carry both local and international meaning. When China became communist, the classical conventions of painting were condemned as aspects of the repressive old order, and Chairman Mao demanded that all artists work in oils and in a style inspired by the Soviet Union's Socialist Realism (see Chapter Five). However, from the 1990s onwards, the Communist Party's policy shifted to invite the cautious

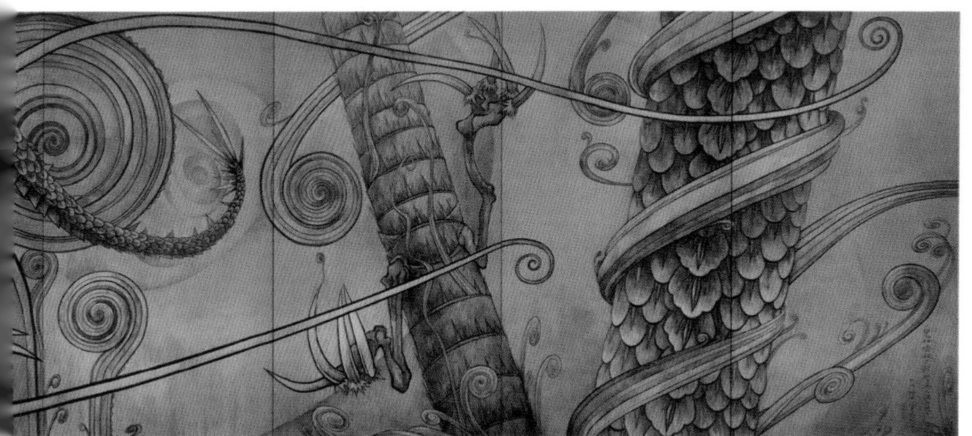

reappraisal of classical Chinese culture. Hao Liang (b. 1983), for example, set out to reinvigorate the classical Chinese tradition of ink painting, especially landscape painting, also working in traditional formats, producing scroll paintings that are intended to be rolled and unrolled, and viewed sequentially, like reading a book. Hao's ink on silk painting *Day and Night (Part II)* (2017–18) is one of two works, the other depicting the night, and evokes a classical Chinese 'mountain-water' landscape painting, as practised by Song Dynasty (960–1279) scholar-painters. But Hao also distances his work from its traditional sources by using characteristically modern elements that allude to abstract art and western cultural influences.

171

Hao's paintings are also a reminder that modern painting is fundamentally *western* painting not only in terms of the ethnicity of the people who created most of it, the culturally specific emphasis on the individualistic attitude, the styles and the limited range of subjects it explored, but also in terms of the material medium itself. Most of the works in this book are made in the quintessentially western medium of oil on canvas, which led to specific styles of painting – permitting, for instance, artists to work with the rigid support propped upright because the viscosity of oil paint means it does not run, rather than flat, which is how traditional Chinese ink paintings were made, because the liquidity of ink requires the paper or silk to be laid horizontally. Oil paint applied to a primed linen or cotton textile surface permits artists to use strongly coloured and layered pigment, whereas ink painting was usually monochrome or used muted water-based colour.

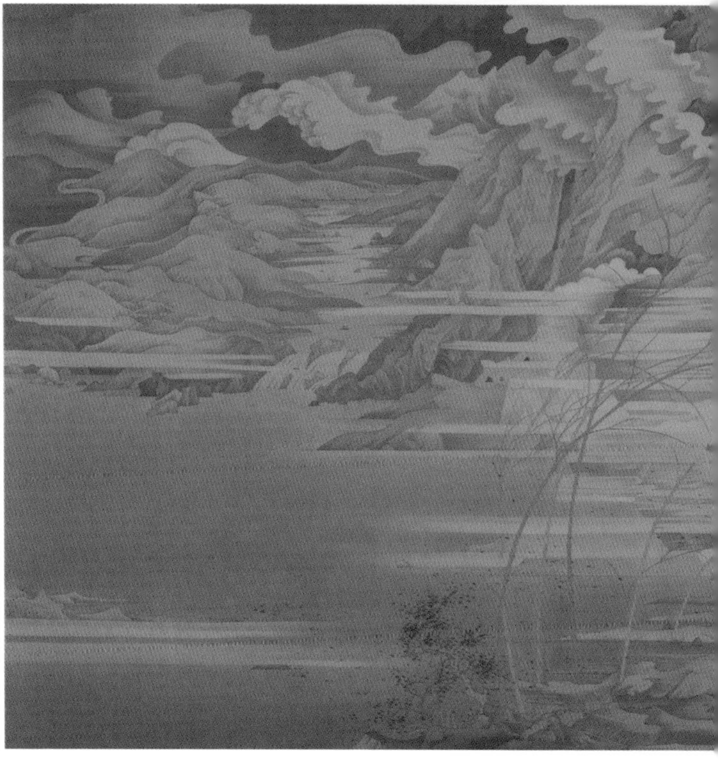

The artists discussed in this section from diverse regions
of the world show that the story of art is no longer written in
the belief that one particular style or 'movement' in a specific
geographical location can monopolize the zeitgeist. The
contemporary artworld is characterized by tolerant global
pluralism. Art practices exist in a technically radical expanded
field, and the result is the unprecedentedly open category
called 'contemporary art' in which art can be made of anything
or nothing. Painting within this global artworld is just one
practice amongst many.

Contemporary Painting and the Market

Some of the artists discussed in this book – the Futurists,
Dadaists, Surrealists and Constructivists – wanted to destroy
museums, comparing them to cemeteries and calling curators
and art historians 'gravediggers'; but now the works of these
same artists are valuable cultural collateral housed within
prestigious 'starchitectural' buildings. They are written about
in catalogues and books and cast as exemplary evidence of

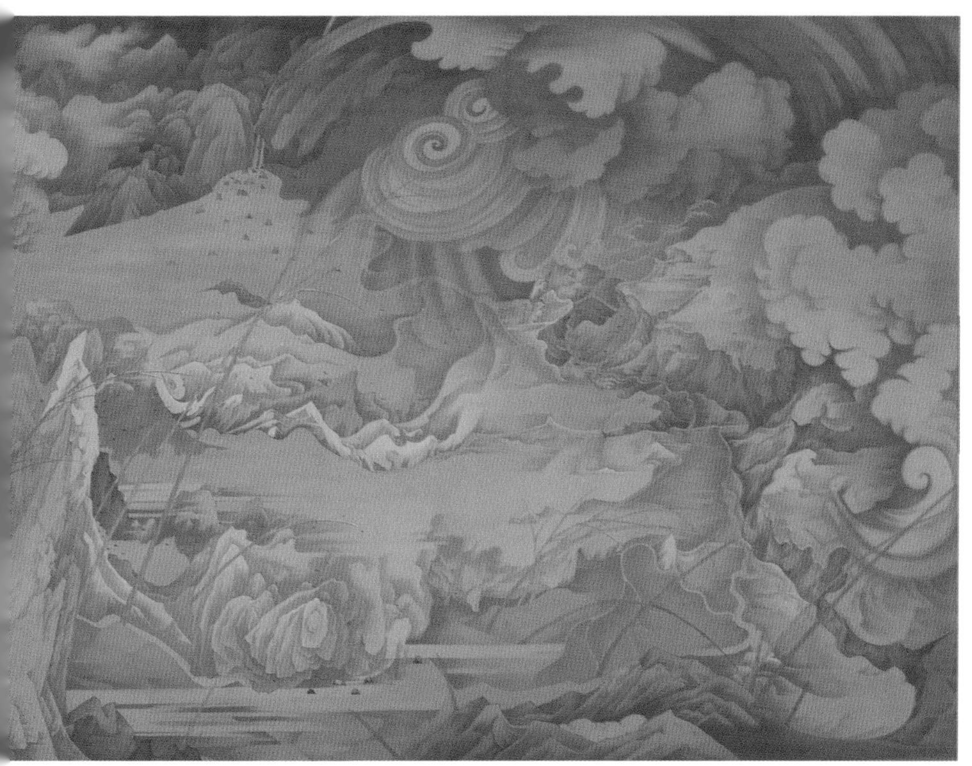

a culture in which resistance to and criticism of traditional values and history and the status quo are understood to be vital to society's continuing evolution and strength.

Today, painting is part of a 'culture industry', a hugely profitable market in which some artists' works are treated as luxury brand commodities. Modern and contemporary art has become a financial investment to be valued alongside stocks, bonds, mutual funds, index funds, exchange-traded funds, options and real estate. Over the past twenty years investments have become increasingly 'derivatives' based, and because the art market remains largely financially unregulated and its products are without any objective measure of value, it has proven an attractive option; the potential for profit is almost limitless, and for the investor, paintings in particular are fascinating propositions because, unlike most contemporary art in the 'post-medium condition', they are finite objects.

93 At the time of writing, Willem de Kooning's 1955 *Interchanged* is the second most expensive painting on earth. It sold at auction in 2015 to a private collector for $300 million.

(The *most* expensive is the Renaissance artist Leonardo da Vinci's recently authenticated *Salvator Mundi*.) The most valuable painting by a living artist at the time of writing is a work from 1972 by David Hockney, which sold at auction in 2019 for $80 million. This bullish market is becoming increasingly global. In 2020, contemporary art represented 15% of the global art market compared to 3% in 2000 and generated $22.7 billion. China and the United States alone generate 68% of global auction turnover, and over 60% of global sales are paintings.

An important characteristic of the contemporary global artworld, and a tell-tale sign of a nation's economic development and liberalization of values, is the emergence of a thriving local art scene supported by collectors and government sponsorship. These have evolved to incorporate both international trends that can be easily monitored via digital media and encountered in international art fairs, and more local pressures and preoccupations. For example, in Indonesia the emergence in 1998 of a more liberal government and rapid modernization led to the emergence of a vibrant market for contemporary art. The Balinese artist I Nyoman Masriadi (b. 1973) became especially popular for satirical paintings like *Juling (Cross-Eyed)* (2005) that mock the aspirations of the westernized middle class in Indonesia following the fall of President Suharto's autocratic regime. He often depicts ludicrous superhuman figures, sometimes posed in the archetypal roles of American comic-book heroes, cowboys, soldiers and athletes. Masriadi was also the first living Southeast Asian artist to top $1 million at auction.

The Role of Painting Today

The commodification of painting within capitalism – its easy assimilation into the 'culture industry' and association with the conspicuous consumption of the wealthy – has led some critics to suggest that the values communicated by many contemporary works are now fully in line with those of the commercial elite, and that more genuinely challenging art is being made in forms that are far removed from painting as a medium. Furthermore, for those who believe that art should be primarily moral and political, painting's aesthetic and historically rooted status make it inherently suspect. Ironically, however, more radical forms of contemporary art are now heavily subsidized by the state as the 'official' art of liberal democratic nations, the preferred image of the values of the 'free world'. By comparison, painting can remain relatively self-sufficient and independent. But it is certainly true that, compared to the newer art media and conceptual practices

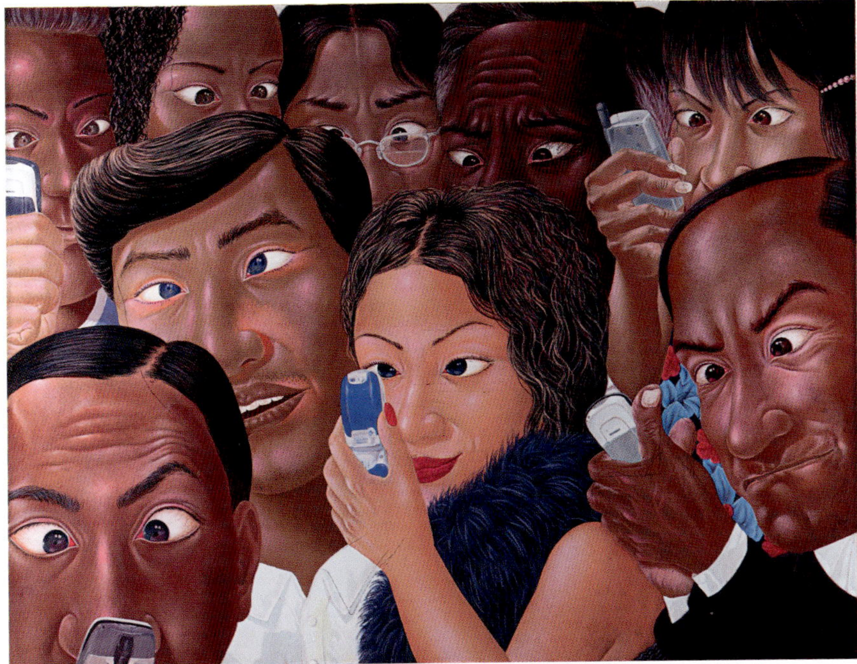

172 | Nyoman Masriadi, *Juling (Cross-Eyed)*, 2005

that seem to know no material or imaginative bounds, offer much greater potential for audience participation, and draw directly on the information technologies with which people are familiar from their daily lives, the inherently 'old-fashioned' nature of painting as a medium can, in some eyes, make it incapable of serving as a challenging and meaningful form of contemporary art.

But it is also possible that painting's very 'conventionality' – especially figurative painting – its familiarity as 'art' within the lives of ordinary people, is what makes such art a potentially viable contemporary medium. One contemporary painter who has managed to engage in a coruscating critique of today's social values while refusing, or at least vociferously resisting, the attempts to domesticate and commodify his work, and at same time becoming immensely popular with the public, is an anonymous artist-provocateur from England who works under the moniker Banksy. Since the 1990s, arresting and witty pictures by Banksy have been appearing in the most unlikely places throughout much of the world. The example illustrated here was at Banksy's Cans Festival in 2008 – a guerrilla takeover of a disused street under London's Waterloo Station where the

173

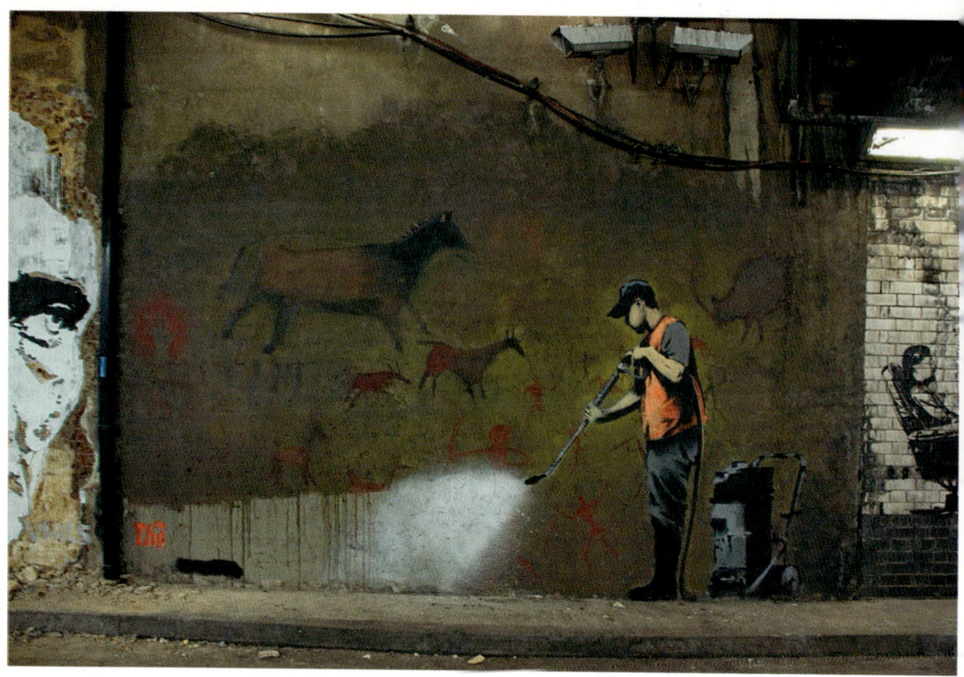

173 Banksy, *Untitled*, The Cans Festival, Leake Street, London, 2008

artist invited some of the world's most renowned street artists
to cover the entire tunnel with their artwork. Today, it is one of
the few places where graffiti is allowed in the UK capital, and
just weeks after the festival finished all the pieces, including
Banksy's, were covered by new graffiti.

By working in a realistic stencil-graffiti style based on
photographs and using witty parody and satire to draw attention
to the obvious problems and prejudices of the society in which
we live, Banksy's work is widely accessible, not just because of
its placement but because of its easily understandable visual
style, and sends a message about intolerance which many
people understand. He reminds us that our world is one of
blatant injustice, of poverty, violence, war, genocide, tribal
hatreds, religious fanaticism, sexism, racism, inequality,
authoritarianism, dehumanizing technology, catastrophic
ecological despoliation, and economic greed and exploitation.
In ways that have broad appeal, Banksy shows a world that is
very far from how it should be, but also that painting can have
a role in imagining it otherwise and provoking change.

Conclusion

Back to the Future

For the first time in human history, it is today possible to adopt something approaching a truly global, multicultural perspective on painting. What do we see? If painting's role is limited to being an artefact of national or personal prestige or financial profit, then obviously it is not a very significant medium for real individual or collective change. But if we acknowledge that painting can be more than this, we also need to recognize that its potential cannot be fully appreciated if it is reduced to functioning as the reflection of an idea, 'issue', social identity or ideology, or is understood as primarily performing a community service by functioning as just the expression of current social and political concerns. However, this does not mean that painting's value is to be found in its resistance to the encroachments of the world, in the preoccupation of the artist with painting's internal constraints – its self-sufficient properties as an aesthetic object detached from the rest of lived experience. Both these antithetical roles risk belittling painting's status as an imaginative and collaborative achievement that touches or calls to us in essential and often inexplicable ways, and to which we respond by reaching out and actively engaging.

The oldest known paintings are the kind parodied by Banksy in the work illustrated here. The first evidence of such ancient art was only discovered in 1868 in Altamira, northern Spain, and initially, because they looked too sophisticated to be made by 'savage' Stone Age humans, the experts dismissed these paintings as fakes. Soon, further spectacular discoveries in Europe were made, but the most recent, and the oldest at the time of writing in late 2022, is in a cave in Indonesia. It is estimated to be 45,500 years old, and depicts a pig that is sufficiently realistic to be recognized as a species that still exists in the region.

We will never know just what these paintings actually meant to the people who made them, but we certainly *do* know how culturally valuable and inspiring they are to the people of the present. We can, of course, see in them the many things that make us different from prehistoric hunter-gatherers. But that in itself is not such a bad thing. As the interactions between European, North American and artists of the wider world charted in this book have shown, encountering art that is very different from one's own can broaden awareness of what it is like to be human. By learning about the very different art of other cultures we learn more about our own. But, as we have also seen is the case in relation to encounters with the wider world during the modern period, it is also possible to see in cave paintings what humanity shares across vast stretches of time and space. After all, like all humans existing throughout the world today, those who made the paintings are biologically identical with us and faced many of the same basic existential dilemmas. They were involved in making something ordinary into the extra-ordinary, and the results are symbolic, expressive, aesthetic, 'site-specific' and participatory.

The discovery of cave paintings means that during the mere 'sixty seconds' of painting's history documented in this book – a period in which there was a bewildering number of far-reaching social, technological, economic, cultural and ecological changes that impacted on the entire world – humanity also became aware for the first time of just how old painting as a meaningful activity really is. And as the first prehistoric paintings were discovered during the period when, for example, Claude Monet and Auguste Renoir were feeling their way towards what became known as Impressionism, they can also be said to be an intrinsic part of the story of modern art. They certainly had an influence on many modern artists. The discovery of cave paintings reminds us that the sampling of the rich diversity of modern paintings presented here belongs within a story that is much longer and more culturally complex than anybody realized until very recently. They are part of a truly global and multicultural human story – one that, barring natural catastrophe and with due diligence in the present, may have only just begun.

Appendix

Here are ten key questions you might want to think about
in relation to the paintings and the ideas discussed in this
book. Each question is broken down into several other related
questions. These do not necessarily reflect the primary
concerns of the artists who made the works in this book. Rather,
they are those that people of the present consider urgently need
asking. Feel free to add your own questions to the list.

**1. What is the role of modern painting in relation to questions of
social identity?**
Who is modern painting for? Who is the audience? What
is its relationship to biography, histories of oppression
and marginalization? Is painting a privileged vehicle for
the expression of personal histories, or is it fundamentally
constrained by its status as a historical practice? To what extent
is modern painting an elite cultural medium that implicitly
condones inequality, and how can it confront this status? How
can modern painting reinforce or critique prejudiced ideas
about identity? Why are so few female or non-white painters
acknowledged before the 1960s? What is the relationship
between the medium of painting and gender and ethnicity? To
what extent is the medium of painting inherently gender and
culturally biased – a specifically male and western art form?
How have women and artists of colour changed the way we
understand painting? To what extent should artists sacrifice
formal and conceptual complexity for the sake of accessibility
and inclusivity?

2. How has globalization affected painting?
Does painting have transcultural and universally binding
characteristics? What role do different worldviews play in

defining how modern painting is understood and practised?
How has globalization changed the way the medium of
painting in the modern period as a whole is understood? How
has the globalization of the artworld changed the way painting
addresses the kinds of issues prioritized within western
culture? What is the relationship between the experience
of painting in a global context and that determined by a
local worldview?

**3. What is the role of modern painting in relation to ideas
about the self?**
What is the relationship between modern painting and
subjectivity, the inner life of the individual? How is modern
painting related to the psychological, or to non-visual
dimensions of human experience? How does modern
painting reflect changing ideas about the self and how has
it functioned as a medium through which to express the
unfolding experience of subjectivity in the modern period?
Are there expressions of subjectivity that are unique to the
medium of painting? To what extent does modern painting
provide access to the inner life of the artist? Is it allied
with, perhaps outdated, concepts of the self? How does
painting address the problem of existential risk and nihilism,
of the loss of meaning in modern society, and how does it
embody existential hope and offer a positive vision of
the future?

4. What is the relationship of modern painting to capitalism?
How do the specific economic conditions of the modern
period, and our different positions within them, impact on
how we perceive modern paintings? What forms of painting
can best critique the dominant economic system, and how is
this critique revealed in terms of content, form and process?
How does the fact that painting is a historical form that is an
intrinsic part of the capitalist system affect what is painted,
and how can artists critique this role? Is the fact that a
painting is an easily commodifiable artefact a definitive sign
of its inability to function as a critical force within culture?
What can artists do to resist this commodification? How does
economic power affect how a painting reaches the public,
the critic, the collector, the museum curator, the art history
book? Why are some paintings much more expensive than
others? How does the art market influence what artists paint,
and what the public sees?

5. **What roles do science and technology play as rival or complementary domains of knowledge to art?**
How have scientific discoveries impacted on modern painting? Can science help us to better understand modern painting? For example, can the neurosciences shed valuable light on the way the brain processes a painting? How does modern painting reflect changing attitudes to science and technology within society? How has the status of painting changed as society has become increasingly mechanized, and now digitalized? What methods do painters have at their disposal to celebrate or condemn the role of science and technology? What effect have changes in visualizing technology, such as analogue photography, the digitalization of photography, film and video, and the development of screen display technologies, had on our understanding of painting and its history?

6. **What is the relationship between modern painting and politics?**
Why is modern painting so influenced by political ideologies? Why are most modern artists progressives? What light does it shed on the dominant nineteenth- and twentieth-century ideological polarities of Left and Right? To what extent should modern painting's role be defined in terms of its explicit engagement with political issues, using these issues as the manifest content of painting? What part does utopian thinking play in art, and how does it determine how attitudes to painting are forged? Is painting a viable medium through which to advance or critique political ideas? If so, what might these ideas be in the 'post-ideological' age, and what forms can this political critique take?

7. **How is painting related to what we call 'nature'?**
What does modern painting tell us about the changing ways in which we perceive and engage with the natural environment? How do artists' works reflect the bias of specific local assumptions about the natural world? What does modern painting tell us about the relationship between the environment and the human nervous system, and the foundations of human culture? Can painting in any effective way be directly activist in relation to our environmental crisis? How are we to move forward when we recognize that the organisation of production, distribution, governance and knowledge that gave birth to modern painting have also brought the world to the brink of catastrophe? What is the role of painting in a period faced with mass extinction?

8.   What is modern painting's relationship to the sacred?
How does modern painting address ultimate reality, the eternal essence of being? How do our religious beliefs affect the way we perceive modern paintings? How has modern painting served to critique orthodox religions? As modern artists often pursue a secular vision of culture, what alternative spiritual forms pertaining to the meaning of life have been explored specifically through the medium of painting? How does it function as a new sacrament within the old religions, or forge new models of the sacred? To what extent are ideas about the spiritual universally binding or culturally specific, and how does modern painting reflect this?

9.   To what extent is painting a self-contained cultural formation?
What is the relationship between modern painting and aesthetics? Just what *is* aesthetic experience? How does modern painting problematize the relationship between form and content? To what extent can we bracket out the wider contexts of the encounter with modern painting and focus purely on an autonomous experience of form? Can the self-critical analysis of the properties of the medium of painting be a step towards establishing painting's progressive value for society? Can form be its own kind of significant content? How has the role of the viewer of paintings changed during the modern period? How have the institutional structures that present painting changed? What theoretical models help to clarify the importance of modern painting as painting? How has excessive focus on the formal properties of painting blinded artists to the wider implications of their practice? How has painting's relationship to itself changed once it was located within a context in which many different forms of art co-exist, many of which, by comparison, have no or little historical depth?

10. How is this history of modern painting biased?
How does the attitude towards modern culture in this book reflect specific interests and prejudices? What is it doing to challenge the familiar structures of inequality, the hierarchies of power? Is it maintaining the status quo or actively displacing and deconstructing it? Is this history inclusive enough? To what extent is it simply playing the 'numbers game' – introducing a more diverse group of artists without questioning the underlying prejudicial core values that exist within the account as a whole? How would the story of modern painting told in this book be different if it was written by, for example, an Asian, Latin American, Middle Eastern or African person? What words have been used that are tacitly assumed to be universally

understood and valid, but in fact are not? Has the *form* of the
art historical account been questioned as well as the content?
What are the unexamined biases of current discussions of
modern painting? How are they different from those of twenty,
fifty, one hundred years ago? How do you think people in
twenty years' time will respond to the choices of the artists and
the themes discussed here?

Further Reading

Note: This booklist does not include monographs about individual artists. The aim is to suggest general titles of interest. The author has included both introductory level texts (like this one) and more academic studies for readers who want to dig deeper.

Modern Art

Altshuler, Bruce. *The Avant-Garde in Exhibition: New Art in the Twentieth Century* (New York: Harry N. Abrams, 1994)

Arnheim, Rudolph. *Art and Visual Perception: A Psychology of the Creative Eye* (Berkeley and Los Angeles: University of California Press, 1954)

Arnheim, Rudolph. *Visual Thinking* (Berkeley and Los Angeles: University of California Press, 1969)

Baas, Jacqueline. *Smile of the Buddha: Eastern Philosophy and Western Art from Monet to Today* (Berkeley: University of California Press, 2005)

Bell, Julian. *What is Painting?* (London and New York: Thames & Hudson, Revised Second Edition, 2017)

Berger, John. *Ways of Seeing* (London: Penguin, 1972)

Berman, Marshall. *All That Is Solid Melts into Air: The Experience of Modernity* (London and New York: Penguin Books, 1988)

Blazwick, Iwona and Magnus af Petersens, eds. *Adventures of the Black Square: Abstract Art and Society 1915–2015* (London: Whitechapel Art Gallery, 2015)

Bois, Yve-Alain. *Painting as Model* (Cambridge, MA and London: The MIT Press, 1993)

Britt, David. *Modern Art. Impressionism to Post-Modernism* (London and New York: Thames & Hudson, 2007)

Chilvers, Ian and John Glaves-Smith. *A Dictionary of Modern and Contemporary Art* (Oxford, 2009)

Chipp, Herschel B., ed. *Theories of Modern Art: A Source Book by Artists and Critics* (Berkeley and Los Angeles: University of California Press, 1984)

Clark, T. J. *Farewell to an Idea: Episodes from a History of Modernism* (New Haven, CT and London: Yale University Press, 1999)

Crow, Thomas. *Modern Art in the Common Culture* (New Haven, CT and London: Yale University Press, 1996)

Danchev, Alex, ed. *100 Artists' Manifestos: From the Futurists to the Stuckists* (London: Penguin Books, 2011)

De Duve, Thierry. *Look, 100 Years of Contemporary Art*, trans. Simon Pleasance and Fronza Woods (Ghent and Amsterdam: Ludion, 2001)

Deepwell, Katy. *Women Artists and Modernism* (Manchester: Manchester University Press, 1998)

Dempsey, Amy. *Styles, Schools and Movement* (London and New York: Thames & Hudson, 2010)

Drucker, Johanna. *Theorizing Modernism: Visual Art and the Critical Tradition* (New York: Columbia University Press, 1996)

Elkins, James. *The Object Stares Back: On the Nature of Seeing* (New York: Harvest Books, 1997)

Elkins, James. *On Pictures and the Words that Fail Them* (Cambridge: Cambridge University Press, 1998)

Elkins, James. *The Domain of Images* (Ithaca, NY: Cornell University Press, 1999)

Elkins, James. *What Painting Is. How to Think about Oil Painting, Using the Language of Alchemy* (New York and London: Routledge, 2000)

Elkins, James. *Stories of Art* (New York and London: Routledge, 2002)

Fer, Briony. *On Abstract Art* (New Haven, CT and London: Yale University Press, 2000)

Fer, Briony. *The Infinite Line: Re-making Art After Modernism* (New Haven, CT and London: Yale University Press, 2004)

Fineberg, Jonathan David. *Art Since 1940: Strategies of Being* (London: Laurence King, 2000)

Flam, Jack, ed. *Primitivism and Twentieth-Century Art: A Documentary History* (Berkeley and Los Angeles: University of California Press, 2003)

Foster, Hal, Rosalind Krauss, Yve-Alain Bois, Benjamin H. D. Buchloh, David Joselit. *Art Since 1900*, vols. I and II (London and New York: Thames & Hudson, Third Edition, 2016)

Frascina, Francis, Tamar Garb, Nigel Blake, Briony Fer, Charles Harrison. *Modernity and Modernism: French Painting in the Nineteenth Century* (New Haven, CT and London: Yale University Press, 1993)

Frascina, Francis and Jonathan Harris, eds. *Art in Modern Culture: An Anthology of Critical Texts* (London and New York: Routledge, 1992)

Frascina, Francis and Charles Harrison, eds. *Modern Art and Modernism: A Critical Anthology* (London: Paul Chapman, 1982)

Gaiger, Jason. *Frameworks for Modern Art* (New Haven, CT and New York: Yale University Press, 2003)

Gaiger, Jason and Paul Wood, eds. *Art of the Twentieth Century: A Reader* (New Haven, CT and New York: Yale University Press, 2003)

Graw, Isabelle. *The Love of Painting: Genealogy of a Success Medium* (Berlin: Sternberg Press, 2019)

Gualidoni, Flaminio. *Art: The Twentieth Century* (New York: Skira, 2008)

Hamilton, George Heard. *Painting and Sculpture in Europe, 1880–1945* (New Haven, CT and London: Yale University Press, 1993)

Harland, Beth and Sunil Manghani, eds. *Painting: Critical and Primary Sources*, vols. 1–4 (London: Bloomsbury Publishing, 2016)

Harrison, Charles and Paul J. Wood, eds. *Art in Theory, 1900–2000: An Anthology of Changing Ideas* (Oxford: Blackwell, 2002)

Harrison, Charles and Paul J. Wood with Jason Gaiger, eds. *Art in Theory, 1815–1900: An Anthology of Changing Ideas* (Oxford: Blackwell, 1998)

Hopkins, David. *After Modern Art 1945–2000* (Oxford: Oxford University Press, 2000)

Hughes, Robert. *The Shock of the New* (London and New York: Thames & Hudson, 1991)

Jones, Amelia, ed. *A Companion to Contemporary Art since 1945* (Oxford: Blackwell, 2006)

Karmel, Pepe. *Abstract Art: A Global History* (London and New York: Thames & Hudson, 2020)

Krauss, Rosalind. *The Originality of the Avant-Garde and Other Modernist Myths* (Cambridge, MA: The MIT Press, 1986)

Krauss, Rosalind. *The Optical Unconscious* (Cambridge, MA and London: The MIT Press, 1994)

Kuspit, Donald. *The Cult of the Avant-Garde Artist* (Cambridge: Cambridge University Press, 1994)

Kuspit, Donald. *The End of Art* (Cambridge: Cambridge University Press, 2005)

Lewandowksa, Karolina, et al. *Woman in Abstraction* (London and New York: Thames & Hudson, 2021)

Lewer, Debbie, ed. *Post-Impressionism to World War II. Blackwell Anthology in Art History* (Oxford: Blackwell, 2005)

Lucie-Smith, Edward. *Lives of the Great Modern Artists* (London and New York: Thames & Hudson, Revised Edition, 2009)

Meecham, Pam and Julie Sheldon. *Modern Art: A Critical Introduction* (London: Routledge, 2000)

Moody, Alys and Stephen Ross, eds. *Global Modernists on Modernism: An Anthology* (London: Bloomsbury Publishing, 2020)

Morley, Simon. *Writing on the Wall: Word and Image in Modern Art* (London and New York: Thames & Hudson, 2003)

Morley, Simon, ed. *The Sublime. Documents in Contemporary Art* (New York and Boston: The MIT Press / London: Whitechapel Art Gallery, 2010)

Morley, Simon. *Seven Keys to Modern Art* (London and New York: Thames & Hudson, 2019)

Morley, Simon. *The Simple Truth. The Monochrome in Modern Art* (London: Reaktion Books, 2020)

Munroe, Alexandra, ed. *The Third Mind, American Artists Contemplate Asia, 1860–1989*, exh.cat. (New York: Solomon R. Guggenheim Museum, 2009)

Murray, Chris. *Key Writers on Art: The Twentieth Century* (London and New York: Routledge, 2003)

Nead, Lynda. *The Female Nude: Art, Obscenity, and Sexuality* (London: Routledge, 1992)

O'Brien, Elaine, et al. *Modern Art in Africa, Asia and Latin America: An Introduction to Global Modernisms* (Chichester: Wiley Blackwell, 2012)

Orton, Fred and Griselda Pollock. *Avant-Gardes and Partisans Reviewed* (Manchester: Manchester University Press, 1996)

Osborne, Richard and Dan Sturgis, eds. and Natalie Turner, illus. *Art Theory for Beginners* (London: Zidane Press, 2009)

Poggiolo, Renato. *The Theory of the Avant-Garde* (Cambridge, MA: Harvard University Press 1968)

Pollock, Griselda. *Vision and Difference: Feminism, Femininity and Histories of Art* (London: Taylor & Francis, 2003)

Powell, Richard J. *Black Art and Culture in the 20th Century* (London and New York: Thames & Hudson, 1997)

Puchner, Martin. *Poetry of the Revolution. Marx, Manifestoes, and the Avant-Gardes* (Princeton and Oxford: Princeton University Press, 2006)

Rainey, Lawrence. *Modernism: An Anthology* (Oxford: Blackwell Publishing, 2005)

Read, Herbert. *A Concise History of Modern Painting* (London and New York: Thames & Hudson, Revised Edition, 1974)

Rhodes, Colin. *Primitivism and Modern Art* (London and New York: Thames & Hudson, 1994)

Rosenblum, Robert. *Modern Painting and the Northern Romantic Tradition: Friedrich to Rothko* (New York: Icon, 1977)

Rosenthal, Mark Lawrence, ed. *Abstraction in the Twentieth Century: Total Risk, Freedom, Disciple*, exh.cat. (New York: Solomon R. Guggenheim Museum, 1996)

Rubin, William. *Primitivism and Twentieth Century Art*, exh.cat. (New York: Museum of Modern Art, 1984)

Salami, Gitti and Monica Blackmun Visonà, eds. *A Companion to Modern African Art* (Chichester: Wiley Blackwell, 2013)

Stangos, Nikos. *Concepts of Modern Art* (London and New York: Thames & Hudson, Third Edition, 1994)

Steinberg, Leo. *Other Criteria: Confrontations with Twentieth-Century Art* (Oxford: Oxford University Press, 1972)

Stiles, Christine and Peter Selz, eds. *Theories and Documents of Contemporary Art: A Sourcebook of Artists' Writings* (Berkeley: University of California Press, 1996)

Taylor, Brandon. *Collage. The Making of Modern Art* (London and New York: Thames & Hudson, 2006)

Tuchman, Maurice, et al. *The Spiritual in Art: Abstract Painting 1890–1985*, exh.cat. (New York: Abbeville Press, 1986)

Underwood, Joseph L. and Chika Okeke-Agulu. *African Artists: From 1882 to Now* (London: Phaidon Press, 2021)

Varnedoe, Kirk, et al. *High and Low: Modern Art, Popular Culture*, exh.cat. (New York: Museum of Modern Art, 1990)

Varnedoe, Kirk. *Pictures of Nothing. Abstract Art Since Pollock* (Princeton and Oxford: Princeton University Press, 2006)

Watson, Peter. *From Manet to Manhattan. The Rise of the Modern Art Market* (New York: Random House, 1992)

Weinberg, H. Barbara. *The Lure of Paris: Nineteenth Century American Painters and Their French Teachers* (New York: Abbeville Press, 1991)

Wiedman, Auguste. *Romantic Roots in Modern Art* (London: Gresham Books, 1979)

Wollheim, Richard. *Painting as an Art* (London and New York: Thames & Hudson, 1989)

Wood, Paul. *The Challenge of the Avant-Garde* (New Haven, CT and London: Yale University Press and the Open University, 1999)

Wood, Paul, ed. *Varieties of Modernism* (New Haven, CT and London: Yale University Press, 2004)

Wood, Paul, Leon Wainwright with Charles Harrison. *Art in Theory. The West in the World. An Anthology of Changing Ideas* (Oxford: Blackwell, 2021)

Chapter 1

Chu, Petra ten-Doesschate. *Nineteenth-Century European Art* (New York: Prentice Hall, 2006)

Clark, Kenneth. *The Romantic Rebellion: Romantics Versus Classic Art* (London: Omega / Futura, 1976)

Clark, Kenneth. *Landscape into Art* (New York: Harper and Row, 1979)

Daniel, Stephen. *Fields of Vision: Landscape Imagery and National Identity in England and the United States* (London: Polity Press, 1993)

Eisenman, Stephen F., ed. *Nineteenth Century Art: A Critical Introduction* (London and New York: Thames & Hudson, 2011)

Ferber, Michael. *Romanticism: A Very Short Introduction* (Oxford: Oxford University Press, 2010)

Harding, James. *Artistes Pompiers: French Academic Art in the Nineteenth Century* (New York: Rizzoli, 1979)

Hemingway, Andrew. *Landscape Imagery and Urban Culture in Early Nineteenth Century Britain* (Cambridge: Cambridge University Press, 1992)

Novak, Barbara. *Nature and Culture: American Landscape Painting 1825–75* (Oxford and New York: Oxford University Press, 1980)

Rosen, Charles and Henri Zerner. *Romanticism and Realism: The Mythology of Nineteenth-Century Art* (New York: Viking, 1984)

Taylor, Joshua, ed. *Nineteenth-Century Theories of Art* (Berkeley and Los Angeles: California University Press, 1992)

Vaughan, William. *Romantic Art* (London and New York: Thames & Hudson, 1978)

Chapter 2

Brettell, Richard, et al. *A Day in the Country: Impressionism and the French Landscape* (New York: Harry N. Abrams, 1984)

Brettell, Richard R. *Impressionism: Painting Quickly in France, 1860–1890*, exh.cat. (New Haven, CT: Yale University Press, 2000)

Champa, Kermit. *The Rise of Landscape Painting in France, Corot to Monet* (New York: Harry N. Abrams, 1991)

Clark, T. J. *Image of the People: Gustave Courbet and the 1848 Revolution* (London and New York: Thames & Hudson, 1982)

Clark, T. J. *The Painting of Modern Life. Paris in the Art of Manet and His Followers* (Princeton, NJ: Princeton University Press, 1984)

Clark, T. J. *The Absolute Bourgeois. Artists and Politics in France, 1848–1851* (Berkeley and Los Angeles: University of California Press, 1999)

Crary, Jonathan. *Techniques of the Observer: On Vision and Modernity in the Nineteenth Century* (Cambridge, MA and London: The MIT Press, 1992)

Fried, Michael. *Courbet's Realism* (Chicago: University of Chicago Press, 1992)

Fried, Michael. *Manet's Modernism: Or, The Face of Painting in the 1860s* (Chicago: University of Chicago Press, 1996)

Herbert, Robert L. *Impressionism: Art, Leisure, and Parisian Society* (New Haven, CT: Yale University Press, 1991)

House, John, *Landscapes of France: Impressionism and its Rivals*, exh.cat. (London: Hayward Gallery, 1995)

Irvine, Gregory. *Japonisme and the Rise of the Modern Art Movement. The Arts of the Meiji Period* (London and New York: Thames & Hudson, 2013)

Nochlin, Linda. *Realism* (Harmondsworth: Penguin Books, 1971)

Nochlin, Linda. *Women, Art and Power and Other Essays* (New York: Westview Press, 1988)

Nochlin, Linda. *The Politics of Vision: Essays on Nineteenth Century Art and Society* (New York: Westview Press, 1989)

Pollock, Griselda. *Avant-Garde Gambits, 1888–1893: Gender and the Colour of Art History* (New York and London: Thames & Hudson, 1993)

Shiff, Richard. *Cézanne and the End of Impressionism* (Chicago: University of Chicago, 1984)

Sjåstad, Øystein. *A Theory of the 'Tache' in Nineteenth-Century Painting* (London: Routledge, 2016)

Thomson, Richard. *Monet to Matisse: Landscape Painting in France 1874–1914*, exh.cat. (Edinburgh: National Galleries of Scotland, 1994)

Chapter 3

Behr, Shulamith, et al., ed. *Expressionism Reassessed* (Manchester: Manchester University Press, 1993)

Cardinal, Roger. *Expressionism* (London: Paladin, 1984)

Claire, Jean and Guy Cogeval. *Lost Paradise: Symbolist Europe*, exh.cat. (Montreal: The Montreal Museum of Fine Arts, 1995)

Cohen, Joshua I. *The 'Black Art' Renaissance. African Sculpture and Modernism across Continents* (Berkeley: University of California Press, 2020)

Denvir, Bernard. *Fauvism and Expressionism* (London and New York: Thames & Hudson, 1975)

Denvir, Bernard. *Post-Impressionism* (London and New York: Thames & Hudson, 1992)

Dorra, Henri. *Symbolist Art Theories: A Critical Anthology* (Berkeley: University of California Press, 1994)

Dube, Wolf-Dieter. *The Expressionists* (London and New York: Thames & Hudson, 1972)

Facos, Michelle. *Symbolist Art in Context* (Berkeley: University of California Press, 2009)

Facos, Michelle and Thor J. Mednik, eds. *The Symbolist Roots of Modern Art* (London and New York: Routledge, 2017)

Freeman, Judi, et al. *The Fauve Landscape*, exh. cat. (New York: Museum of Modern Art, 1990)

Gualidoni, Flaminio. *Post-Impressionism* (New York: Skira, 2008)

Herbert, James D. *Fauve Painting: The Making of a Cultural Landscape* (New Haven, CT and London: Yale University Press, 1992)

Lewis, Mark Tompkins, ed. *Impressionism and Post-Impressionism. An Anthology* (Berkeley and Los Angeles: California University Press, 2007)

Parsons, Thomas and Ian Gale. *Post-Impressionism: The Rise of Modern Art, 1880–1920* (London: NDE Pub., 1999)

Rapetti, Rodolphe, *Symbolism* (New York: Flammarion, 2005)

Thomas, Belinda. *Post-Impressionism* (Cambridge: Cambridge University Press, 1998)

Weikop, Christian, ed. *New Perspectives on Brücke Expressionism* (London: Ashgate, 2011)

Werenskiold, Marit. *The Concept of Expressionism: Origins and Metamorphosis* (Oxford: Oxford University Press, 1985)

Chapter 4

Anliff, Mark and Patricia Leighton. *Cubism and Culture* (London and New York: Thames & Hudson, 2001)

Chambers, Emma. *Aftermath: Art in the Wake of World War One*, exh.cat. (London: Tate Britain, 2018)

Clark, T. J. *Picasso and Truth* (Princeton and Oxford: Princeton University Press, 2013)

Cottington, David. *Cubism and its Histories* (Manchester and New York: Manchester University Press, 2004)

Dickerman, Leah, *Inventing Abstraction 1910–1925. How a Radical Idea Changed Modern Art* (London and New York: Thames & Hudson, 2013)

Duve, Thierry de. *Kant After Duchamp* (Cambridge, MA and London: The MIT Press, 1998)

Cooper, Douglas. *The Cubist Epoch* (London: Phaidon, 1971)

Cork, Richard. *Vorticism and Abstract Art in the First Machine Age* (Berkeley: University of California Press, 1976)

Golding, John. *Cubism: A History and an Analysis, 1907–1914* (Cambridge, MA: Harvard University Press, 1988)

Gough, Maria. *The Artist as Producer. Russian Constructivism in Revolution* (Berkeley: University of California Press, 2005)

Gualidoni, Flaminio. *Futurism* (New York: Skira, 2009)

Hopkins, David. *Dada and Surrealism: A Very Short Introduction* (Oxford: Oxford University Press, 2004)

Hughes, Gordon and Philip Blom, eds. *Nothing but the Clouds Unchanged. Artists in World War 1* (Los Angeles: Getty Research Institute, 2014)

Humphreys, Richard. *Futurism* (London: Tate Publishing, 1999)

Kern, Stephen. *The Culture of Time and Space 1880–1918* (Cambridge, MA: Harvard University Press, 1983)

Perry, Gill, Francis Frascina, Charles Harrison. *Primitivism, Cubism, Abstraction* (New Haven, CT and London: Yale University Press, 1993)

Poggi, Christine. *In Defiance of Painting: Cubism, Futurism, and Invention of Collage* (New Haven, CT: Yale University Press, 1992)

Poggi, Christine. *Inventing Futurism: The Art and Politics of Artificial Optimism* (Princeton and Oxford: Princeton University Press, 2009)

Rosenblum, Robert. *Cubism and Twentieth Century Art* (Englewood Cliffs, NJ: Harry N. Abrams, 1976)

Rubin, William. *Dada and Surrealism*, exh.cat. (New York: Museum of Modern Art, 1968)

Taylor, Michael, ed. *The Invention of Abstraction, 1910–1925*, exh.cat. (New York: Museum of Modern Art)

Chapter 5

Ades, Dawn, Michael Richardson, Krzysztof Fijalowski, eds. *Surrealism Reader: An Anthology of Ideas* (Chicago and London: University of Chicago Press, 2016)

Bann, Stephen, ed. *The Tradition of Constructivism* (New York: Viking Press, 1974)

Batchelor, David, Briony Fer and Paul Wood. *Realism, Rationalism, Surrealism: Art between the Wars* (New Haven, CT and London: Yale University Press, 1993)

Bradley, Fiona. *Surrealism* (London: Tate Publishing, 1997)

Caws, Mark Ann. *Surrealism* (London: Phaidon Press, 2010)

Corbett, David Peters. *The Modernity of English Art 1914–1930* (Manchester: Manchester University Press, 1997)

Corn, Wanda. *The Great American Thing: Modern Art and National Identity, 1915–1935* (Berkeley: University of California Press, 1999)

D'Alessandro, Stephanie and Matthew Gale. *Surrealism Beyond Borders*, exh.cat. (New York and London: Metropolitan Museum of Art / Tate Modern, 2021)

Droste, Magdalen. *Bauhaus* (Cologne: Taschen, Updated Edition, 2019)

Edwards, Steve and Paul Woods, eds. *Art of the Avant-Gardes (Art of the Twentieth Century)* (New Haven, CT and London: Yale University Press, 2004)

Fijalowski, Krzysztof. *Surrealism: Key Concepts* (London and New York: Routledge, 2016)

Foster, Hal. *Compulsive Beauty* (Boston: The MIT Press, 1995)

Golomstock, Igor. *Totalitarian Art* (New York: Abrams, Inc., 1990)

Gualidoni, Flaminio. *Surrealism* (New York: Skira, 2008)

Hauptman, Jodi, ed. *Engineer, Agitator, Constructor: The Artists Reinvented: 1918–1938*, exh.cat. (New York: Museum of Modern Art, 2020)

Powell, Richard and David A. Bailey. *Rhapsodies in Black: Art of the Harlem Renaissance* (Berkeley: University of California Press, 1997)

Chapter 6

Anfam, David, Susan Davidson, Jeremy Lewison, Carter Ratcliff. *Abstract Expressionism*, exh. cat. (London: Royal Academy of Arts, Reprint Edition, 2019)

Doss, Erika. *Benton, Pollock, and the Politics of Modernism: From Regionalism to Abstract Expressionism* (Chicago: University of Chicago Press, 1991)

Dossin, Catherine. *The Rise and Fall of American Art, 1940s–1980s* (London and New York: Routledge, 2016)

Frascina, Francis, ed. *Pollock and After: The Critical Debate* (London and New York: Routledge, Second Edition, 2000)

Gibson, Anne. *Abstract Expressionism: Other Politics* (New Haven, CT: Yale University Press, 1997)

Greenberg, Clement. *Art and Culture: Critical Essays* (Boston: Beacon Press, 1961)

Guilbaut, Serge. *How New York Stole the Idea of Modern Art: Abstract Expressionism, Freedom and the Cold War* (Chicago: University of Chicago Press, 1983)

Harris, Jonathan, Francis Frascina, Charles Harrison, Paul Wood. *Modernism in Dispute. Art Since the 1940s* (New Haven, CT and London: Yale University Press, 1993)

Hillings, Valerie, et al. *Zero. Countdown to Tomorrow, 1950s–60s*, exh.cat. (New York: Solomon R. Guggenheim Museum, 2014)

Kurczynski, Karen. *The Cobra Movement in Postwar Art* (London and New York: Routledge, 2021)

Leja, Michael. *Reframing Abstract Expressionism: Subjectivity and Painting in the 1940s* (New Haven, CT: Yale University Press, 1993)

Marter, Joan, ed. *Women of Abstract Expressionism* (New Haven, CT: Yale University Press, 2016)

Morris, Frances, et al. *Paris Post War: Art and Existentialism 1945–55*, exh.cat. (London: Tate Gallery, 1993)

Neofetou, Daniel. *Rereading Abstract Expressionism. Clement Greenberg and the Cold War* (London: Bloomsbury, 2022)

Piery, Lucienne. *Art Brut. The Origins of Outsider Art* (New York: Random House, 2001)

Rosenberg, Harold. *The Tradition of the New* (New York: da Capo, 1994)

Sandler, Irving. *The Triumph of American Painting: A History of Abstract Expressionism* (New York: Taylor & Francis, 1970)

Schimmel, Paul, et al. *Destroy the Picture: Painting the Void, 1949–1962*, exh.cat. (New York: Rizzoli International Publications, 2012)

Tiampo, Ming, ed. *Gutai: Decentering Modernism* (Chicago and London: University of Chicago Press, 2011)

Westgeest, Helen. *Zen in the Fifties: Interactions in Art between East and West* (Amstelveen: Cobra Museeum voor Moderne Kunst, 1996)

Chapter 7

Archer, Michael. *Art since 1960* (London and New York: Thames & Hudson, 2002)

Baas, J. and M. J. Jacob, eds. *Buddha Mind in Contemporary Art* (Berkeley and Los Angeles: University of California Press, 2004)

Battock, Gregory, ed. *Minimal Art: A Critical Anthology* (Berkeley: University of California Press, Reprint, 1995)

Buchloh, Benjamin. *Neo-Avantgarde and Culture Industry: Essays on European and American Art from 1955 to 1975* (Boston: The MIT Press, 2003)

Cane, Simon and Otto Lenze. *Photorealism: 50 Years of Hyperrealistic Painting*, exh.cat. (Stuttgart and Berlin: Hatje Cantz, 2013)

Chase, Linda. *Hyperrealism* (New York: Rizzoli, 1975)

Frigeri, Flavia. *Pop Art* (London and New York: Thames & Hudson, 2018)

Goldie, Peter and Elisabeth Schellekens, eds. *Who's Afraid of Conceptual Art?* (London and New York: Routledge, 2010)

Jones, Caroline A. *The Machine in the Studio. Constructing the Postwar American Artist* (Chicago and London: The University of Chicago Press, 1996)

Lippard, Lucy. *Six Years: The Dematerialization of the Art Object* (Berkeley: University of California Press, 1997)

Livingstone, Marco. *Pop Art: A Continuing History* (New York: Harry N. Abrams, 1990)

Madoff, Steven, ed. *Pop Art: A Critical History* (Berkeley: University of California Press, 1997)

Newman, Michael and Jon Bird, eds. *Rewriting Conceptual Art* (London: Reaktion Books, 1999)

Osterwold, Tilman. *Pop Art* (Cologne: Taschen, 2003)

Rosen, Randy and Catherine Brawer. *Making Their Mark: Women Artists Move into the Mainstream, 1970–1985* (New York: Abbeville Press, 1989)

Sooke, Alistair. *Pop Art: A Colourful History* (London: Penguin, 2015)

Stich, Sidra. *Made in U.S.A.: An Americanization in Modern Art, the '50s and '60s* (Berkeley: University of California Press, 1987)

Wallis, Brian, et al., ed. *Modern Dreams: The Rise and Fall and Rise of Pop* (Cambridge, MA and London: The MIT Press, 1988)

Chapter 8

Belting, Hans. *Art after Modernism* (Chicago: University of Chicago Press, 2003)

Bianchi, Lorenzo Sassoli de. *China: Contemporary Painting* (Bologna: Damiani, 2005)

Bourriaud, Nicholas. *Relational Aesthetics*, trans. Simon Pleasance and Fronza Wood (Dijon: Les Presses du reel, 2002)

Caruana, Wally. *Aboriginal Art* (London and New York: Thames & Hudson, 2012)

Chiu, Melissa and Benjamin Genocchio. *Contemporary Asian Art* (London and New York: Thames & Hudson, 2010)

Clearwater, Bonnie. *Defining the Nineties: Consensus-Making in New York, Miami, and Los Angeles*, exh.cat. (Miami: Museum of Contemporary Art, 1996)

Colpitt, Frances, ed. *Abstract Art in the Late Twentieth Century* (Cambridge: Cambridge University Press, 2002)

Costello, Diarmuid and Jonathan Vickery, eds. *Art: Key Contemporary Thinkers* (London: Bloomsbury, 2007)

Danto, Arthur C. *After the End of Art: Contemporary Art and the Pale of History* (Princeton and Oxford: Princeton University Press, 1997)

Danto, Arthur C. *After the End of Art: Contemporary Art and the Pale of History* (Princeton: Princeton University Press, 1997)

Docherty, Thomas, ed. *Postmodernism: A Reader* (New York: Harvester Wheatsheaf, 1993)

Doherty, Claire. *Contemporary Art: From Studio to Situation* (London: Black Dog Publishing, 2004)

Drucker, Johanna. *Sweet Dreams: Contemporary Art and Complicity* (Chicago: University of Chicago Press, 2005)

Foster, Hal, ed. *The Anti-Aesthetic: Essays on Postmodern Culture* (New York: New Press, 1984)

Foster, Hal. *The Return of the Real: The Avant-Garde at the End of the Century* (Cambridge, MA: The MIT Press, 1996)

Foster, Hal, ed. *Discussions in Contemporary Culture* (New York: New Press, 1998)

Gilbert-Rolfe, Jeremy. *Beyond Piety: Critical Essays on the Visual Arts, 1986–1993* (Cambridge: Cambridge University Press, 1995)

Grovier, Kelly. *Art Since 1989* (London and New York: Thames & Hudson, 2015)

Harris, Jonathan, ed. *Critical Perspectives on Contemporary Painting: Hybridity, Hegemony, Historicism* (Liverpool: Liverpool University Press, 2003)

Harvey, David. *The Condition of Postmodernity: An Enquiry in the Origins of Cultural Change* (Cambridge, MA and Oxford: Blackwell, 1989)

Hickey, Dave. *Air Guitar: Essays on Art & Democracy* (New York: Art Issues Press, 1997)

Hudson, Suzanne and Alexander Dumbadze, eds. *Contemporary Art: 1989 to the Present* (Oxford: Wiley Blackwell, 2013)

Joachimides, Christos M., ed. *A New Spirit in Painting*, exh.cat. (London: Royal Academy of Arts, 1981)

Kocur, Zoya and Simon Leung, eds. *Theory in Contemporary Art since 1985* (Oxford: Blackwell, 2005)

Krauss, Rosalind. *A Voyage on the North Sea: Art in the Age of the Post-Medium Condition* (London and New York: Thames & Hudson, 1999)

Leduc, Marie. *Dissidence. The Rise of Chinese Contemporary Art in the West* (Cambridge, MA: The MIT Press, 2018)

McEvilley, Thomas. *Capacity: History, the World and the Self in Contemporary Art and Criticism* (Amsterdam: OPA, 1996)

Owen, Craig. *Beyond Recognition: Representation, Power, and Culture* (Berkeley: University of California Press, 1994)

Perry, Gill, ed. *Themes in Contemporary Art* (New Haven, CT and London: Yale University Press, 2004)

Robertson, Jean and Craig McDaniel. *Themes of Contemporary Art: Visual Art after 1980* (Oxford: Oxford University Press, 2005)

Stallabrass, Julian. *Art Incorporated* (Oxford: Oxford University Press, 2004)

Stallabrass, Julian. *Contemporary Art. A Very Short Introduction* (Oxford: Oxford University Press, 2004)

Taylor, Brandon. *Contemporary Art: Art since 1970* (New Jersey: Prentice Hall, 2004)

Wallis, Brian and Marcia Tucker. *Art after Modernism: Rethinking Representation* (New York: David R. Godine, 1992)

Waugh, Patricia, ed. *Postmodernism: A Reader* (London: Hodder Arnold, 1992)

Weintraub, Linda. *Making Contemporary Art: How Today's Artists Think and Work* (London and New York: Thames & Hudson, 2003)

Welchman, John. *Art after Appropriation: Essays on Art in the 1990s* (London and New York: Routledge, 2001)

Chapter 9

Belting, Hans, Andrea Buddesieg, Peter Weibel. *The Global Contemporary and the Rise of New Art Worlds*, exh.cat. (Karlsruhe: ZKM / Boston: The MIT Press, 2012)

Bradway, Todd, ed. *Landscape Painting Now: From Pop Abstraction to New Romanticism* (New York: D.A.P, 2019)

Deitch, Jeffrey, et al. *Unrealism: New Figurative Painting* (New York: Rizzoli Electa, 2019)

Favell, Adrian. *Before and After Superflat: A Short History of Japanese Contemporary Art, 1990–2011* (Hong Kong: Blue Kingfisher Ltd., 2011)

Foster, Hal. *Bad New Days: Art, Criticism, Emergency* (London: Verso, 2015)

Gnyp, Marta. *New Waves: Contemporary Art and the Issues Shaping Its Tomorrow* (New York: Skira, 2021)

Godfrey, Tony. *Painting Today* (London: Phaidon, 2009)

Godfrey, Tony. *The Story of Contemporary Art* (Cambridge, MA: The MIT Press, 2020)

Graw, Isabelle and Ewa Lajer-Burcharth, eds. *Painting Beyond Itself. The Medium in the Post-Medium Condition* (Berlin: Sternberg Press, 2016)

Harris, Jonathan, ed. *Globalization and Contemporary Art* (Chichester: Wiley Blackwell, 2011)

Hudson, Suzanne, *Painting Now* (London and New York: Thames & Hudson, 2015)

Hudson, Suzanne. *Contemporary Painting* (London and New York: Thames & Hudson, 2021)

Iskin, Ruth. *Re-Envisioning the Contemporary Canon. Perspectives in a Global World* (London and New York: Routledge, 2016)

Jones, Caroline. *The Global Work of Art: World's Fairs, Biennials and the Aesthetics of Experience* (Chicago: University of Chicago Press, 2017)

Kee, J. *Contemporary Korean Art: Tansaekhwa and the Urgency of Method* (Minnesota, MN: University of Minnesota Press, 2013)

Mullins, Charlotte. *Picturing People: The New State of the Art* (London and New York: Thames & Hudson, 2015)

Pietropaolo, Francesca, ed. *Writings on Art 2006–2021* (London: HENI Publishing, 2021)

Scala, Mark, ed. *Chaos and Awe. Painting for the 21st Century*, exh.cat. (Cambridge, MA and London: The MIT Press / Nashville, TN: Frist Center for the Visual Arts, 2018)

Schwabsky, Barry. *Vitamin P: New Perspectives in Painting* (Oxford: Phaidon, 2007, revised 2016)

Seed, John. *Disrupted Realism: Paintings for a Distracted World* (Atglen, PA: Schiffer, 2019)

Shnayerson, Michael. *Boom: Mad Money, Mega Dealers, and the Rise of Contemporary Art* (New York: PublicAffairs, 2019)

Smith, Terry. *What is Contemporary Art?* (Chicago: University of Chicago Press, 2009)

Thomson, Don. *The $12 Million Stuffed Shark: The Curious Economics of Contemporary Art* (New York: Macmillan, 2010)

Thornton, Sarah. *Seven Days in the Art World* (New York: W. W. Norton, 2009)

Yee, Lydia, ed. *Radical Figures: Painting in the New Millennium*, exh.cat. (London: Whitechapel Art Gallery, 2020)

Zhu, Lao. *Introduction to Contemporary Art in China* (London: Routledge, 2022)

Websites

All the major museums have websites where it is possible to view their collections and read about specific paintings.

General websites dedicated to modern art:

https://www.wikiart.org

https://www.theartstory.org

https://artsandculture.google.com

https://www.khanacademy.org/humanities/art-history

https://smarthistory.org

https://artincontext.org

Contemporary art magazines:

https://frieze.com

https://whitehotmagazine.com

http://www.artinamericamagazine.com

https://www.artspace.com/magazine

https://www.artsy.net/articles

https://news.artnet.com

http://www.artnews.com

http://artforum.com

http://theartnewspaper.com

http://hyperallergic.com

https://www.widewalls.ch

The following are dedicated to contemporary painting:

http://www.twocoatsofpaint.com

https://www.turpsbanana.com/magazine

List of Illustrations

Measurements are given in centimetres and inches, height before width before depth, where applicable

27 Henri de Toulouse-Lautrec, *Marcelle Lender Dancing the Bolero in 'Chilpéric'*, 1895–96. Oil on canvas, 145 × 149 (57⅛ × 58¾). National Gallery of Art, Washington, D.C. Collection of Mr and Mrs John Hay Whitney
28 Paul Gauguin, *Nevermore*, 1897. Oil on canvas, 96 × 130 (38 × 51). The Courtauld, London (Samuel Courtauld Trust)
29 Henri Rousseau, *Tiger in a Tropical Storm (Surprised!)*, 1891. Oil on canvas, 130 × 162 (51⅛ × 63¾). The National Gallery, London. Bought, with the aid of a substantial donation from the Hon. Walter H. Annenberg, 1972
30 Arnold Böcklin, *Island of the Dead*, 1880. Oil on wood, 73.7 × 121.9 (29 × 48). The Metropolitan Museum of Art, New York. Reisinger Fund, 1926
31 Odilon Redon, *The Cyclops*, c. 1914. Oil on cardboard mounted on panel, 65.8 × 52.7 (25 × 20). Kröller-Müller Museum, Otterlo
32 Suzanne Valadon, *Adam and Eve*, 1909. Oil on canvas, 162 × 131 (63 × 51⅝). Centre Pompidou, Paris. Photo Centre Pompidou, MNAM-CCI, Dist. RMN-Grand Palais/Jacqueline Hyde
33 André Derain, *Mountains at Collioure*, 1905. Oil on canvas, 81.3 × 100.3 (32⅛ × 39½). National Gallery of Art, Washington, D.C. John Hay Whitney Collection. © ADAGP, Paris and DACS, London 2023
34 Henri Matisse, *The Dessert: Harmony in Red*, 1908. Oil on canvas, 180.5 × 221 (70 × 86⅝). The State Hermitage Museum, St Petersburg. © Succession H. Matisse/DACS 2023
35 Edvard Munch, *The Scream*, 1893. Oil, tempera and pastel on cardboard, 91 × 73.5 (36 × 28). Nasjonalmuseet, Oslo. Photo Børre Høstland
36 James Ensor, *Death and the Masks*, 1897. Oil on canvas, 78.5 × 100 (31 × 39⅜). Musee d'art moderne et d'art contemporain, Liège
37 Emil Nolde, *Masks Still Life III*, 1911. Oil on canvas, 73 × 77.5 (28¾ × 30½). Nelson-Atkins Museum of Art, Kansas City. Photo Album/Scala, Florence
38 Franz Marc, *Blue Horse I*, 1911. Oil on canvas, 112 × 84.5 (44⅛ × 33⅜). Lenbachhaus, Städtische Galerie im Lenbachhaus und Kunstbau München. Bernhard und Elly Koehler Stiftung 1965
39 Gustav Klimt, *The Kiss*, 1908–9. Oil on canvas, 180 × 180 (70 × 70). Belvedere, Vienna. Photo Belvedere, Vienna
40 Egon Schiele, *The Self-Seers II (Death and Man)*, 1911. Oil on canvas, 80 × 80.5 (31½ × 31¾). Leopold Museum, Vienna
41 Hilma af Klint, *The Ten Largest, No. 2, Childhood*, 1907. Oil tempera and paper, 315 × 234 (124 × 92⅛). Hilma af Klint Foundation

42 Wassily Kandinsky, *Composition VI*, 1913. Oil on canvas, 195 × 300 (76 × 118⅛). The State Hermitage Museum, St Petersburg
43 Georges Braque, *Still Life (Violin and Candlestick) (Nature Morte (Violon et Compotier))*, 1910. Oil on canvas, 61 × 50.2 (24⅛ × 19⅞). San Francisco Museum of Modern Art. Gift of Rita B. Schreiber in loving memory of her husband, Taft Schreiber. © ADAGP, Paris and DACS, London 2023
44 Pablo Picasso, *Still Life with Compote and Glass*, 1914–15. Oil on canvas, 63.5 × 78.7 (25 × 31). Columbus Museum of Art, Ohio. Gift of Ferdinand Howald. © Succession Picasso/DACS, London 2023
45 Fernand Léger, *The City*, 1919. Oil on canvas, 231.1 × 298.4 (91 × 117½). Philadelphia Museum of Art. A. E. Gallatin Collection, 1952. © ADAGP, Paris and DACS, London 2023
46 Marc Chagall, *I and the Village*, 1911. Oil on canvas, 192.1 × 151.4 (75⅝ × 59½). The Museum of Modern Art, New York. © ADAGP, Paris and DACS, London 2023
47 Robert Delaunay, *Homage to Blériot (Hommage à Blériot)*, 1914. Tempera on canvas, 250 × 251 (98½ × 98⅞). Kunstmuseum Basel
48 František Kupka, *Amorpha, Fugue in Two Colours*, 1912. Oil on canvas, 211 × 220 (83⅛ × 86⅝). National Gallery Prague. © ADAGP, Paris and DACS, London 2023
49 Gino Severini, *Dynamic Hieroglyphic of the Bal Tabarin*, 1912. Oil on canvas with sequins, 161.6 × 156.2 (63⅝ × 61½). The Museum of Modern Art, New York. Acquired through the Lillie P. Bliss Bequest (by exchange). © ADAGP, Paris and DACS, London 2023
50 David Bomberg, *Ju-Jitsu*, c. 1913. Oil on board, 61.9 × 61.9 (24⅜ × 24⅜). Tate. Photo Tate. © Tate
51 Liubov Popova, *Painterly Architectonic (Still Life: Instruments)*, 1915. Oil on canvas, 105.5 × 69.2 (41½ × 27¼). Museo Nacional Thyssen-Bornemisza, Madrid. Photo Museo Nacional Thyssen-Bornemisza/Scala, Florence
52 Kazimir Malevich, *Black Square*, 1915. Oil on linen, 79.5 × 79.5 (31⅜ × 31⅜). The State Tretyakov Gallery, Moscow
53 Paul Nash, *We Are Making a New World*, 1918. Oil on canvas, 71.1 × 91.4 (28 × 36). Imperial War Museum, London
54 Max Beckmann, *The Night*, 1918–19. Oil on canvas, 133 × 154 (52 × 60⅝). Kunstsammlung Nordrhein-Westfalen, Düsseldorf. Photo Scala, Florence/bpk, Bildagentur für Kunst, Kultur und Geschichte, Berlin
55 Kurt Schwitters, *Merz Picture 25A: Star Picture (Merz Picture 25A: The Constellation)*, 1920. Collage, oil on cardboard, 104.5 × 79 (41½ × 31⅛).

Kunstsammlung Nordrhein-Westfalen, Düsseldorf. Photo Scala, Florence/bpk, Bildagentur für Kunst, Kultur und Geschichte, Berlin

56 Francis Picabia, *Machine tournez vite* (*Machine Turn Quickly*), 1916/18. Brush and ink with watercolour and shell gold over a 19th-century French lithographic illustration; laid down on canvas, 49.6 × 32.7 (19⅝ × 12⅞). National Gallery of Art, Washington, D.C. Patrons' Permanent Fund. © ADAGP, Paris and DACS, London 2023

57 Marcel Duchamp, *The Bride Stripped Bare by her Bachelors, Even (The Large Glass)*, 1915–23. Oil, varnish, lead foil, lead wire, and dust on two glass panels, 277.5 × 177.8 (109⅜ × 70). Philadelphia Museum of Art. Bequest of Katherine S. Dreier, 1952. © Association Marcel Duchamp/ADAGP, Paris and DACS, London 2023

58 Max Ernst, *Celebes*, 1921. Oil on canvas, 125.4 × 107.9 (49⅜ × 42½). Tate. Photo Tate. © ADAGP, Paris and DACS, London 2023

59 Giorgio de Chirico, *The Soothsayer's Recompense*, 1913. Oil on canvas, 135.6 × 180 (53⅜ × 70). Philadelphia Museum of Art. The Louise and Walter Arensberg Collection, 1950. © DACS 2023

60 René Magritte, *The Central Story*, 1928. Oil on canvas, 116 × 81 (45⅝ × 31⅞). Private collection. Photo Photothèque René Magritte/Adagp Images, Paris/Scala, Florence. © ADAGP, Paris and DACS, London 2023

61 Salvador Dalí, *The Great Masturbator*, 1928. Oil on canvas, 110 × 150 (43¼ × 59). Museo Nacional Centro de Arte Reina Sofía, Madrid. © Salvador Dalí, Fundació Gala-Salvador Dalí, DACS 2023

62 Adolf Wölfli, *Japan Tower (Japan=Thurm)*, 1920. Pencil and coloured pencil on paper, 45.3 × 32.5 (17 × 12¾). Adolf Wölfli Foundation, Museum of Fine Arts Bern

63 Paul Klee, *Bird Garden*, 1924. Mixed media on cardboard, 27 × 39 (10⅝ × 15⅜). Bayerische Staatsgemäldesammlungen – Sammlung Moderne Kunst in der Pinakothek der Moderne München

64 Joan Miró, *Composition (Painting)*, 1933. Oil on canvas, 130 × 162 (51¼ × 63⅞). National Gallery Prague. © Successió Miró/ADAGP, Paris and DACS London 2023

65 El Lissitzky, *Proun Room*, 1923 (reconstruction, 1971). Painted wood, 320 × 364 × 364 (126 × 143⅜ × 143⅜). Van Abbemuseum, Eindhoven. Photo Peter Cox, Eindhoven

66 Piet Mondrian, *Painting I (Tableau I)*, 1921. Oil on canvas, 96.5 × 60.5 (38 × 23⅞). Museum Ludwig, Cologne

67 Ben Nicholson, *1934 (painted relief)*, 1934. Oil on composite board, 92.5 × 92.5 (36½ × 36½). Courtesy the University of Hertfordshire Art Collection. © Angela Verren Taunt. All rights reserved, DACS 2023

68 Josef Albers, *Frontal*, c. 1927. Sandblasted flashed glass with black paint, 34.8 × 47.9 (13¾ × 18⅞). Musée d'Art Moderne de Paris. Photo Tim Nighswander/Imaging4Art. © The Josef and Anni Albers Foundation/DACS 2023

69 Sophie Taeuber-Arp, *Rising, Falling, Flying*, 1934. Oil on canvas, 99.8 × 73.3 (39⅜ × 28). Kunstmuseum Basel

70 Pierre Bonnard, *The Open Window*, 1921. Oil on canvas, 118.1 × 95.9 (46½ × 37⅞). The Phillips Collection, Washington, D.C. Acquired 1930

71 Otto Dix, *Portrait of the Journalist Sylvia von Harden*, 1926. Oil and tempera on wood, 121 × 89 (47¾ × 35⅛). Centre Pompidou, Paris. Photo Centre Pompidou, MNAM-CCI, Dist. RMN-Grand Palais/Audrey Laurans. © DACS 2023

72 Edward Hopper, *Nighthawks*, 1942. Oil on canvas, 84.1 × 152.4 (33⅛ × 60). Art Institute of Chicago. Friends of American Art Collection

73 Georgia O'Keeffe, *Ram's Head, White Hollyhock-Hills (Ram's Head and White Hollyhock, New Mexico)*, 1935. Oil on canvas, 76.2 × 91.4 (30 × 36). Brooklyn Museum, New York. © Georgia O'Keeffe Museum/DACS 2023

74 Stuart Davis, *Swing Landscape*, 1938. Oil on canvas, 220.3 × 439.7 (86¾ × 173⅛). Eskenazi Museum of Art, Indiana University. Allocated by the U.S. Government, commissioned through the New Deal Art Projects. Photo Eskenazi Museum of Art/Kevin Montague

75 Aaron Douglas, *Aspects of Negro Life: Song of the Towers*, 1934. Oil on canvas, 274.3 × 274.3 (108 × 108). The New York Public Library. Schomburg Center for Research in Black Culture, Art and Artifacts Division. © Heirs of Aaron Douglas/VAGA at ARS, NY and DACS, London 2023

76 Leonor Fini, *Two Women*, 1939. Oil on canvas, 34 × 24.5 (13½ × 9¾). Sammlung Ulla und Heiner Pietzsch, Berlin. © ADAGP, Paris and DACS, London 2023

77 Joaquín Torres-García, *Composición constructiva*, 1936. Oil on canvas, 46 × 38.1 (18⅛ × 15). Carmen Thyssen-Bornemisza Collection

78 Diego Rivera, *In the Arsenal* (detail), 1928. Mural, overall 203 × 398 (80 × 156¾). Secretaria de Educacion Publica, Mexico City. Photo Schalkwijk/Art Resource/Scala, Florence. © 2023 Banco de México Diego Rivera Frida Kahlo Museums Trust, Mexico, D.F./Artists Rights Society (ARS), New York

79 Frida Kahlo, *The Two Fridas*, 1939. Oil on canvas, 173.5 × 173 (68⅜ × 68⅜). Museo de Arte Moderno, Mexico City. © 2023 Banco de México

Diego Rivera Frida Kahlo Museums Trust, Mexico, D.F./Artists Rights Society (ARS), New York
80 Amrita Sher-Gil, *Hill Women*, 1935. Oil on canvas, 89 × 147.3 (35⅛ × 58). Vivan and Navina Sundaram collection, Delhi
81 Isaak Brodsky, *Lenin in Smolny*, 1930. Oil on canvas, 190 × 287 (74¾ × 113). The State Tretyakov Gallery, Moscow
82 Pablo Picasso, *Guernica*, 1937. Oil on canvas, 349 × 776 (137¼ × 305½). Museo Nacional Centro de Arte Reina Sofía. © Succession Picasso/DACS, London 2023
83 Jean Fautrier, *Head of a Hostage*, 1945. Oil on paper mounted on canvas, 35 × 27 (13 × 10¾). Centre Pompidou, Paris. Photo Centre Pompidou, MNAM-CCI, Dist. RMN-Grand Palais/Philippe Migeat. © ADAGP, Paris and DACS, London 2023
84 Giorgio Morandi, *Still Life*, 1948–49. Oil on canvas, 26 × 35 (10¼ × 13). Carmen Thyssen Collection, on loan to the Museo Nacional Thyssen-Bornemisza, Madrid. Photo Colección Carmen Thyssen-Bornemisza en depósito en el Museo Nacional Thyssen-Bornemisza/Scala, Florence. © DACS 2023
85 André Fougeron, *Atlantic Civilization*, 1953. Oil on canvas, 380 × 559 (149¾ × 220). Tate. Photo Tate. © ADAGP, Paris and DACS, London 2023
86 Francis Bacon, *Study after Velázquez's Portrait of Pope Innocent X*, 1953. Oil on canvas, 153 × 118 (60¼ × 46½). Des Moines Art Center. © The Estate of Francis Bacon. All rights reserved, DACS/Artimage 2023. Photo Prudence Cuming Associates Ltd
87 Alberto Giacometti, *Jean Genet*, 1954/55. Oil on canvas, 65.3 × 54.3 (25¾ × 21⅜). Tate. Photo Tate. © Succession Alberto Giacometti/DACS 2023
88 Jean Dubuffet, *Fautrier spider on the forehead (Fautrier araignée au front)*, 1947. Oil on canvas, 116 × 89 (45¾ × 35⅛). Private collection. © ADAGP, Paris and DACS, London 2023
89 Karel Appel, *Hip, Hip, Hoorah!*, 1949. Oil on canvas, 81.7 × 127 (31¼ × 50). Tate. Photo Tate. © Karel Appel Foundation/DACS 2023
90 Pierre Soulages, *3 April 1954 (3 Avril 1954)*, 1954. Oil on canvas, 194.9 × 130.2 (76¾ × 51⅜). Albright-Knox Art Gallery, Buffalo, New York. Gift of Mr and Mrs Samuel M. Kootz, 1958. Photo Buffalo AKG Art Museum/Art Resource, NY/Scala, Florence. © ADAGP, Paris and DACS, London 2023
91 Antoni Tàpies, *Great Painting*, 1958. Oil with marble dust and sand on canvas, 200.7 × 262.9 (79⅛ × 103⅝). Solomon R. Guggenheim Museum, New York. © Foundation Antoni Tàpies, Barcelona/VEGAP, Madrid and DACS, London 2023
92 Jackson Pollock, *Autumn Rhythm (Number 30)*, 1950. Enamel paint on canvas, 266.7 × 525.8 (105 × 207⅛). The Metropolitan Museum of Art, New York. George A. Hearn Fund, 1957. Photo The Metropolitan Museum of Art/Art Resource/Scala, Florence. © The Pollock-Krasner Foundation ARS, NY and DACS, London 2023
93 Willem de Kooning, *Interchanged*, 1955. Oil on canvas, 200 × 175 (78¾ × 69). Private collection. Photo courtesy Mnuchin Gallery, New York. © The Willem de Kooning Foundation/Artists Rights Society (ARS), New York and DACS, London 2023
94 Joan Mitchell, *Untitled*, 1952. Oil on canvas, 162.5 × 152.4 (64 × 60). Joan Mitchell Foundation. © Estate of Joan Mitchell
95 Cy Twombly, *Untitled*, 1955. Oil-based house paint, wax crayon, coloured pencil, lead pencil on canvas, 127 × 147 (50 × 57⅞). Private collection. © Cy Twombly Foundation
96 Helen Frankenthaler, *Mountains and Sea*, 1952. Oil and charcoal on unsized, unprimed canvas, 219.4 × 297.8 (86½ × 117¼). Helen Frankenthaler Foundation, New York, on extended loan to the National Gallery of Art, Washington, D.C. © Helen Frankenthaler Foundation, Inc./ARS, NY and DACS, London 2023
97 Mark Rothko, *Green and Maroon*, 1953. Oil on canvas, 231.5 × 139.4 (91¼ × 54⅞). The Phillips Collection, Washington, D.C. © 1998 Kate Rothko Prizel & Christopher Rothko ARS, NY and DACS, London
98 Barnett Newman, *Vir Heroicus Sublimis*, 1950–51. Oil on canvas, 242.2 × 541.7 (95⅜ × 213¼). The Museum of Modern Art, New York. Gift of Mr and Mrs Ben Heller. © The Barnett Newman Foundation, New York / DACS, London 2023
99 Wifredo Lam, *The Jungle*, 1943. Gouache on paper mounted on canvas, 239.4 × 229.9 (94¼ × 90½). The Museum of Modern Art, New York, NY. © ADAGP, Paris and DACS, London 2023
100 Fahrelnissa Zeid, *Resolved Problems*, 1948. Oil on canvas, 130 × 97 (51¼ × 38¼). Istanbul Museum of Modern Art. Eczacıbaşı Group Donation. © Raad Bin Zeid Al-Hussein
101 Robert Rauschenberg, *Collection*, 1954/55. Fabric, metal, oil, paper and wood on canvas, 203.2 × 243.8 (80 × 96). San Francisco Museum of Modern Art. Gift of Harry W. and Mary Margaret Anderson. Photo Ben Blackwell. © Robert Rauschenberg Foundation/VAGA at ARS, NY and DACS, London 2023
102 Jasper Johns, *Flag*, 1954–55. Encaustic, oil and collage on fabric mounted on plywood, three panels, 107.3 × 153.8 (42¼ × 60⅝). The Museum of Modern Art, New York. Gift of Philip Johnson in honour of Alfred H. Barr, Jr. © Jasper Johns/VAGA at ARS, NY and DACS, London 2023

103 Richard Hamilton, *$he*, 1958–61. Oil, cellulose, collage on panel, 122 × 81 (48⅛ × 32). Tate. © R. Hamilton. All Rights Reserved, DACS/Artimage 2023
104 David Hockney, *Two Boys in a Pool, Hollywood*, 1965. Acrylic on canvas, 152.4 × 152.4 (60 × 60). Private collection. © David Hockney
105 Andy Warhol, *Campbell Soup Cans*, 1962. Acrylic with metallic enamel paint on canvas, 32 panels, each canvas 50.8 × 40.6 (20 × 16). The Museum of Modern Art, New York. Partial gift of Irving Blum. Additional funding provided by Nelson A. Rockefeller. Bequest, gift of Mr and Mrs William A. M. Burden, Abby Aldrich Rockefeller. Fund, gift of Nina and Gordon Bunshaft, acquired through the Lillie P. Bliss Bequest, Philip Johnson Fund, Frances R. Keech Bequest, gift of Mrs Bliss Parkinson, and Florence B. Wesley Bequest (all by exchange). © 2023 The Andy Warhol Foundation for the Visual Arts, Inc./Licensed by DACS, London
106 Ed Ruscha, *Large Trademark with Eight Spotlights*, 1962. Oil, house paint, ink and graphite pencil on canvas, 170 × 338.1 (67 × 133⅛). Whitney Museum of American Art, New York. Purchase, with funds from the Mrs Percy Uris Purchase Fund. Photo Whitney Museum of American Art/Licensed by Scala. © Ed Ruscha
107 Chuck Close, *Phil*, 1969. Acrylic on gessoed canvas, 274.3 × 213.4 (108 × 84). Photo courtesy Pace Gallery. © Chuck Close
108 Gerhard Richter, *Uncle Rudi*, 1965. Oil on canvas, 87 × 49.5 (34¼ × 19½). Lidice Memorial. On loan to The Metropolitan Museum of Art, New York. © Gerhard Richter
109 Ellsworth Kelly, *Green Blue Red*, 1963. Oil on canvas, 171.5 × 228.6 (67½ × 90). The Eli and Edythe L. Broad Collection. © Ellsworth Kelly Foundation. Courtesy Matthew Marks Gallery
110 Ad Reinhardt, *Abstract Painting*, 1962. Oil on canvas with artist's frame, framed 158.1 × 158.1 (62⅛ × 62⅛). Collection Museum of Contemporary Art Chicago. Gift of William J. Hokin, 1981.44. Photo Nathan Keay/MCA Chicago. © ARS, NY and DACS, London 2023
111 Frank Stella, *Avicenna*, 1960. Alkyd paint on canvas, 189.2 × 182.9 (74½ × 72). The Menil Collection, Houston. Photo Paul Hester. © Frank Stella. ARS, NY and DACS, London 2023
112 Robert Ryman, *Untitled*, 1969. Oil on fibreglass, 48 × 48 (19 × 19). Mercedes-Benz Art Collection, Stuttgart/Berlin. Photo I. Kalkkinen, Geneva. © Robert Ryman/DACS, London 2023
113 Bridget Riley, *Movement in Squares*, 1961. Synthetic emulsion on board, 123.2 × 121.2. Arts Council Collection, Southbank Centre, London. © Bridget Riley 2023. All rights reserved

114 Lynda Benglis, *Contraband*, 1969. Pigmented latex, overall (irregular) 7.6 × 295.3 × 1011.6 (3 × 116¼ × 398¼), overall (thickness of latex) 0.3 (⅛). Whitney Museum of American Art, New York. Purchase, with funds from the Painting and Sculpture Committee and partial gift of John Cheim and Howard Read. Courtesy Locks Gallery. © Lynda Benglis/VAGA at ARS, NY and DACS, London 2023
115 Agnes Martin, *Night Sea*, 1963. Oil, crayon and gold leaf on linen, 182.9 × 182.9 (72 × 72). The Doris and Donald Fisher Collection at the San Francisco Museum of Modern Art. Photo Katherine Du Tiel. © Agnes Martin Foundation, New York/DACS 2023
116 Yves Klein, *Untitled Blue Monochrome (IKB 47)*, 1956. Dry pigment and synthetic resin on gauze mounted on panel, 31 × 27 (12¼ × 10¾). © Succession Yves Klein c/o ADAGP, Paris and DACS, London 2023
117 Yayoi Kusama, *Infinity Nets (2)*, 1958. Oil on canvas, 125.2 × 91 (49⅜ × 35⅞). © YAYOI KUSAMA
118 Kim Whanki, *10-VIII-70 #185*, 1970 ('Where, in what form, shall we meet again' series). Oil on cotton, 292 × 216 (115 × 85⅛). © Whanki Foundation·Whanki Museum
119 Mohamed Melehi, *Pink Flame*, 1972. Celluloid paint on panel, 110 × 95 (43⅜ × 37½). Photo courtesy Meem Gallery, Dubai. © ADAGP, Paris and DACS, London 2023
120 Hélio Oiticica, *Spatial Relief*, 1960. Oil on plywood, 98 × 124.5 × 15.2 (38⅝ × 49 × 6). Collection César and Claudio Oiticica. © César and Claudio Oiticica
121 Photo Souvenir: Daniel Buren, *Hommes/Sandwichs, work in situ*, Paris (detail), April 1968. Photo Bernard Boyer. © DB – ADAGP, Paris and DACS, London 2023
122 On Kawara, *Title*, 1965. Acrylic and collage on canvas, triptych, left panel: 117.8 × 155.9 (46⅜ × 61⅜); centre panel: 130.2 × 159.4 (51¼ × 62¾); right panel: 117.5 × 155.9 (46¼ × 61⅜). National Gallery of Art, Washington, D.C. Patrons' Permanent Fund. Courtesy One Million Years Foundation and David Zwirner. © One Million Years Foundation
123 Christopher Wool, *Apocalypse Now*, 1988. Enamel and flashe on aluminium, 213.4 × 182.9 (84 × 72). © Christopher Wool, courtesy the artist
124 David Salle, *Poverty Is No Disgrace*, 1982. Oil, acrylic and chair on canvas, 248.9 × 520.7 (98 × 37½). Akron Art Museum. Museum Acquisition Fund and gift of Larry Gagosian. © David Salle/VAGA at ARS, NY and DACS, London 2023
125 Peter Halley, *Prison with Conduit*, 1986. Oil on canvas, 147.6 × 284.8 (58⅛ × 112¼). Museum of Contemporary Art, Los Angeles. Gift of The Douglas S. Cramer Foundation. © Peter Halley, courtesy the artist

126 Glenn Ligon, *White #13*, 1994. Paint stick on linen, 213.4 × 152.4 (84 × 60). San Francisco Museum of Modern Art. Gift of Vicki and Kent Logan. Photo Ben Blackwell. © Glenn Ligon; Courtesy of the artist, Hauser & Wirth, New York, Regen Projects, Los Angeles, Thomas Dane Gallery, London, and Galerie Chantal Crousel, Paris

127 Lucian Freud, *Esther*, 1980. Oil on canvas, 48.9 × 38.3 (19⅜ × 15⅛). Private collection. © The Lucian Freud Archive. All Rights Reserved 2023/Bridgeman Images

128 Alice Neel, *Jackie Curtis and Ritta Redd*, 1970. Oil on canvas, 152.4 × 106.4 (60 × 41⅞). The Cleveland Museum of Art. Courtesy The Estate of Alice Neel and David Zwirner. © The Estate of Alice Neel

129 Alex Katz, *Islesboro Ferry Slip*, 1975. Oil on canvas, 198 × 213 (78 × 83⅞). Private collection. © Alex Katz/VAGA at ARS, NY and DACS, London 2023

130 Faith Ringgold, *The American People Series #18: The Flag is Bleeding*, 1967. Oil on canvas, 182.9 × 243.8 (72 × 96). National Gallery of Art, Washington, D.C. Gift of Glenstone Foundation and Patrons' Permanent Fund. © Faith Ringgold/ARS, NY and DACS, London, Courtesy ACA Galleries, New York 2023

131 Leon Golub, *Mercenaries I*, 1979. Acrylic on unstretched linen, 304.8 × 421.6 (120 × 166). Museum of Contemporary Art Chicago. Gift of Lannan Foundation. Photo MCA Chicago. © The Nancy Spero and Leon Golub Foundation for the Arts/VAGA at ARS, NY and DACS, London 2023

132 Eric Fischl, *Bad Boy*, 1981. Oil on canvas, 168 × 244 (66 × 96). Private collection. © Eric Fischl/ARS, NY and DACS, London 2023

133 Jean-Michel Basquiat, *Untitled (Two Heads in Gold)*, 1982. Acrylic and oil paintstick on canvas, 203 × 317.5 (79⅞ × 125). Private collection. Photo Adagp Images, Paris/Scala, Florence. © The Estate of Jean-Michel Basquiat/ADAGP, Paris and DACS, London 2023

134 Philip Guston, *Tears*, 1977. Oil on canvas, 172.7 × 290.8 (68 × 114½). Private collection. Photo Genevieve Hanson. © The Estate of Philip Guston, courtesy Hauser & Wirth

135 Julian Schnabel, *Hope*, 1982. Oil and velvet on velvet, 279.4 × 401.3 (110 × 158). Whitney Museum of American Art, New York. Photo Whitney Museum of American Art/Licensed by Scala. © Julian Schnabel/ARS, New York/DACS 2023

136 Mimmo Paladino, *Baal* 1986. Mixed media on canvas, diameter 259 cm. Private collection. © Mimmo Paladino

137 Anselm Kiefer, *Innenraum*, 1981. Oil, acrylic, emulsion and shellac on canvas with woodcut, 287.5 × 311 (113¼ × 122⅜). Stedelijk Museum Amsterdam. © Anselm Kiefer, courtesy White Cube

138 Sigmar Polke, *Watchtower*, 1984. Enamel paint on bubble wrap, 300 × 225 (118⅛ × 88⅝). Instituto Valenciano de Arte Moderno. © The Estate of Sigmar Polke, Cologne/DACS 2023

139 Martin Kippenberger, *Untitled (from the series The Raft of Medusa)*, 1996. Oil on canvas, 200 × 240 (78¾ × 94½). Museum of Modern Art, New York. Gift of Leon D. and Debra Blac. © Estate of Martin Kippenberger, Galerie Gisela Capitain, Cologne

140 Marlene Dumas, *The Painter*, 1994. Oil on canvas, 200 × 100 (78¾ × 39⅜). The Museum of Modern Art, New York. Fractional and promised gift of Martin and Rebecca Eisenberg, 2005. Courtesy Zeno X Gallery, Antwerp. Photo Peter Cox

141 Luc Tuymans, *Gas Chamber (Gaskamer)*, 1986. Oil on canvas, 50 × 70 (19¾ × 27⅝). The Over Holland Collection. Courtesy Zeno X Gallery, Antwerp. Photo © Studio Luc Tuymans

142 Bernard Frize, *Pacifique*, 1991. Acrylique and resin on canvas, 256 × 364 (100 × 143⅜). Private collection. Courtesy Perrotin and Bernard Frize. © ADAGP, Paris and DACS, London 2023

143 Gary Hume, *Close-Up (Green)*, 1999. Gloss paint on aluminium panel, 250 × 180 (98⅜ × 70⅞). Private collection. © Gary Hume. All rights reserved, DACS/Artimage 2023. Image courtesy White Cube

144 Jessica Stockhlolder, *Your Skin in this Weather Bourne Eye-Threads and Swollen Perfume*, 1995–96. Paint, concrete, structolite, misc. building material, carpet lamps, electrical cord, purple plastic stacking crates, swimming pool liner, welded steel, stuffed shirts pillows, papier-mâché and balls. Installation view at Dia Center for the Arts, New York, 1995. Courtesy the artist and Mitchell-Innes & Nash, New York. © Jessica Stockholder

145 Chéri Samba, *The Officials of Black Africa*, 1994. Acrylic on canvas, 128 × 199 (50½ × 78⅜). Courtesy The Jean Pigozzi African Art Collection and MAGNIN-A, Paris

146 Tim Leura Tjapaltjarri and Clifford Possum Tjapaltjarri, *Spirit Dreaming through Napperby Country*, 1980. Synthetic polymer paint on canvas, 207.7 × 670.8 (81⅞ × 264). National Gallery of Victoria. Melbourne Felton Bequest, 1988. © Tim Leura Tjapaltjarri/Copyright Agency. Licensed by DACS 2023 and © The Estate of Clifford Possum Tjapaltjarri/Copyright Agency. Licensed by DACS 2023

147 Zhang Xiaogang, *Bloodline – Big Family No. 3*, 1995. Oil on canvas, 179 × 229 (70½ × 90¼). Private collection. © Zhang Xiaogang, courtesy Pace Gallery

148 Damien Hirst, *Anthraquinone-1-Diazonium Chloride*, 1994. Household gloss on canvas, 205.7 × 251.5 (81 × 99⅛). © Damien Hirst and

Science Ltd. All rights reserved, DACS/Artimage 2023. Photo Prudence Cuming Associates Ltd

149 Komar and Melamid, *America's Most Wanted*, 1994. Oil and acrylic on canvas, 61 × 81.3 (24 × 32). Courtesy the artists and Ronald Feldman Gallery, New York. Photo D. James Dee

150 Julie Mehretu, *Retopistics: A Renegade Excavation*, 2001. Ink and acrylic on canvas, 257.2 × 529.6 (101⅜ × 99⅛). Crystal Bridges Museum of American Art, Bentonville. Courtesy the artist and Marian Goodman Gallery. © Julie Mehretu

151 Wade Guyton, *Untitled*, 2007. Epson UltraChrome inkjet on linen, 213 × 175 (84 × 69). © Wade Guyton. Courtesy Matthew Marks Gallery

152 Albert Oehlen, *More Fire and Ice*, 2001. Inkjet print and mixed media on canvas, 350.2 × 340 (137 × 133). Private collection. Photo Archive Galerie Max Hetzler Berlin | Paris | London. © Albert Oehlen. All Rights Reserved, DACS 2023

153 R. H. Quaytman, *Point de Gaze, Chapter 23*, 2011. Silkscreen ink and gesso on wood, dimensions variable. Purchased with funds contributed by the International Director's Council, 2012. Solomon R. Guggenheim Museum, New York. Photo The Solomon R. Guggenheim Foundation/Art Resource, NY/Scala, Florence © R. H. Quaytman, courtesy R. H. Quaytman and Gladstone Gallery

154 Mary Reid Kelley with Patrick Kelley, Still from *The Syphilis of Sisyphus*, 2011. High definition video, sound, 11 min, 2 sec. Courtesy the artists and Fredericks & Freiser, New York

155 Cecily Brown, *When this kiss is over*, 2020. Oil on linen, 226.1 × 210.8 (89 × 83). Photo Genevieve Hanson. © Cecily Brown. Courtesy the artist and Thomas Dane Gallery

156 Dana Schutz, *Bound*, 2019. Oil on canvas 223.5 × 223.5 (88 × 88). Photo Jason Mandella. © Dana Schutz. Courtesy the artist, David Zwirner, Thomas Dane Gallery and CFA Berlin

157 Peter Doig, *Gasthof zur Muldentalsperre*, 2000–2. Oil on canvas, 196 × 296 (77⅛ × 116½). Art Institute of Chicago. Gift of Nancy Lauter McDougal and Alfred L. McDougal. Photo The Art Institute of Chicago/Art Resource, NY/Scala, Florence. © Peter Doig. All Rights Reserved, DACS 2023

158 Neo Rauch, *Der Blaue Fisch*, 2014. Oil on canvas, 301.6 × 502 (118¾ × 197⅝). National Gallery of Canada, Ottawa. © Courtesy Galerie EIGEN + ART, Leipzig/ Berlin und Zwirner, New York/DACS 2023

159 Chris Ofili, *Princess of the Posse*, 1999. Acrylic, oil, paper collage, glitter, polyester resin, map pins and elephant dung on linen, 243.8 × 182.8 (96 × 72). San Francisco Museum of Modern Art. John Caldwell, Curator of Painting and Sculpture (1989–93), Fund for Contemporary Art purchase. Photo Ben Blackwell.
© Chris Ofili. Courtesy the artist and Victoria Miro

160 Hurvin Anderson, *Is it OK to be black?*, 2016. Acrylic on canvas, 130 × 100 (51¼ × 39⅜). A 70th Anniversary Commission for the Arts Council Collection with New Art Exchange, Nottingham and Thomas Dane Gallery, London. © Hurvin Anderson. All Rights Reserved, DACS/Artimage 2023

162 Salman Toor, *The Bar on East 13th*, 2019. Oil on panel, 91.4 × 121.9 (36 × 48). Museum of Contemporary Art Chicago. Promised Gift of Keith Fox and Tom Keyes. © Salman Toor; courtesy the artist and Luhring Augustine, New York

163 Tomma Abts, *Lüür*, 2015. Acrylic and oil on canvas, 48 × 38 (19 × 15). Private collection, San Francisco. Courtesy greengrassi, London. Photo Marcus Leith

164 Charline von Heyl, *Slow Tramp*, 2012. Oil, acrylic and charcoal on canvas, 208.3 × 182.9 (82 × 72). Collection of Evan Snyderman & Zesty Meyers, R & Company. Courtesy the artist and Petzel, New York

165 Mark Bradford, *Tomorrow Is Another Day*, 2016. Mixed media on canvas, 315 × 546.1 (124 × 215). The Museum of Modern Art, New York. Gift of Kenneth C. Griffin. Photo Joshua White/JWPictures. © Mark Bradford. Courtesy the artist and Hauser & Wirth

166 Y. Z. Kami, Installation view, *Y. Z. Kami: Geometry of Light*, Gagosian, rue de Ponthieu, Paris, 2018. Courtesy Gagosian. Photo Zarko Vijatovic. Artworks © Y. Z. Kami

167 Wangechi Mutu, *Double Fuse*, 2003. Ink and collage on Mylar, diptych, each 114.3 × 91.4 (45 × 36). Hood Museum of Art, Hanover, New Hampshire. Purchased through the Charles F. Venrick 1936 Fund. © Wangechi Mutu. Courtesy the artist and Gladstone Gallery

168 Beatriz Milhazes, *Banho de Rio*, 2017. Acrylic on canvas, 280 × 300 (110¼ × 118⅛). Tate. Photo Manuel Águas and Pepe Schettino. © Studio Beatriz Milhazes

169 Lee Ufan, *Dialogue*, 2014. Oil on canvas 227 × 182 (89⅜ × 71⅝). Courtesy the artist and Lisson Gallery. Photo Jack Hems/Adagp images. © ADAGP, Paris and DACS, London 2023

170 Takashi Murakami, *Dragon in Clouds – Indigo Blue*, 2010. Acrylic on canvas mounted on board, 363.2 × 1,799.9 (143 × 708⅝). Collection of Larry Gagosian. © 2010 Takashi Murakami/Kaikai Kiki Co., Ltd. All Rights Reserved

171 Hao Liang, *Day and Night (Part II)*, 2017–18. Ink and colour on silk, 173 × 441 (68⅛ × 175⅝). © Hao Liang. Courtesy the artist and Gagosian

172 I Nyoman Masriadi, *Juling (Cross-Eyed)*, 2005. Mixed media on canvas, 150 × 200 (59 × 78¾). Collection of Museum MACAN, Jakarta. Photo courtesy Museum MACAN. © I Nyoman Masriadi

173 Banksy, *Untitled*, The Cans Festival, Leake Street, London, 2008. Spray paint. Courtesy Pest Control Office, Banksy

Index

photography 43
Photorealism 194–5
Picabia, Francis 104; *56*
Picasso, Pablo 86, 89–90, 126,
    143, 148; *44, 82*
Pointillism 56
Polke,Sigmar 238–9; *138*
Pollock, Jackson 163, 168; *92*
Pop Art 189–91
Popova, Liubov 98; *51*
popular art (most and least
    wanted) 254–6
poster-artists (Affichistes)
    185–6
postmodernism 219–25
postmodernity 216–19
Pre-Raphaelite Brotherhood
    37–9
Primitivism 62–3, 66–7, 76–8
Prince, Richard 221–2, 243

Q
Quaytman, R. H. 263–4; *153*

R
Ramsden, Mel 214
Rauch, Neo 271; *158*
Rauschenberg, Robert 181; *101*
Realism 33–5
Redon, Odilon 68; *31*
Reinhardt, Ad 198; *110*
Renaissance art 15, 25
Renoir, Pierre-Auguste 49–50;
    21
Richter, Daniel 270–1
Richter, Gerhard 194–5, 243;
    108
Riley, Bridget 202; *113*
Ringgold, Faith 228; *130*
Ritchie, Matthew 261
Rivera, Diego 137–8; *78*
Rodchenko, Alexander 119
Romanticism 19–29
Rosenberg, Harold 162–3, 173
Rothko, Mark 170; *97*
Rousseau, Henri 66; *29*
Ruscha, Ed 191; *106*
Russia 117–19, 140
Ryman, Robert 201–2; *112*

S
Saatchi, Charles 252
Salle, David 219–20; *124*
Salon painters 33–4
Samba, Chéri 248; *145*

Sartre, Jean-Paul 152–5
Schiele, Egon 80; *40*
Schnabel, Julian 234; *135*
Schutz, Dana 268–9; *156*
Schwitters, Kurt 103–4; *55*
Scull auction 252
Second World War 146–8
Seurat, Georges 56, 61; *24*
Severini, Gino 96; *49*
Sher-Gil, Amrita 140; *80*
Shiraga, Kasuo 179
silk-screening 190
Sillman, Amy 260
sketches 25, 44
slavery 27
social change, 1880–1910 90–1
social class 70
social identity 271–6
Socialist Realism 140
Soulages, Pierre 159, 180; *90*
Spanish Civil War, the 143
Stella, Frank 199–201; *111*
Stijl, De 120
Stockholder, Jessica 245;
    144
Strzemiński, Władysław 123
sublime, the 22–5
Superflat style 287–8
Support/Surface group 203–4
Suprematism 98–9
Surrealism 108–17, 137
Symbolism 67–9, 92

T
Taeuber-Arp, Sophie 125; *69*
Tàpies, Antoni 159–61, 175; *91*
Tjapaltjarri, Clifford Possum
    248–9; *146*
Toor, Salman 275–6; *162*
Torres-García, Joaquín 137; *77*
totalitarianism 140–3
Toulouse-Lautrec, Henri de
    61; *27*
Turner, J. M. W. 17–19; *5*
Tuymans, Luc 241; *141*
Twombly, Cy 167, 252; *95*

U
Unism 123
United States of America
    129–34, 161–3

V
Valadon, Suzanne 70; *32*
Van Gogh, Vincent 58–63; *26*

Velázquez, Diego 152
Vienna Secession 79
Vorticism 96–7

W
Warhol, Andy 190–1; *105*
Whistler, James Abbott McNeill
    46; *20*
Wiley, Kehinde 274–5; *1, 161*
windscreen analogy 42
Wölfli, Adolf 115–16; *62*
women artists and
    discrimination 50–3, 70
Wool, Christopher 216, 243; *123*

Y
Yoshihara, Jiro 179
Young British Artists (YBAs)
    252

Z
Zeid, Fahrelnissa 179; *100*
Zen Buddhism 180, 207
Zero group 202
Zhang Xiaogang 251; *147*

"This kind of book at this kind of price
is what art publishing should be about"
—*New York Times Book Review*

"An extraordinarily rich and varied series"
—Linda Nochlin

The World of Art series is a comprehensive,
accessible, indispensable companion to the history
of art and its latest developments, covering themes,
artists and movements that span centuries and
the gamut of visual culture around the globe.

You may also like:

Abstract Expressionism
David Anfam

Art in California
Jenni Sorkin

**The Art of Contemporary
China**
Jiang Jiehong

Art Since 1960
Michael Archer

Art Since 1989
Kelly Grovier

Black Art
Richard J. Powell

**Central and Eastern
European Art Since 1950**
Maja and Reuben Fowkes

Color in Art
John Gage

Contemporary African Art
Sidney Littlefield Kasfir

Contemporary Painting
Suzanne Hudson

Fauvism
Sarah Whitfield

Graffiti and Street Art
Anna Waclawek

Movements in Art Since 1945
Edward Lucie-Smith

**The Photograph as
Contemporary Art**
Charlotte Cotton

World of Art

For more information about
Thames & Hudson, and the World of Art
series, visit **thamesandhudsonusa.com**